S█████S
OF THE
CODE

SECRETS
OF THE
CODE

**The Unauthorized Guide
to the Mysteries Behind
The Da Vinci Code**

Edited by DAN BURSTEIN

ORION

For Julie,
who represents the spirit of the sacred feminine
in my life every day
D.B.

An Orion paperback

First published in Great Britain in 2004
by Weidenfeld & Nicolson
This paperback edition published in 2005
by Orion Books Ltd,
Orion House, 5 Upper St Martin's Lane,
London WC2H 9EA

First published in the USA in 2004 by CDS Books
in association with Squibnocket Partners LLC

1 3 5 7 9 10 8 6 4 2

A CIP catalogue record for this book
is available from the British Library.

ISBN 0 75286 450 5

Printed in Great Britain by Clays Ltd, St Ives plc

www.orionbooks.co.uk

Contents

Part II
Echoes of the Hidden Past

Part III
Keeping the Secrets Secret

BOOK II
The Da Vinci Code Revealed

Part I
24 Hours, Two Cities, and the Future of Western Civilization

Part II
Reviews and Commentaries on The Da Vinci Code

Part III
Underneath the Pyramid

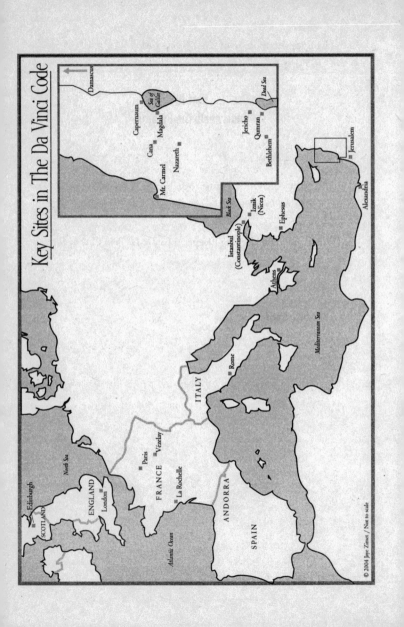

Key Sites in The Da Vinci Code

Damascus

Capernaum
Sea of Galilee
Cana
Magdala
Nazareth
Mt. Carmel
Dead Sea
Jericho
Qumran
Bethlehem
Jerusalem

Black Sea
Iznik (Nicea)
Ephesus
Istanbul (Constantinople)
Athens
Alexandria
Mediterranean Sea

Rome
ITALY

North Sea
Edinburgh
SCOTLAND
ENGLAND
London
Paris
Vézelay
FRANCE
La Rochelle
ANDORRA
SPAIN
Atlantic Ocean

© 2004 Jaye Zimet / Not to scale

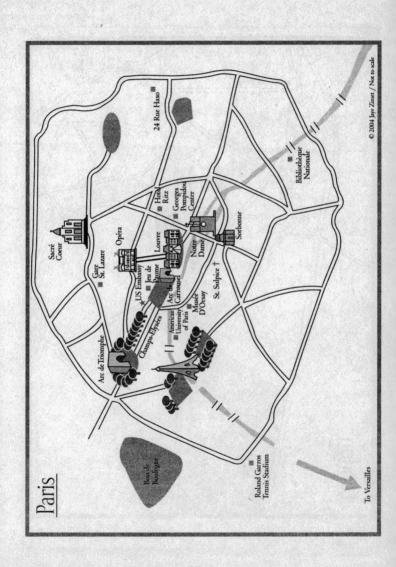

Paris

24 Rue Haxo

Sacré Coeur

Gare St. Lazare

Opéra

Hôtel Ritz

Georges Pompidou Center

Bibliothèque Nationale

Sorbonne

Louvre

US Embassy

Jeu de Paume

Arc du Carrousel

American University of Paris

Musée D'Orsay

Notre Dame

St. Sulpice †

Arc de Triomphe

Champs-Elysées

Bois de Boulogne

Roland Garros Tennis Stadium

To Versailles

© 2004 Joye Zimet / Not to scale

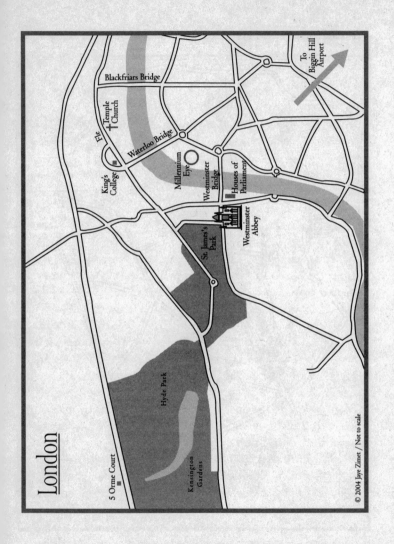

London

Blackfriars Bridge

Temple Church

Flt

King's College

Waterloo Bridge

Millennium Eye

Westminster Bridge

Houses of Parliament

St. James's Park

Westminster Abbey

To Biggin Hill Airport

5 Orme Court

Hyde Park

Kensington Gardens

© 2004 Jaye Zimet / Not to scale

Editor's Note

Secrets of the Code: The Unauthorized Guide to the Mysteries Behind The
Da Vinci Code is a compendium of original thought and writing, excerpts from numerous books, websites, and magazines,
and interviews with key writers and scholars active in their
fields. Working with such a wide range of source materials,
including transcriptions of ancient texts, we have tended
to regularize spellings and naming conventions in our own
work, while leaving undisturbed the original spellings
and conventions that appear in the many works that are
excerpted here from other books or materials. In some cases,
we have renumbered footnotes for ease of reading.

The careful reader will enjoy some variations within the
book. For example, references to the name Leonardo da Vinci
within the text generally follow the convention art history has
assigned to Leonardo, but when the name is reproduced as part
of the title of *The Da Vinci Code*, the *D* is capitalized, as it was
throughout Dan Brown's book. Elsewhere, some sources spell
Magdalene with the final *e*, some without. Wherever possible,
we have tried to leave original material from other sources
untouched, even at the risk of inconsistencies.

We have taken great care to set off each type of material
so that it will be clear when we are excerpting from previously
published works and when we are providing our own original
writing and speaking in our own editorial voice. Readers
should note that we, the editors, are speaking in introductions
to chapters, interstitial discussions, questions in interviews,
sidebars, boxes, captions, and explanatory notes within

brackets. Guest contributions, interviews, and excerpts from previously published materials should be clearly identified with bylines and/or copyright and reprint permission notices. If we have inadvertently missed any explanations of the provenance of the material or otherwise misidentified any of the pieces in this text, the editors apologize in advance.

Throughout the book, we have tried to find short selections and excerpts from much larger bodies of works to give our readers a quick taste of the content in a certain book, or the ideas of a certain expert. It was incredibly difficult to make these editorial decisions and to have to leave so much great material on the cutting room floor. We want to thank all the authors, publishers, periodicals, websites, and experts who have so generously made their content available to us for this book. And we want to encourage readers to buy the books that are excerpted here, visit the websites that are mentioned, and pursue all the multitude of ideas referred to within these pages from the original source.

The exigencies of our production schedule made it impossible to include certain interviews and excerpts, as well as bibliographies, timeline, and index materials. We expect to post some of these items on our website: www.secretsofthecode.com.

Introduction
Searching for Sophia

Like many of you, I came across *The Da Vinci Code* by Dan Brown in the summer of 2003. It was already the number one book on the *New York Times* bestseller list. It sat by my bedside for a while, along with dozens of other unread books, piles of magazines, business presentations I needed to review, and all the other things typical of the competition for mind share in the complex, chaotic, information-intense world in which we all live.

Then one day I picked up *The Da Vinci Code* and started reading. I read all night, fascinated. I literally couldn't put it down. It is an experience I used to have frequently, but not so often in this season of my life, as I was turning fifty. At one point, around 4:00 a.m., as I read Leigh Teabing's explanation to Sophie Neveu of why and how he saw Mary Magdalene in the *Last Supper*, I got out of bed and pulled the art books down from our library shelves. I looked at the Leonardo painting that I had encountered, of course, hundreds of times previously. *Yes, it really does look like a woman seated next to Jesus!* I thought.

By morning, when I had finished the book, I was as intellectually challenged as I had been by any book I had read in a long time. I wanted to know what was true and what was not, what was fact, what was fiction, what was informed speculation and what was pure flight of literary fancy. As soon as my local bookstore opened, I was there, sipping latte and rummaging through scores of books that had been mentioned or alluded to in *The Da Vinci Code: Holy Blood, Holy Grail, The Templar Revelation, Gnostic Gospels, The Woman With the Alabaster Jar, The Nag Hammadi*

Library, and many more. I discovered, to my surprise, that there were dozens of recent books about Mary Magdalene, Goddess culture, the sacred feminine, the roots of Christianity, and about how the Bible was written and codified, as well as all the Gnostic and other alternative Gospels. I found shelves full of occult books on Templar traditions, secret societies, and several places mentioned by *The Da Vinci Code* that I had never heard of before, including Rennes-le-Château in France and Rosslyn Chapel in Scotland. I left the store with hundreds of dollars' worth of books and went home to absorb all this material, only later discovering that Dan Brown had a website with a bibliography on it.

For weeks, I continued to buy books that I discovered were relevant to *The Da Vinci Code.* I raced through Elaine Pagels's new book, *Beyond Belief,* having already had my eyes opened to the world of alternative scriptures through her path-breaking 1979 book, *The Gnostic Gospels.* I discovered a world of scholars who were experts in Coptic, Greek, Hebrew, and Latin, and who had painstakingly translated and parsed ancient documents to discern new information and discover new possible interpretations of events described in the Bible. I read all of the books by Baigent, Leigh, and Lincoln, Lynn Picknett, and others who have been mining much of the same raw material as Dan Brown for years. I soaked up the richly detailed book on Mary Magdalene by Susan Haskins, that documented two thousand years of myth and metaphor about the woman who Dan Brown suggests was the bride of Christ.

I rediscovered books I had read previously: Jonathan Kirsch's powerful biography *Moses,* in which he tried to tease the true story of Moses's life out of oblique passages from the Old Testament, including fascinating references to the idea that Miriam was not the sister of Moses, as the Bible tells us, but a priestess with her own cult following and her own role in liberating the Jewish slaves from Egypt. I reread the following passage: "Some scholars argue that Miriam is real but Moses is made up. Others suggest that both of them existed but were not really brother and sister—Miriam, they argue, was a priestess and prophetess in her own right," who was ultimately merged into the Bible story as the "sister" of Moses as a kind of ancient form of politically correct storytelling. Perhaps this longstanding habit of biblical redactors—changing relationships, merging deeds performed by women with deeds performed by men, changing the earlier forms of the story to fit later political needs—had manifested itself in the way New Testament redactors edited the story of Jesus, Mary Magdalene, and the others in their circle.

I reread Umberto Eco's *Foucault's Pendulum* (a literary pastiche and send-up of much of the same occult material treated in *The Da Vinci Code*). Eco would later tell interviewers from *Jesus, Mary, and da Vinci* (the ABC news special that was devoted to exploring Dan Brown's thesis) that *The Da Vinci Code*'s premises were based on nineteenth-century fairy tales equivalent to Pinocchio and Little Red Riding Hood—"wrong theories," as false as believing that the world was flat.

I recommuned with Norman O. Brown's 1960s classic, *Love's Body*, a favorite of mine at an earlier time in my life, with all its brilliant synthesis of myth and archetype concerning the sacred feminine and the role of mythic ideas in the creation of Western consciousness. Many of the quotations from interdisciplinary fields and diverse cultures that Brown assembled seemed to be right up Robert Langdon's symbological alley. Langdon sees *chalices* and *blades* as universal male and female symbols. And, he sees them everywhere: from the adoption of the six-pointed Star of David in ancient Jewish history, to the interplay of the space between Jesus and the person seated next to him in *The Last Supper*, to I. M. Pei's downward- and upward-pointed pyramids at the Louvre. As Norman O. Brown argued, "All metaphors are sexual; a penis in every convex object and a vagina in every concave one." Langdon would have also appreciated Brown's frequent invocation of Yeats, seeking to understand how the sacred unity that was divided into male and female may someday be restored to a unified state: "Nothing can be sole or whole / That has not been rent."

I revisited a 1965 bestseller, *The Passover Plot*, that I remember my parents reading and discussing. The vintage copy I bought had these interesting words emblazoned on the flap copy: "*The Passover Plot* asserts—and presents detailed evidence from the Bible and from the newly discovered Dead Sea Scrolls to prove—that Jesus planned his own arrest, crucifixion, and resurrection, that he arranged to be drugged on the cross, simulating death so that he could later be safely removed and thus bear out the Messianic prophecies . . . Never before has so eminent an authority presented so challenging a thesis—or backed it up with such irrefutable evidence ." Déjà vu all over again for readers of Dan Brown's bestselling book forty years later.

I read Nikos Kazantzakis's *The Last Temptation of Christ* from half a century ago, and watched the Martin Scorsese movie adaptation of it, which I had never seen. These works certainly painted a vivid picture of a possible romantic relationship between Jesus and Mary Magdalene (or Willem Dafoe and Barbara Hershey, as the case may be).

As I absorbed all these books and materials and as I continued to talk to friends about their experience of reading *The Da Vinci Code (DVC)*, the idea occurred to me that I should try to bring some of these diverse strands together into a single volume, so that other *DVC* readers and enthusiasts could benefit from the same body of knowledge and criticism that I was exploring. Thus, the idea for this book was born.

Shortly after I decided to dig into this material with the vision of creating an unauthorized reader's guide to the novel, I read a report that indicated there were approximately ninety books that were selling better at bookstores around the country because of the proximity of their subject matter to *DVC*. I realized that other readers were indeed embarked on exactly the same quest that I was, reaffirming my instinct and desire to create this book. Fortunately, Gilbert Perlman and his colleagues at CDS shared my vision and were ready to move heaven and earth to support the publication of this book on a time cycle sufficiently accelerated to provide relevant context to the thousands of new readers who are buying *The Da Vinci Code* with each passing day.

In my "day job" as a venture capitalist, our firm often hears interesting but outlandish claims about new technologies and innovations. We then undertake what is known as the "due diligence" process to evaluate these claims. We look to see if, beneath all the hype, there is a real business that can be built successfully. Our approach usually begins with a list of questions.

My research on *The Da Vinci Code* was somewhat analogous. Here was my initial list:

- What do we really know about Mary Magdalene? Was she a prostitute, as Christian tradition has portrayed her? If she was not, why was she portrayed as such for so long in church history, and why did the Vatican change its mind in the 1960s?

- Is there real evidence that Jesus and Mary Magdalene were married? When Gospel accounts in the New Testament speak of a woman anointing Jesus with luxurious aromatic oils from an alabaster jar and drying his feet with her hair—was this Mary Magdalene or a different Mary, who may have actually been a reformed prostitute? And if it was Mary Magdalene who performed these acts, are they ritual acts of respect or metaphors for sexual relations?

- Does the *Gospel of Philip* found at Nag Hammadi really say that Jesus frequently kissed Mary Magdalene on the mouth—and if we have the right translation and the right words, is this too a metaphor? Or is it an actual reference to a romantic relationship?

❧ Is it possible Jesus and Mary Magdalene had a child and fostered a bloodline that continued into modern times? How valid are the many legends about Mary Magdalene's escape to France? Could her progeny have been the basis for the Merovingian kings? And what of the cults of the "black Madonna" in France and elsewhere? Could Mary Magdalene have possibly been a black woman from Egypt or Ethiopia?

❧ Was the historical Jesus essentially a Jewish rabbi, teacher, or spiritual leader and, as such, would it be likely and even probable that he would be married? Or was there already a tradition at that time of celibacy and asceticism among Jewish male leaders?

❧ Is it possible that Mary Magdalene was an important spiritual figure in her own right, the romantic companion and/or wife of Jesus, and the person whom he wished to lead his movement after his death? Is there a historical record of arguments and jealousies on the part of the male apostles over Mary Magdalene's role? Is the *DVC*'s assertion that Jesus was the "original feminist" plausible in any way?

❧ Are the Gnostic Gospels and other alternative scriptures credible—or at least as credible as the mainstream, traditional Gospels? Do they really tell a significantly different story? What do they add to our understanding of the intellectual and philosophical ferment of the first few hundred years of the Common Era?

❧ Did leaders of the Roman church, from Constantine to Pope Gregory, carry out a concerted attack on alternative beliefs and scriptures? Did they edit what became the accepted canon for political purposes? Did they deliberately conflate Mary Magdalene with another Mary in the

Gospels who was, indeed, a prostitute?

- Did these early church fathers not only slander Mary Magdalene as a prostitute, but do so as part of a larger effort to cover up Christianity's archaic inheritances from Goddess cults and in order to suppress the role of women in the church?

- Did the Gnostics practice sacred sexual rituals? Is there a tradition of *hieros gamos* that runs from Egypt through Greece, through early Christianity and on to the Templars and Priory of Sion members?

- Who were the Knights Templar and what might they have found in excavating the Temple Mount during the crusades?

- How did the Templars gain power and influence and how did they lose it? Is there any evidence that the Templars ever found the Holy Grail?

- Is there any evidence that the Templars or other secret societies of that time believed the Holy Grail to be related not to a chalice or wine cup, but to Mary Magdalene, her relics, documents about her role in the early church, her progeny, and the future of the Jesus-Mary bloodline?

- Is the Priory of Sion a real organization in history? If so, did it continue uninterrupted into modern-day France, with the involvement of the great figures of European culture alleged by *DVC* to have been grand masters: Leonardo, Newton, Victor Hugo, Claude Debussy, Jean Cocteau, etc.?

- What is going on within the church today to reevaluate doctrine, reconsider fundamental principles, and rethink the role of women? Why do movies like *The Passion* stir such passion? How is the church responding to sex abuse and other scandals, and what does history tell us is likely to happen? What is Opus Dei, and what role does it play in the Catholic Church?

- Did Leonardo da Vinci embed secret symbolic messages in

The Last Supper and other works? And does *The Last Supper* depict a female Mary Magdalene to the right of Christ, rather than the male apostle John?

In this volume, readers will find materials that address all of these questions and more. The materials include excerpts from books, periodicals, websites, original articles, commentaries, and interviews with scholars, experts, and thinkers who have been working on aspects of these issues for years. It is my sincere hope that readers will find these resources as useful to the process of drawing their own conclusions and formulating their own ideas as I have found them to mine.

Before setting readers off into the stacks contained in this volume of what we like to call "Sophie's Library," I would like to share a variety of observations about why I think *The Da Vinci Code* has struck such a nerve among the reading public and resonates so deeply with the contemporary zeitgeist.

1). *DVC* is a novel of *ideas*. Say what you will about some of the ham-fisted dialogue and improbable plot elements, Dan Brown has wrapped large complex ideas, as well as minute details and fragments of intriguing thoughts into his action-adventure-murder mystery. Our culture is hungry for the opportunity to feed the collective mind with something other than intellectual junk food. Even among much higher-brow, more literary writers, all too few are writing novels that deal with big philosophical, cosmological, or historical concepts. And among those who are, most of the books they are producing are simply too inaccessible for even the average sophisticated, educated reader. Dan Brown has given us an incredible array of fascinating ideas and concepts. We get to partake in all this with no academic prerequisites. We open the first page with Saunière staggering through the Louvre's Grand Gallery at 10:46 p.m. and we then get swept away into Brown's fast-paced scavenger hunt through the history of Western civilization. We never have to do any heavy mental lifting if we don't want to, but for those who want to pursue the ideas, the novel leaves the key words at every turn.

2) Like James Joyce's *Ulysses*, *DVC* takes place essentially in one twenty-four-hour period. Like Joyce's *Finnegan's Wake*, it ends where it begins. Clearly, Dan Brown takes literary form quite seriously. He may play faster and looser with facts than some would like, but his ability to compress extensive intellectual and religious arguments into quickly accessible sound bites is an art form. This is not to say that *DVC* is "great literature." I am not certain it will stand the test of time, popular as it is right now. But our society should appreciate, more highly than it does, the artistry of the great mystery, spy thriller, and action-adventure novelists. Dan Brown, it will turn out, is this type of literary artist.

3) Our materialistic, technological, scientific, information-flooded culture is hungry, not only for the intellectual allure of big ideas, but for a sense of mission and meaning. People are looking for a recovery of their spiritual sensibility, or at least a context for their lives. *DVC*, like the Harry Potter novels that parallel it in this same zeitgeist, is a classic hero's journey (only in this case the heroine is not only a full and equal partner, she is actually more important). *DVC* can be read as a modern *Odyssey* through myth, archetypes, symbolic language, and religious practice. The characters will not only save the most precious secrets from falling into the wrong hands, in the process they will gain knowledge of self, identity, and a place in the world.

4) Like other times in history—the legendary days of Arthur, the Crusades, the nineteenth century—we are living in an era when the romance of the hunt for the Holy Grail is being renewed. This is true in the narrow sense of a huge flourishing of new literature about the Holy Grail of Christian

history. Dan Brown draws extensively on this body of occult, New Age, and mysterious work. But there is also a flourishing of the Holy Grail hunt in the widest, most metaphoric sense. The search to unlock the secrets of the human genome, to go to Mars, understand the Big Bang, and shrink communication into wireless digital bits—all of these are Holy Grail quests of a kind. Perhaps this is all a bit of delayed millennialism: when the actual change of the millennium occurred a few years ago, many trend-watchers were surprised at how little millennial fever was exhibited. But then came the shock of September 11, apocalyptic acts of terrorism, wars in Afghanistan and Iraq, explosions of violence throughout the Middle East, all accented by religious extremism and Crusades-era rhetoric about faith and infidels. The birth of our new era has started to look more millennial after all. *DVC* strikes right into this vein, drawing its key plot elements from one thousand and two thousand years ago—the birth of the Christian era and the Crusades. In a remarkable book that came out shortly after *DVC, The Holy Grail: Imagination and Belief*, Britain's leading medieval historian, Richard Barber, traces the role of the Holy Grail in firing artistic imaginations from Wagner to T. S. Eliot to Monty Python. He also charts the use of the phrase *Holy Grail* by mainstream newspapers not usually given to spending much time on religious matters. According to Barber, the *New York Times* mentioned the Holy Grail only 32 times in 1995–96, but 140 in 2001–2. The *Times* of London upped its Grail score from 14 in 1985–86 to 171 in 2001–2; *Le Figaro* from 56 in 1997–98 to 113 in 2001–2.

5) Women are a large constituency of *DVC* readers, and the book responds in many ways to new thinking about women in our culture. Dan Brown has rescued Mary Magdalene from the reputation of sin, pentitence, and prostitution. In the book, even the smart, sophisticated Sophie Neveu still thinks of Mary Magdalene as a prostitute until Langdon and Teabing

set her straight. I am willing to go out on a limb and guess that far more people may have learned from *The Da Vinci Code* that Mary Magdalene is no longer considered a prostitute than from the official church clarifications of the 1960s. Fourteen hundred years of being seen as a fallen woman is a tough reputation to overcome. But *DVC* has moved the church's correction off the proverbial page 28 of the third section and on to the front page of the public's consciousness. Not only that. *DVC* makes the case that Mary Magdalene was much more than "not a prostitute." In the novel's estimation, she was a strong, independent figure, patron of Jesus, cofounder of his movement, his only believer in his greatest hour of need, author of her own Gospel, his romantic partner, and the mother of his child. To the millions of women who feel slighted, discriminated against, or unwelcome in churches of all faiths today, the novel is a chance to see early religious history in an entirely different light. Just as women have found new pioneering female heroines in every pursuit from science to the arts to sports over the last thirty years, *The Da Vinci Code* opens everyone's eyes to a startlingly different view of the powerful role of women in the birth of Christianity. These themes have become mainstream at Harvard's divinity school and other intellectual centers, but it is *DVC* that brought this perspective into focus for literate women (and men) who dwell outside academe. For Catholic women in particular—many of whom have long been embittered by the church's stance against abortion, birth control, divorce, and women being ordained as priests—the book illuminates how the feminine half of the human equation may have been deliberately suppressed for political reasons by the rise of the institutional, centralized power of the Roman church. Facts presented in *DVC*—real, verifiable facts—tell a story many people do not know. For example, there was no prohibition against women being priests in the early years of the church, and male celibacy in the priesthood did not become the rule until six centuries after Christ. Moreover, it was not only Mary Magdalene who was an important figure in the traditional Gospels. There are a variety of other leading women mentioned by name, most of whom have remained ciphers even to the faithful all these years. Of course the Virgin Mary, mother of Jesus, has long had a deeply devoted following. In recent years, she has emerged as an even more important figure in the church—a trend Pope John Paul II has encouraged. But the new vision of Mary Magdalene that Dan Brown paints—powerful, strong, independent, smart, the standard-bearer of Christianity long after the death of Jesus and yes, sexy—makes Mary Magdalene a much more accessible, more human character to contemplate than the aloof, saintly, perfect Virgin Mary.

6) In a time of growing fundamentalism and religious extremism in the world, *DVC* offers an important study of Western history. First, it highlights the diversity and ferment that existed in the Judeo-Christian world two thousand years ago—diversity and ferment that was later suppressed by the antiheresy campaigns of the church. It suggests that some of the pagan and Eastern ideas that found their way into eastern Mediterranean thought may have had value and validity. In reminding us of the Crusades and Inquisitions as well as the intense ideological battles over interpretation, and in contrast to Mel Gibson's 2004 movie, *The Passion of the Christ*, which seeks to present a version of *the* true way these well-known events unfolded, *DVC* challenges readers to imagine that what they have always heard or believed may *not* be the truth after all. The novel suggests a multitude of conspiracies and covert worlds: the mainstream church's great cover-up and conspiracy to eradicate the Priory of Sion, the Priory's own conspiracy of secrecy, Opus Dei's conspiracy to gain power in the church, and the Teacher's conspiracy to murder and bring forward his own version of the truth. In doing so, *DVC* is an implicit critique of

intolerance, of madness in the name of God, and of all those who believe there is only one true God, one true faith, and one true way to practice religious devotion.

7) Tapping into recent archaeological finds—such as the Nag Hammadi texts and the Dead Sea Scrolls—as well as doing art history analysis of Leonardo and other painters, symbol interpretation, and cryptography, *DVC* weaves together various strands from the scientific and archaeological reports of our times. In doing so, the novel sketches out elements of the greatest detective story ever told: we are living in an era where we are uncovering authentic evidence about human origins as well as the origins of many ideas and beliefs. Sophie's journey of self-discovery is really an analog of our own. Sophie may be descended directly from Jesus, but we are all descended from people who walked the earth at that time, thought those thoughts, practiced those customs. When we are able to share the insights that Gnostic philosophers may have had sitting in the Egyptian desert sixteen or eighteen centuries ago, it is a startling experience. We are simultaneously cracking the codes of our biological DNA as well as our cultural DNA. With new research and with new scientific tools, we may well learn what Leonardo was trying to tell us—or if he was trying to tell us anything at all.

8) The idea that Robert Langdon is a *symbologist*—an academic pursuit that appears to be Dan Brown's own coinage—and that Langdon has such a terrific knack for explaining signs and symbols, is another aspect of the book's appeal. We are moving at full throttle out of the Gutenberg age and into the webified world of interactive media. It is a transition from the world of hierarchical, literal, structured, rational thought into a futuristic soup of image, idea, motion, emotion, randomness, and interconnection. In a sense, we are moving backward in time to a period when visual signs and symbols were much more important. The icons on our computer screens are the

reincarnation of cave paintings in France. That Dan Brown is attuned to the rich meanings and inputs coming into our lives from nonliteral, nonrational sources, is a critical part of the experience of reading the book. Indeed, reading *DVC* is similar to the experience Langdon describes when he says that, for him, watching a Disney movie is like being "barraged by an avalanche of allusion and metaphor." The Langdon character, as pointed out elsewhere in this book, is an attractive mix of Indiana Jones and Joseph Campbell. The fact that Brown has strewn codes, symbols, and anagrams throughout the book makes it all the more interesting and interactive for us as participants in the experience.

9) Conspiracy, secrecy, privacy, identity theft, technology and its problems—these are themes in all of Dan Brown's books, and they are very appropriate themes for our time. Reading *DVC* stimulates thought and discussions on all these subjects. The modern American church concealed heinous cases of sexual abuse for years; the president of the United States may have launched an invasion of a foreign country based on concocted evidence of weapons of mass destruction; executives of companies like Enron and Worldcom deceived shareholders and regulators about billions and billions in nonexistent value. One can't read *The Da Vinci Code* without hearing the echoes of these contemporary incidents of lying and cover-up—and the truth coming out in the end.

Is *The Da Vinci Code* fact or fiction? My primary goal is to give you the materials so you can draw your own conclusion. Let me make it perfectly clear that I do not claim to have great prior expertise on the subjects covered by *The Da Vinci Code.* I have an intense interest and abiding curiosity about these subjects, but no academic, religious, or artistic credentials. I see myself as very much like most of the novel's readers. I became engaged with these ideas and I went out to research them in more depth,

find the most well-regarded experts I could to interview, identify the most compelling source material, and bring it all
together in a handy single volume designed for other interested, curious readers.

As a business person, however, I feel I owe my readers at
least an executive summary of the case I think the materials in
this book present in aggregate. My personal conclusion is that
the novel is a fascinating, well-crafted work of fiction that is
informed throughout by interesting bits of little-known facts
and stimulating, but highly speculative thought provocations.
It is most valuable when read as a book of ideas and
metaphors—a notebook, Leonardo style, that helps the reader
think through his or her own philosophy, cosmology, religious
beliefs, or critiques.

With those caveats, let me offer a quick overview of my
personal conclusions on the "fact versus fiction" question.
There are at least two very different parts to answering this
question.

First, I would say that the further Dan Brown goes back in
time, the more he stands on credible intellectual ground. For
example, you can find many anthropologists, archaeologists,
and other experts who would endorse the broad strokes of the
argument made in *DVC* about the sacred feminine. Serious academic literature abounds making the case that prior to the
emergence of Judeo-Christian monotheism, many polytheistic
pagan belief systems tended to pay much more attention to
goddesses as well as gods, and to the spiritual and divine nature
of sex, procreation, fertility, and birth. Similarly, on the question of Mary Magdalene not being confused with the prostitute of the New Testament, or on the matter of Mary having a
much more important role in the founding moments of Christianity than has been previously emphasized, you can find a
large body of independent academic work, as well as research
by religious scholars and theologians, making the same points.

Of course serious academics are not going to leap to a conclusion for which there is no hard evidence, so you don't find a lot of mainstream academics who are positively *convinced* that Jesus and Mary were married. But you can find very serious, credible academics—and even theologians—who are open to the *possibility* of a romantic relationship between them.

Thus, much of what *The Da Vinci Code* has to say about the role of the sacred feminine in prehistory, Mary Magdalene, early Christianity, the diversity of thought two thousand years ago, the ensuing consolidation of the institution of the Roman church—most of this discussion starts, at least from the work of serious scholars and bits of real evidence, such as the Nag Hammadi finds. Dan Brown interprets this material in the most dramatic, exaggerated, plot-driven way possible. Of course he does: this is a novel. But the roots of the ideas for these themes seem to me to have validity.

However, as we fast forward through history, *The Da Vinci Code* remains a fascinating story, but it becomes further and further uncoupled from serious scholarship. The early history of the Crusades and the Templars, as it is presented, is not out of synch with mainstream views. But by the time we get to matters such as the Holy Grail being synonymous with Mary Magdalene and the royal bloodline of Jesus, or the Priory of Sion's enduring commitment to the spirit of the sacred feminine, or the argument that *The Last Supper* is a coded message from Leonardo about the real history of Jesus and Mary, or that the Priory continued into modern times with an unbroken chain of grand masters from Leonardo to Pierre Plantard, Dan Brown has left mainstream scholarship behind. He has plunged into the world of the medieval and New Age myths. Almost all of this is recycled from legend and lore documented by other writers over the last few decades. A great deal of it falls so far below the standards of evidence for historical credibility that it's not worth discussing as history or as fact. To some, it is a lot of occult hogwash. To me, and perhaps many others, it is hogwash as history, but great material for storytelling and folklore, endlessly fascinating to discuss from the point of view of myth, metaphor, and our cultural DNA.

Many commentators are arguing over Dan Brown's portrayal of religious doctrine and Christian history. In fact, several other books offering readers a critique of *DVC* from a religious point of view are being written and published. I encourage you to read those too. But whether or not Dan Brown got his theology right is not the focus of this book, although we have presented some arguments along those lines here. Instead, I have chosen to emphasize the ideas, metaphors, and their interconnections that can be discerned by engaging in the dialogue over this book. It is not my desire to enter into polemics or to be critical or disrespectful of anyone's religious beliefs. Nor is it my desire to uphold or disparage the works that *DVC* relies on for source material that are excerpted here. The fact that material is presented here doesn't mean I think the arguments presented are true. It only means I think you should hear the arguments and make up your own mind.

What follows in *Secrets of the Code* is a compilation of ideas and opinions from a wide spectrum of thinkers. This book is designed to help the reader on his or her hunt for personal knowledge and insight—*sophia*, if you will.

Let me be crystal clear: *The Da Vinci Code* is a novel. It is an entertainment. It is something to enjoy. Part of the enjoyment, for me anyway, is to follow upon its threads and ideas, to pursue its interconnections. That's what this book is all about.

—Dan Burstein
April, 2004

BOOK I

The Drama
of Herstory,
History, and
Heresy

Part I

Mary Magdalene and the Sacred Feminine

1 Mary Magdalene

How a Woman of Substance Was Harlotized by History

Christ loved her more than all the disciples and used to kiss her often on the [mouth]. The rest of the disciples were offended by it and expressed disapproval. They said to him, "Why do you love her more than all of us?" The Savior answered and said to them, "Why do I not love you like I love her?"

—GOSPEL OF PHILIP

Mary Magdalene is, in many ways, the star of *The Da Vinci Code*, and it is fitting that she should be the starting point for this book's odyssey into exploring the histories and mysteries in Dan Brown's novel. But who was this woman who plays such a key role at critical moments in the traditional Gospels? She is clearly one of the closest companions of the itinerant Jesus. She is mentioned twelve times by name in the New Testament. She is among the only followers of Jesus to be present at his crucifixion and she attends to him after his death. She is the person who returns to his tomb three days later and the person to whom the resurrected Jesus first appears. When he appears, he instructs—indeed, he empowers—her to spread the news of his resurrection and to become, in effect, the most important apostle, the bearer of the Christian message to the other apostles and to the world.

All of that is according to statements made in the officially accepted New Testament accounts. If you study the alternative accounts—various lost scriptures and the Gnostic Gospels—you quickly find the hints that Mary Magdalene and Jesus may have had an extremely close relationship, an intimate relationship of man and wife. You find that she may have been a leader and thinker in her own right to whom Jesus may have entrusted secrets that he did not even share with the male apostles. She may have been caught up in a jealous rivalry among the other apostles, some of whom, notably Peter, may have disdained her role in the movement on the basis of her gender and found her relationship with Jesus problematic. She may have represented a more humanistic, individualized philosophy, perhaps closer to that which Jesus actually preached than to what became accepted by the Roman Empire in the time of Constantine as official, standardized, mainstream Christian thinking.

She is perhaps best known in history as a prostitute. But was she ever a prostitute? Did Jesus simply forgive her—and did she simply repent and change her ways—to illustrate traditional Christian principles about sin, forgiveness, penance, and redemption? Or was she not a prostitute at all, but a wealthy financial patron and supporter of the Jesus movement who was later declared by Pope Gregory in the sixth century to be identical to a different Mary in the Gospels who was, indeed, a prostitute? And when Pope Gregory conflated three different Marys in the Gospels into one, did he do this deliberately to brand Mary Magdalene with the stigma of prostitution? Was it an honest mistake of interpretation in a dark age when few original documents were in hand and biblical language was a mélange of Hebrew, Aramaic, Greek, and Latin? Did the church need to simplify and codify the Gospels and to play up the themes of sin, penance and redemption? Or was it a far more Machiavellian stratagem (a millennium before Machiavelli) to ruin Mary Magdalene's reputation in history and, by doing so, destroy the last vestiges of the influences of pagan goddess cults and the "sacred feminine" on early Christianity, to undermine the role of women in the church and bury the more humanistic side of Christian faith?

Did it go even further? When Pope Gregory placed the scarlet letter of prostitution on Mary Magdalene—who would remain officially a reformed prostitute for the next fourteen centuries—was it the beginning of the great cover-up to deny the marriage of Jesus and Mary Magdalene and, ultimately, the royal, sacred bloodline of their offspring?

Their offspring? Well, yes. If Jesus and Mary Magdalene were married or at least had an intimate relationship, there might well have been a child or children. And what did happen to Mary Magdalene after the crucifixion? The Bible is silent, but around the Mediterranean, from Ephesus to Egypt, there is legend and lore suggesting Mary Magdalene, with her child (or children), escaped from Jerusalem and eventually settled down to the life of an evangelist. The most interesting stories have her living out her years in France . . . a theme Dan Brown picks up and makes integral to the plot of *The Da Vinci Code*.

Representing issues about sin and redemption, the Madonna and the whore, penitence and virtue, the faithful and the fallen, it is no surprise that Mary Magdalene has always been a towering figure in literature and culture. Male churchgoers took to the stage to portray her in the passion plays, the very first theater works produced in Western Europe over a thousand years ago. And she has been a constant figure in church art ever since.

In much more recent times, Dan Brown is not the first author to be fascinated with Mary Magdalene, nor the first to play up the issue of her possible marriage to Jesus. Nikos Kazantzakis posited a romantic relationship between them in his novel *The Last Temptation of Christ* more than fifty years ago (well before Martin Scorsese turned it into a movie in the 1980s and raised the issue again). William E. Phipps addressed many of these same issues in his book *Was Jesus Married?*, more than thirty years ago. The rock opera *Jesus Christ Superstar*, another work that hails from more than thirty years ago, also assumes a romantic relationship between Jesus and Mary Magdalene. Given our society's interest in issues about gender roles, women as leaders, and all the permutations of love, marriage and sex one can imagine, the "new" Mary Magdalene fits right in, and *The Da Vinci Code* is right on time.

In the pages of this chapter, some of the world's leading experts on Mary Magdalene discuss and debate different versions of who she may have been in history, the meaning of her role in the traditional Gospels, and how the Gnostic and other alternative Gospels may further augment our ability to understand her today. Some of the experts are interested in teasing out the meaning of only what is in the Bible. Others want to deepen and enrich the debate with new evidence and new interpretations. Still others are focused less on what texts say and much more on the meaning of Mary Magdalene in the context of archetype, myth, and metaphor.

Every issue that could be debated has come into the twenty-first century debate about Mary Magdalene. Was she from Magdala on the Sea of Galilee and was she therefore likely to be a Jewish woman? Or was she from a similarly named town in Egypt or Ethiopia? Was she fair and auburn-haired as she was often depicted in medieval times or was she a black African woman? Was she an "insider" to the Holy Land's customs and way of life or was she an outsider, much like Jesus is sometimes portrayed? Was she very wealthy and able to finance Jesus' movement from her personal means? How do we know that she was wealthy—because she came from a prosperous fishing town? Because *spikenard*, the perfume she used to anoint Jesus, was considered an expensive luxury product? Because she appears to have arranged for the food and lodging of Jesus and his followers who had renounced worldly things? Since she is just one of several women who appear to be patrons of Jesus, what of the other women, several of whom are mentioned by name? Was she descended from the House of Benjamin, as some accounts suggest Jesus was descended from the House of David, and would their marriage have been politically important, bringing these two clans together? Would Jesus have been married in the normal course of events anyway? After all, most of the rabbis of Jewish culture in those days were married, and Jesus is called "rabboni" by Mary Magdalene and many of his followers in the New Testament. If he was a Jewish rabbi, wouldn't the expectation be that he would be married? Weren't Peter and several of the other apostles explicitly referred to as married? Why would Jesus have practiced celibacy when biblical language is so full of the injunctions to be "fruitful" and "to go forth and multiply"?

In the scene in the Gospels where Mary Magdalene anoints Jesus with perfumed unguents from an alabaster jar and washes his feet with her tears, drying them with her hair—is this really she or a different Mary? If it is Mary Magdalene, are these actions indicators of ceremonial respect or metaphors for sexual relations? And if sexual relations, is this an allusion to her former life as a prostitute? Is it a clue that Jesus and Mary Magdalene are actually married? Is it a poetic metaphor not just for sexual relations, but specially charged, sacred sexual relations, such as the *hieros gamos* (sacred marriage) practices that come from even more ancient Greek, Minoan, and Egyptian cultures? Could she be a "prostitute" in the sense that in some

ancient cultures, men engaged in sexual acts with "temple prostitutes" in order to have ecstatic, divine, mystical, religious
experiences? Is the wedding at Cana, described in the New Testament, really a metaphoric description of the wedding of
Mary Magdalene and Jesus Christ and does it, in turn, hearken
back to the Song of Solomon in the Old Testament? And don't
these stories, in turn, harken even further back to what Carl
Jung or Joseph Campbell would see as universal archetypes and
myths of sacred unity between male and female, of the need
for wholeness and the need for love—not just love in the New
Testament sense, but love in the full-bodied, erotic, humanistic
sense as well?

Are there sacred texts and other kinds of documents that
shed light on the true history of what happened in Israel in the
time of Christ and what happened between Jesus, Mary Magdalene, and their followers? Could documents and relics referring to these events have been buried under the Temple Mount
in Jerusalem and become the Holy Grail sought by crusading
knights? Could the Knights Templar have found this material,
spirited it out of the Holy Land, and taken it to France in
medieval days? And if this material is ever found—whether in
the cavity under Rosslyn Chapel in Scotland or under the Louvre's pyramid, or anywhere else—will it fundamentally change
Christian history and belief the way the fragmentary Gnostic
Gospels and Dead Sea Scrolls have already proven influential?

Dan Brown has done quite a job in *The Da Vinci Code* of
alluding to many of those questions. In a handful of pages, in
the midst of a murder mystery–thriller–detective story, he
manages to refer to all of the key issues above and much more
... most notably the possibility that Leonardo da Vinci knew
and understood the real history of Jesus Christ and Mary
Magdalene and that's why he painted Mary Magdalene into
The Last Supper. Moreover, the image of a leering Peter, slicing
his bladelike hand in Mary Magdalene's direction in the paint-

ing, is meant, according to *The Da Vinci Code*, to suggest the animosity between Peter and Mary Magdalene over the future of the church. In the novel, Sophie Neveu asks her late-night teachers, Teabing and Langdon, "You're saying the Christian Church was to be carried on by a woman?"

"That was the plan," says Teabing. "Jesus was the original feminist. He intended for the future of His Church to be in the hands of Mary Magdalene."

One can see why the issues of *The Da Vinci Code* have people talking, arguing, searching—however improbable some aspects of the plot may be and however rewoven or spun out of whole cloth the religious history may be. In this chapter, we hear from a wide range of experts on many aspects of the Mary Magdalene debate. Some, like Lynn Picknett and Margaret Starbird are part of the original source material for the ideas in *The Da Vinci Code*. Their ideas may be at the extreme end of the continuum, but they are always thought-provoking and challenging. Authorities like Susan Haskins, Esther de Boer, Deirdre Good, Karen King, and Richard McBrien are well-credentialed academics who have spent years studying the most arcane details from the available information about Mary Magdalene and related issues. They all believe that she has been mistreated in history. They eschew the most extreme ideas about her, but are consciously working to create a new multifaceted, nuanced view of Mary Magdalene restored to her rightful place in history. Katherine Ludwig Jansen and Kenneth Woodward are more conservative. Yet even the conservatives today are willing to assign a dramatically stronger role to Mary Magdalene in history than the traditional church view.

We start the discussion off with a mainstream, up-the-middle piece from *Time* magazine, occasioned by the extraordinary fascination with Mary Magdalene and the ideas of *The Da Vinci Code* in 2003.

Mary Magdalene: Saint or Sinner?

By David Van Biema, Reported by Lisa McLaughlin
Excerpted from *Time* magazine, August 11, 2003. © 2003 Time Inc. reprinted by permission.

The gorgeous female cryptographer and the hunky college professor are fleeing the scene of a ghastly murder they did not commit. In the midst of their escape, which will eventually utilize an armored car, a private jet, electronic-surveillance devices and just enough unavoidable violence to keep things interesting, our heroes seek out the one man who holds the key not only to their exoneration but also to a mystery that could change the world. To help explain it to them, crippled, jovial, fabulously wealthy historian Sir Leigh Teabing points out a figure in a famous painting.

"Who is she?" Sophie asked.

"That, my dear," Teabing replied, "is Mary Magdalene."

Sophie turned. "The prostitute?"

Teabing drew a short breath, as if the word had injured him personally. "Magdalene was no such thing. That unfortunate misconception is the legacy of a smear campaign launched by the early Church."

Summer page turners tend to sidestep the finer points of sixth century church history. Perhaps that is their loss. *The Da Vinci Code*, by Dan Brown ... is one of those hypercaffeinated conspiracy specials with two-page chapters and people's hair described as "burgundy." But Brown, who by book's end has woven Magdalene intricately and rather outrageously into his plot, has picked his MacGuffin cannily. Not only has he enlisted one of the few New Testament personages whom a reader might arguably imagine in a bathing suit (generations of Old Masters, after all, painted her topless). He has chosen a character whose actual identity is in play, both in theology and pop culture.

Three decades ago, the Roman Catholic Church quietly admitted what critics had been saying for centuries: Magdalene's standard image as a reformed prostitute is not supported by the text of the Bible. Freed of this lurid, limiting premise and employing varying ratios of scholarship and whimsy, academics and enthusiasts have posited various other Magdalenes: a rich and honored patron of Jesus, an apostle in her own right, the mother of the Messiah's child and even his prophetic successor. The wealth of possibilities has inspired a wave of literature, both academic and popular, including Margaret George's 2002 best-selling historical novel *Mary, Called Magdalene*. And it has gained Magdalene a new following among Catholics who see in her a potent female role model and a possible argument against the all-male priesthood. The woman who three Gospels agree was the first witness to Christ's resurrection is having her own kind of rebirth. Says Ellen Turner, who played host to an alternative celebration for the saint on her traditional feast day on July 22: "Mary [Magdalene] got worked over by the church, but she is still there for us. If we can bring her story forward, we can get back to what Jesus was really about."

In 1988, the book *Mary Magdalene: A Woman Who Showed Her Gratitude*, part of a children's biblical-women series and a fairly typical product of its time, explained that its subject "was not famous for the great things she did or said, but she goes down in history as a woman who truly loved Jesus with all her heart and was not embarrassed to show it despite criticism from others." That is certainly part of her traditional resume. Many Christian churches would add her importance as an example of the power of Christ's love to save even the most fallen humanity, and of repentance. (The word *maudlin* derives from her reputation as a tearful penitent.) Centuries of Catholic teaching also established her colloquial identity as the bad girl who became the hope of all bad girls, the saved siren active not only in the overheated imaginations of parochial-school students but also as the patron of institutions for wayward women such as the grim nun-run laundries featured in the new movie *The Magdalene Sisters* ...

The only problem is that it turns out that she wasn't bad, just interpreted that way. Mary Magdalene (her name refers to Magdala, a city in Galilee) first appears in the Gospel of Luke as one of several apparently wealthy women Jesus cures of possession (seven demons are cast from her), who join him and the apostles and "provided for them out of their means." Her name does not come up again until the crucifixion, which she and other women witness from the foot of the cross, the male disciples having fled. On Easter Sunday morning, she visits Jesus' sepulcher, either alone or with other women, and discovers it empty. She learns—in three Gospels from angels and in one from Jesus himself—that he is risen. John's recounting is the most dramatic. She is solo at the empty tomb. She alerts Peter and an unnamed disciple; only the latter seems to grasp the Resurrection, and they leave. Lingering, Magdalene encounters Jesus, who asks her not to cling to him, "but go to my brethren and say unto them, I ascend unto my Father ... and my God." In Luke's and Mark's versions, this plays out as a bit of a farce: Magdalene and other women try to alert the men, but "these words seemed to them an idle tale, and they did not believe them." Eventually they came around.

Discrepancies notwithstanding, the net impression is of a woman of substance, brave and smart and devoted, who plays a crucial—perhaps irreplaceable—role in Christianity's defining moment. So where did all the juicy stuff come from? Mary Magdalene's image became distorted when early church leaders bundled into her story those of several less distinguished women whom the Bible did not name or referred to without a last name. One is the "sinner" in Luke who bathes Jesus' feet with her tears, dries them with her hair, kisses them and anoints them with ointment. "Her many sins have been forgiven, for she loved much," he says. Others include Luke's Mary of Bethany and a third unnamed woman, both of whom anointed Jesus in one form or another. The mix-up was made official by Pope Gregory the Great in 591: "She whom Luke calls the sinful woman, whom John calls Mary [of Bethany], we believe to be the Mary from whom seven devils were ejected according to Mark," Gregory declared in a sermon. That position became church teaching, although it was not adopted by Orthodoxy or Protestantism when each later split from Catholicism.

What prompted Gregory? One theory suggests an attempt to reduce the number of Marys—there was a similar merging of characters named John. Another submits that the sinning woman was appended simply to provide missing backstory for a figure of obvious importance. Others blame misogyny. Whatever the motivation, the effect of the process was drastic and, from a feminist perspective, tragic. Magdalene's witness to the Resurrection, rather than being acclaimed as an act of discipleship in some ways greater than the men's, was reduced to the final stage in a moving but far less central tale about the redemption of a repentant sinner. "The pattern is a common one," writes Jane Schaberg, a professor of religious and women's studies at the University of Detroit Mercy and author of last year's *The Resurrection of Mary Magdalene*, "the powerful woman disempowered, remembered as a whore or whorish." As shorthand, Schaberg coined the term "harlotization."

In 1969, in the liturgical equivalent of fine print, the Catholic Church officially separated Luke's sinful woman, Mary of Bethany and Mary Magdalene as part of a general revision of its missal. Word has been slow in filtering down into the pews, however. (It hasn't helped that Magdalene's heroics at the tomb are still omitted from the Easter Sunday liturgy, relegated instead to midweek.) And in the meantime, more scholarship has stoked the fires of those who see her eclipse as a chauvinist conspiracy. Historians of Christianity are increasingly fascinated with a group of early followers of Christ known broadly as the Gnostics, some of whose writings were unearthed only fifty-five years ago. And the Gnostics were fascinated by Magdalene. The so-called Gospel of Mary [Magdalene], which may date from as early as A.D. 125 (or about forty years after John's Gospel), describes her as having received a private vision from Jesus, which she passes on to the male disciples. This role is a usurpation of the go-between status the standard Gospels normally accord to Peter, and Mary depicts him as mightily peeved, asking, "Did [Jesus] really speak with a woman without our knowledge?" The disciple Levi comes to her defense, saying, "Peter, you have always been hot-tempered . . . If the Savior made her worthy, who are you to reject her? Surely, the Savior loves her very well. That is why he loved her more than us."

Them's fightin' words, especially when one remembers that the papacy traces its authority back to Peter. Of course, the Gnostic Gospels are not the Bible. In fact, there is evidence that the Bible was standardized and canonized precisely to exclude such books, which the early church leaders regarded as heretical for many non-Magdalene reasons. Nonetheless, feminists have been quick to cite Mary as evidence both of Magdalene's early importance, at least in some communities, and as the virtual play-by-play of a forgotten gender battle, in which church fathers eventually prevailed over the people who never got the chance to be known as church mothers. "I think it was a power struggle," says Schaberg, "And the canonical texts that we have [today] come from the winners."

Schaberg goes further. In her book, she returns to John in light of the Gnostic writings and purports to find "fragments of a claim" that Jesus may have seen Magdalene as his prophetic successor. The position is thus far quite lonely. But it serves nicely to illustrate the way in which any retrieval of Magdalene as a "winner" inevitably shakes up current assumptions about male church leadership. After Pope John Paul II prohibited even the discussion of female priests in 1995, he cited "the example recorded in the Sacred Scriptures of Christ choosing his Apostles only from among men . . ." That argument would seem weakened in light of the "new" Magdalene, whom the Pope himself has acknowledged by the once unfashionable title "Apostle to the Apostles." Chester Gillis, chair of the department of theology at Georgetown University, says conventional Catholics still feel that Mary Magdalene's absence from many biblical scenes involving the male disciples, and specifically from the ordination-like ritual of the Last Supper, rule her out as a priest precedent. Gillis agrees, however, that her recalibration "certainly makes a case for a stronger role for women in the church."

Meanwhile, the combination of Catholic rethinking and Gnostic revelations have reanimated wilder Magdalene speculations, like that of a Jesus-Magdalene marriage. ("No other biblical figure," Schaberg notes, "has had such a vivid and bizarre postbiblical life.") The Gnostic Gospel of Philip describes Magdalene as "the one who was called [Jesus'] companion," claiming that he "used to kiss her on her [mouth]." Most scholars discount a Jesus-Magdalene match because it finds little echo in the canonical Gospels once the false Magdalenes are removed. But it fulfills a deep narrative expectation: for the alpha male to take a mate, for a yin to Jesus' yang or, as some neopagans have suggested, for a goddess to his god. Martin Luther believed that Jesus and Magdalene were married, as did Mormon patriarch Brigham Young.

The notion that Magdalene was pregnant by Jesus at his crucifixion became especially entrenched in France, which already had a tradition of her immigration in a rudderless boat, bearing the Holy Grail, his chalice at the Last Supper into which his blood later fell. Several French kings promoted the legend that descendants of Magdalene's child founded the Merovingian line of European royalty, a story revived by Richard Wagner in his opera *Parsifal* and again in connection with Diana, Princess of Wales, who reportedly had some Merovingian blood....The idea that Magdalene herself was the Holy Grail—the human receptacle for Jesus' blood line—popped up in a 1986 bestseller *Holy Blood, Holy Grail*, which inspired Brown's *Da Vinci Code*. When Brown said recently, "Mary Magdalene is a historical figure whose time has come," he meant a figure with a lot of mythic filagree....

Sacred Sex and Divine Love
A Radical Reconceptualization of Mary Magdalene

BY LYNN PICKNETT

This excerpt is taken from *Mary Magdalene* by Lynn Picknett. Appears by permission of Carroll & Graf Publishers, an imprint of Avalon Publishing Group. Copyright © Lynn Picknett 2003. Lynn Picknett is a writer, researcher, and lecturer on the paranormal, the occult and historical and religious mysteries.

Who was the mysterious Mary Magdalene, so carefully squeezed to the very outside edge of the New Testament by the Gospel writers? Where did she come from, and what made her so threatening to the men of the emergent Roman Church?

In *The Templar Revelation* . . . I write about the enduring controversy surrounding this pivotal biblical character:

> The identification of Mary Magdalene, Mary of Bethany (Lazarus' sister) and the 'unnamed sinner' who anoints Jesus in Luke's Gospel has always been hotly debated. The Catholic Church decided at an early date that these three characters were one and the same, although it reversed this position as recently as 1969. Mary's identification as a prostitute stems from Pope Gregory I's *Homily 33*, delivered in 591 C.E. in which he declared:
>
> 'She whom Luke calls the sinful woman, whom John calls Mary, we believe to be Mary from whom seven devils were ejected according to Mark. And what did these seven devils signify, if not all the vices? . . . It is clear, brothers, that the woman previously used the unguent to perfume her flesh in forbidden acts.'

The Eastern Orthodox Church has always treated Mary Magdalene and Mary of Bethany as separate characters.

The Catholic Church has always been canny in its presentation of the Magdalene, recognizing her value as role model for the hopeless women under their control, such as the Magdalene laundresses. As David Tresemer and Laura-Lea Cannon write in their Preface to Jean-Yves Leloup's 1997 translation of the Gnostic *Gospel of Mary Magdalene*:

> Only in 1969 did the Catholic Church officially repeal Gregory's labeling of Mary as a whore, thereby admitting their error—though the image of Mary Magdalene as the penitent whore has remained in the public teachings of all Christian denominations. Like a small erratum buried in the back pages of a newspaper, the Church's correction goes unnoticed, while the initial and incorrect article continues to influence readers.

Yet perhaps it would be unduly hasty to dissociate her from all suspicion of 'prostitution' in an excess of modern zeal to rehabilitate her. Several researchers have pointed out that the 'seven devils' that were allegedly cast out of her may be a garbled reference to the seven underworld gatekeepers of the pagan mysteries, and may provide a valuable clue about her real background. Indeed, in the pagan world there were the so-called 'temple prostitutes,' women who literally embodied and passed on the sacred 'whore wisdom' through transcendental sex: clearly, outside their own culture they would be viewed as little more than streetwalkers, especially among the male disciples, imbued with the moral and sexual strictures of the Judaic Law, in the Holy Land . . .

Luke's choice of words in describing her moral status is

very interesting: it is *harmartolos*, meaning one who has committed a crime against the Jewish law, although this does not necessarily imply prostitution. It is a term taken from the sport of archery, meaning missing the target and may refer to someone who for whatever reason does not keep the religious observances—or does not pay the taxes, possibly because she was not actually Jewish.

Mary of Bethany is also described as having unbound or uncovered hair, which no self-respecting Judaean Jewish woman would do, for it represented sexual licence, as it does to Orthodox Jews and Muslims in today's Middle East. Indeed, Mary wipes Jesus' feet with her hair—a curiously intimate, not to say iconoclastic, action for an apparently unknown woman to perform in public. This would have been regarded as utterly scandalous by the disciples. . . .

A woman could even be divorced on the grounds of appearing in public with unbound hair—so heinous was the sin—and here Mary of Bethany, a 'harmartolos' woman, one who somehow misses the Jewish mark or is outside the religious law, seems utterly oblivious to the outcry her actions would cause. More significantly, not only does Jesus not rebuke her for flouting the Judaic law, but he tacitly encourages her by turning on those who criticize her behaviour.

Both of them are behaving like foreigners in a strange land: no wonder they are not understood, particularly by the Twelve who, time after time, we are told, fail to understand Jesus' teaching or the whole point of his mission. Mary of Bethany may be an outsider, but she appears to share some kind of private secret with Jesus—and they are both outsiders.

If the anointing were not a Jewish custom, then to what tradition did it belong? In their time there was a sublimely sacred *pagan* rite that involved a woman anointing a chosen man both on the head and feet—and also on the genitals—for a very special destiny. This was the anointing of the sacred king, in which the priestess singled out the chosen man and anointed him, before bestowing his destiny upon him in a sexual rite known as the *hieros gamos* (sacred marriage). The anointing was part of the ritual preparation for penetration during the rite—which did not have the same emotional or legal ramifications as the more usual form of marriage—in which the priest-king was flooded with the power of the god, while the priestess-queen became possessed by the great goddess. Without the power of the woman, the chosen king could never reign and would be powerless. . . . This was the original meaning of 'holy matrimony' *(hieros gamos)*. . . .

The concept of the sacred marriage is essential to the understanding of Jesus and his mission, and his relationship with the most important woman in his life—not to mention two highly significant men . . . The persistent image of Mary of Bethany/Mary Magdalene as a whore begins to make sense when it is realized that this ritual is the ultimate expression of what the Victorian historians called 'temple prostitution'—of course with their arrogant and hypocritical puritanism and sexual repression, this should not surprise us—although the original term for the priestess involved was *hierodule*, or 'sacred servant.' It was only through her that a man could achieve knowledge of himself and of the gods. In the epitome of the sacred servant's work, the *hieros gamos*, the king is sanctified and set apart—and of course immediately after the biblical anointing, Judas betrays Jesus and the machinery for his ultimate destiny through the crucifixion is set in motion . . .

The sacred marriage was a familiar concept to pagans of Jesus' day: versions of it were commonly performed by the devotees of various other dying-and-rising god cults, such as that of Tammuz (to whom there was a temple in Jerusalem at that time), and the Egyptian god Osiris, whose consort Isis breathed life into his dead body long enough for her to conceive the magical child, the hawkheaded god of courage,

Horus. Indeed, Tresemer and Cannon state unequivocally that: 'Her appearances with special oils to use in anointing Jesus Christ place her in the tradition of priests and priestesses of Isis, whose unguents were used to achieve the transition over the threshold of death while retaining consciousness.'[1] Indeed, this places her in the specific context of the shamanic tradition of Egypt, which is only now being acknowledged. . . .

In all versions of the sacred marriage, the representative of the goddess, in the form of her priestess, united sexually with the chosen king before his sacrificial death. Three days afterwards the god rose again, and the land was fertile once more. . . .

Clearly, this woman who anointed Jesus was very special, a great priestess of some ancient pagan tradition—but was she also Mary Magdalene, as the Church claimed until 1969? . . . Let us consider the clues concerning the true nature of the mysterious woman known as the Magdalene.

Where was Magdala?

This enigmatic woman, who was so obviously a central part of the mission of Jesus, is referred to in the Bible as 'Mary Magdalene' or simply 'the Magdalene,' which conveys a pervasive sense that the Gospel writers expected their readers to know who she was, recognizing her name immediately. . . . This early twentieth century analysis gives a largely conventional interpretation which is still generally accepted today:

> Mary Magdalene is probably named from the town of Magdala or Magadan . . . now Medjdel, which is said to mean "a tower." It was situated at a short distance from Tiberias, and is mentioned . . . in connection with the

1. Leloup, pp. xx–xxi

miracle of the seven loaves. An ancient watchtower still marks the site. According to Jewish authorities it was famous for its wealth, and for the moral corruption of its inhabitants.[2/3] ...

In fact, nowhere in the New Testament does it spell out where Mary comes from, which has led scholars and churchgoers merely to assume that she hailed from the shores of Lake Galilee—even though it must be said that there are more compelling reasons to believe she may have come from elsewhere: perhaps as a truly exotic foreigner. Indeed, ... there is persuasive evidence that Jesus himself was not from those parts, although the assumption that he was a Jew from Galilee is so entrenched as to be deemed an unassailable fact. ...

In fact, there is no necessity to endeavour to crowbar her into a Galilean setting, for there are at least two other intriguing alternatives for her place of origin: although there was no 'Magdala' in Judaea in her day, there was a Magdolum in Egypt—just across the border—which was probably the Migdol mentioned in Ezekiel. There was a large and flourishing Jewish community in Egypt at that time, which was particularly centred on the great sea port of Alexandria, a seething cosmopolitan melting pot of many races, nationalities and religions, where John the Baptist had his headquarters, and perhaps where the Holy Family had fled to escape the depredations of Herod's men. ... If the Magdalene really was from the Egyptian town of Magdolum, this could provide a clue as to why she was so sidelined—after all, despite the exciting mix of nations and religions in Galilee at that time, human nature has always been suspicious of foreigners, and the gospels make it clear that few were more insular in their

2. Edersheim, vol. i. p. 571.
3. *A Dictionary of the Bible: Dealing with its language, literature, and contents including the Biblical theology*, edited by James Hastings, M.A., D.D., Edinburgh, 1900, p. 284.

attitudes than the likes of Simon Peter, at least at the beginning of the mission ...

However, if the Magdalene was a *priestess* from Egypt, that would increase the Jewish men's hostility to her a thousandfold. Not only was she an outspoken and independent woman of means, but also invested with pagan authority! ... They would have had great reservations about the foreign priestess who constantly tagged along. ...

Perhaps there was another reason why the Magdalene was treated so badly by the men of Jesus' following. While she may have lived in Egypt—after all, we know that both the Baptist and Jesus himself lived there for several years—perhaps that is not where she came from originally. Indeed, it may be significant that for many years there was a Magdala in Ethiopia ... This rocky outcrop is now called Amra *Mariam* (Mary): although the Ethiopians today generally revere the Virgin Mary over Mary Magdalene, these place names indicate that there is a long association with the latter in that area, perhaps—unthinkably to many—it may even have been her birthplace or home.

An Ethiopian background would certainly have made her extremely exotic and perhaps disturbing to the insular men of Jesus' mission such as Simon Peter. Despite what politically correct revisionists may claim now, the British Empire did not invent racism: if the Magdalene were *black*, outspoken, rich, a pagan priestess—and Jesus' closest ally (to say the least)—the Twelve might well have floundered in a sea of uneducated emotions at the sight of her, born of fear of the alien, the unknown. ...

Bride of Christ?

Was the obviously close relationship between the Magdalene and Jesus due to their being legally man and wife, as some—

most seminally Baigent, Leigh and Lincoln in their 1982 book *Holy Blood, Holy Grail*—have claimed? If they were, there is a very strange silence about it in the New Testament, for despite what Christians (especially Catholics) may think today, priests and rabbis in the Holy Land were *supposed* to be married, for to abstain from procreation was (and still is, among Orthodox Jews) seen as an insult to God. Indeed, celibacy won censure from the elders of the synagogue, and perhaps also mutterings about unnatural lusts among the congregation. For a Jewish rabbi, it would have been very odd if Jesus were *not* married, but if he had a wife, surely she would have been mentioned— as 'Miriam the wife of the Saviour,' or 'Mary the wife of Jesus.' There is never any phrase that might remotely be interpreted as alluding to his legal spouse, but was this because there was no such person, or because his wife was known but disliked so intensely and on such a scale that the canonical Gospel writers decided to ignore her? Or because they had married in a cere- mony that the Jews did not recognize? But if, as the Gnostic Gospels overwhelmingly suggest, Jesus and the Magdalene were committed and passionate lovers, why did they stop short of putting their relationship on an official footing? . . .

Apart from there being some kind of legal proscription on their love—such as being close blood relatives or being legally married to someone else at the time—there seems little reason for them not to have made a public commitment to each other. Could this reluctance to tie the knot have been because they were not, in fact, Jewish at all in the generally accepted sense and therefore could not be married in a synagogue? And it is significant that pagan priestesses, even those involved in sacred sex, were often required to be otherwise celibate and remain unmarried. . . .

The French Connection

There are several legends about Mary Magdalene travelling to France (or Gaul as it was then) after the crucifixion, together with a varied assortment of people, including a black servant girl called Sarah, and Mary Salome and Mary Jacobi— allegedly Jesus' aunts—besides Joseph of Arimathea, the rich man who owned the tomb in which Christ was laid prior to the resurrection, and St Maximin (Maximus), one of the seventy-two closest disciples of Jesus and the first bishop of Provence. Although the details of the story differ from version to version, it appears that the Magdalene and her party were forced to flee from Palestine under less than perfect conditions—their boat was leaky, rudderless, oarless and without a sail, which is believed to have been the result of deliberate sabotage on the part of certain factions in their homeland. Even allowing for the inevitable exaggeration of myth-making—the ruinous state of their boat seems rather unlikely—given the Gnostic Gospels' depiction of the volatile situation between Mary and Simon Peter, it is not difficult to hazard a guess at the possible, even probable, identity of at least one of the plotters who would have wished her and her companions at the bottom of the sea. In the light of the legend of the leaky boat, it is chilling to recall Mary's words from the *Pistis Sophia*: 'I am afraid of Peter, because he threatened me and hateth our sex.' But whoever sought to kill them, miraculously they survived, allegedly ending up on the wild coast of what is now Provence . . .

The story goes that they landed (no doubt very gratefully, after wallowing about in floods of seawater for weeks) at what is now the town of Saintes-Maries-de-la-Mer in the Camargue, in the wetlands where the Rhone meets the Mediterranean. Three Marys—Magdalene, Mary Jacobi and Mary Salome— are the focus for great reverence in the grand church that rises like a stately sailing ship from the surrounding marshes, while in the crypt there is an altar dedicated to Sarah the Egyptian, allegedly the Magdalene's black servant girl, now the much-loved patron saint of the gypsies, who converge on the town for her annual feast day of 25 May. Surrounded by thousands of adoring devotees, Sarah's statue is paraded to the sea, where it is ceremoniously dipped. As medieval folk thought of gypsies as being from Egypt—'egypsies'—it made sense for them to venerate this young woman who originated from that country. Indeed, the colour of her skin, and the fact that Egypt was known as the land of *'Khem,'* or blackness, may be very significant. Judging by the New Testament's division of one woman into three—the Magdalene, Mary of Bethany and the unnamed 'sinner'—perhaps the assorted women in the leaky boat were also merely different aspects of one woman . . .

The Woman With the Alabaster Jar
Mary Magdalen and the Holy Grail

BY MARGARET STARBIRD

The Woman With the Alabaster Jar: Mary Magdalen and the Holy Grail. Copyright © 1993 by Margaret Starbird. Reprinted by permission of Bear & Company, a division of Inner Traditions International, www.innertraditions.com. Margaret Starbird holds a master's degree from the University of Maryland and has studied at Christian Albrechts University in Kiel, Germany, and at Vanderbilt Divinity School. She is also author of *The Goddess in the Gospels*.

I have come to suspect that Jesus had a secret dynastic marriage with Mary of Bethany and that she was a daughter of the tribe of Benjamin, whose ancestral heritage was the land surrounding the Holy City of David, the city Jerusalem. A dynastic marriage between Jesus and a royal daughter of the Benjamites would have been perceived as a source of healing to the people of Israel during their time of misery as an occupied nation.

Israel's first anointed King Saul was of the tribe of Benjamin, and his daughter Michol was the wife of King David. Throughout the history of the tribes of Israel, the tribes of Judah and Benjamin were the closest and most loyal of allies. Their destinies were intertwined. A dynastic marriage between a Benjamite heiress to the lands surrounding the Holy City and the messianic Son of David would have appealed to the fundamentalist Zealot faction of the Jewish nation. It would have been seen as a sign of hope and blessing during Israel's darkest hour.

In the novel *King Jesus* (1946), Robert Graves, the twentieth-century mythographer, suggests that Jesus' lineage and marriage were concealed from all but a select circle of royalist leaders. To protect the royal bloodline, this marriage would have been kept secret from the Romans and the Herodian tetrarchs, and after the crucifixion of Jesus, the protection of his wife and family would have been a sacred trust for those few who knew their identity. All reference to the marriage of Jesus would have been deliberately obscured, edited, or eradicated. Yet the pregnant wife of the anointed Son of David would have been the bearer of the hope of Israel—the bearer of the Sangraal, the royal bloodline.

Magdal-eder, the Tower of the Flock

In chapter 4 of the Hebrew prophet Micah, we read a beautiful prophecy of the restoration of Jerusalem, when all nations shall beat their swords into plowshares and be reconciled under God. Beginning with verse 8 we find:

> As for you, O [Magdal-eder], watchtower of the flock,
> O stronghold of the Daughter of Zion!

the former dominion will be restored to you;
kingship will come to the Daughter of Jerusalem.
Why do you now cry aloud—
have you no king?
Has your counselor perished,
that pain seizes you like that of a woman in labor?
Writhe in agony, O Daughter of Zion,
like a woman in labor,
for now you must leave the city
and camp in the open field.

It is probable that the original references to Mary Magdalen in the oral tradition, the "pericopes" of the New Testament, were misunderstood before they were ever committed to writing. I suspect that the epithet "Magdalen" was meant to be an allusion to the "Magdal-eder" found in Micah, the promise of the restoration of Sion following her exile. Perhaps the earliest verbal references attaching the epithet "Magdala" to Mary of Bethany's name had nothing to do with an obscure town in Galilee, as is suggested, but were deliberate references to these lines in Micah, to the "watchtower" or "stronghold" of the daughter of Sion who was forced into political exile.

The place name *Magdal-eder* literally means "tower of the flock," in the sense of a high place used by a shepherd as a vantage point from which to watch over his sheep. In Hebrew, the epithet *Magdala* literally means "tower" or "elevated, great, magnificent." This meaning has particular relevance if the Mary so named was in fact the wife of the Messiah. It would have been the Hebrew equivalent of calling her "Mary the Great," while at the same time referring to the prophesied return of dominion to "the daughter of Jerusalem" (Mic. 4:8).

In Old French legend, the exiled "Magdal-eder," the refugee Mary who seeks asylum on the southern coast of

France, is Mary of Bethany, the Magdalen. The early French legend records that Mary "Magdalen," traveling with Martha and Lazarus of Bethany, landed in a boat on the coast of Provence in France. Other legends credit Joseph of Arimathea as being the custodian of the Sangraal, which I have suggested may be the *royal bloodline of Israel* rather than a literal chalice. The vessel that contained this bloodline, the archetypal chalice of medieval myth, must have been the wife of the anointed King Jesus.

The image of Jesus that emerges in our story is that of a charismatic leader who embodies the roles of prophet, healer, and Messiah-King, a leader who was executed by the Roman Army of Occupation and whose wife and bloodline were secretly taken from Israel by his loyal friends and transplanted in Western Europe to await the fullness of time and the culmination of prophecy. The friends of Jesus who believed so fervently that he was the Messiah, the Anointed of God, would have perceived the preservation of his family as a sacred duty. The vessel, the chalice that embodied the promises of the Millennium, the "Sangraal" of medieval legend, was, I have come to believe, Mary Magdalen . . .

But tradition derived from [another] Old French legend from the Mediterranean coast tells us that . . . Joseph of Arimathea, was the custodian of the "Sangraal" and that the child on the boat was Egyptian, which means quite literally "born in Egypt." It seems likely that after the crucifixion of Jesus, Mary the Magdalen found it necessary to flee for the sake of her unborn child to the nearest refuge. The influential friend of Jesus, Joseph of Arimathea, could very well have been her protector.

If our theory is correct, the child actually *was* born in Egypt. Egypt was the traditional place of asylum for Jews whose safety was threatened in Israel; Alexandria was easily reached from Judea and contained well-established Jewish

communities at the time of Jesus. In all probability, the emergency refuge of Mary Magdalen and Joseph of Arimanthea
was Egypt. And later—years later—they left Alexandria and
sought an even safer haven on the coast of France.

Scholars of archaeology and linguistics have found that
place names and legends of an area contain "fossils" from that
area's remote past. The truth may be embellished by changes
and stories may suffer abridgment through the years of
telling, but traces of the truth remain in fossil form, buried in
the names of people and places. In the town of Les Saintes-
Maries-de-la-Mer in France, there is a festival every May 23 to
25 at a shrine in honor of Saint Sarah the Egyptian, also
called Sara Kali, the "Black Queen." Close scrutiny reveals that
this festival, which originated in the Middle Ages, is in honor
of an "Egyptian" child who accompanied Mary Magdalen,
Martha, and Lazarus, arriving with them in a small boat that
came ashore at this location in approximately A.D. 42. The
people seem to have assumed that the child, being "Egyptian,"
was dark-skinned and, by further interpolation, that she must
have been the servant of the family from Bethany, since no
other reasonable explanation could be found for her presence.

The name Sarah means "queen" or "princess" in Hebrew.
This Sarah is further characterized in local legends as "young,"
no more than a child. So we have, in a tiny coastal town in
France, a yearly festival in honor of a young, dark-skinned girl-
child called Sarah. The fossil in this legend is that the child is
called "princess" in Hebrew. A child of Jesus, born after
Mary's flight to Alexandria, would have been about twelve
years of age at the time of the voyage to Gaul recorded in the
legend. She, like the princes of David's line, is *symbolically* black,
"unrecognized in the streets" (Lam. 4:8). The Magdalen was
herself the "Sangraal," in the sense that she was the "chalice"
or vessel that once carried the royal bloodline *in utero*. The symbolic blackness of the Bride in Canticles and the Davidic

princes of Lamentations is extended to this hidden Mary and her child. . . .

In summary, the two royal refugees from Israel, mother and daughter, might logically be represented in early European art as a dark-skinned mother and child, the hidden ones. The Black Madonnas of the early shrines in Europe (fifth to twelfth centuries) might then have been venerated as symbolic of this other Mary and her child, the Sangraal, which Joseph of Arimathea brought in safety to the coast of France. The symbol for a male of the royal house of David would be a flowering or budding staff, but the symbol for a woman would be the chalice—a cup or vessel containing the royal blood of Jesus. And that is exactly what the Holy Grail is said to have been!

Mary Magdalene
The Model for Women in the Church

An Interview with Susan Haskins

Susan Haskins is the author of *Mary Magdalen: Myth and Metaphor*. An excerpt from that 1993 book follows the interview.

In your opinion, who was the true Mary Magdalene?

The true Mary Magdalene is the figure in the Gospels: the leading woman follower of Christ, who, together with the other women named in Luke, supported and contributed to the living expenses of the itinerant group. She was present at his crucifixion, witnessed it, and according to John's Gospel, was one of the privileged few, along with the Virgin Mary, wife of Cleophas, and St. John, to be beneath the cross. She was witness to the putting of his body in Joseph of Arimathea's sepulcher; she came at dawn with either one or two other Marys to bring unguents. In John's Gospel, it was to her alone and first that Christ appeared after his resurrection, and it was to her alone and first that he gave the message of the new Christian life. Mark's Gospel, in a later addition, says that she had had seven devils driven from her. We have no idea of what she looked like. She is shown with long red or golden hair in medieval and later art, because blond hair was the attribute of ideal feminine beauty. We do not know what her life was like. It is assumed that because she, along with the other women followers, supported the group "of their own substance," that she was mature— among the other women were ones who were married or separated—and comparatively well off and independent. So I agree with those who see her as a patron and supporter of Jesus.

What are the representations of Mary Magdalene that have occurred throughout history? Do any of them fit with Dan Brown's theory in The Da Vinci Code *that she may have been married to Jesus and had his child?*

Dan Brown's theory that Mary Magdalene may have been married to Jesus and had his child has a long history. It was made particularly public by *Holy Blood, Holy Grail,* and followed up by Bishop Spong and others. Luther seems to have thought that she had a sexual relationship with Christ as far back as the sixteenth century! As there is no concrete evidence of either a marriage or child, I would give no credence to this hypothesis.

Why did the church depict Mary Magdalene as a prostitute for so many years? Was she simply a victim of bad luck to be confused with all of the other Marys in the New Testament, or was there a kind of foul play involved?

The church depicted Mary Magdalene as a prostitute

because of the various commentaries on the Gospels made by early church fathers from the third century, trying to work out who all the Gospel characters were. There are several females called Mary in the New Testament, which led to confusion. Because Luke's first mention of Mary Magdalene, following Christ from Galilee with the other women, and the male disciples follows his account of the unnamed woman named as a sinner, forgiven by Christ in the house of the Pharisee, Pope Gregory the Great (A.D. 595) conflated these two figures, as well as that of Mary of Bethany. Although the woman is only called a "sinner," the assumption was that her sin was that of the flesh, even though the word *porin*, used to describe her, does not mean "prostitute." Making Mary Magdalene a repentant prostitute diminished her role as first apostle, an otherwise extremely powerful and important role. We cannot know for sure whether foul play was involved, but certainly ecclesiastical politics were. The early church had women priests and bishops, but by the fifth century the sacerdotal role was not allowed to women, although tomb monuments in southern Italy show that women were still carrying out the priestly role. Diminishing Mary Magdalene's role to both penitent and prostitute puts her on a par with Eve, whose sexuality and gender were deemed by the male ecclesiastical hierarchy as being responsible for the Fall.

Do you think that Jesus and Mary Magdalene could have been married?

I personally do not think Jesus and Mary Magdalene were married. That an important relationship existed between them is undeniable, but was it any more than the fact that she was his leading woman disciple? People find the idea compelling for many reasons: there is this enigmatic relationship in the Gospels—even more so in the Gnostic

Gospels—so a kind of logical progression would be marriage. Rabbis were often, if not usually, married, so it has often been suggested that Christ must also have been, although there is nothing in the Gospels to suggest this. We have no evidence of a child, and the Merovingian link is very unlikely.

How does The Da Vinci Code *character of Mary Magdalene fit in with other characters in prior religious belief systems? Is there a woman comparable to Mary Magdalene in Greek, Egyptian, Jewish, or pagan/tribal cultures?*

The Da Vinci Code is interesting for its narrative re: the goddess figure, suppressed by the early church. The theme of resurrection is found in Egyptian, Sumerian, and Christian belief systems: Isis and Osiris, Ishtar and Tammuz, Mary Magdalene and Christ. Mary Magdalene can be seen as the Christian goddess.

What do you think the Gospel of Philip *tells us about the relationship between Jesus and Mary Magdalene, and about the rivalries with Peter for control of the church?*

The *Gospel of Philip* is regarded by scholars as an allegory of the relationship between Christ and his church, his love for his church. Elaine Pagels sees the antagonism between Peter and Mary Magdalene as—if I remember rightly—a metaphor of the antagonism between the evolving early church in the second and third centuries, based on a hierarchy of bishops, deacons, and priests, and Gnosticism, which valued individual inspiration or knowledge, without the intermediary of the church. Peter was also jealous of Mary Magdalene because of gender issues.

Why was Mary Magdalene one of the few at the crucifixion? Why might she have attended when other disciples did not? And what is the importance of Mary Magdalene being the first to see Jesus after the resurrection?

It is interesting that Mary Magdalene was one of the few at the crucifixion. But this is only in John's account; in the others, she witnesses it from a distance, with other women. We do not know who edited the Gospel texts or why they are only approximately identical, but presumably they come from different oral traditions. The women disciples were there, but not the males because the males had taken fright, particularly Peter, who denied Jesus thrice.

It is, or should be, of the utmost importance to Christians that it was to Mary Magdalene that Jesus appeared first after the resurrection, because the keystone to Christianity is the promise of everlasting life—the very message Christ gave to her to tell the world. It was male prejudice in both the Judaic and Hellenistic systems that disallowed women as witnesses and therefore allowed the male disciples to claim the right to give the news of the resurrection. But, of course, it can be seen as equally important—as a matter of editing the canon, Christian apologetics, and ecclesiastical politics—for the church to deny this role and to assert the premise that "You are Peter and upon this rock I will found my church."

Why is the topic of Mary Magdalene so compelling in itself?

She is a beautiful image of an independent woman, who follows a charismatic preacher and offers an ethical and theological framework for his followers. She is also dynamic, a leader and a model of fidelity. She witnesses the crucifixion, unlike the male disciples. She is courageous. She goes alone, or with others, to the sepulcher at dawn. She meets Christ. Christ is egalitarian. He heals women of their afflictions without criticism and social stigma—the "sinner" in Luke; the Samaritan woman, the woman with the issue of blood, the woman taken in adultery, Mary Magdalene with her seven devils. He appears to a woman, Mary Magdalene, first after his resurrection, and he gives one woman, Mary Magdalene, the role of delivering the Christian message of everlasting life.

She has represented the sinner redeemed since the sixth century, and for this reason has been a model for all Christians, male and female. She offers them hope. Her closeness to Christ has been a topic of fascination since early Christianity; her cult burgeoned from the eleventh century. She represents the fallible female redeemed, as well as her role as intercessor with God. Renewed interest in her in our times is due in part to feminism, particularly in recent scholarship about women's roles in religion and the reassertion of their right to be priests, which has been denied for seventeen centuries. Mary Magdalene, as first apostle and disciple, is the model for women in the church, both Catholic and Protestant, and in the synagogue.

In four excerpts from Susan Haskins's seminal book, *Mary Magdalen: Myth and Metaphor,* we sample the author's view on the role of the female apostles, how Mary's relationship to Christ is portrayed in the *Gospel of Philip,* what the exact relationship between Jesus and Mary Magdalene might have been, and where Mary went after the crucifixion—and how French towns built mini-industries around worshipping Mary Magdalene. Haskins does not mince words. She states her case baldly:

And so the transformation of Mary Magdalen was complete. From the gospel figure with her active role as her-

ald of the New Life—the Apostle before the Apostles—
she became the redeemed whore and Christianity's
model of repentance: a manageable, controllable figure,
an effective weapon and instrument of propaganda
against her own sex.

Mary Magdalen
Myth and Metaphor

BY SUSAN HASKINS
Copyright © 1993 by Susan Haskins. Used by permission.

De Unica Magdalena

We know very little about Mary Magdalen. The predominant
image we have of her is of a beautiful woman with long golden
hair, weeping for her sins, the very incarnation of the age-old
equation between feminine beauty, sexuality and sin. For nearly
two thousand years, the traditional conception of Mary Magdalen has been that of the prostitute who, hearing the words of
Jesus Christ, repented of her sinful past and henceforth
devoted her life and love to him. She appears in countless devotional images, scarlet-cloaked and with loose hair, kneeling
below the cross, or seated at Christ's feet in the house of Mary
and Martha of Bethany, or as the beauteous prostitute herself,
sprawled at his feet, unguent jar by her side, in the house of the
Pharisee. Her very name evokes images of beauty and sensuality, yet when we look for this creature in the New Testament,
we look for her in vain. All we truly know of her comes from
the four gospels, a few brief references which yield an inconsistent, even contradictory vision. These shifting reflections

converge, however, on four salient aspects: that Mary Magdalen was one of Christ's female followers, was present at his crucifixion, was a witness—indeed, according to the gospel of St. John, *the* witness—of his resurrection, and was the first to be charged with the supreme ministry, that of proclaiming the Christian message. She brought the knowledge that through Christ's victory over death, life everlasting was offered to all who believe . . .

One of the most striking aspects about the gospel accounts is the role given to Christ's female followers as supporters and witnesses during the events of that first Easter. Their faith and tenacity were acknowledged by early Christian commentators, but later cast into the background as new emphases and interpretations increasingly reduced their importance. The true significance of their witness was for the most part ignored, while Mary Magdalen herself was in the late sixth century recreated as an entirely different character to serve the purposes of the ecclesiastical hierarchy. This refashioning by the early Church Fathers has distorted our view of Mary Magdalen and the other women; we need therefore to turn again to the gospels in order to see them more clearly.

Mark tells us that Mary Magdalen was among the women who when Christ was in Galilee "followed him and *ministered* unto him" (my italics; 15:41; see also Matt. 27:55). "To minister" is translated from the Greek verb *diakonein*, to serve or to minister. It is also the root of the word "deacon," which establishes the important function given to the women within the group of both female and male disciples. Luke, from whom we also hear that the group has been part of Christ's entourage for some considerable time before the crucifixion (8:1–4), corroborates their ministering role, and amplifies it with the words "of their own substance" (v.3). This role has often been assumed to have been domestic, as women's lives in Jewish society of the first century A.D. were circumscribed within their traditional household environment. They carried out such tasks as grinding flour, baking and laundering, feeding children, bedmaking and wool-working. Until modern times the role of the women amongst Christ's followers has also been taken to have been merely domestic, and therefore less important, an assumption which has only recently been questioned by scholars. But "of their own substance" indicates that the women contributed the means to enable the travelling preachers to carry out their work. Whilst women are known to have supported rabbis with money, possessions and food, their participation in the practice of Judaism was negligible. Although they were allowed to read the Torah at congregational services, they were forbidden to recite lessons in public in order to "safeguard the honor of the congregation."

In the first century A.D., one Rabbi Eliezer was quoted as saying, "Rather should the words of the Torah be burned than entrusted to a woman!"[1] It was for much the same reason that in the synagogue itself, women were seated apart from the men. They were restricted to a gallery above, unable to wear the phylactery—the small leather box containing verses from the Old Testament attached to the head and arm by leather thongs—or to carry out any liturgical functions. Their exclusion from the priesthood was based on their supposed uncleanness during menstruation, as defined in a Temple ordinance (Leviticus 15), a taboo which was also invoked by the Christian Church and still used until recently as a powerful weapon against the entry of women into ecclesiastical office. A priest, according to Leviticus 21 and 22, was to be clean and holy at all times to offer sacrifice. Women were, nonetheless, allowed to be prophetesses, as the Old Testament bears

---

1. Mishnah Sotah 3, 4, quoted in Leonard Swidler, *Biblical Affirmations of Woman*, Philadelphia, 1979, p. 163.

witness, and even, as in the case of Anna, daughter of Phanuel, celebrated as such in Christ's day (Luke 2:36–8).

It is in this context that Luke's phrase has a special significance, as it suggests that Christ's women followers were central to the group as a whole, in that they donated their own property and income to provide Christ and the male disciples with the means to live as they travelled around the countryside preaching and healing. This, in turn, sheds further light on the women, since their ability to dispose of their money presupposes their financial independence, and possibly their maturity, which is corroborated by the statement that one of the Marys is the "mother of James," presumably referring to the apostle (Mark 15:40 and 16:1). Even more important is the recent suggestion that, contrary to a general assumption that the women disciples did not preach, and in this way differed from their male counterparts, they may well have done so, since the term "to follow" as used by Mark to describe those at the crucifixion— "who also when he was in Galilee followed him, and ministered unto him" (15:41)—was used technically to imply their full participation, both in belief and in the activities of the travelling preachers, as is borne out by the accounts in Acts and in Paul's letters of the women's involvement. Nowhere in the texts is there any indication that Christ regarded the women's contribution as inferior or subsidiary to that of his male disciples. Indeed, it could be argued that the women's contribution both during and after the crucifixion showed greater tenacity of purpose and courage, though not necessarily greater faith, than that of the men who fled. Unlike the eleven male disciples who feared for their own lives, the women disciples followed, were present at the crucifixion, witnessed the burial, discovered the empty tomb and, as true disciples, were rewarded with the first news of the resurrection and, in the case of Mary Magdalen, the first meeting with the risen Christ.

Christ's disinterest in the conventions of his day and his desire to radically alter certain social *mores*, are made manifest in his treatment of women, not least because they actually formed part of his retinue. Although women might assist rabbis financially, it was certainly uncommon for them to accompany preachers as travelling disciples. Christ also welcomed into the group the kind of women whom Luke describes as having been healed of "evil spirits and infirmities" (8:2–3), those who might otherwise have been regarded as social outcasts. Of the few women in the community who are named, one, Joanna, is or has been married to Chuza, Herod's steward, and must therefore have left her family and the royal court to follow Christ. It perhaps should be noted that the reference to Joanna's social status, as a married woman, has the effect of further determining that of Mary Magdalen: of the women described, she alone stands out undefined by a designation attaching her to some male as wife, mother or daughter; and she is the only one to be identified by her place of birth. It is therefore as an *independent* woman that she is presented: this implies that she must also have been of some means, to have been able to choose to follow and support Christ. . . .

Mary Magdalen's "seven devils" to which both Luke and Mark refer were a focus for speculation amongst early Christian commentators; their link with the "evil spirits and infirmities" ascribed to some of the women may well have led to their identification with the seven deadly sins. It has been suggested that Mary Magdalen was the best known of the women because her "healing was the most dramatic," as the seven demons may have indicated a "possession of extraordinary malignity."[2] However, nowhere in the New Testament is demoniacal possession regarded as synonymous with

2. Ben Witherington III, *Women in the Ministry of Jesus*, Cambridge, 1984, p. 117.

sin.[3] That Mary Magdalen's condition might have been psychological, that is, seen as madness, rather than moral or sexual, seems never to have entered into the considerations of the early biblical commentators, although it preoccupied her interpreters from the nineteenth century onwards. There is, after all, no implication in the story of the man possessed of devils that his "unclean spirit" is sexual (Luke 8:26–39) ... Mrs. Balfour, the noted nineteenth-century Evangelical, was one of the first to deny that Mary Magdalen's malaise was anything other than psychological, and more recently J. E. Fallon has written that rather than being in a state of sinfulness, she probably suffered from a "violent and chronic nervous disorder."

To the ascription to her of the ambiguous "seven devils" was added the putative disadvantage of her birthplace: Mary Magdalen's second name, *Magdalini* in Greek, signified her belonging to el Mejdel, a prosperous fishing village on the north-west bank of the lake of Galilee, four miles north of Tiberias. Its apparent notoriety in the early centuries of Christianity—it was destroyed in A.D. 75 because of its infamy and the licentious behaviour of its inhabitants—may have helped later to colour the name and reputation of Mary Magdalen herself.[4] (Today, a rusting sign by the lake tells the passing tourist that Magdala, or Migdal, had been a flourishing city at the end of the period of the Second Temple, and was also the birthplace of Mary of Magdala who "followed and ministered to Jesus.'")

It might be argued that none of the elements detailed above offers sufficient grounds in itself for proving that Mary Magdalen was a sinner or prostitute. Indeed, these assertions might never have achieved currency—at least not to the extent they did—had she not also been confused with other female

3. Although in John 8:46–9 direct comparison is made between being a sinner and having a devil.
4. J. E. Fallon, "Mary Magdalen," *NCE*, vol. IX, p. 387.

characters from the gospels, some of whom are explicitly described as sinners; and one who, from her story, appears to have been a prostitute. To later commentators, and in an ecclesiastical environment which was becoming more entrenched in its attachment to the ideal of celibacy, her femaleness would only have served to lend credence to this misidentification. By such means could the seven devils with which she was possessed assume the social and moral stigma, the monstrous proportions, of lust and temptation—those vices which early Christian interpreters of Genesis traditionally associated with the Female—that they did. Mary Magdalen, chief female disciple, first apostle and beloved friend of Christ, would become transformed into a penitent whore . . .

Companion of the Saviour

Her close relationship to Christ is emphasised in the *Gospel of Philip* where she is depicted as one of the "three who always walked with the Lord: Mary his mother, her sister and Magdalene [*sic*], the one who was called his companion. His sister and his mother and his companion were each a Mary. And the companion of the Saviour is Mary Magdalene." The Greek word *koinonōs* used to describe Mary Magdalen, whilst often rendered as "companion," is more correctly translated as "partner" or "consort," a woman with whom a man has had sexual intercourse. Two pages on is another passage, which amplifies in sexual imagery the relationship already described:

> But Christ loved her more than all the disciples and used to kiss her often on the mouth. The rest of the disciples were offended by it and expressed disapproval. They said to him, "Why do you love her more than all of us?" The Saviour answered and said to them, "Why do I not love you like [I love] her?"

Erotic love has often been the vehicle used to express mystical experiences, perhaps most notably in that great spiritual epithalamium, the *Canticle of Canticles*, or *Song of Songs*, which describes in the most sensual and voluptuous imagery what the rabbis were to read as an allegory of Yahweh's love for Israel, and early Christian commentators to interpret as Christ's love for the Church, for the Christian soul—sometimes in the person of Mary Magdalen—and for the Virgin Mary. In the *Gospel of Philip*, the spiritual union between Christ and Mary Magdalen is couched in terms of human sexuality; it is also a metaphor for the reunion of Christ and the Church which takes place in the bridal chamber, the place of fullness or *pleroma*. While the tractate itself deals with sacramental and ethical arguments, its main theme is the idea, common to many Gnostic and later Christian writings, that mankind's woes had been brought about by the differentiation of the sexes caused by the separation of Eve from Adam, which destroyed the primal androgynous unity found in Genesis 1:27, after which the Gnostic spirit would forever yearn. As the author of the *Gospel of Philip* explains: "When Eve was still in Adam death did not exist. When she was separated from him, death came into being. If he again becomes complete and attains his former self, death will be no more." The *Gospel of Philip* uses the bridal chamber as a metaphor for the reunion between "Adam" and "Eve," in which the polarities of male and female would be abolished, and androgyny, or the spiritual state, would be effected through the coming of Christ, the Bridegroom.[5] The relationship between Christ and Mary Magdalen symbolises that perfect spiritual union. Some Gnostics, however, were believed by their adversaries to put erotic concepts into practice, and to take part in sexual orgies which were profane re-enactions of Christian ritual: according to Epiphanius,

5. Wesley W. Isenberg, introd., *Gospel of Philip*, NHL, p. 131.

the Gnostics had a book called the "Great Questions of Mary" which represented Christ as a revealer to Mary Magdalen of obscene ceremonies which a sect had to perform for its salvation. He wrote indignantly:

> For in the Questions of Mary which are called "Great" . . . they assert that he [Jesus] gave her [Mary] a revelation, taking her aside to the mountain and praying; and he brought forth from his side a woman and began to unite with her, and so, forsooth, taking his effluent, he showed that "we must so do, that we may live"; and how when Mary fell to the ground abashed, he raised her up again and said to her: "Why didst thou doubt, O thou of little faith?"[6]

The sequence in the *Gospel of Philip* can be seen at two different levels, one symbolic of the love of Christ for the Church—in the person of Mary Magdalen—and the other as representing an historical situation in which she symbolises the feminine element in the Church. As we have seen, the preferential treatment that Mary Magdalen receives from Christ in both the *Gospel of Mary* and the *Gospel of Philip* gives rise to jealousy among the other disciples, notably Peter. In the *Pistis Sophia*, one of the few tractates found before the writings at Nag Hammadi, a similar argument breaks out between Mary and Peter, who complains on behalf of the male disciples that Mary dominates the conversation about Pistis Sophia's fall from the realm of Light, and so prevents them from speaking. Jesus rebukes him. Mary later tells Jesus that she fears Peter, "because he is wont to threaten me, and he hateth our sex." (Jesus tells her that anyone who is inspired by the divine spirit

6. Epiphanius (*Panarion*, 26.8. 2–3), quoted in H.-Ch. Puech, "Gnostic Gospels and Related Documents," in *NTA*, vol. I, pp. 338–9.

may come forward to speak, implying that inspiration nulli-fies sexual differentiation, and reiterating the theme of androgyny found in the *Gospel of Philip*.) It has been suggested that Peter's antagonism towards Mary Magdalen may reflect the historical ambivalence of the leaders of the orthodox community towards the participation of women in the Church. But by the end of the second century, the egalitarian principles defined in the New Testament, and adhered to in this context by St. Paul, had been discarded in favour of a return to the patriarchal system of Judaism which had pre-ceded them. Thus at the level of historical interpretation, the Gnostic texts may have referred to a political tension in the early Church. It is a situation inferred in the synoptics through the disciples' disbelief of the women's account of the resurrection, and in Paul's omission of the women's witness of the resurrection, but never alluded to directly by the orthodox Christians, namely the suppression of the feminine element within the Church which had gradually been taking place from the second century.

Much Malign'd Magdalen

Christ's genuine humanity, and therefore his sexuality, have been the subject of several serious studies over the past three decades. Unlike the Renaissance images which drew attention to his genitalia in order to stress his humanity, recently the problem has been how to deal with his sexuality in the context of his human existence. The suggestion that he may have been married, as a rabbi of his age would probably have been, has led one writer, as we have seen, to conjecture that he might even have been married to Mary Magdalen. This was argued by the Protestant theologian William E. Phipps in his book *Was Jesus Married? The Distortion of Sexuality in the Christian Tradi-tion*, first published in 1970, and reissued in 1989. Marriage to Mary Magdalen, he suggests, might have taken place during the second decade of Christ's life; she may even, in a further extension of the hypothesis, have been unfaithful, and Christ out of unwavering love, may well have duly forgiven her. This experience, according to Phipps, rendered Christ far more understanding about the nature of adultery and love, *agape*, and convinced him to reject all notion of divorce. Phipps's "intriguing conjecture" could therefore be taken to accord to Mary Magdalen the power to influence to some extent Christ's views of human relationships, a theme which has been resumed recently, and with rather less authority, by other more populist writers. A book published in 1992, Dr. Barbara Thiering's *Jesus the Man*, goes so far as to claim that Mary Magdalen was not only married to Jesus, but left him after the crucifixion (which he survived for thirty years), having borne him a girl and two boys. Christ it seems, then married again. The author, a lecturer in the school of divinity at Sydney University, bases her claims on a new reading of the Dead Sea Scrolls.

The idea that Mary Magdalen might have been married to Christ, and the bearer of his children, receives an airing in [Baigent, Leigh and Lincoln's] *Holy Blood, Holy Grail*, one of the more bizarre manifestations of the late twentieth-century popular interest both in the story of Christ and in conspiracy theory. Following a staged crucifixion, in which Jesus is either taken down from the cross in a drugged state, or replaced by Simon of Cyrene, his family is obliged to flee from those, headed by St. Peter, who were not part of the plot and are bent on preserving the reputation of Christ the Messiah. Mary Magdalen, together with brother Lazarus and others, arrive in the south of France, she bearing the *Sang Raal*, or Holy Grail, which the authors interpret as the holy blood of Christ in the form of his child or children. Once established within the Jewish community in the south of France, the family intermarries with the Merovingian kings and so on down through Godfroi de Bouillon (who almost becomes king of Jerusalem), the house of Lorraine, the Hapsburgs and the ever shadowy, but ever present, Prieuré de Sion, who hold the secret of it all, whatever it may be (and are also poised to create a unified state of Europe with a descendant of Christ, and of course Mary Magdalen, on its throne), which is rumoured to be hidden near the town of Rennes-le-Château, whose *curé* Saunière discovered coded documents in the church, and constructed the mysterious Tour de Magdala to house his library. The authors breathlessly bend to their purpose whatever information comes their way, and the book offers no new insights into the historical figure of Mary Magdalen, but concentrates on trying to assemble proof for some of the more far-fetched of the legends which have accumulated around her over the centuries, using as their guiding principle the idea that there is no smoke without a fire. . . .

[In a dense, complex and brilliant analysis, Susan Haskins recounts the many-faceted history of how a cult of Mary Magdalene came to be so prominent in France. She traces the arc of far-flung myth and legend that has Mary fleeing Jerusalem and heading in all directions—Ephesus, where there was a long-standing Greek goddess cult around Diana and where the Virgin Mary is thought to have gone (visitors today are still shown the house where the Virgin Mary allegedly lived); thirty years in the Egyptian desert as a hermit; and even to Northumbria in England, where she, Joseph of Arimathea, and the Holy Grail become bound up in the legends of Avalon and King Arthur. But in medieval France, an industry arose, creating provenance about how Mary Magdalene arrived and lived in France. The fascinating tale of human mythmaking, fraud, and credulity that Haskins tells is worth every *Da Vinci Code* reader's attention. If you think Pierre Plantard and the Dossier Secrets are a fraud, or if you think Baigent, Leigh, and Lincoln—or Dan Brown, for that matter—have played too fast and loose with history, you should have seen what the abbots, bishops, and enterprising noblemen did during the Crusades: they dreamed up relics having to do with Mary Magdalene—some bits of her hair, some of her teardrops. They brought back alleged holy objects from the Holy Land, made big profits in the trade in relics, and mined them for the snake oil of purported medicinal value. They also created processionals, pilgrimages, festivals, and some of the first outdoor theater productions, all of which brought tourist dollars, trade and commerce to small French towns. And wherever Mary Magdalene's name and image as a penitent were invoked, it was usually to provide a cover for festivals of debauchery. As Haskins puts it:]

The Grandes Heures *of Vézelay*

In the twelfth and thirteenth centuries, huge pilgrimages grew around the more famous shrines, with vast crowds in the hope of cures, deliverance from demons, and other such manifestations of divine intervention. These were not the only purposes, however, of such festivities, for dissoluteness and debauchery were often companions to the relics being processed . . . Seduction, it seems, was rife, and procuresses plying their trade were often much in evidence. But . . . the local town council would have been extremely loath to abolish its pilgrimage, since such processions brought the town large profits as all the pilgrims had to be fed and lodged, and anyway, it seemed such decadence was all part of the occasion.

Pilgrims flocked from all over France to touch the tomb of Mary Magdalen at Vézelay; some even came from as far as

England to be healed, forgiven, and dispossessed of their devils at the holy site. And with these faithful came the merchants too, ever ready to profit from the pious . . .

[The cult of Mary Magdalene was so potent, and her spirit was credited with such intercessory powers with God, that Mary received credit for everything from bringing peace to Burgundy to putting dead knights back in the saddle. Papal bulls issued by Lucius III, Urban III, and Clement III all confirmed that Mary Magdalene's body was, indeed, resting in the French town of Vézelay. But how did she get from Jerusalem to France, and what did she do during her years there? Haskins picks up the story as follows:]

There was always, however, the awkward question of how Mary Magdalen's body had come to its resting place in Burgundy, so far way from her birthplace in Judaea. Reverence was paid to a tomb, but although the body of the "blessed Magdalen" was said to rest in the monastery's church, it had never been seen, and nor had adequate account been given of its arrival from Palestine after the ascension. In the eleventh century, the simple answer given to tiresome questions could be "summed up in a few words," as a document issued by Vézelay rather testily pointed out. "All is possible to God who does what he pleases. Nothing is difficult for him when he has decided to do it for the well-being of men." When this reply proved unsatisfactory, the narrator told of how Mary Magdalen had appeared to him standing outside her tomb, saying, "It is me, whom many people believe to be here." Warnings of the divine chastisement which had befallen previous doubters were given to those who queried the existence of the Magdalen's body. An excuse for not exposing the remains appears in a late twelfth-century manuscript which told of the occasion when Geoffrey [abbott of Vézelay] himself had decided to remove the Magdalen's relics from the little crypt where they had been found to put them in a precious reliquary. The church had suddenly been plunged into thick darkness, and the people assisting had fled terrified, and all those present had suffered; it had henceforth been decided to relinquish all ideas of opening the holy tomb as such acts clearly provoked wrath from above. Faith was all that was required, the monks at Vézelay told their faint-hearted pilgrims.

Remembrance of Things Past

The famous French sweet, the madeleine, is associated with Mary Magdalene. This cross between a cookie and a pastry is traditionally made of eggs, butter, flour, and sugar. It is the act of biting into the madeleine, with all the nostalgic memories it conjures, that sets Marcel Proust off on the telling of his long, long novel, *Remembrance of Things Past*. Legend holds that the nuns of a convent dedicated to Mary Magdalene in the town of Commercy either invented or perfected the madeleine, later selling their recipe to commercial bakers for a fabulous sum in order to support themselves after their convent was abolished in the wake of the French revolution. Madeleines became ubiquitous in France, but were made in particularly great quantity on Mary Magdalene's feast day, July 22.

Documents issued by the abbey in the thirteenth century to justify its claims to possess Mary Magdalen's relics relate how the pilgrims' faith had so dwindled that it was clear to the monks that they had to engineer some way of making their claim credible. A flood of hagiographical material henceforth issued from the abbey in which a new element in the Magdalen story emerged. Tales, often entirely contradictory, were told of how the body had arrived, not directly from Palestine, but from somewhere in Provence where she had been buried between the years 882 and 884, and how a "holy theft" by one Aléaume had been perpetrated to bring the precious remains to their final resting place. . . .

However, the most widely believed story was that she had arrived by boat, like other saints and apostles who made their way to France, and had been accompanied by Maximinus—in the first account—one of the seventy-two disciples (for, as Duchesne wryly remarked, "a woman could not have come alone as she always has need of support"). They had disembarked at Marseille and there preached the gospel. In this account, our saint had once more become the *apostola apostolorum* who, having been the first apostle of the gospels, now, through her arrival in France, and her preaching, continued her apostolic career, and in the process had converted the pagan prince of Marseille. (A later monkish narrator, however, clearly felt it his duty to explain discreetly how a woman could have taken part in these apostolic and by definition masculine activities, remembering that ecclesiastical discipline was disinclined to favour female apostolacy, and told instead of how, having arrived on French soil, Mary Magdalen had not preached but retired in solitude.[7]) According to this same legend, Maximinus had subsequently become the first bishop of Aix. Mary Magdalen had predeceased her companion who buried her and was then himself buried near her. A special altar at the church of St. Sauveur at Aix was dedicated to Maximinus and Mary Magdalen as first founders of the city, which also claimed the honour of having been evangelised in the first century. A false charter purporting to be dated 7 August 1103 refers to this consecration, written by the archbishop

7. Baudouin de Gaiffier, "Hagiographie bourguignonne," *Anlaecta Bollandiana*, vol. LXIX, 1951, p. 140.

and canons of the church in support of their claims at the end of the twelfth century that the bones of its illustrious founders were still in the tomb from which Vézelay had fabricated its *furtum sacrum*.

A later version, recalling the Magdalen's relationship to Lazarus and Martha, recounted the family from Bethany's flight from Palestine during the Jewish persecution—where, as close friends of Christ, they would have been prime targets—their journey across the sea, and arrival at Aix. In this, Lazarus had become first bishop of Marseille, Martha had lived at Tarascon, and overcome the wicked dragon, and they had all died; the bones of Lazarus and Mary Magdalen had been taken to Burgundy, but those of Martha had remained in Provence, where they were "discovered" in 1187.

By the thirteenth century, an alarmingly confusing array of versions existed of Mary Magdalen's voyage, sometimes featuring Maximinus, sometimes Lazarus and Martha, sometimes including Sidonius and Marcellina, Martha's servant, and sometimes apostolising Marseille and lower Gaul. But the results were uniform: the relics were now at Vézelay, brought by Badilon in an heroic "holy" theft. . . .

Without the monastic rivalries of the Middle Ages, and the pilgrimage to Vézelay, Mary Magdalen might never have become as popular as she did. Without the claim of the monks of St. Maximin, and her consequent adoption by the Dominicans, the concept of the penitent Magdalen, who had spent thirty years in the desert, might never have been taken to Italy, where it appeared in liturgica and in frescoes painted in churches and monasteries all over the peninsula from the thirteenth century. Through Charles of Anjou, king of Naples and Sicily, the idea of Mary Magdalen was taken to Naples, and through marriage alliances between his own royal house and that of Spain, she also reached the Iberian peninsula. And the movement founded in her name in Germany in 1225 for the moral relief of prostitutes and fallen women, which grew to enormous proportions throughout the Middle Ages, and lasted in various forms until early in the twentieth century, might never have existed had it not been for Vézelay's claims to have in its possession the relics of Christianity's most loved and illustrious penitent.

[In the next excerpt, de Boer takes a painstaking, rigorously researched approach to sifting the textual evidence supplied by the Gospels and other historic documents about Mary Magdalene. She has many insights into who Mary Magdalene may have been, where she may have been from, and what kind of relationship she may have had with Jesus. But, in the end, she draws more circumspect conclusions than other experts whose views are represented in this book, insisting on avoiding the last tempting jump to conclusions where there is no hard evidence.]

Mary Magdalene
Beyond the Myth

By ESTHER DE BOER

Excerpted from *Mary Magdalene: Beyond the Myth* by Esther de Boer. Used by permission of Trinity Press International. Copyright © 1996 by Meinema. Translation © 1997 by John Bowden. Esther De Boer studies theology at the Free University of Amsterdam and is now a minister of the Dutch Reformed Churches in Ouderkerk aan de Amstel.

Was Mary also deliberately banished to the background in the Middle Ages because of the role of women? It is worth remembering the precise moment when Mary Magdalene officially became the penitent.

Before the Council of Trent (1545–1563) there were still calendars of saints which gave Mary Magdalene no predicate, or which celebrated her as the first witness to the resurrection of the Lord. Local customs to mark her day differed from place to place. However, on the authority of the Council, liturgical books were produced which were binding on the whole Roman Catholic Church. Thus the Roman Missal appeared in 1570. In that first compulsory missal Mary Magdalene is given the epithet 'penitent.' Here the missal was not just taking up the image of Mary Magdalene which had been disseminated by Gregory the Great and others. This image also emerged from the Counter-Reformation church. Over against the Reformation with its doctrine of grace, the Counter-Reformation emphasized the doctrine of penance and merits. Here St Mary Magdalene could play an important role as a penitent and one who was favoured *par excellence*.

The Second Vatican Council (1962–1965) commissioned a revision of the Roman Missal, which came out in 1970. The Gospel reading on the feast day of Mary Magdalene in the revised edition of the Missal is John 20.1–18. The encounter of Mary Magdalene with the Risen Lord stands at the centre. The word 'penitent' is no longer used. The further explanation now given by the Missal is:

> Mary Magdalene was one of the women who followed Christ on his travels. She was present when he died and was the first to see him after his resurrection (Mark 16.9). Veneration of her spread in the Western church above all in the twelfth century.[1]

1. Dutch National Council for the Liturgy, *Altaarmissaal voor de Nederlandse kerkprovincie*, 1978, 864.

So you could say that Mary Magdalene was officially passed off as a penitent for precisely 400 years ... Anyone in quest of Mary Magdalene must feel some disappointment at the sparse light that the earliest sources shed on her. Who Mary Magdalene was before she met Jesus, what kind of life she led, how old she was, how she came to be converted, what became of her later: the earliest sources leave us guessing.

This brings us to a first crossroads in our quest. What conclusion are we to draw from the fact that the evangelists tell us so little? ... The most obvious reply would be that the evangelists thought that any further information about her was unimportant for the story of the belief in Jesus that they wanted to tell. ...

Reading through the birth or death notices in the papers one hardly ever comes across the name 'Magdalene' or 'Magdalena.' However, the names Magda and Madeleine do appear, and these are derivatives. So you could suppose that 'Magdalena' is a first name. Nothing is further from the truth. The four New Testament Gospels also never speak of Mary Magdalene, the name we are used to, but of Mary the Magdalene. The Gospel of Luke put this even more emphatically, speaking of Mary who 'was called the Magdalene' (Luke 8.2). The addition 'the Magdalene' is intended to make it clear which Mary this is. It is the Mary who comes from Magdala.

Mary Magdalene: her name conjures up a picture of her background.

The town of Magdala is not mentioned in the New Testament, at least in the text of the New Testament as we normally read it. But the New Testament has been handed down in a great many manuscripts, and in a few of them Magdala does occur, in a version of Mark (8.10) and one of Matthew (15.39). These read Magdala where the official text has Dalmanutha and Magadan respectively. These are two place names which scholars have not been able to identify more closely. If

Mark and Matthew indeed meant Magdala, that is the place to which Jesus and his disciples crossed after he had fed four thousand people with seven loaves and a few fishes.

There, in the region of Magadan/Dalmanutha or Magdala, Pharisees asked him for a sign from heaven 'to tempt him' (Matt. 16.1–4; Mark 8.11–13). If anything, we can only conclude from the New Testament that there were scribes in the region of Magdala and that the region could be reached by ship.

There has been a long discussion about the possible location of Magdala. It becomes clear from the rabbinic literature that we have to look for Magdala in the neighbourhood of Tiberias, by the sea of Galilee.

Nowadays, north of Tiberias lies the small town of Meidel. The name could recall Magdala. That is an assumption which fits closely with testimonies of earlier pilgrims who locate Magdala between Tiberias and Capernaum to the north.

There are reports of pilgrimages between the sixth and the seventeenth centuries. Without exception they bear witness that Magdala was equidistant between Tiberias and Tabga, a place close to Capernaum. Pilgrims talk of the house of Mary Magdalene that they could inspect and the church that the empress Helena (fourth century) had had built in her honour. Ricoldus de Monte Crucis in his travel account (1294) tells us that the church was no longer in use at the end of the thirteenth century. He writes:

> Then we arrived in Magdala . . ., the town of Mary Magdalene by the Sea of Gennesaret. We burst into tears and wept because we found a splendid church, completely intact, but being used as a stable. We then sang in this place and proclaimed the gospel of the Magdalene there.[2]

2. Manns, "Magdala" (n.4), 335.

If Magdala in fact lay on the site of Mejdel, then Jesus *must* have been there. The city was on the road from Nazareth, the small village where Jesus grew up (around twenty miles from Magdala) to Capernaum, where he later went to live.

Capernaum was about six miles from Magdala. It is not unthinkable that Jesus knew the town well. At all events, it seems possible that he taught and perhaps healed people there, as the Gospel of Mark relates:

> And he went throughout all Galilee, preaching in their synagogues and casting out demons (Mark 1.3 9; cf. Matt. 4.23 and Luke 8.1–3) . . .

It also appears from the rabbinic literature that Magdala had a synagogue. Next to it was a *beth ha-midrash*, a school for the explanation and application of holy scripture (at all events at the beginning of the second century, perhaps earlier). . . .

In a midrash on Lamentations 2.2 which begins with the words 'The Lord has destroyed without mercy all the habitations of Jacob,' Magdala is cited as an example. The sages give an extensive description of the piety of the town. There were 300 stalls where you could buy the birds necessary for ritual purification. And the religious tax which went to Jerusalem weighed so much that it had to go by wagon. Yet the city was devastated. Why? While the answer to the question given in the case of two other towns is 'disunity' and 'witchcraft,' in Magdala 'adultery' is cited as the reason (Ika Rabbah II, 2,4). So the city was not just associated with piety, but also with adultery. . . .

Should we then think of a Mary of Magdala who sought to please men from near and far? The only reference to sexual promiscuity in Magdala . . . is to be found in the Midrash on Lamentations mentioned [above]. The sages give 'adultery' as the reason for the destruction of Magdala. However, the adultery is mentioned in the context of piety. Despite this piety, Magdala was devastated because of adultery. There is no obvious reason for associating Mary Magdalene in particular with adultery, just as there is no special reason for describing her as extraordinarily pious because of the piety of Magdala.

However, we may allow her name to conjure up the general atmosphere of Magdala. This was the atmosphere of a trading town on an international route, in which people of all kinds of religions and customs met one another at the market. It was the atmosphere of a prosperous town which had to suffer under the occupation and the opposition to it, under the violence and political upheaval which came with the occupation. It was also the atmosphere of a tolerant city, in which both Jewish and Hellenistic culture were known from the inside.

Mary Magdalene owes her name to the Hebrew name for the city. She is specifically called Mary of Magdala and not Mary of Tarichea. This strengthens the impression that she was a Jew. . . .

The New Testament Gospels agree in telling us that Mary Magdalene was one of the followers of Jesus. She was not the only woman; there were others too. The Gospels do not give us any indication of precisely how this came about. . . .

To be a disciple of Jesus and to belong to the small group of his permanent followers had far-reaching consequences for everyday life, certainly for a woman. To follow Jesus meant travelling around, leaving everything behind and following him. It meant living in a poverty and simplicity which one had chosen for oneself. It meant having dealings with the other disciples, rich and poor, from the city or the country, whether zealot, toll collector or fisherman. It meant abstaining from sex. It also meant incurring danger from both Jews and Romans. Mary Magdalene had to accept all this in order to follow Jesus . . .

What moved Mary Magdalene to follow Jesus? She will

have come under the spell of his authority, like so many others. But we can say yet more in view of what we have so far come to know about her.

She had grown up in a city in which the Roman occupation, the opposition to it and the suffering which that brought were tangible. That could have made her receptive precisely to the non-violent, the spiritual and the healing element of the kingdom of God as this took shape in Jesus.

She had grown up in a place where Jewish and Hellenistic culture lived side by side. She had also grown up with people from different countries and of different religions who came to Magdala with their trade. That could have made her receptive to Jesus' emphasis on people's dispositions, on their inner life and the way in which they really acted, rather than external differences. And this could have made her receptive to the conviction that God has mercy on all without distinction, because God is a God of the whole creation: the God of human beings is also the God of nature, which particularly around Magdala proved to be so abundant and rich . . .

Mary Magdalene came from the town of Magdala, by the sea of Galilee; it was a centre of trade on an international route, where people of all kinds of religions and customs met one another at the market. It was a prosperous town where trade was done in salt fish, dyed material and a selection of agricultural products. It was a tolerant town, where both Jewish and Hellenistic culture were known from the inside.

Mary, Mary

Mary is the number one most common female name in the United States. According to census statistics, over three million American women—almost three percent of all females in the United States—are named Mary.

It was a fortified town in a strategic location, in an area which suffered much under the Roman occupation and opposition to it. By contrast, nature was rich and abundant in the region. Mary Magdalene's background was in all probability Jewish. However, she is not defined by her family ties as is the case with the other Marys in the four Gospels. She is defined by the city of Magdala from where she comes. From her youth upward she was familiar with violence, with poverty and riches, with injustice, with different cultures and religions, all this in a splendid and extraordinarily fertile natural environment. At a particular moment she began to follow Jesus. It is not inconceivable that she met him in the synagogue at Magdala. Luke is the only Gospel which relates that through Jesus seven evil spirits went out of her. We do not know precisely what that says about her, except that contact with Jesus must have been very liberating and uplifting for her. John depicts her as one of the closest acquaintances of Jesus. She stood just beneath the cross with his family. On the basis of Mark's description of the women at the cross, on the basis of what the Gospels show us about Jesus' attitude towards women, and on the basis of the resurrection stories in Luke and John, we conclude that Mary Magdalene must have belonged to the small circle of disciples who were Jesus' permanent followers. She was under the impact of his authority and his message about the coming of the kingdom of God. She was under the impact of his teaching: the importance that he attached to a good disposition in people rather than to good external behaviour, and also the emphasis that he placed on the overflowing goodness of God, not limited to some but addressed to all.

The evangelists mention Mary Magdalene in their story about Jesus because she is the key witness to his death, to the burial of his body, the empty tomb and the revelation which goes with it. We have seen that her presence at Jesus' tomb showed courage in the face of both the Jewish and the Roman authorities.

It is striking that Mark, Luke and John invite the reader to compare Mary Magdalene with Peter. In Mark she is on the same footing as Peter; in Luke, Peter is clearly more important than Mary Magdalene, whereas in John, Peter pales by comparison ...

Whereas the later church fathers and the two church orders emphasize the distance between Mary Magdalene and Jesus, the other writings show the intimacy between them.

This already begins in the Letter of the Apostles. As in the Gospel of Luke, the women's story about the resurrection is not believed. However, in contrast to Luke, they have been given the command to speak by the Lord himself. He has Mary Magdalene and Mary the sister of Martha going one by one. When they are still not believed, the Lord appears to the eleven disciples. However, he is not alone but takes the two Marys with him. They go together. So with his solidarity the Lord shows that they are right. In the Gospel of Thomas, Jesus promises to give Mary Magdalene special guidance. In answer to Peter's request to exclude her from the circle of the disciples he says:

> I myself shall lead her in order to make her male, so that she too may become a living spirit resembling you males. For every woman who will make herself male will enter the kingdom of heaven (Gospel of Thomas, Logion 114).

The *Gospel of Philip* says that Mary Magdalene was called the companion of Jesus. Together with Mary the mother of Jesus and her sister she was always with him. The author writes:

> The Saviour loved Mary Magdalene more than all the disciples, and kissed on her mouth often (*Gospel of Philip* 63.34–35).

We must not understand this 'kissing' in a sexual sense, but in a spiritual sense. The grace which those who kiss exchange makes them born again. This is already described earlier in the Gospel:

> If the children of Adam are numerous, although they die, how much more the children of the perfect man who do not die but are continually born anew ... They receive nourishment from the promise, to enter into the place above. The promise comes from the mouth, for the Word has come from there and has been nourished from the mouth and become perfect. The perfect conceive through a kiss and give birth. Because of this we also kiss one another. We receive conception from the grace which we have among us (Gospel of Philip 58.20–59.6).

Mary Magdalene is made fruitful through the grace which is in Christ. Receiving his grace makes her born again.

The distance between Jesus and Mary Magdalene in the later church fathers is a distance between the sinful woman and God. The intimacy shown by the writings mentioned here is the intimacy of teacher and pupil. ...

We concluded that Mary Magdalene was a courageous and persistent disciple, as is witnessed by the fact that she seems to have been one of the few at the crucifixion and the burial and that she also went to look at the tomb later ...

The fact that Mary Magdalene was a woman played a role in our quest in all kinds of ways. It already began with the earliest sources. We noted that above all the first three New Testament Gospels proved ambivalent over the women disciples. They have to be mentioned as witnesses, but the way in which they are introduced is abrupt and restrained. We compared that with the not particularly positive Roman and Jewish view of women as witnesses. We also saw that the fact that there were women disciples cannot have been regarded warmly. Both Jewish tradition and Roman legislation propagated motherhood as the only worthy content of a woman's life. Nor do the Gospels anywhere call Mary Magdalene and the other women real disciples, unless they are included when the masculine plural of the word 'disciples' is used. However, in the church fathers and the Gospel literature outside the Bible the female form of the word 'disciple' does appear.

The fact that Mary Magdalene was a woman made it possible for the church fathers to portray her as a counterpart of Eve, the woman who brought sin into the world. For the church fathers Mary Magdalene is the 'new Eve'; she may bring the message of redemption. So she seems to be almost in a line with Christ, who is seen as the new Adam. However, nothing is less true. From Origin to Augustine the great distance between the two is emphasized . . .

In some writings Peter is the personification of the orthodox view of women. Mary Magdalene is afraid of him 'because he hates our sex,' and he is afraid of Mary; he is anxious that this 'new Eve' should not become influential. 'Let Mary depart from us,' he says, 'since women are not worthy of Life', and he asks the brothers, 'Are we to turn about and all listen to her? Has he chosen her above us?'

We can ask how far the fact that Mary Magdalene was a woman also consciously played a role for herself. Did she attach herself to Jesus among other things because of the open way in which he dealt with women? I have found no texts which might confirm the conjecture. Moreover according to the Dialogue of the Saviour she is unprotestingly a conversation partner in the doctrinal discussion about the 'works of femininity' which must be destroyed. She does not react when Matthew cites as words of the Lord, 'Pray where there is no woman.' The other question which keeps occupying people down the centuries is whether Mary Magdalene felt attracted as a woman to Jesus. We have not come across any texts which indicate this . . .

"*The Da Vinci Code* uses fiction as a means to interpret historical obscurity . . ."

AN INTERVIEW WITH DEIRDRE GOOD

Deirdre Good is a professor of the New Testament at the General Theological Seminary of the Episcopal Church in New York. She earned her doctorate at Harvard Divinity School. Recently, she has held numerous speaking events on Mary Magdalene and *The Da Vinci Code*.

Who was the true Mary Magdalene and what was her life like?
According to Luke's Gospel, she was a wealthy follower and disciple of Jesus from whom he cast out seven demons. Her name suggests whence she came: from Magdala, a city on the shore of Galilee known in Roman times for fish salting. Migdal is just north of Tiberias. She was one of a group of women disciples who came to the tomb in the early morning of the third day after Jesus' death, perhaps to bring spices. In several Gospel accounts, the women were met by an angel who announced, "He is risen!" She had a vision of the resurrected Jesus according to John's Gospel. This makes her both prophet and apostle. We do not know what she looked like, but we certainly have representations of her in art of the Christian East and West and in the medieval mystery plays.

As a scholar of Christian Origins, I can identify Mary Magdalene in the Gospels of Luke, John, the longer text of Mark, and the extracanonical *Gospels of Thomas, Mary,*

Philip, Peter, and in the later *Pistis Sophia* and the *Manichaean Psalms.* In early texts, her fidelity to Jesus causes her, along with two other women, to visit his tomb. Subsequently, in several texts, she is apostle and prophet to whom the resurrected Jesus appears. Her insight is conveyed in reports of her vision of Jesus (John 20; *Gospel of Mary*). In John 20, Jesus addresses her by her Semitic name: Mariam! She recognizes him by replying: Rabboni! In a few texts (longer ending of Mark; *Gospel of Mary; Gospel of Thomas; Pistis Sophia*) she encounters hostility from other apostles (Peter especially) and her testimony is disbelieved. But other apostles (Levi) speak on her behalf. Thus in Christian tradition, she is the apostle to the apostles. In the *Manichaean Psalms,* Jesus reminds her of their resurrection encounter and confirms that she is to go to the other disciples, especially Peter.

What do you think of the picture that is painted of Mary Magdalene in The Da Vinci Code?

What *The Da Vinci Code* does is use fiction as a means to interpret historical obscurity and fill the gaps. This is an approach used successfully by other—and better—novelists: Charles Dickens, for example. It's an approach worth pursuing, once we dismiss Brown's claim that what he writes is true. Thus the claim that Jesus and Mary Magdalene were married is a fiction designed to express the particularity of their relationship. However, Jesus also had distinctive relationships with others—for example, the "Beloved Disciple" of John's Gospel, with Peter, and so on. Thus one must ask whether Brown's assertion that Jesus and Mary Magdalene were married is a restrictive way to describe the particular relationship of a man Jesus with a woman Mary Magdalene. If one assumes this limited particularity, one then looks for it anywhere and everywhere. Actually it isn't in da Vinci's *Last Supper* because art historians, looking at sketches of figures drawn by the artist to prepare for the painting, identify the figure to Jesus' right with John. Representations of John always depict him as young and thus beardless.

Why do you think there is so much contemporary interest in Mary Magdalene?

New interest in Mary Magdalene coincides with the appearance of feminist research—now established as a credible discipline in its own right—on the role of women and the subject of gender as culturally constructed in the field of Christian origins. In this regard, the discovery and publication of original Coptic texts from Nag Hammadi in English have stimulated interest in early material outside the canon among those interested in gender categories and women. The success of Elaine Pagels' book *The Gnostic Gospels,* and publication of these Nag Hammadi texts on the Internet created access to a new body of material. Investigating all the historical material about Mary Magdalene raised the question about the role of women in the early Christian movements. Mary Magdalene was clearly identified as a prominent apostle and prophet.

You have worked on the comparative names and meaning of Mary Magdalene of the New Testament and Miriam of the Old Testament. What is your thesis on this subject?

I believe there is a connection in name and function between Miriam of the Hebrew Bible and both Mary Magdalen and Mary, the mother of Jesus. This is the argument of my new book, *Mariam, the Magdalen, and the Mother,* to be published in 2005 by Indiana University Press. The name Miriam in the Greek translation of Hebrew Scripture is Mariam. This form of the name is used to describe the women to whom Gabriel speaks in Luke 2 and the woman to whom Jesus appears in the garden in John 20. Moreover, like Miriam the prophet, Jesus' mother praises God (in the song called the Magnificat) for the reversal of fortunes God has accomplished in the past. She also anticipates what God will accomplish in the ministry of her son, Jesus, described in Luke's Gospel. The prophetic role of Jesus' mother continues in the *Protevangelium* of James, one of the noncanonical birth stories.

Like Miriam, Mary Magdalen is disbelieved when she proclaims her vision of the resurrected Lord, undoubtedly because of her gender. Ultimately, she is vindicated. This feature resonates with the experience of most women who have felt a call to ministry.

Can you comment on the background of celibacy versus marriage that would have prevailed in biblical times?

In Matthew 19:12, in a discussion of marriage and divorce, Jesus tells his disciples:

> For there are some eunuchs which were so born from their mother's womb: and there are some eunuchs, which were made eunuchs of men: and there be eunuchs, which have made themselves eunuchs for the kingdom of heaven's sake. He that is able to receive it, let him receive it.

Some commentators interpret this passage as a commendation of celibacy. And when celibacy was viewed as a higher state than marriage in subsequent Christian tradition, Jerome could understand Matthew 19:10–12 to indicate that "Christ loves virgins more than others."

Modern commentators have tended to follow this view by interpreting this passage as an invitation to celibacy for some or by linking the passage explicitly to Paul's teaching in I Cor. 7 commending celibacy over marriage. But in Matthew's Gospel, eunuchs, like someone voluntarily humbling him- or herself, forego being "great" or exercising authority over others. Since Matthew 20:26–7 equates status within the Matthean community to being a servant or a slave, we can entertain the thesis that the eunuch within the Matthean community is the perfect servant. Eunuchs in the Matthean community, having voluntarily given up all honor deriving from their own family, possessions, and wealth, are exclusively loyal to the kingdom. To Peter's question: "Look, we have left everything and followed you. What then will we have?" Jesus offers status and power not in this world, but in the next: "At the renewal of all things, when the Son of Man is seated on the throne of his glory, you who have followed me will also sit on twelve thrones, judging the twelve tribes of Israel. And every one who has left houses or brothers or sisters or father or mother or children or lands, for my name's sake, will receive a hundredfold, and inherit eternal life"(19:27–30).

Many people believe the fragmentary Gospel of Philip *to say that Jesus kissed Mary Magdalene often on her mouth. Do you believe that to be true? And, if so, what is its meaning?*

The *Gospel of Philip* is actually in far better shape than the *Gospel of Mary*! Although both texts were published in the same collection, *The Nag Hammadi Library in English,* they presuppose different symbolic worlds. For example, we should not assume, because the *Gospel of Philip* speaks of men and women, that it is describing real men and women. The *Second Apocalypse of James* reports that Jesus called James his beloved and grants him deeper understanding of things that others have not known. In both the *Second* and the *Third Apocalypse of James*, Jesus and James kiss and embrace each other as an indication of their special relationship. In the so-called *Secret Gospel of Mark*, Jesus reveals the mystery of the kingdom of God to a young man he loves. In the fourth-century Coptic text *Pistis Sophia*, Philip, John, James, and Matthew, along with Mariamne (Mary), are all spoken of as beloved by Jesus. This probably indicates their special capacity for spiritual insight. It is easy to imagine that others would be jealous of such people.

Critiquing the Conspiracy Theory about Pope Gregory

AN INTERVIEW WITH KATHERINE LUDWIG JANSEN
Katherine Ludwig Jansen is Associate Professor of History at Catholic University. She is the author of *The Making of the Magdalen: Preaching and Popular Devotion in the Later Middle Ages.*

Like Esther de Boer, Jansen emphasizes facts that come from the texts of accepted biblical documents and official church history. She argues against the cover-up thesis and presents the defense for Pope Gregory and church officialdom on the issue of Mary Magdalene, sin and penitence. On the other hand, she also concludes that the Dark Ages may have been more enlightened than our own times in one respect: Mary Magdalene, a woman, was understood to be an apostle in her own right, whereas today there remains a battle in many religious groups over whether women should assume leadership roles in preaching their faiths.

In your opinion, who was the true Mary Magdalene?

As a historian, I am trained to base my opinions and analysis on historical evidence. In the case of Mary Magdalene, the only evidence we have to document her existence is that which is contained in the New Testament. All told, the four Gospels contain just twelve references to this woman, eleven of which are directly related to the passion and resurrection narratives. Only Luke 8:2–3 adds the detail that "Mary who is called Magdalene" was the woman from whom Jesus cast out seven demons. After he did so, Mary from Magdala became one of Jesus' most steadfast disciples, ministering to him from her own financial resources (Luke 8:3). Based on this textual evidence, it seems clear that Mary Magdalene was a financially independent woman who used her resources to support Jesus and his band of disciples.

Why did the church depict Mary Magdalene as a prostitute for so many years? Do you feel that they benefited from this "cover-up" in any way?

In my view, "cover-up" and "conspiracy" are not useful ways to understand the historical confusion about Mary Magdalene's identity. We must begin by noting that, in addition to the Virgin Mary and Mary Magdalene, there are five women mentioned in the Gospels who are also called Mary—that very fact has created ample room for confusion. Nonetheless, early church writers tended to keep all these women distinct in their discussions of Mary Magdalene, as does the Eastern Orthodox Church, which never conflated the figure of Mary of Magdala with Mary of Bethany, let alone the unnamed sinner of Luke (7:37–50). Indeed, the Orthodox Church has always kept separate feasts for separate women.

It was only at the end of the sixth century that the figure of Mary Magdalene was fused together with the figures of Mary of Bethany and the unnamed sinner in Luke. Pope Gregory the Great collapsed into one individual the identities of three distinct Gospel figures. The moment Pope Gregory the Great grafted Luke's sinner onto Mary Magdalene's identity, was the moment at which Mary Magdalene was transformed into a prostitute, largely because women's sins were inevitably construed as sexual sins. Had Mary Magdalene been married, that sin might have been construed as adultery. As a single woman, her sin was construed as wantonness, which was tantamount to prostitution.

What were Gregory's motives for compounding the characters of sinners with Mary Magdalene?

It would be a gross misrepresentation of history to view it as a conspiracy or an act of maliciousness on his part. One has to see Gregory in his own context, a period beset by intense dislocation: Germanic invasions, plague, and famine were just a few of the major catastrophes he had to face during his pontificate, which demanded that he be not only a spiritual leader, but a political leader, as well. In this period of flux and uncertainty, Gregory was attempting to create some sort of stability and certainty for his community. The text in which Gregory creates a new identity for Mary Magdalene was a sermon in which he was clearly responding to questions about Magdalenian identity that had been posed by the people of his community, who were, it seems, looking for clarity in their faith to serve as a bulwark against the late Roman world crumbling beneath their feet. Gregory's composite Magdalene figure had the virtue of seeming to answer definitively all the questions that his Christian community had been asking about the relation of one Mary to another.

The identification stuck because it filled a deep-seated need, theologically speaking. Mary Magdalene, now reconfigured as the great sinner, was poised to become the great saint. Gregory suggested that she achieved this through penance, which in her case was the penitential act of washing Christ's feet with her tears and drying them with her hair. As the sacrament of penance continued to be reformulated and given primacy during the Middle Ages and the early modern period, so Mary Magdalene's image as sinner-saint grew correspondingly. The image of the sinner-saint became increasingly important at historical moments when the sacrament of penance came to the fore. In my view, the image of the sinner-saint was certainly one of the reasons that so many people were attracted to Mary Magdalene through-out the centuries: She provided hope to ordinary sinners—both men and women—that they too could be redeemed.

Why was Mary Magdalene one of the few at the crucifixion? Why might she have attended when other disciples did not? What is the importance of Mary Magdalene being the first to see Jesus after the resurrection?

After Jesus' arrest, most of the other disciples went into hiding for fear that they too would be arrested. Mary Magdalene and the other women did not. Whether this is because the Romans did not consider the female disciples a danger or because the women were more steadfast in their loyalty to Jesus is an open question. Nonetheless, their faith did not waiver. They appeared at and witnessed the crucifixion. In my view, Mary Magdalene's most important role is as first witness to Jesus' resurrection. Jesus charges her with the duty of bearing the news of his resurrection to the other disciples. At that moment, she earned the title given her by medieval scriptural commentators: *apostolorum apostola*—the apostle of the apostles, a title that endured throughout the Middle Ages. Thus, one of the most important tenets of Christianity—the resurrection—was both witnessed and announced by a woman. The title "apostle of the apostles" is as appropriate now to celebrate her role in the history of Christianity as it was in the medieval period.

The Beliefnet Debate

KENNETH WOODWARD VS. KAREN L. KING

Beliefnet.com describes itself as a "multi-faith e-community" designed to help individuals meet their religious and spiritual needs. Since the publication of *The Da Vinci Code*, a number of Beliefnet articles and postings have focused on discussions about Mary Magdalene and other issues raised by the book. Here, we excerpt key arguments from a point-counterpoint between Kenneth L. Woodward and Karen King. Woodward is a contributing editor at *Newsweek*. King is Winn Professor of Ecclesiastical History at Harvard University Divinity School.

A Quite Contrary Mary

BY KENNETH WOODWARD

Like Jesus, Mary Magdalene is now the subject of a cultural makeover.
What agenda do feminist scholars have in mind?

Why the sudden interest in Mary Magdalene? Yes, I know about the two or three new books on the subject, as well as the bestselling book *The Da Vinci Code* and the new movie *The Magdalene Sisters*. But is anything new being said about this familiar Biblical figure?

Not really. Scholars have known for decades, if not longer, that Mary Magdalene was not a prostitute, and that she had been erroneously conflated in early Christian tradition with the penitent woman in Luke who anoints the feet of the soon-to-be-crucified Jesus and dries them with her hair. It's certainly not news that her greatest claim to fame was the commission she received from Christ to go tell the apostles the news of his resurrection. Those kinds of "redefinitions" were readily available in the entry under her name in the *New Catholic Encyclopedia*, published in 1967—hardly an arcane resource for any journalist willing to check out claims that something new is being said.

That Jesus was married—possibly to Mary Magdalene—is also a hoary notion going well beyond William E. Phipps' theological potboiler of 1970, *Was Jesus Married?* Phipps' answer—that he probably was, since most Jewish men of the time married—was hardly persuasive. Nor is the contrary view, that Jesus was gay and had a thing for John, the "beloved disciple," a new idea; I came upon it in the 1960s, when the notion of Jesus as the ultimate "outsider" was popular in Existentialist circles. The conceit was that by virtue of his "illegitimate birth" and his rural origins, Jesus was an outsider to the power groups of his day. Anglican bishop Hugh Montefiore added homosexuality to the mix so as to complete the outsider image. Like Jesus, Mary Magdalene is now the subject of a cultural makeover.

When it comes to Biblical figures, it is not enough to say that every generation entertains notions already imagined and discarded by previous generations. In the case of Mary Magdalene, the news is not what is being said about her, but the new context in which she is being placed—and who is doing the placing and why. In other words, Mary Magdalene has become a project for a certain kind of ideologically committed feminist scholarship. That's the real news . . .

In the 13th century, no less a figure than Peter Abelard preached a sermon in which he saw symmetry between Miriam and Mary Magdalene as proclaimers of good news. (Even then, Mary Magdalene was known as "apostle to the apostles.") Finding symmetries between Old and New Testament figures was an important aspect of medieval Biblical exegesis. In the current context, some exegetes focus on Exodus 15:20–21, where Miriam is called a "prophet" and leads the Israelite women in dance and song. For those feminists who are looking for any signs of female leadership in the Hebrew Bible (not to mention grounds for doing their own song and dance), this passage has led to the creation of a story of their own. According to that narrative, Miriam was regarded as a prophet, just as her brother Moses was, producing a rivalry among the ancient Israelites between the party of Moses and the party of Miriam.

But—so the story goes—the male editors of the Bible expunged the stories of Miriam's leadership that they believe existed in ancient oral traditions. Moreover, a few feminist scholars insist that the ancient Israelites actually created an egalitarian society before the rise of male kingship. Thus, we have a classic case of patriarchy—feminism's equivalent of original sin—excising the evidence of female leadership, indeed, of female prophethood. Similarly, the Biblical myth of an original Eden is replaced by the feminist idea of an original egalitarian society which was eventually covered up by the male redactors of the Exodus story, Judaism's foundation event.

Whether any of this is true—or even likely—is not something a mere journalist is equipped to judge. Nonetheless, a journalist might note that not many Biblical scholars, male or female, give these speculations credence. The evidence simply isn't there, which is why those who advance them rely on what is called "rhetorical analysis" of Biblical texts rather than historical or archeological evidence. A journalist might also note that within religious feminism, the truth or falsity of these speculations doesn't matter. Thus, at least since the late 1970s, some Jewish women have staged feminist seders in which a cup is set aside for Miriam as well as the traditional one for Elijah. They do this not because they believe that Miriam, like Elijah, was taken bodily into heaven and so will return in the fullness of time, but just to make things, well, egalitarian.

We find the same pattern in the feminist redefinition of Mary Magdalene. Here the narrative framework functions like this: the early movement led by Jesus was egalitarian and gender-inclusive (though some second-generation Jewish feminists now reject this on the grounds that it makes Jesus an exception among Jewish men of his day and so is anti-Semitic). Among the women who follow Jesus, Mary of Magdala is the most prominent: she is mentioned more often (12 times) than any other woman but the mother of Jesus. The most important mention is in John 20:11–18, where the resurrected Jesus appears to Mary alone and commissions her to relay the news to his (male) apostles. Hence her traditional title: "apostle to the apostles."

Now, it should be clear to any reader of the New Testament that the women who followed Jesus often acted more like disciples than did some of Jesus' chosen Twelve. For example, the synoptic gospels (Mark, Matthew and Luke) have *only* women at the foot of the cross. (The Gospel of John adds

John, the beloved disciple.) But a small cadre of feminist scholars—especially those tutored and credentialed at Harvard Divinity School—go much further. Their headline-making claim is that in the early church there was a party of Magdalene and a party of Peter—again, men versus women, as in the case of Miriam—and that the party of Peter not only won, but also proceeded to expunge the evidence and memory of the Magdalene faction from the New Testament and to tarnish the reputation of Magdalene to boot. A sermon preached by Pope Gregory in 591 is frequently cited on the latter point, as if he had invented an anti-woman tradition and sealed it with (retroactive) infallibility. Blaming a pope fits the feminist agenda here, injecting an anti-hierarchical, indeed, anti-papal note. In short, patriarchy is again the culprit.

But there is a difference between the two Marys—Miriam and the Magdalene. To make their case, Mary Magdalene's feminist defenders have switched to a different deck of cards. Just as a feminist hermeneutics of suspicion—biblical scholarship based on suspicion of male authorship—dictates that the text of the New Testament, being the work of males, must be distrusted for that very reason, so a feminist hermeneutics of retrieval—in this case, retrieving the suppressed evidence of the party of Mary Magdalene—must go to other sources. These sources are the various texts that did not make it into the New Testament as it was fixed in the 4th century. And the very fact of this exclusion by male church hierarchs makes the extra texts all the more authoritative for scholars whose aim is showing that patriarchy suppressed female leadership in the church. Among these texts, The *Gospel of Mary* is paramount; it reads as if the author had obtained a D.D. degree from Harvard Divinity School.

As second-century documents, the *Gospel of Mary*, the *Gospel of Philip* (in which Jesus and Mary kiss), and other apocryphal texts come much too late to provide any reliable historical information about Jesus, Peter, or Mary Magdalene. But they do suggest what some groups—traditionally considered Gnostics—understood about the story of Jesus and his followers . . .

Karen King, a professor at the Harvard Divinity School, argues that there is a relationship between the *Gospel of Mary*, which exalts the role of Mary Magdalene, and Paul's Letter to Timothy, which counsels women to be silent in church. Her argument is that both were produced about the same time, 125 C.E., and taken together reflect a raging gender war in the early church. But she does this by taking certain liberties with the dating of these two texts. No one knows when either was written, but some scholars put Timothy in the 90s C.E., and some scholars put the *Gospel of Mary* in the late—not early—second century. King maximizes the dates of both, like bookends with nothing in between, for her purposes. In short, the new Mary Magdalene is an old Gnostic.

Even so, how credible is the assumption that the church's rejection of Gnosticism in all its forms was essentially a gender war? In his rigorously balanced "Introduction to the New Testament," the late scholar Raymond E. Brown summarizes how the scriptures written by Christians were preserved and accepted—and what criteria were used. Among them were apostolic origin, real or putative, and conformity to the rule of faith. None of them involved gender. Furthermore, there is no reason to believe that whole communities of Christians used the *Gospel of Mary*, or, of *Phillip*, as authoritative texts. Yes, they were in circulation, but so are a number of books in my own library, several of them including the Gnostic gospels, but that does not make me a Gnostic . . .

For several years I have kept an anthology of selections from the various world religions that on the cover invites the reader to choose from them those that they find appealing and thereby "create your own scriptures." That anyone would package this material, I thought, was indicative of one wind blowing in the mixed weather pattern of contemporary American religion. The operative assumption is that all sacred texts are of equal value and the reader is free to make sacred those that provide personal appeal . . . It is the ultimate in consumer-oriented religion, of course, and has the added advantage of bypassing the authority of any community as to which texts count as sacred and which do not.

Something similar is, I think, happening with the Gnostic texts that support poor Mary Magdalene in the role thrust upon her as a leader of the church—and, if author Lynn Picknett is to be believed, as "Christianity's Hidden Goddess." At least the minority of feminist scholars pushing the Gnostic texts as equal in standing to those of the New Testament can argue that at an early period in Christian history they were available to Christians and occasionally read. From that it apparently follows that if you don't like the established canon, create one of your own. If the *Gospel of Mary* is just as authoritative as, say, the Gospel of Mark, then of course Mary Magdalene can be whatever today's feminists want her to be.

Were I to write a story involving Mary Magdalene, I think it would focus on this: that a small group of well-educated women decided to devote their careers to the pieces of Gnostic literature discovered in the last century, a find that promised a new academic specialty within the somewhat overtrodden field of Biblical studies, on which they could build a career. They became experts in this literature, as others become experts in the biology of the hermit crab. But unlike those who study marine decapod crustaceans, some of them came to identify with the objects of their study—in some cases, perhaps, because they had no other religious community to identify with other than that formed by common academic pursuit; others perhaps because they were in rebellion against whatever authoritative religious community nurtured their interest in religion in the first place . . .

And the next step? That is already upon us in the form of a new book from Harvard's Karen King, *What Is Gnosticism?* which aims at showing the great diversity among Gnostics— true and pluralizing Gnosticism—fair enough—but also at divesting Gnostics of their opposition to orthodox Christianity, thereby dissolving the very category of heresy. In short, if there is no error, then anything can be true. How very American. How inclusive and nonjudgmental. And in this age of postmodernism, so Now. In this kind of environment, even the figure of Mary Magdalene can be prostituted for polemical purposes.

Letting Mary Magdalene Speak

By KAREN L. KING

> *Tradition is not fixed. Newly discovered texts like the* Gospel of Mary *let us hear other voices in an ancient Christian debate.*

In an article about recent interest in Mary Magdalene, Kenneth Woodward writes: "The news is not what is being said about her, but the new context in which she is being placed—and who is doing the placing and why." As he points out, scholars have agreed at least since the 1960s that she was not a prostitute. Likewise, the speculation that Mary and Jesus were married is hardly new. "The real news," he says, is found in the work of "ideologically committed feminist scholarship"— a statement I heartily agree with.

The rest of his article, however, is more an expression of Woodward's distaste for feminism than a review or even a critique of that scholarship. Readers may want to evaluate for themselves examples of the best work in rhetorical criticism and feminist scholarship on Mary of Magdala, such as Elisabeth Schussler Fiorenza's classic work, *In Memory of Her*, and Jane Schaberg's recent book, *The Resurrection of Mary Magdalene*.

Part of the recent excitement about Mary Magdalene has to do with discoveries of previously unknown early Christian writings from Egypt, like the *Gospel of Mary*, the *Dialogue of the Savior*, and the *Gospel of Thomas*. The *Gospel of Mary* is found in a fifth-century C.E. papyrus book that came onto the Cairo antiquities market in 1896. It was purchased by a German scholar and taken to Berlin, where it was first published in 1955. In 1945, two Egyptian peasants made an astonishing discovery while digging for fertilizer at the foot of the Jabel al-Tarif, a cliff near the town of Nag Hammadi in Middle Egypt. They uncovered a sealed clay jar containing a hoard of papyrus manuscripts. Known as the Nag Hammadi Codices, these fourth-century C.E. papyrus books included a wealth of ancient Christian literature, a total of forty-six different works in all, almost all of which were previously unknown. These and other original writings are offering new perspectives on Christian beginnings. They show that early Christianity was much more diverse than we had ever imagined.

Early Christians intensely debated such basic issues as the content and meaning of Jesus' teachings, the nature of salvation, the value of prophetic authority, the roles of women and slaves, and competing visions of ideal community. After all, these first Christians had no New Testament, no Nicene Creed or Apostles Creed, no commonly established church order or chain of authority, no church buildings, and indeed no single understanding of Jesus. All of the elements we might consider essential to define Christianity did not yet exist. Far from being starting points, the Nicene Creed and the New Testament were the end products of these debates and disputes. They represent the distillation of experience and experimentation—and not a small amount of strife and struggle.

One consequence of these struggles is that the winners were able to write the history of this period from their perspective. The viewpoints of the losers were largely lost since their ideas survived only in documents denouncing them. Until now. The recent discoveries provide a wealth of primary works that illustrate the plural character of early Christianity and offer alternative voices. They also help us to understand the winners better because their ideas and practices were shaped in the crucible of these early Christian debates . . .

Placing the figure of Mary Magdalene in this new context helps us understand how the erroneous portrait of her as a prostitute could have been invented and how it could have flourished in the West for well over a millennium without any evidence to support it. Several of the newly discovered works portray her as a favored disciple of Jesus and apostle after the resurrection. In the *Gospel of Mary*, for example, she calms the other disciples when they are afraid and gives them special teaching that Jesus had conveyed to her alone. The text states that Jesus knew her completely and loved her more than the others. It also draws upon a tradition of Peter in conflict with Mary, a topic handled with great sophistication by Anne Brock in her new book, *Mary Magdalene, the First Apostle: The Struggle for Authority*.

But in these newly discovered books, Mary is the apostolic guarantor of a theological position that lost out in the battle for orthodoxy. The *Gospel of Mary*, for example, presents a radical interpretation of Jesus' teachings as a path to inner spiritual knowledge, not apocalyptic revelation; it acknowledges the reality of Jesus' death and his resurrection, but it rejects his suffering and death as the path to eternal life; it also rejects the immortality of the physical body, asserting that only the soul will be saved; it presents the most straightforward and convincing argument in any early Christian writing for the legitimacy of women's leadership; it offers a sharp critique of illegitimate power and a utopian vision of spiritual perfection; it challenges our romantic views about the harmony of the first Christians; and it asks us to rethink the basis for church authority. All written in the name of a woman.

The *Gospel of Mary* lets us see that by making Mary Magdalene into a repentant prostitute, the leaders of the Church could achieve two aims at once. They succeeded both in undermining appeals to Mary Magdalene to support women's leadership, and at the same time they were able to undermine the kind of theology being promoted in her name—theology which the Church Fathers condemned as heresy.

Mr. Woodward is quite right that the discovery of such sources challenges the traditional portrait of Christian history, a history which states that Jesus gave the true teaching to male apostles who passed it down untainted to the bishops who succeeded them. The purity of this gospel is secured especially through the Nicene Creed and orthodox interpretation of the Biblical canon.

While the new texts do not show a "raging gender war" in the early churches, they do provide evidence that one issue being debated concerned women's leadership. In the *Gospel of Mary*, Peter is portrayed as a hothead—just as he is in many episodes in the New Testament gospels. Here he is jealous of Mary and refuses to believe that Jesus would give her special teaching. This portrait seems to suggest that Christians who, like Peter, reject women's right to teach do so out of jealousy and lack of understanding . . .

Mary Magdalene, Patron Saint of Elite Education

Both Oxford and Cambridge, the tradition-steeped leading universities of England, have colleges named for Mary Magdalene.

Oxford's Magdalen College was founded in 1448 and was among the first colleges in the world to teach science. Magdalen Choir—with a history that goes back to the beginnings of the college—is famous for welcoming of spring ceremonies held in May at its famed tower. The movie *Shadowlands*, about the life of C. S. Lewis, depicted these tower ceremonies. Some of the experts whose work we present in this volume would, no doubt, see intriguing connections of myth and metaphor between the pagan-influenced spring rites of pre-Christian history, the Magdalen College tower (recall the etymology of Magdala is derived from an ancient word for tower), and the interests of C. S. Lewis in faith, theology, symbolism, and myth. Magdalen College counts nine Nobel laureates as among its students or professors.

At Cambridge, Magdalene College, founded in 1542, is spelled with a final *e* to differentiate it from Oxford. Historically, however, this college's name was pronounced Maudleyn, a compressed double meaning in the word (Dan Brown fans, take note) having to do with its founder, Lord Audley. Meanwhile, the word *maudlin* (excessively sentimental, often teary-eyed) comes into English from this Renaissance era pronunciation of Mary Magdalene, whose tears are among the most famous in history.

The *Gospel of Mary* lets us hear another voice in the ancient debate, one that was lost for almost two thousand years. It expands our understanding of the dynamics of early Christianity, but it does not offer a voice that is beyond criticism. For example, the *Gospel of Mary*'s rejection of the body as one's true self is highly problematic for contemporary feminism which affirms the dignity of the human body.

Of course the issue of women's leadership has not gone away. It is not just anancient controversy. In our own time, feminists are working to ensure that the true story of Mary Magdalene, as well as other ancient alternative voices, are heard—not only by readers of the 1967 *New Catholic Encyclopedia*, but also by a broader range of the public as well. On the other hand, scholars and others who find these new works challenging tend to dismiss them as heresy and try to marginalize their impact on current debates. It would seem, then, that all this commotion about Mary Magdalene is just another episode in the long history of Christians arguing amongst themselves. Why should anyone pay attention?

This is why: Since so much in Christian belief and practice rests upon historical claims, an accurate view of history is crucial. One criterion for good history is accounting for all the evidence and not marginalizing the parts one doesn't like or promoting unfairly the parts one does like. Whether or not communities of faith embrace or reject the teaching found in these newly discovered texts, Christians will better understand and responsibly engage their own tradition by attending to an accurate historical account of Christian beginnings.

Moreover, given the importance of religion in today's world—especially notable in the intersection of religion and violence—I believe it is important for non-Christians as well as Christians to recognize that all religious traditions contain many voices and offer a variety of possibilities for addressing the complex issues of our day. In that sense, tradition is not fixed, but is continually being constructed as believers draw upon the past to address the present ... Therefore religion is not simply given—something one can only accept or reject. Religions are constantly being interpreted ... An accurate historical account will not ensure that the figure of Mary Magdalene won't continue to be prostituted for polemical purposes as she has been for centuries—but it does restore some dignity to this important woman disciple of Jesus.

"Is it sinful to engage in sex within marriage?"

AN INTERVIEW WITH REV. RICHARD P. McBRIEN

Richard McBrien is a professor of theology at the University of Notre Dame. He appeared on the ABC television program *Jesus, Mary and da Vinci* in 2003, triggering considerable controversy over his logical explanation of why Jesus could well have been married. In the interview that follows, he elaborates on his explanation and on Mary Magdalene as a character in Christian history.

What do you think of the possibility that Mary Magdalene is depicted in The Last Supper?

I'm open to it. There is no evidence in the New Testament that she was present. The question is whether da Vinci put her there. That's at least arguable, given the highly feminine features of the one resting her/his head against Jesus.

Why did the church depict Mary Magdalene as a prostitute for so many years?

Perhaps it's because some church leaders couldn't face up to the fact that she was one of Jesus' main disciples, a close friend, and a primary witness of the resurrection.

In the ABC special, Jesus, Mary and da Vinci, *you mention that it would not have compromised the divinity of Jesus for him to have been married. Can you explain why?*

I don't mean to be flippant, but why not? The Epistle to the Hebrews (4:15) says that Jesus was like us in all things except sin. Is it sinful to engage in sexual relations within marriage?

You also said that if Jesus was married, it's just "a short putt" to Mary Magdalene. Why Mary Magdalene?

Because she was the female disciple closest to him during his life. Unlike the cowardly males, she and other women stuck by him to the end. She is the one who, according to at least three traditions in the New Testament, was the first to see him after his resurrection. He also had to warn her not to "touch" him because he had not yet ascended to his Father in heaven.

Would all the leading religious figures of the time have been married?

Perhaps not all, but certainly most. It is clear that some of the apostles were married, including Peter.

Why do so many people find Mary Magdalene such a compelling character today?

Perhaps because they have been so alienated from the church for its negative, rigid, and censorious views on human sexuality. Thinking about Mary Magdalene raises the question of Jesus' sexuality and also makes people reconsider the place of women in the church. If Jesus had been married, that would undermine centuries of bias against sexual intimacy.

To what do you attribute the renewed interest in Mary Magdalene?

Recent writings by reputable scholars and the women's movement have been influential. But obviously nothing has done more to draw attention to her than *The Da Vinci Code.*

2 The Sacred Feminine

The sacred feminine is that other face of God that has not been honored over the two millennia of Christianity—at least not as a fully equal partner.

—MARGARET STARBIRD

In this chapter, we explore the background to the "sacred feminine" thesis that lies at the heart of *The Da Vinci Code*'s plot. As readers of the novel will recall, almost on arrival in the middle of the night at Leigh Teabing's Château Villette, Sophie Neveu finds herself immersed in explanations and theoretical pyrotechnics from Teabing and Langdon about the Holy Grail, Mary Magdalene, and the sacred feminine. Langdon tells Sophie: "The Holy Grail represents the sacred feminine and the goddess . . . The power of the female and her ability to produce life was once very sacred, but it posed a threat to the rise of the predominantly male Church, and so the sacred feminine was demonized and called unclean . . . When Christianity came along, the old pagan religions did not die easily. Legends of chivalric quests for the lost Grail were in fact stories of forbidden quests to find the lost sacred feminine. Knights who claimed to be 'searching for the chalice' were speaking in code as a way to protect themselves from a Church that had subjugated women, banished the Goddess, burned nonbelievers, and forbidden the pagan reverence for the sacred feminine."

The case for the sacred feminine-suppressed goddess-Mary Magdalene analysis that Langdon and Teabing lay out for Sophie raises some of the most intellectually fascinating questions in the novel. To be sure, it is implausible in many respects, especially the way this set of mysteries has been wrapped into the enigmas of the plot. But it is profoundly interesting. In making his late-night case, the fictional Langdon draws heavily on several of the experts whose work is represented in this chapter—Margaret Starbird, Elaine Pagels, Timothy Freke and Peter Gandy, Riane Eisler, and others.

In the following pages, these experts put forward their own arguments about the role of the sacred feminine in the development of Western culture, thought, politics, philosophy, and religion. They recall the goddess-worshipping cults in Egypt, Greece, Crete, Rome, and gender roles in the context of the Judeo-Christian biblical era. They sift through the Christian experience of the early and medieval church. And they examine spirituality, myths, legends, and traditions that associate special sacred significance with women in general—and with Mary Magdalene in particular.

Readers should note: much of this material is, by definition, mystical, mythical, and poetic; much of the original source material comes in fragments and has been handed down through a variety of languages and translations. In many cases, a short passage from a biblical or Gnostic source has been the subject of extensive analysis and commentary elsewhere. We can only give it shorthand treatment here.

God Does Not Look Like a Man

AN INTERVIEW WITH MARGARET STARBIRD
Copyright © 2004 by Margaret L. Starbird

Two of Margaret Starbird's real-life books are specifically mentioned in *The Da Vinci Code* when they attract Sophie Neveu's interest on Leigh Teabing's library shelves in Château Villette: *The Woman With the Alabaster Jar: Mary Magdalen and the Holy Grail* and *The Goddess in the Gospels: Reclaiming the Sacred Feminine.* In the interview below for this book, Starbird briefly explains her view of the sacred feminine. She also declares that "characterizing Mary Magdalen as an apostle, equal to Peter, or perhaps even more important than Peter, does not go nearly far enough." Our interview presents an introduction to Starbird's thinking. Following the interview, we present brief excerpts from the aforementioned books.

How does the concept of the sacred feminine differ from the way most religions seem to assume the primacy of male deities?

More and more, we are becoming aware that the Divine we call "God" does not really look like the patriarch on the ceiling of the Sistine Chapel in the Vatican. For two millennia Christians have been attributing exclusively masculine images to God, using masculine pronouns when speaking of the Creator. But intellectually, we realize that God is not male. God is beyond gender, the "weaver" beyond "the veil" and beyond our ability to conceive God. So we limit God by ascribing attributes to "Him." God is neither male nor female, which is why the Jews were always told never to make images of God. But Christians dropped this idea, and ascribed to God and Jesus the epithets "Father" and "Son." When the Greek words for "Holy Spirit" were translated into Latin, they became masculine: *Spiritus Sanctus.* The entire trinity was characterized as masculine from the fifth century onward in Western Europe.

The sacred feminine is that *other* face of God that has not been honored over the two millennia of Christianity—at least, not as a fully equal partner. The Virgin Mary certainly embodies one aspect of "God" as feminine: the Blessed Mother, our advocate at the throne of her Son. But in Christianity, the paradigm of partnership, the life-giving principle on planet earth, has not been celebrated or even acknowledged.

I believe we need to reclaim the lost feminine at all levels: physical, psychological, emotional, and spiritual. We have been gravely impoverished by the loss of the bride and the mandala of sacred partnership that was to have been the birthright of Christians. We have suffered the loss of Eros/relationship and deep connection with the feminine—the body, the emotions, the intuitive, the kinship of all the living, the blessings of the beautiful and bountiful planet.

Who is "the lost bride" of the Christian tradition? How does she tie in with the concept of the sacred feminine?

There is only one model for life on planet earth—and that model is "sacred union." In ancient cultures, this fundamental reality was honored in cults that celebrated the mutuality and "symbiosis" of the masculine and feminine as intimate partners. Examples are Tammuz/Ishtar, Ba'al/Astarte, Adonis/Venus, Osiris/Isis. In these cultures, the joy from their bridal chambers spread out into the crops and herds, and into the people of their realm.

Similar rites were acknowledged in various liturgies throughout the Near East. The Song of Songs is a redaction of ancient liturgical poetry from the *hieros gamos* rites of Isis and Osiris. Invariably the king is executed and his bride seeks him, mourning his death, and is eventually reunited with him. In the Song of Songs, the fragrance of the bride is nard [spikenard, an eastern perfume or ointment] which wafts around the bridegroom at the banquet table. And in the Gospel, again it is nard with which Mary anoints Jesus, and the fragrance "filled the house." (John 12:3)

On seven of eight lists of women who accompanied Jesus, Mary Magdalene is mentioned first, and yet, her status as "first lady" was later denied. It suited the church fathers of the fourth century to officially elevate the mother of Jesus as "Theotokos" (God-bearer, Mother of God) but to ignore his bride/beloved. The result has been a distortion of the most basic model for life on our planet—the "sacred union" of devoted partners.

You just referred to heiros gamos, *which is mentioned in* The Da Vinci Code *and is understood to be a translation from the Greek of "sacred marriage." But what does it really mean? And how is it connected to Jesus?*

I believe that Jesus embodied the archetype of the sacred bridegroom and that he and his bride together manifested the mythology of *hieros gamos*. Their union was, in my opinion, the cornerstone of the early Christian community, a radical new way of living a partnership. In I Corinthians 9:5, Paul mentions that the brothers of Jesus and the other apostles travel around with their "sister-wives," a phrase that is often translated as "Christian sisters." But it actually says "sister-wives." What is a "sister-wife"? There is another place in Scripture where sister and wife occur together and that is in the Song of Songs. There, the bridegroom calls his beloved "my sister, my bride." This phrase speaks of an intimate relationship that is beyond that of an arranged marriage. It is a relationship of mutual interest, affection, and special kinship. According to Paul, these apostles were traveling as missionary couples, not as pairs of men as we have been inclined to believe. I firmly believe the model for this relationship was Jesus traveling with his own beloved. It is this intimacy to which the *Gospel of Philip* alludes when it states: "There were three Marys who walked with Jesus. His mother, his sister, and his consort were each a Mary," and goes on to say that Jesus used to kiss Mary Magdalene and the other disciples were jealous.

What is the significance of the chalice—or grail—symbolism?

The chalice or vessel is ubiquitous as a symbol for the feminine "container." I have a picture of a pitcher with breasts from about 6000 B.C.E. It represents the feminine as nurturer. Marija Gimbutas [pioneering archaeologist and commentator on goddess symbols and goddess-worshipping cultures of pre-historic Europe and the Near East] noted examples of the letter *V* on cave walls dating from prehistoric times. The downward-pointing triangle is universally understood as the female pubic triangle, and the hexagram is a very ancient symbol for the cosmic dance of the chalice and the blade, the male and female triangles representing the deities Shiva and Shakti in India.

What role did women play in the earliest days of the Christian church?

Before the Gospels were ever written, women were apparently very much involved in the leadership of the early Christian communities. In his epistles, written in the

50s C.E., Paul mentions various women, including Phoebe, a deaconess, Prisca, and Junia, who exercised leadership in early Christian communities. In the epistle to the Romans (16:6,12), Paul commends several women—Mary, Persis, Tryphosa, and Tryphena—for their hard work. Wealthy women supported Jesus' ministry from the beginning, and were faithful to him until the end, standing at the foot of the cross while the male apostles cowered in hiding. Women opened their homes as meeting places and communal living space in the early community, and some served as deaconesses and even priests in the early days of the church. Dr. Dorothy Irvin has discovered and published numerous murals and mosaics from early Christian communities depicting women in priestly robes and regalia. Following the guidelines found in the epistle I Timothy, the hierarchy later denied women the right to teach and prophecy in the assembly.

How do you feel about efforts by modern feminist scholars to recast Mary Magdalene as the preeminent apostle?

Although I'm very much in sympathy with research establishing Mary Magdalene as the most faithful of all those who accompanied Jesus during his ministry, I don't think that styling her as an apostle, equal to Peter, or perhaps even more important than Peter, goes nearly far enough. There is no doubt that Mary Magdalene shows total devotion and faithfulness to Christ. But the Gospel also tells a different story. In the earliest Christian texts, Mary Magdalene is not merely equal in status to Peter. She is identified as the archetypal bride of the eternal bridegroom and provides the model for the quest and desire of the human soul (and the entire human community) for union with the Divine. She models the way of "eros" relatedness, the way of the heart, and together with her bridegroom, provides the paradigm for imaging the Divine as partners. Her role of apostle or "emissary" fades in comparison.

Some people, taking this argument too literally, seem to feel that styling Mary Magdalene as the wife of Jesus somehow demeans her. The argument seems to be that it defines her in terms of her relationship with a man which somehow diminishes her own stature. I believe this is far too narrow a view. One needs to realize that the "sacred marriage" we are discussing here is not merely about a first-century Jewish rabbi and his wife. It is really about the archetypal pattern for wholeness, the harmony of the polarities and the "syzygy" of *logos/sophia* (reason/wisdom) representing the Divine as a union of opposites.

Throughout the Gospels Jesus is presented as bridegroom, but it is now widely claimed that he had no bride. In the ancient rites of *hieros gamos*, the royal bride proclaimed and even conferred kingship by her anointing of the bridegroom. Clearly the woman with the alabaster jar who anointed Jesus embodies that ancient archetype, immediately recognized in every corner of the Roman Empire. There was nothing subservient in the mythic act of recognition and endorsement Mary performed in anointing Jesus in the rite of *hieros gamos*.

Mary and Jesus
Re-Enacting Ancient Fertility Cults?

BY MARGARET STARBIRD

Excerpted from *The Goddess in the Gospels: Reclaiming the Sacred Feminine.* Copyright © 1998 by Margaret Starbird. Reprinted by permission of Bear & Company, a division of Inner Traditions International.

Early Christian renderings of the Virgin and her child were modeled on the far more ancient images of the Egyptian goddess Isis, the Sister-Bride of Osiris, holding the sacred child Horus, god of light, on her lap. Ritual poetry from the cult of Isis and Osiris parallels the Song of Songs, in some places word for word. Both lunar and Earth goddesses of the ancient world were often rendered dark to represent feminine principle in juxtaposition to the solar/masculine, a dualism common in the early civilizations of the Mediterranean. Numerous goddesses were rendered black: Inanna, Isis, Cybele, and Artemis, to name only a few.

For the earliest Christians, the goddess in the Gospels was Mary Magdalene, whose epithet meant "elevated" or "watchtower/stronghold"...

After peaking in the twelfth century, the unique importance of the Magdalene in Western Europe was gradually downgraded from around the mid-thirteenth century—a date that corresponds rather dramatically with the Albigensian crusade against the Cathars and the adherents of the "Church of Love." The rise of the Inquisition in the thirteenth century was especially virulent in southern France in response to several Gospel-oriented versions of Christianity, popular heretical sects that severely threatened the hegemony of the Church of Rome. With collaboration from the French king, the pope mounted a crusade against the Albigensian heretics, a bloody war of devastation that lasted for a generation, wiping out whole towns and destroying the cultural flowering of the region known as the Languedoc.

During this same era, beautiful and important epithets that once belonged to the Magdalene were shifted to the Blessed Virgin Mary and churches built to "Our Lady" ostensibly honored the mother of Jesus as the preeminent bearer of the archetypal feminine—"alone of all her sex." Statues and effigies of the Virgin proliferated, most often with her child on her lap, reminiscent of the Egyptian statues of Isis and Horus. After the mid–thirteenth century, the "voice of the Bride" was effectively silenced, although it is whispered that the masons of Europe kept the true faith and built its symbols into the very stones of their Gothic cathedrals . . .

The anointing of Jesus in the Gospels is an enactment of rites from the prevailing fertility cult of the ancient Middle East. In pouring her precious unguent of nard over the head of Jesus, the woman whom tradition has identified with "the Magdalene" ("the Great"!) performed an act identical to the marriage rite of the *hieros gamos*—the rite of the anointing of the chosen Bridegroom/King by the royal representative of the Great Goddess!

Jesus recognized and acknowledged this rite himself, in the context of his role as the sacrificed king: "She has anointed me in preparation for burial" (Mark 14:8b). Those who heard the Gospel story of the anointing at the feast in Bethany would certainly have recognized the rite as the ceremonial anointing of the Sacred King, just as they would have recognized the woman, "the woman with the alabaster jar," who came to the garden sepulcher on the third day to finish the anointing for burial and to lament her tortured Bridegroom. She found an empty tomb. . . .

In the pagan rituals surrounding the ancient myths, the Goddess (the Sister-Bride) goes to the tomb in the garden to lament the death of her Bridegroom and rejoices to find him resurrected. "Love is stronger than death" is the poignant promise in the Song of Songs and similar love poetry of the Middle East celebrating these ancient rites of the Sacred Marriage. . . .

Royal Blood and Mary's Vine

By Margaret Starbird

Excerpted from *The Woman With the Alabaster Jar: Mary Magdalen and the Holy Grail*. Copyright © 1993 by Margaret Starbird. Reprinted by permission of Bear & Company, a division of Inner Traditions International.

The Sangraal

Medieval poets writing in the twelfth century, when the Grail legends first surfaced in European literature, mention a "Grail Family," presumably the custodians of the chalice who were later found unworthy of this privilege. A connection is sometimes drawn by Grail scholars between the word *sangraal* and *gradales*, a word that seems to have meant "cup," "platter," or "basin" in the Provençal language. But it has also been suggested that if one breaks the word *sangraal* after the *g*, the result is *sang raal*, which in Old French means "blood royal."

This second derivation of the French *sangraal* is extremely provocative, and perhaps enlightening. Suddenly one is faced with a new reading of the familiar legend: Instead of a cup or chalice, the story now states that Mary Magdalen brought the "blood royal" to the Mediterranean coast of France. Other legends credit Joseph of Arimathea with bringing the blood of Jesus to France in some kind of vessel. Perhaps it was really Mary Magdalen, under the protection of Joseph of Arimathea, who carried the royal bloodline of David the King to the Mediterranean coast of France.

The Merovingian Connection

There is evidence to suggest that the royal bloodline of Jesus and Mary Magdalen eventually flowed in the veins of the

Merovingian monarchs of France. The name *Merovingian* may itself be a linguistic fossil. The lore surrounding the royal family of the Franks mentions an ancestor Merovee. But the word *Merovingian* breaks down phonetically into syllables that we can easily recognize: *mer* and *vin*, Mary and the vine. Broken down this way, it may be seen to allude to the "vine of Mary" or perhaps the "vine of the Mother."

The royal emblem of the Merovingian King Clovis was the fleur-de-lis (the iris). The Latin name for the iris flower, which grows wild in countries of the Middle East, is *gladiolus*, or "small sword." The trefoil fleur-de-lis of the royal house of France is a masculine symbol. In fact, it is a graphic image of the covenant of circumcision in which are inherent all the promises of God to Israel and to the House of David. Thomas Inman discusses the masculine nature of the "flower of light" at length in his nineteenth-century work, *Ancient Pagan and Modern Christian Symbolism*. It is almost amusing that this same male symbol, the "little sword," is today the international emblem for the Boy Scouts!

The Gnostic Tradition and the Divine Mother

By ELAINE PAGELS

Excerpted from *The Gnostic Gospels* by Elaine Pagels Copyright © 1979 by Elaine Pagels. Used by permission of Random House, Inc.

One group of gnostic sources claims to have received a secret tradition from Jesus through James and through Mary Magdalene. Members of this group prayed to both the divine Father and Mother: "From Thee, Father, and through Thee, Mother, the two immortal names, Parents of the divine being, and thou, dweller in heaven, humanity, of the mighty name . . ."

Since the Genesis account goes on to say that humanity was created "male and female" (1:27), some concluded that the God in whose image we are made must also be both masculine and feminine—both Father and Mother.

How do these texts characterize the divine Mother? I find no simple answer, since the texts themselves are extremely diverse. Yet we may sketch out three primary characterizations. In the first place, several gnostic groups describe the divine Mother as part of an original couple. Valentinus, the teacher and poet, begins with the premise that God is essentially indescribable. But he suggests that the divine can be imagined as a dyad; consisting, in one part, of the Ineffable, the Depth, the Primal Father; and, in the other, of Grace, Silence, the Womb and "Mother of the All." Valentinus reasons that Silence is the appropriate complement of the Father, designating the former as feminine and the latter as masculine because of the grammatical gender of the Greek words. He goes on to describe how Silence receives, as in a womb, the seed of the Ineffable Source; from this she brings forth all the emanations of divine being, ranged in harmonious pairs of masculine and feminine energies.

Followers of Valentinus prayed to her for protection as the Mother, and as "the mystical, eternal Silence." For example, Marcus the magician invokes her as Grace (in Greek, the feminine term *charis*): "May She who is before all things, the incomprehensible and indescribable Grace, fill you within, and increase in you her own knowledge." In his secret celebration of the mass, Marcus teaches that the wine symbolizes her blood. As the cup of wine is offered, he prays that "Grace may flow"into all who drink of it. A prophet and visionary, Marcus calls himself the "*womb* and *recipient* of Silence" (as she is of the Father). The visions he received of the divine being appeared, he reports, in female form.

Another gnostic writing, called the *Great Announcement*, quoted by Hippolytus in his *Refutation of All Heresies*, explains the origin of the universe as follows: From the power of Silence appeared "a great power, the Mind of the Universe, which manages all things, and is a male ... the other ... a great Intelligence ... is a female which produces all things." Following the gender of the Greek words for "mind" (*nous*-masculine) and "intelligence" (*epinoia*-feminine), this author explains that these powers, joined in union, "are discovered to be duality ... This is Mind in Intelligence, and these are separable from one another, and yet are one, found in a state of duality." This means, the gnostic teacher explains, that

> there is in everyone [divine power] existing in a latent condition ... This is one power divided above and below; generating itself, making itself grow, seeking itself, finding itself, being mother of itself, father of itself, sister of itself, spouse of itself, daughter of itself, son of itself—mother, father, unity, being a source of the entire circle of existence.

How did these gnostics intend their meaning to be understood? Different teachers disagreed. Some insisted that the divine to be considered masculofeminine—the "great male-female power." Others claimed that the terms were meant only as metaphors, since, in reality, the divine is neither male nor female." A third group suggested that one can describe the primal Source in either masculine or feminine terms, depending on which aspect one intends to stress. Proponents of these diverse views agreed that the divine is to be understood in terms of a harmonious, dynamic relationship of opposites—a concept that may be akin to the Eastern view of *yin* and *yang*, but remains alien to orthodox Judaism and Christianity ...

If some gnostic sources suggest that the Spirit constitutes the maternal element of the Trinity, the *Gospel of Philip* makes an equally radical suggestion about the doctrine that later developed as the virgin birth. Here again, the Spirit is both Mother and Virgin, the counterpart-and consort-of the Heavenly Father: "Is it permitted to utter a mystery? The Father of everything united with the virgin who came down"—that is, with the Holy Spirit descending into the world. But because this process is to be understood symbolically, not literally, the Spirit remains a virgin. The author goes on to explain that "Adam came into being from two virgins, from the Spirit and from the virgin earth" so "Christ, therefore, was born from a virgin" (that is, from the Spirit). But the author ridicules those literal-minded Christians who mistakenly refer the virgin birth to Mary, Jesus' mother, as though she conceived apart from Joseph: "They do not know what they are saying. When did a woman ever conceive by a woman?" Instead, he argues, virgin birth refers to that mysterious union of the two divine powers, the Father of All and the Holy Spirit.

In addition to the eternal, mystical Silence and the Holy Spirit, certain gnostics suggest a third characterization of the divine Mother: as Wisdom. Here the Greek feminine term for "wisdom," *sophia*, translates a Hebrew feminine term, *hokhmah*. Early interpreters had pondered the meaning of certain Biblical passages—for example, the saying in Proverbs that "God made the world in Wisdom." Could Wisdom be the feminine power in which God's creation was "conceived"? According to one teacher, the double meaning of the term conception—physical and intellectual—suggests this possibility: "The image of thought [*ennoia*] is feminine, since . . . [it] is a power of conception."

The Godman and the Goddess

An Interview with Timothy Freke

Timothy Freke has a degree in philosophy. Peter Gandy has an M.A. in classical civilizations, specializing in ancient pagan mystery religions. They are the coauthors of *Jesus and the Lost Goddess: The Secret Teachings of the Original Christians,* as well as *The Jesus Mysteries: Was the "Original Jesus" a Pagan God?* and more than twenty other books.

In this interview, Freke introduces some of the argument in *Jesus and the Lost Goddess,* excerpts from which follow. Freke and Gandy are key architects of the argument that holds that the belief system of the original Christians was thoroughly subverted as the Roman Empire institutionalized Christianity. The early Christian movement's beliefs in the Gnostic experience of mystical enlightenment and the mystical union of the Godman (Jesus) and the Goddess (Mary Magdalene) were so threatening to the Roman church's vision that they had to be brutally suppressed. The Goddess as well as the mystical and Gnostic traditions, was then written out of the documents, beliefs, and practices of Christianity. For the original Christians, as Teabing tells Sophie in *The Da Vinci Code* about the Priory of Sion's efforts to keep alive the Goddess tradition, Mary Magdalene represents "the Goddess, the Holy Grail, the Rose, and the Divine Mother."

What was the importance of Goddess worship in pagan cultures?

Along with the myth of the Godman, the pagan mysteries told an allegorical myth of the lost and redeemed Goddess, that was an allegory about the fall and redemption of the soul. The most famous pagan version of this myth is Demeter and Persephone. The original Christians adapted this into their myth of Sophia—the Christian Goddess whose name means "wisdom."

What is distinctly "feminine" about Sophia?

The Goddess represents the All, the universe, all that we sense, all that we imagine—the flow of appearances, forms, experience. God—the male archetype—represents the One, the mysterious source of all consciousness which conceives and witnesses the flow of appearances we call life. (Life, or Zoë, was another name of the Christian Goddess.) Sophia was already being venerated by Jewish and pagan mystics before the rise of Christianity.

But the Goddess is not always portrayed in only one light.

Christian mythology is deep and multilayered. This relationship plays out in many ways on many levels. From the arising of something from nothing, it eventually becomes the relationship between Jesus and the two Marys who represent the two aspects of the Goddess—virgin mother and fallen and redeemed whore. Again, these are images taken from ancient pagan mythology.

How does Eve fit into the "lost Goddess" tradition?

She represents half (not a rib as is often mistranslated) of Adam (whose name means "human"). Her myth mirrors pagan myths of the fall of the soul into incarnation, which the Jesus myth seeks to redress.

What is the philosophical concept behind the sacred feminine?

The male principle for the ancients was indivisible consciousness. The female principle was the multitude of appearances, experiences, what is being witnessed. This duality is fundamental to life. Without it there is nothing.

Wisdom is the state of the soul (feminine principle) when it is pure enough to recognize its true nature, to be the One Consciousness in all, which was symbolized for Paul and company by the Christ or "King."

Sophia's Journey
The Pagan Goddess of the Centuries Lost in the Modern Christian World

BY TIMOTHY FREKE AND PETER GANDY

Excerpted from *Jesus and the Lost Goddess: The Secret Teachings of the Original Christians*, by Timothy Freke and Peter Gandy. Copyright © 2001 by Timothy Freke and Peter Gandy. Used by permission of Harmony Books, a division of Random House, Inc.

In this excerpt from Freke and Gandy's *Jesus and the Lost Goddess*, the authors trace the tradition of the Goddess back to the Greek myths and Jewish sources. They build their image of the Goddess from Old Testament quotations, Greek myths, and pagan traditions that range from Helen of Troy to Plato's view of Psyche as female, to mysteries of Eleusis that regularly re-enacted the myth of Demeter and Persephone. In the end, they find the theme of the lost Goddess even in the Sleeping Beauty legend.

The Christian Goddess

The myth of the Godman Jesus can only be properly understood alongside the myth of the Goddess Sophia. After so many centuries of patriarchal Christianity it is both shocking

Did Early Gnostic Christians Engage in Sacred Sexual Acts?

Most of our experts find little evidence on this subject. However Freke and Gandy comment briefly, noting that "Gnostics deliberately violated social norms as a way of deconditioning themselves from their social personae and so becoming aware of their true spiritual identity. For some, such as the Cainite school, this was done through ascetic abstinence. For others, such as the Carpocratian school, this was done through libertine indulgence . . ."

Apparently Carpocrates, an Alexandrian Platonist Gnostic, who founded a sect of Gnostic Christians in the early second century C.E.—a group described by Freke and Gandy as radical communists who abhorred private property—taught students to "enjoy life, including the pleasures of sex that are so often condemned by religious Literalists . . . Such Gnostics saw sexuality as a celebration of the union of God and Goddess, from which all life springs. They are said to have sometimes practiced sacramental nudity in church and even ritual intercourse."

and reassuring to discover a Goddess at the very heart of Christianity. She is, like her son/brother/lover Jesus, a syncretic figure created from both Pagan and Jewish sources.

Sophia, whose name means "wisdom," had been the Goddess of pagan philosophers for centuries. Indeed, the word for "philosopher," first used by Pythagoras, means "lover of Sophia." Although often pictured today as dry academics, these brilliant intellectuals were actually mystics and devotees of the Goddess. Parmenides, for example, is usually remembered as the founder of Western logic, yet his masterwork is a visionary poem in which he descends to the underworld to be instructed by the Goddess.

Sophia was also an important mythical figure for Jewish Gnostics, such as Philo [Jewish-Hellenistic philosopher based in Alexandria, 25 B.C.E.–50 C.E.]. Although later rejected by Jewish literalists, there had always been a Jewish Goddess tradition. At one time Israelites had worshipped the Goddess Asherah as the consort of the Jewish God Jehovah. In the fifth century B.C.E. she was known as Anat Jahu. In texts written between the fourth and fifth centuries B.C.E., such as *Proverbs*, *The Sophia of Solomon,* and the *Sophia of Jesus the Son of Sirach*, she becomes God's companion and cocreator Sophia.

Origins of the Christian Goddess

As with all Christian mythology, the myth of the lost Goddess is a synthesis of preexisting Jewish and Pagan myths. Let's examine some of these sources.

Jewish Sources

The Exegesis on the Soul [one of the most intriguing lost gospels found among the books in the Nag Hammadi Library] draws attention to some of the Jewish mythological motifs which it develops in the myth of Sophia. It quotes *Jeremiah*, in which God proclaims to Israel, as if to the lost Goddess:

> You prostituted yourself to many shepherds and then you returned to me. Take an honest look and see where you prostituted yourself. You became shameless with everyone. You did not call on me as kinsman or as Father or author of your virginity.

Likewise, in *Ezekiel* God announces:

> You built yourself a brothel on every lane, and you wasted your beauty, and you spread your legs in every alley, and you multiplied your acts of prostitution. You prostituted yourself to the sons of Egypt, those who are your neighbors, men great of flesh.

The *Exegesis on the Soul* decodes the allegorical meaning of this text:

> What does "the sons of Egypt, men great of flesh" mean, if not the world of the body and the realm of the senses and the affairs of this Earth, by which the psyche has become contaminated?"

The *Exegesis on the Soul* also points out the resonance between the myth of Sophia and the *Genesis* myth. In *Genesis* Adam represents Consciousness and Eve represents psyche. In the beginning there was originally a primordial human being, Adam, from whom God took "one side" and created Eve (not a "rib" as it says in traditional translations!) This represents the projection of psyche from Consciousness. The two are essentially one, but appear as opposites. The psyche (Eve) leads Consciousness (Adam) into identification with the body. This is symbolized by the Fall from Eden. The mystical marriage repairs the primal separation of Adam and Eve, Consciousness and psyche. *The Exegesis on the Soul* quotes Paul's teaching, "They will become a single body," and comments:

> They were originally joined one to another when they were with the Father, before the woman led astray the man, who is her brother. This marriage has brought them back together again and the psyche has been joined to her true lover.

In another Jewish text, *Proverbs*, the two fundamental states of the psyche are represented by Lady Wisdom and Lady Folly, According to Philo, Lady Folly is like a whore who leads those who listen to her to Hell. Lady Wisdom, however, is compared to an invitation to a wedding and a faithful wife—images which refer to the motif of the mystical marriage.

The Myth of Helen

As with the Jesus story, the most important source for the Christian Goddess myth is Pagan mythology. *The Exegesis on the Soul* compares the Christian myth of Sophia to Homer's initiatory tales *The Iliad* and *The Odyssey*, in which Helen has been abducted and must be rescued. According to the Pythagoreans, Helen is a symbol of the psyche and her abduction represents the fall of the psyche into incarnation ...

The Helen myth was important to the first Christians ... Deliberately imitating the myth of Jesus and the Goddess, these Gnostic masters identified themselves with the role of the savior come to reveal Gnosis to their lost followers, symbolized by Helen/Sophia.

Plato's Phaedo

In *Phaedo* Plato gives us an account of the fall and redemption of the psyche which was undoubtedly drawn on by the original Christians when they created their own version of the myth of the lost Goddess:

> The Psyche is dragged by the body into the region of the changeable, where she wanders in confusion. The world spins around her and she is like a drunkard under its influence. But returning to herself, she reflects. Then she passes into the realm of purity, eternity, immortality and

unchangeableness, which are her kindred. When she is herself and not obstructed or hindered she is ever with them. When she ceases from her erring ways and is in communion with the unchanging, she is herself unchanging. This state of the psyche is called Sophia.

The Myth of Aphrodite

The Pagan myth of the Goddess Aphrodite tells fundamentally the same tale as the later Christian myth of the lost Goddess. Like Sophia, Aphrodite has a pristine and fallen nature. Plotinus [Egyptian-Roman philosopher of the third century C.E.] explains that in essence she is "Aphrodite of the Heavens," but "here she has turned whore." He writes, "Zeus represents consciousness and Aphrodite his daughter who issues from him is psyche," commenting:

> The nature of the psyche is to love God and long to be at one with Him in the noble love of a daughter for a noble Father. But coming to human birth and lured by the courtships of this sphere, she takes up with another lover, a mortal, leaves her Father and falls. But one day, coming to hate her shame, she puts away the evil of Earth, once more seeks her Father and finds peace. The psyche's true good lies in devotion to Consciousness its kin. Evil to the psyche lies in frequenting strangers. But suppose the psyche has attained the highest, or rather it has revealed its presence to her. Then as long as the presence holds all distinctions fade. It is like the merging of lover and beloved. Once she has this she would not trade it for anything in the whole universe.

The Myth of Demeter and Persephone

The most influential of all the myths of the Goddess in her two aspects is the myth of Demeter and Persephone, taught in the Mysteries of Eleusis. The Pagan Gnostic Sallustius [who lived around 360 C.E. was an advisor to the Roman Emperor Julian and sought a Pagan revival] tells us that this myth is an allegory for descent of the Psyche into incarnation. Olympiodorus likewise explains, "The Psyche descends after the manner of Persephone." Lucius Apuleius talks of the "dark descending rites" and "luminous ascending rites" of Persephone , writing of his own initiation:

> I approached the confines of death, and trod on the threshold of Persephone, and being carried through all the elements, I came back again to my pristine condition.

The Literalist Christian Hippolytus describes the teachings of the descent and ascent of the Psyche as the mystery revealed to those "admitted to the highest grade of the Eleusinian rites" and states that initiates of the Naassene school [Gnostic sect during the time of Hadrian—110–140 C.E.—which believed in the divinity of the serpent and held mystery rites dedicated to the Great Mother] of Christian Gnosticism had developed their teachings specifically from this source.

Plato tells us the name "Persephone" comes from *sophe* and means "wise," so it derives from the same root as "Sophia." Persephone, who was known as Kore, meaning "Daughter" or "Girl," represents the fallen psyche. In the Christian *Acts of Thomas*, the psyche is called Kore. Demeter means "Mother." She is the Celestial Queen who represents the pure psyche.

In the myth, Demeter's daughter Persephone is abducted by Hades, god of the underworld. This represents the fall into incarnation. Before they were initiated, initiates into the Mysteries of Eleusis had to imitate the grief felt by Demeter and Persephone at their separation. This represents the experience of *metanoia* which results from the initiates' grief at becoming separated from their deeper nature and lost in the world. Hermes goes to the underworld to rescue Persephone and reunite her with her mother Demeter. This represents rescuing the psyche from identification with the circumference of the circle of self and reuniting it with its true nature at the center.

Hades secretly gives Persephone pomegranate seeds to eat, however, and because she eats these seeds she must return to the underworld for a third of every year. The pomegranate seeds represent the seeds of future lives which we create in this life, which bring us back into human incarnation to continue the journey of awakening. They represent what the ancients called our "fate," which in modern spiritual jargon is generally known as our "karma." The motif of returning to the underworld for "a third of the year" is an allusion to the threefold nature of the Self: Consciousness, psyche, body. A third of our identity—the body—is in the underworld.

The figures of Demeter and Persephone were developed by the Greeks from ancient Egyptian mythology. Porphyry [pagan philosopher, 232–303 c.e.] tells us that the Egyptian Isis is equivalent to both Demeter and Persephone . . . In Egyptian mythology the higher and lower aspects of the Goddess are represented by Isis and her sister Nephthys, the wife of the evil god Set, who, like Hades, represents the material world.

These Egyptian myths are the earliest sources of what was to become the Christian myth of the lost and redeemed Goddess. Although this perennial story has been expunged from Christianity, it survived in the form of fairy tales such as *Sleeping Beauty*. As her name suggests, Sleeping Beauty is an image of the psyche fallen asleep in the world. The story portrays her as a princess cursed to sleep forever, imprisoned in a dark castle surrounded by deep impenetrable forest, but finally rescued by her lover, the hero prince.

The Goddess in the Gospels

In the Christian myth of Sophia, the Goddess, representing the psyche, is the central figure, while her brother-lover, representing Consciousness, is an incidental character. In the Jesus myth, it is the opposite. The Godman is the central character. Yet the myth of the lost Goddess forms an important subtext to the Jesus story, which would have been obvious to Christian initiates familiar with both allegories. The Sophia myth makes clear the nature of Jesus' mythical mission—he comes to rescue his sister-lover Sophia, the psyche lost in identification with the body. "Christ came for her sake," states *The Tripartate Tractate* [another of Nag Hammadi's Gnostic Gospels].

Virgin and Prostitute

In the gospels the Virgin Mary and Mary Magdalene represent the higher Sophia and the fallen Sophia. They are called by the same name to emphasize the fact that mythologically they are aspects of the same figure. As in the Sophia myth, the first Mary is a virgin, like Sophia when she was living with her Father, and the second is a prostitute who is redeemed by her lover Jesus, like Sophia when lost in the world.

The Goddess as mother and prostitute is alluded to in the genealogy created for Jesus by *The Gospel of Matthew.* As we would expect, this genealogy follows the patriarchal line, but breaks this pattern to specifically mention four famous Jewish "fallen women." Tamar was a temple prostitute. Ruth indulged in shameless sexual exploitation. Baathsheba was committed for adultery with King David. Rahab was the madam of a brothel. In the *Exodus* allegory, when Jesus/Joshua arrives in the Promised Land he rescues the prostitute Rahab, symbolizing the psyche, from the walled city of Jericho, symbolizing the body. By specifically naming Rahab as one of Jesus Christ's ancestors *The Gospel of Matthew* points to the mythological resonance between this story and the gospel story of Jesus redeeming the prostitute Mary Magdalene.

Mary Magdalene, representing Jesus' sister-lover Sophia, is the "Beloved Disciple" who is consistently portrayed in Christian texts as having a particularly close relationship with Jesus. *The Gospel of the Beloved Disciple* (aka *The Gospel of John*) [another Gnostic work] portrays Jesus and Mary as so close that, during the Last Supper, she is lying in his lap. *The Gospel of Philip* relates that Jesus "loved her more than the other disciples, and often used to kiss her on the lips." In *The Gospel of Luke* Mary wipes her hair on Jesus' feet.' According to Jewish law, only a husband was allowed to see a woman's hair unbound and if a woman let down her hair in front of another man, this was a sign of impropriety and grounds for mandatory divorce. This incident, then, can be seen as portraying Jesus and Mary either as man and wife or as libertine lovers with scant regard for moral niceties.

Images of the Awakening Psyche

Women play a prominent role throughout the Jesus story, particularly in *The Gospel of the Beloved Disciple*, and all of them represent Sophia in her various states of awakening. *The Exegesis on the Soul* portrays Sophia at her most desperate as a barren old woman. It is in this state that she experiences *metanoia* and calls out to the Father to rescue her. In the Jesus story this aspect of Sophia is represented by Elizabeth, the mother of John the Baptist. She is a partner figure to the Virgin Mary. Mary is young and unimpregnated. Elizabeth is old and barren. In this condition, like Sophia, she calls out to the Father for help, representing the barren psyche in which the call for help arises, The answer is John the Baptist, who represents the *psychic* initiation of purification through baptism with water, which is the start of the Gnostic path of self-knowledge.

Throughout his mission Jesus has various encounters with women who are Sophia figures and symbolize the progressive states of awakening of the psyche. In one incident Jesus prevents an adulterous woman from being stoned to death by pointing out that none of her accusers are themselves blameless. This is an allusion to the fallen Sophia being abused by her adulterous lovers. The woman in this story is a helpless victim surprised to be rescued. This represents the early stage of awakening in which the embodied psyche is a recipient of unasked for assistance from essential Self, which it experiences as "grace."

In a further incident, Jesus meets an adulterous Samaritan woman representing the fallen Sophia. Jesus reveals to the woman that he is Christ and offers her the "waters of life." This story takes the relationship between Sophia, representing the psyche, and Jesus, representing Consciousness, a step further. Here, Jesus directly offers the teaching which lead to Gnosis, represented by the waters of eternal life, and reveals that he is the Christ. This represents a state in which initiates glimpse their true nature for the first time, and understand the possibility of knowledge. The scene is set at Jacob's Well, which is designed to reinforce the allusion to the Sophia myth. In Jewish mythology, Rebecca, the mother of Jacob, draws water from this well, which Philo tells us represents receiving the wisdom of Sophia.

In the next episode, we meet two important Sophia figures, Martha and her sister Mary. Their brother Lazarus has died, but they believe that if Jesus had been present he could have saved him. Moved by their faith, Jesus goes to the cave in which Lazarus is buried and miraculously raises him from the dead. In this remarkable little story Lazarus represents the *hylic* [i.e., material, corporeal] state of being spiritually dead in the underworld. He is brought to life by the power of the Christ, representing Consciousness, through the faith of Martha and Mary, representing the *psychic* and *pneumatic* stages of awakening . . .

Another significant episode also happens whilst Jesus is visiting the house of Lazarus, Martha and Mary. Martha is again serving whilst Lazarus, now returned from the dead, sits at the table. Meanwhile, Mary takes "very costly ointment" and anoints Jesus, thus formally making him the "Anointed" or Christ/King. These events represent the stage of awakening in which initiates are no longer spiritually dead in the *hylic* state, which is represented by the resurrected Lazarus eating at the table. They are engaged in the *psychic* process of awakening, represented by Martha, who is serving, and have progressed sufficiently in the *pneumatic* level of awakening to clearly recognize their true identity as Consciousness, represented by Mary anointing Jesus as the Christ/King.

Jesus is portrayed as having expelled "seven demons" from "Mary called Magdalene." The number seven is significant. In the Gnostic mythical schema, the cosmos has seven levels, represented by the sun, moon, and five visible planets. These were sometimes imagined as demonic forces which entrap us in materiality. Above these is the *ogdoad* or "eighth," represented by the starry skies, which is the mythological home of the Goddess. The Gnostic journey of awakening from incarnation is sometimes conceived of as mounting a sevenfold ladder to the *ogdoad*. That Mary has been freed from seven demons represents Jesus having helped her to ascend the seven rungs of the ladder to the heavens.

At the culmination of the Jesus story, it is Mary Magdalene who finds Jesus' empty tomb and to whom the resurrected Christ first appears. This represents the fulfillment of the process of initiation. For the Gnostics the body is a "tomb" in which we exist as the spiritually dead. Mary finding that the tomb is empty represents the understanding that we are not the physical body. Her encounter with the resurrected Christ represents the realization that our essential nature is the one Consciousness of God.

After this Mary represents the wise psyche, truly worthy of the name "Sophia." As *The Dialogue of the Saviour* puts it, Mary is now "a woman who completely understands." In *The Gospel according to Mary* the resurrected Jesus imparts the Inner Mysteries of Christianity to Mary, who reveals these secret teachings to the other disciples. They then go forth to preach "the gospel according to Mary." Despite the misogyny of the Christian Literalists, the tradition of Mary Magdalene as the *apostola apostolorum*, the "apostle to the apostles," remains Catholic doctrine to this day.

Motifs of the Mystical Marriage

According to the Christian Gnostics, there are many allusions to the mystical marriage in the Jesus story. The most important is the Eucharist ritual, which is based on the ancient rites of the mystical marriage in the Pagan Mysteries. In the Mysteries of Eleusius, the Goddess Demeter was represented by bread and the Godman Dionysus by wine. The original Christians, likewise, associated bread with Mary and wine with Jesus, who is called "the true vine" in *The Gospel of John*. The Literalist Epiphanius records with horror that initiates of the Colyridian school of Christianity celebrated the Eucharist in the name of "Mary Queen of Heaven," writing:

> They adorn a chair or a square throne, spread a linen cloth over it, and, at a certain solemn time, place bread on it and offer it in the name of Mary; and all partake of this bread.

In the act of ceremonially eating the bread and drinking the wine, the Godman and the Goddess, representing Consciousness and psyche commune in the mystical marriage. It is obviously significant that as Jesus officiates at the Last Supper Eucharist celebration, the "Beloved Disciple" Mary Magdalene rests intimately in his lap.

Earlier, Jesus miraculously turns water into wine at a marriage ceremony at Cana, which according to Christian Gnostics represents the mystical marriage. Water becoming wine is an archaic symbol representing the ecstatic intoxication of spiritual transformation. The creators of the Jesus story borrowed this motif from Pagan mythology, in which the Godman Dionysus turns water into wine at his marriage to Ariadne. In the Christian version of this tale Jesus is not portrayed as the bridegroom. However, in the New Testament Jesus refers to himself, and is repeatedly referred to by others, as "the bridegroom." . . .

In one intriguing non-canonical Christian tale, Jesus takes Mary Magdalene up a mountain, whereupon one side of him becomes a woman with whom he makes love. Going up a mountain is a perennial image of walking the spiritual path to Heaven. The image of Jesus producing a woman from his side is an allusion to the *Genesis* myth in which Eve is created from one side of Adam, representing Consciousness objectifying itself as psyche. In the Christian parable, Jesus (Consciousness) shows Mary (fallen psyche) the magical woman (higher psyche), who is Mary's original nature. Jesus then makes love with the woman, representing the consummation of the mystical marriage in which Consciousness and psyche commune in the realization of their essential Oneness.

Summary

&❧ The Christian myth of the lost Goddess is the partner

myth to the Jesus myth. Jesus and the Goddess represent Consciousness and psyche, or spirit and soul. The Goddess is portrayed as having two aspects, representing the pure psyche and the embodied psyche. These two aspects can be thought of as the two ends of the radius circle of self, one connecting to Consciousness at the center and the other to the body at the circumference.

❧ The myth of Sophia tells the story of the fall of the psyche into incarnation and her redemption by her lover-brother, representing Consciousness. Sophia's fall, repentance, redemption and marriage represent the *hylic, psychic* and *pneumatic* states of awareness an initiate passes through on their journey towards the realization of Gnosis.

❧ The myth of Sophia forms the subtext to the Jesus story. The most important Sophia figures in the gospels are the two Marys, Jesus' virgin mother and prostitute lover, representing the higher Sophia and the fallen Sophia. . . .

The Chalice and the Blade
Archaelogy, Anthropology, and the Sacred Feminine

Including excerpts from *The Chalice and the Blade: Our History, Our Future,* by Riane Eisler. Copyright © 1987 by Riane Eisler. Quotations by permission of HarperCollins Publishers, Inc.

In her well-known work, *The Chalice and the Blade: Our History, Our Future,* Riane Eisler lays the archeological and historical foundation for the central role of the Goddess and the feminine in early culture—a role she argues was later pushed aside by hierarchies that implicitly fostered domination, patriarchy, and rigidity. Eisler is a cofounder of the Center for Partnership Studies, which promotes a way of life based on "harmony with nature, nonviolence, and gender, racial, and economic equity." Her book is mentioned in Dan Brown's bibliography for *The Da Vinci Code* and informs some of *The Da Vinci Code's* discussion of symbols and representations of goddess culture in history.

"There is abundant evidence that spirituality, and particularly the spiritual vision characteristic of wise seers, was once associated with woman," writes Eisler. "From Mesopotamian archaeological records we learn that Ishtar of Babylon ... was still known as the Lady of Vision, She Who Directs Oracles, and the Prophetess." In Egypt, where there is ample evidence of strong queens and female pharaohs, records show that "the picture of a cobra was the hieroglyphic sign for the word *goddess* and the cobra was known as the Eye, *uzait*, a symbol of mystic insight and wisdom . . ."

Turning to Greece, Eisler points out that, "the well-known oracular shrine at Delphi also stood on a site originally identified with the worship of the Goddess. And even in classical Greek times, after it was taken over for the worship of Apollo, the oracle still spoke through the lips of a woman."

Archaeological records from many Near East and eastern Mediterranean countries note a propensity to associate justice (law) and medicine (healing powers) with women. Apparently, the Egyptian goddess Isis was associated with these traits. "Even writing, long assumed to date back to around 3200 B.C.E. in Sumer, appears to have much earlier, and possibly feminine, roots. In Sumerian tablets the Goddess Nidaba is described as the scribe of the Sumerian heaven as well as the inventor of both clay tablets and the art of writing. In

Indian mythology the Goddess Sarasvati is credited with inventing the original alphabet."

The Minoan society left an artistic and archaeological record that indicates its daily life centered on the worship of the Goddess. "The evidence indicates that in Crete power was primarily equated with the responsibility of motherhood," says Eisler, arguing that Minoan Crete offered a male-female "partnership model of society in which women and traits associated with women were not systematically devalued. " Democracy was practiced before its rise in Athens, the arts flourished, peace prevailed, and the culture exhibited a love for life that included what Eisler refers to as a "pleasure bond" between males and females. Clothing and art emphasized a relaxed and uninhibited sexuality, according to Eisler and many other researchers. Some scholars suggest that Minoan civilization was particularly successful, artistic, rich, and peaceful because the aggressive tendencies of its males were well channeled into sports, ecstatic dancing, music, and sex, rather than warfare.

While other goddess-worshipping cultures were abandoning their female deities for male gods of war, the Crete of four thousand years ago clung to its goddess traditions. Perhaps that is why, as Eisler puts it, "In the island of Crete where the Goddess was still supreme, there are no signs of war. Here the economy prospered and the arts flourished." The Goddess remained at the center of religious and ritual practice in Minoan society for hundreds more years, before the Goddess was lost here too and male God figures gained sway. The process of the fall of the Goddess is one that may well have echoes in the story of the Christian experience and how Mary Magdalene was treated by the early church and even today. Langdon, Teabing and Sauniere are no doubt on to one of male-written history's greatest cover-ups.

If you go to Knossos, the Minoan palace in Crete, even today, the limestone frescoes still tell the story of the Goddess, her priestesses, and sacred, mystical practices—including sacred sexual practices. These and other archaeological finds give us many clues to understanding that looking for the "sacred feminine" in the collective unconscious of Western thought or the Judeo-Christian experience is an intriguing, productive, and historically important endeavor.

Part II

Echoes of the Hidden Past

3 The Lost Gospels

> *What I find interesting about Dan Brown's book is that it raises a very important question: If they—meaning the leaders of the church—suppressed so much of early Christian history, what else don't we know about? What else is there to be known? And as a historian, I think it's a really important question because the answer means a great deal.*
>
> —ELAINE PAGELS

The religious girders that frame the edifice of Dan Brown's plot are built upon the foundations of early Christian history and, in particular, the set of Gnostic Gospels found in 1945 near the Egyptian town of Nag Hammadi. These documents, which have led to remarkable discoveries about an alternate tradition later suppressed, form the backdrop of another artful blending of fact and fiction in *The Da Vinci Code*. In Chapter 58, which takes place in Lee Teabing's sumptuous study, Sophie Neveu and Robert Langdon are handed a copy of these lost Gospels in a "leather-bound ... poster-sized" edition to demonstrate with irrevocable proof that "the marriage of Jesus and Mary Magdalene is part of the historical record."

As the following excerpts and interviews with some of world's leading experts elaborate, there is no doubt the Nag Hammadi texts have yielded a treasure trove of documents permitting a richer, more nuanced and, perhaps, even more radical interpretation of the words of Jesus, the role of his followers, and the interpretation of early Christianity. They help shed light on a time when the many contending schools of Christian worship were interwoven and the definitive canon had not yet been created. Specifically, they give our era a glimpse into a different tradition—the Gnostic Tradition—that conflicted with the interpretation of Jesus' preaching found today in the orthodoxy of the New Testament. More explosively, in terms of the history of the church, they suggest a much more important role for Mary Magdalene as a disciple and close companion to Jesus. They also suggest more interest in seeking inner knowledge and self-development than what we traditionally understand as the philosophy of the New Testament. And the Gnostics of Nag Hammadi seemed to feel less need for churches and priests. They seemed perfectly comfortable interpreting their own Gospels and sacred books without intermediation—an idea institutionalized Christianity would find threatening.

In this chapter, we invite readers to join in the search for the meaning and implications of these lost Gospels. Certainly they seem to emphasize a balance between the masculine and the feminine, the good and the evil in mankind, and the importance of Mary Magdalene as an apostle. Beyond that, did the word *companion* mean "marriage" or was it simply a fellow traveler? What of the seemingly explicit reference in the *Gospel of Philip* to Jesus kissing Mary Magdalene frequently on the mouth? Factual description or metaphor? And if metaphor, metaphor for what? Are these Gnostic Gospels really telling us that a more humane, more "the spirit is within you" emphasis and a strongly anti-authoritarian, pro-feminine tradition existed that was purposely marginalized and shoved aside as heresy by history's Christian "winners"?

In the hands of the experts who have lived and breathed

this material their whole professional lives, the reader will be guided through the existing scholarship as well as translations of the original documents that play such a prominent role in *The Da Vinci Code*.

An Astonishing Find
The Keys to the Alternate Tradition and Their Meaning for Today

BY ELAINE PAGELS

Elaine Pagels is Harrington Spear Paine Professor of Religion at Princeton University and author of the bestselling *Beyond Belief* as well as *The Gnostic Gospels*, which won the National Book Critics Circle Award and the National Book Award.

Excerpted from *The Gnostic Gospels* by Elaine Pagels. Copyright © 1979 by Elaine Pagels. Used by permission of Random House, Inc.

In December 1945 an Arab peasant made an astonishing archeological discovery in Upper Egypt. Rumors obscured the circumstances of this find—perhaps because the discovery was accidental, and its sale on the black market illegal. For years even the identity of the discoverer remained unknown. One rumor held that he was a blood avenger; another, that he had made the find near the town of Naj 'Hammadi at the Jabal al-Tārif, a mountain honeycombed with more than 150 caves. Originally natural, some of these caves were cut and painted and used as grave sites as early as the sixth dynasty, some 4,300 years ago.

Thirty years later the discoverer himself, Muhammad 'Alī al-Samman, told what happened. Shortly before he and his brothers avenged their father's murder in a blood feud, they had saddled their camels and gone out to the Jabal to dig for *sabakh*, a soft soil they used to fertilize their crops. Digging around a massive boulder, they hit a red earthenware jar, almost a meter high. Muhammad 'Alī hesitated to break the jar, considering that a *jinn*, or spirit, might live inside. But realizing that it might also contain gold, he raised his mattock, smashed the jar, and discovered inside thirteen papyrus books, bound in leather. Returning to his home in al-Qasr, Muhammad 'Alī dumped the books and loose papyrus leaves on the straw piled on the ground next to the oven. Muhammad's mother, 'Umm-Ahmad, admits that she burned much of the papyrus in the oven along with the straw she used to kindle the fire.

A few weeks later, as Muhammad 'Alī tells it, he and his brothers avenged their father's death by murdering Ahmed Ismā'īl. Their mother had warned her sons to keep their mattocks sharp: when they learned that their father's enemy was nearby, the brothers seized the opportunity, "hacked off his limbs . . . ripped out his heart, and devoured it among them, as the ultimate act of blood revenge."

Fearing that the police investigating the murder would search his house and discover the books, Muhammad 'Alī asked the priest, al-Qummus Basiliyus Abd al-Masïh, to keep one or more for him. During the time that Muhammad 'Alī and his brothers were being interrogated for murder, Raghib, a local history teacher, had seen one of the books, and suspected that it had value. Having received one from al-Qummus Basiliylus, Raghib sent it to a friend in Cairo to find out its worth.

Sold on the black market through antiquities dealers in Cairo, the manuscripts soon attracted the attention of officials of the Egyptian government. Through circumstances of high drama, as we shall see, they bought one and confiscated ten and a half of the thirteen leather-bound books, called codices, and deposited them in the Coptic Museum in Cairo. But a large part of the thirteenth codex, containing five extraordinary texts, was smuggled out of Egypt and offered for sale in

America. Word of this codex soon reached Professor Gilles Quispel, distinguished historian of religion at Utrecht, in the Netherlands. Excited by the discovery, Quispel urged the Jung Foundation in Zürich to buy the codex. But discovering, when he succeeded, that some pages were missing, he flew to Egypt in the spring of 1955 to try to find them in the Coptic Museum. Arriving in Cairo, he went at once to the Coptic Museum, borrowed photographs of some of the texts, and hurried back to his hotel to decipher them. Tracing out the first line, Quispel was startled, then incredulous, to read: "These are the secret words which the living Jesus spoke, and which the twin, Judas Thomas, wrote down." Quispel knew that his colleague H.-C. Puech, using notes from another French scholar, Jean Doresse, had identified the opening lines with fragments of a Greek *Gospel of Thomas* discovered in the 1890's. But the discovery of the whole text raised new questions: Did Jesus have a twin brother, as this text implies? Could the text be an authentic record of Jesus' sayings? According to its title, it contained the *Gospel According to Thomas*; yet, unlike the gospels of the New Testament, this text identified itself as a *secret* gospel. Quispel also discovered that it contained many sayings known from the New Testament; but these sayings, placed in unfamiliar contexts, suggested other dimensions of meaning. Other passages, Quispel found, differed entirely from any known Christian tradition: the "living Jesus," for example, speaks in sayings as cryptic and compelling as Zen *koans*:

> Jesus said, "If you bring forth what is within you, what you bring forth will save you. If you do not bring forth what is within you, what you do not bring forth will destroy you."

What Quispel held in his hand, the *Gospel of Thomas*, was only one of the fifty-two texts discovered at Nag Hammadi (the usual English transliteration of the town's name). Bound into the same volume with it is the *Gospel of Philip*, which attributes to Jesus acts and sayings quite different from those in the New Testament:

> ... the companion of the [Savior is] Mary Magdalene. [But Christ loved] her more than [all] the disciples, and used to kiss her [often] on her [mouth]. The rest of [the disciples were offended] ... They said to him, "Why do you love her more than all of us?" The Savior answered and said to them, "Why do I not love you as [I love] her?"

Other sayings in this collection criticize common Christian beliefs, such as the virgin birth or the bodily resurrection, as naïve misunderstandings. Bound together with these gospels is the *Apocryphon* (literally, "secret book") of *John*, which opens with an offer to reveal "the mysteries [and the] things hidden in silence" which Jesus taught to his disciple John.

Muhammad 'Alī later admitted that some of the texts were lost—burned up or thrown away. But what remains is astonishing: some fifty-two texts from the early centuries of the Christian era—including a collection of early Christian gospels, previously unknown. Besides the *Gospel of Thomas* and the *Gospel of Philip*, the find included the *Gospel of Truth* and the *Gospel to the Egyptians*, which identifies itself as "the [sacred book] of the Great Invisible [Spirit]." Another group of texts consists of writings attributed to Jesus' followers, such as the *Secret Book of James*, the *Apocalypse of Paul*, the *Letter of Peter to Philip*, and the *Apocalypse of Peter*.

What Muhammad 'Alī discovered at Nag Hammadi, it soon became clear, were Coptic translations, made about 1,500 years ago, of still more ancient manuscripts. The originals themselves had been written in Greek, the language of the New Testament: as Doresse, Puech, and Quispel had recognized, part of one of them had been discovered by archeologists about fifty years earlier, when they found a few fragments of the original Greek version of the *Gospel of Thomas*.

About the dating of the manuscripts themselves there is little debate. Examination of the datable papyrus used to thicken the leather bindings, and of the Coptic script, place them c. A.D. 350–400. But scholars sharply disagree about the dating of the original texts. Some of them can hardly be later than c. A.D. 120–150, since Irenaeus, the orthodox Bishop of Lyons, writing c. 180, declares that heretics "boast that they possess more gospels than there really are," and complains that in his time such writings already have won wide circulation— from Gaul through Rome, Greece, and Asia Minor.

Quispel and his collaborators, who first published the *Gospel* of *Thomas*, suggested the date of c. A.D. 140 for the original. Some reasoned that since these gospels were heretical, they must have been written later than the gospels of the New Testament, which are dated c. 60–110. But recently Professor Helmut Koester of Harvard University has suggested that the collection of sayings in the *Gospel of Thomas*, although compiled c. 140, may include some traditions even *older* than the gospels of the New Testament, "possibly as early as the second half of the first century" (50–100)—as early as, or earlier, than Mark, Matthew, Luke, and John.

Scholars investigating the Nag Hammadi find discovered that some of the texts tell the origin of the human race in terms very different from the usual reading of Genesis: the *Testimony of Truth*, for example, tells the story of the Garden of Eden from the viewpoint of the serpent! Here the serpent, long known to appear in gnostic literature as the principle of divine wisdom, convinces Adam and Eve to partake of knowledge while "the Lord" threatens them with death, trying jealously to prevent them from attaining knowledge, and expelling them from Paradise when they achieve it. Another text, mysteriously entitled the *Thunder, Perfect Mind*, offers an extraordinary poem spoken in the voice of a feminine divine power:

> For I am the first and the last.
> I am the honored one and the scorned one.
> I am the whore and the holy one.
> I am the wife and the virgin . . .
> I am the barren one,
> and many are her sons . . .
> I am the silence that is incomprehensible . . .
> I am the utterance of my name.

These diverse texts range, then, from secret gospels, poems, and quasi-philosophic descriptions of the origin of the universe, to myths, magic, and instructions for mystical practice.

Why were these texts buried—and why have they remained virtually unknown for nearly 2,000 years? Their suppression as banned documents, and their burial on the cliff at Nag Hammadi, it turns out, were both part of a struggle critical for the formation of early Christianity. The Nag Hammadi texts, and others like them, which circulated at the beginning of the Christian era, were denounced as heresy by orthodox Christians in the middle of the second century. We have long known that many early followers of Christ were condemned by other Christians as heretics, but nearly all we knew about them came from what their opponents wrote attacking them. Bishop Irenaeus, who supervised the church in Lyons, c. 180, wrote five volumes, entitled *The Destruction and Overthrow of Falsely So-called Knowledge*, which begin with his promise to

> set forth the views of those who are now teaching heresy
> . . . to show how absurd and inconsistent with the truth
> are their statements . . . I do this so that . . . you may urge

all those with whom you are connected to avoid such an abyss of madness and of blasphemy against Christ.

He denounces as especially "full of blasphemy" a famous gospel called the *Gospel of Truth*. Is Irenaeus referring to the same *Gospel of Truth* discovered at Nag Hammadi? Quispel and his collaborators, who first published the *Gospel of Truth*, argued that he is; one of their critics maintains that the opening line (which begins "The gospel of truth") is not a title. But Irenaeus does use the same source as at least one of the texts discovered at Nag Hammadi—the *Apocryphon* (Secret Book) *of John*—as ammunition for his own attack on such "heresy." Fifty years later Hippolytus, a teacher in Rome, wrote another massive *Refutation of All Heresies* to "expose and refute the wicked blasphemy of the heretics."

This campaign against heresy involved an involuntary admission of its persuasive power; yet the bishops prevailed. By the time of the Emperor Constantine's conversion, when Christianity became an officially approved religion in the fourth century, Christian bishops, previously victimized by the police, now commanded them. Possession of books denounced as heretical was made a criminal offense. Copies of such books were burned and destroyed. But in Upper Egypt, someone, possibly a monk from a nearby monastery of St. Pachomius, took the banned books and hid them from destruction—in the jar where they remained buried for almost 1,600 years.

But those who wrote and circulated these texts did not regard *themselves* as "heretics." Most of the writings use Christian terminology, unmistakably related to a Jewish heritage. Many claim to offer traditions about Jesus that are secret, hidden from "the many" who constitute what, in the second century, came to be called the "catholic church." These Christians are now called gnostics, from the Greek word *gnosis*, usually translated as "knowledge." For as those who claim to know nothing about ultimate reality are called agnostic (literally, "not knowing"), the person who does claim to know such things is called gnostic ("knowing"). But *gnosis* is not primarily rational knowledge. The Greek language distinguishes between scientific or reflective knowledge ("He knows mathematics") and knowing through observation or experience ("He knows me"), which is *gnosis*. As the gnostics use the term, we could translate it as "insight," for *gnosis* involves an intuitive process of knowing oneself. And to know oneself, they claimed, is to know human nature and human destiny. According to the gnostic teacher Theodotus, writing in Asia Minor (c. 140–160), the gnostic is one who has come to understand

> who we were, and what we have become; where we were .
> .. whither we are hastening; from what we are being
> released; what birth is, and what is rebirth.

Yet to know oneself, at the deepest level, is simultaneously to know God; this is the secret of *gnosis*. Another gnostic teacher, Monoimus, says:

> Abandon the search for God and the creation and other
> matters of a similar sort. Look for him by taking your-
> self as the starting point. Learn who it is within you who
> makes everything his own and says, "My God, my mind,
> my thought, my soul, my body." Learn the sources of sor-
> row, joy, love, hate ... If you carefully investigate these
> matters you will find him *in yourself*.

What Muhammad 'Alī discovered at Nag Hammadi is, appar-ently, a library of writings, almost all of them gnostic. Although they claim to offer secret teaching, many of these texts refer to the Scriptures of the Old Testament, and others to the letters of Paul and the New Testament gospels. Many of

them include the same *dramatis personae* as the New Testament—
Jesus and his disciples. Yet the differences are striking.

Orthodox Jews and Christians insist that a chasm separates humanity from its creator: God is wholly other. But some
of the gnostics who wrote these gospels contradict this: self-
knowledge is knowledge of God; the self and the divine are
identical.

Second, the "living Jesus" of these texts speaks of illusion
and enlightenment, not of sin and repentance, like the Jesus of
the New Testament. Instead of coming to save us from sin, he
comes as a guide who opens access to spiritual understanding.
But when the disciple attains enlightenment, Jesus no longer
serves as his spiritual master: the two have become equal—even
identical.

Third, orthodox Christians believe that Jesus is Lord and
Son of God in a unique way: he remains forever distinct from
the rest of humanity whom he came to save. Yet the gnostic
Gospel of Thomas relates that as soon as Thomas recognizes him,
Jesus says to Thomas that they have both received their being
from the same source:

> Jesus said, "I am not your master. Because you have
> drunk, you have become drunk from the bubbling
> stream which I have measured out. . . . He who will drink
> from my mouth will become as I am: I myself shall
> become he, and the things that are hidden will be
> revealed to him."

Does not such teaching—the identity of the divine and
human, the concern with illusion and enlightenment, the
founder who is presented not as Lord, but as spiritual guide—
sound more Eastern than Western? Some scholars have suggested that if the names were changed, the "living Buddha"
appropriately could say what the *Gospel of Thomas* attributes to

the living Jesus. Could Hindu or Buddhist tradition have influenced gnosticism?

The British scholar of Buddhism, Edward Conze, suggests that it had. He points out that "Buddhists were in contact with the Thomas Christians (that is, Christians who knew and used such writings as the *Gospel of Thomas*) in South India." Trade routes between the Greco-Roman world and the Far East were opening up at the time when gnosticism flourished (A.D. 80–200); for generations, Buddhist missionaries had been proselytizing in Alexandria. We note, too, that Hippolytus, who was a Greek-speaking Christian in Rome (c. 225), knows of the Indian Brahmins—and includes their tradition among the sources of heresy . . .

Could the title of the *Gospel of Thomas*—named for the disciple who, tradition tells us, went to India—suggest the influence of Indian tradition? These hints indicate the possibility, yet our evidence is not conclusive. Since parallel traditions may emerge in different places at different times, such ideas could have developed independently. What we call Eastern and Western religions, and tend to regard as separate streams, were not clearly differentiated 2,000 years ago. Research on the Nag Hammadi texts is only beginning: we look forward to the work of scholars who can study these traditions comparatively to discover whether they can, in fact, be traced to Indian sources.

Even so, ideas that we associate with Eastern religions emerged in the first century through the gnostic movement in the West, but they were suppressed and condemned by polemicists like Irenaeus. Yet those who called gnosticism heresy were adopting—consciously or not—the viewpoint of that group of Christians who called themselves orthodox Christians. A heretic may be anyone whose outlook someone else dislikes or denounces. According to tradition, a heretic is one who deviates from the true faith. But what defines that "true faith"? Who calls it that, and for what reasons?

We find this problem familiar in our own experience. The term "Christianity," especially since the Reformation, has covered an astonishing range of groups. Those claiming to represent "true Christianity" in the twentieth century can range from a Catholic cardinal in the Vatican to an African Methodist Episcopal preacher initiating revival in Detroit, a Mormon missionary in Thailand, or the member of a village church on the coast of Greece. Yet Catholics, Protestants, and Orthodox agree that such diversity is a recent—and deplorable—development. According to Christian legend, the early church was different. Christians of every persuasion look back to the primitive church to find a simpler, purer form of Christian faith. In the apostles' time, all members of the Christian community shared their money and property; all believed the same teaching, and worshiped together; all revered the authority of the apostles. It was only after that golden age that conflict, then heresy emerged: so says the author of the Acts of the Apostles, who identifies himself as the first historian of Christianity.

But the discoveries at Nag Hammadi have upset this picture. If we admit that some of these fifty-two texts represent early forms of Christian teaching, we may have to recognize that early Christianity is far more diverse than nearly anyone expected before the Nag Hammadi discoveries.

Contemporary Christianity, diverse and complex as we find it, actually may show more unanimity than the Christian churches of the first and second centuries. For nearly all Christians since that time, Catholics, Protestants, or Orthodox, shared three basic premises. First, they accept the canon of the New Testament; second, they confess the apostolic creed; and third, they affirm specific forms of church institution. But every one of these—the canon of Scripture, the creed, and the institutional structure—emerged in its present form only toward the end of the second century. Before that time, as

Irenaeus and others attest, numerous gospels circulated among various Christian groups, ranging from those of the New Testament, Matthew, Mark, Luke, and John, to such writings as the *Gospel of Thomas*, the *Gospel of Philip*, and the *Gospel of Truth*, as well as many other secret teachings, myths, and poems attributed to Jesus or his disciples. Some of these, apparently, were discovered at Nag Hammadi; many others are lost to us. Those who identified themselves as Christians entertained many—and radically differing—religious beliefs and practices. And the communities scattered throughout the known world organized themselves in ways that differed widely from one group to another.

Yet by A.D. 200, the situation had changed. Christianity had become an institution headed by a three-rank hierarchy of bishops, priests, and deacons, who understood themselves to be the guardians of the only "true faith." The majority of churches, among which the church of Rome took a leading role, rejected all other viewpoints as heresy. Deploring the diversity of the earlier movement, Bishop Irenaeus and his followers insisted that there could be only one church, and outside of that church, he declared, "there is no salvation." Members of this church alone are orthodox (literally, "straight-thinking") Christians. And, he claimed, this church must be *catholic*—that is, universal. Whoever challenged that consensus, arguing instead for other forms of Christian teaching, was declared to be a heretic, and expelled. When the orthodox gained military support, sometime after the Emperor Constantine became Christian in the fourth century, the penalty for heresy escalated.

The efforts of the majority to destroy every trace of heretical "blasphemy" proved so successful that, until the discoveries at Nag Hammadi, nearly all our information concerning alternative forms of early Christianity came from the massive Orthodox attacks upon them. Although gnosticism is perhaps the earliest—and most threatening—of the heresies, scholars had known only a handful of original gnostic texts, none published before the nineteenth century. The first emerged in 1769, when a Scottish tourist named James Bruce bought a Coptic manuscript near Thebes (modern Luxor) in Upper Egypt. Published only in 1892, it claims to record conversations of Jesus with his disciples—a group that here includes both men and women. In 1773 a collector found in a London bookshop an ancient text, also in Coptic, that contained a dialogue on "mysteries" between Jesus and his disciples. In 1896 a German Egyptologist, alerted by the previous publications, bought in Cairo a manuscript that, to his amazement, contained the *Gospel of Mary* (Magdalene) and three other texts. Three copies of one of them, the *Apocryphon* (Secret Book) *of John* were also included among the gnostic library discovered at Nag Hammadi fifty years later . . .

Yet even the fifty-two writings discovered at Nag Hammadi offer only a glimpse of the complexity of the early Christian movement. We now begin to see that what we call Christianity—and what we identify as Christian tradition—actually represents only a small selection of specific sources, chosen from among dozens of others. Who made that selection, and for what reasons? Why were these other writings excluded and banned as "heresy"? What made them so dangerous? Now, for the first time, we have the opportunity to find out about the earliest Christian heresy; for the first time, the heretics can speak for themselves.

Gnostic Christians undoubtedly expressed ideas that the orthodox abhorred. For example, some of these gnostic texts question whether all suffering, labor, and death derive from human sin, which, in the orthodox version, marred an originally perfect creation. Others speak of the feminine element in the divine, celebrating God as Father *and* Mother. Still others suggest that Christ's resurrection is to be understood symbolically, not literally. A few radical texts even denounce catholic Christians themselves as heretics, who, although they "do not understand mystery . . . boast that the mystery of truth belongs to them alone." Such gnostic ideas fascinated the psychoanalyst C. G. Jung: he thought they expressed "the other side of the mind"—the spontaneous, unconscious thoughts that any orthodoxy requires its adherents to repress.

Yet orthodox Christianity, as the apostolic creed defines it, contains some ideas that many of us today might find even stranger. The creed requires, for example, that Christians confess that God is perfectly good, and still, he created a world that includes pain, injustice, and death; that Jesus of Nazareth was born of a virgin mother; and that, after being executed by order of the Roman procurator, Pontius Pilate, he arose from his grave "on the third day."

Why did the consensus of Christian churches not only accept these astonishing views but establish them as the only true form of Christian doctrine? Traditionally, historians have told us that the orthodox objected to gnostic views for religious and philosophic reasons. Certainly they did; yet investigation of the newly discovered gnostic sources suggests another dimension of the controversy. It suggests that these religious debates—questions of the nature of God, or of Christ—simultaneously bear social and political implications that are crucial to the development of Christianity as an institutional religion. In simplest terms, ideas which bear implications contrary to that development come to be labeled as "heresy"; ideas which implicitly support it become "orthodox."

By investigating the texts from Nag Hammadi, together with sources known for well over a thousand years from orthodox tradition, we can see how politics and religion coincide in the development of Christianity. We can see, for example, the *political* implications of such orthodox doctrines as the bodily resurrection—and how gnostic views of resurrection bear opposite implications. In the process, we can gain a startlingly new perspective on the origins of Christianity.

What the Nag Hammadi Texts Tell Us about "Liberated" Christianity

AN INTERVIEW WITH JAMES M. ROBINSON

James Robinson is Professor of Religion Emeritus, Claremont Graduate University, and general editor, *The Nag Hammadi Library*. He is one of the world's leading authorities on early Christianity and supervised the team of scholars and translators who brought the lost Gospels to life.

As one of the leading scholars of what we know as the lost Gospels, what is your reaction to seeing these historic ideas suddenly being propelled onto the bestseller list with the popularity of The Da Vinci Code?

The book has had a sensationalist kind of success, which worries scholars such as myself who are trying to stick to the facts. I think there is a certain built-in problem of this book being a novel, and therefore saying it's fiction but, at the same time, using enough facts, well-known names and things like the Nag Hammadi discovery to give it a semblance of factual accuracy. It is hard for the lay public to distinguish where one begins and the other leaves off. So, strictly from that point of view, it's very misleading.

Moreover, it is clear to me that Dan Brown doesn't know much about the scholarly side of things in my field and he sort of fudges the evidence to make it more sensational than it is. As an example, he refers to the Nag Hammadi find as "scrolls," but they are not. They are codexes—books with individual pages. Indeed, it is actually the oldest example we have of leather-bound books. Elsewhere, Dan Brown refers to the *Gospel Q*, writing, "Allegedly it is a book of Jesus' teachings, possibly written with His own hand." What is interesting is that while it is mentioned, it is not discussed—perhaps because it would not help his argument since we know Jesus didn't write it. These are just some of the ideas thrown into the novel that are more sensational than factual.

So how would you characterize the Nag Hammadi texts?

The canonical Gospels, Matthew, Mark, Luke, and John are a sort of theological biography of Jesus. By contrast, the Nag Hammadi Gospels are not Gospels in the traditional use of that word to mean narrative history, but what we now call a sayings Gospel. The *Gospel of Philip*, for example, is a scattering of materials that is not an original document, but some sort of collection of excerpts from various sources. The *Gospel of Truth* is a quasi-philosophical theological treatise, but it doesn't tell the story of Jesus in any sense of the word. The only one that can claim in some sense to be what we might call a Gospel is the fourth Nag Hammadi text (the *Gospel of Thomas*), which uses the word *Gospel* as a secondary title appended at the end. The opening of the text, however, calls it "secret sayings." It's a collection of sayings, like the sayings behind Matthew and Luke, which is called theoretically *Q*, and which is mentioned once in *The Da Vinci Code*.

Do we know anything about the people who might have written these texts?

They were most likely written by different people at different times. If they were written in the second and third centuries, the authors would likely have been Gnostics, part of a Gnostic movement that was almost competing with emerging orthodox Christianity for who had the right form of Christianity. The orthodox movement had books called Gospels that are known as Mathew, Mark, Luke, and John. The Gnostic side attached the word *Gospel* to some of their tracts, which really weren't Gospels, like those in the New Testament, since the canonical Gospels are narratives that speak to the theological biography of Jesus. The Nag Hammadi Gospels are more like a collection of scattered excerpts.

Would you flesh out this idea of competing Christianities?

The writers of these codices were attempting to influence what we might call left-wing Christianity—somewhat similar to the New Age phenomenon in our time. They thought that the dominant church of the day (in *The Da Vinci Code* called the Roman Catholic Church) was too earth bound, too worldly, too materialistic, too physical and had missed the spiritual, allegorical, higher, heavenly secret meaning of all of this. And that's what they were supporting.

Talking about New Age, does the word companion *in the* Gospel of Philip *imply for you, as it does for some students of these documents, that Jesus and Mary were married? And even that they kissed?*

No, it doesn't automatically mean married or unmarried. *Companion* is not necessarily a sex-related term as it might be construed in our day and age. It seems to me it might have been simply a way to pump up the story, to make it more intriguing. If one reads the entire *Gospel of Philip* it becomes clear that the writer disdains physical sex as beastly, literally comparing it to animals. In the early church, a kiss was known as a metaphor for giving birth.

And too much has been made out of this kiss. It was also called the Kiss of Peace, somewhat analogous to a modern church service where they ask you to shake hands with everybody and say, "May the peace of Christ be with you."

Regarding designating Mary Magdalene as Jesus' companion, Brown says Aramaic scholars know this means wife. But the *Gospel of Philip* is in Coptic, translated from Greek, so there is no word in the text for Aramaic scholars to consider.

I think the only relevant text for historical information about Mary Magdalene is the New Testament, and it does not go beyond saying that she was one of the circle of women who accompanied the wandering Jesus and his male followers. I think the seven demons that Jesus cast out of her may have referred to some sort of nervous problem or mental illness, like epilepsy. She was challanged, he helped her, and she became a disciple, loyal to the bitter end. I also think she was alone after the execution because the other disciples were cowards. They were likely to have been arrested. The Romans felt women were not important enough to arrest, so they let Mary grieve, figuring she would soon enough melt into the crowds. No doubt the New Testament gives an accurate protrayal of all of these Marys having been there at the time of the crucifixion and on Easter Sunday, to the extent that one gives historical credence to any of the empty-tomb stories.

While you seem to believe her role to be more circumscribed than some of the radicals would have it, would you nevertheless agree that whoever wrote the Gnostic Gospels was more sympathetic to women and their role in spiritual life than was the case with the orthodox tradition?

Yes, certainly. I think the Gnostics were more liberated—

if I can use a more modern term—on many issues. Their view of women in the church, for example, was based more on the perceived quality of their religious experience than on the relationship between bishop and supplicant or other forms of authority. They believed women to have religious experiences, spiritual insights, and even visions. The idea that the men were keeping the women in their place, I think, is a historically accurate description of those early centuries, and the fact that there were some women who were trying to get everybody (including the men) to accept them as equal partners is a historical fact of the second and third centuries. The *Gospel of Mary* is a good documentation for that.

That said, people should not override that which is known with that which can only be speculated about. Even with these texts in hand, one must not interpret the specific role of Mary beyond what is known about her as related in the New Testament—and the New Testament does not say anything about Jesus having more time with Mary than the other disciples. This starts to get into the realm of what could be called wishful thinking, about which we historians have to be cautious. It is not the scholarly method to use wishful thinking to weigh the evidence one way or the other—as saint or sinner, married or not. That's not the method that we historians can use.

What Was Lost Is Found
A Wider View of Christianity and Its Roots

AN INTERVIEW WITH ELAINE PAGELS

Elaine Pagels is Harrington Spear Paine Professor of Religion at Princeton University and author of the bestselling *Beyond Belief* as well as *The Gnostic Gospels*, which won the National Book Critics Circle Award and the National Book Award.

Why do you think The Da Vinci Code *has captured the public's imagination?*

What I find interesting about Dan Brown's book is that it raises a very important question: if they—meaning the leaders of the church—suppressed so much of early Christian history, what else don't we know about it? What else is there to be known? As a historian, I think this is a really important question because the answer would mean a great deal. So I'd rather not say anything negative about his book. I simply am not an expert on it, but I'd like to say it raises an important question.

But what do *we know about early Christianity and its roots now that we didn't a generation or so ago?*

The earliest accounts we have about Jesus of Nazareth were written twenty years after his death at the earliest, and those are from letters. Then we have the New Testament Gospels, which were written maybe forty to seventy years after his death. So everything we have is from later accounts. These accounts are not neutral; they're either written by people devoted to Jesus or people hostile to Jesus, such as the Roman historian Suetonious, the Roman senator and historian Cassiodorus, and some polemical Jewish sources from late in the first century. So it's interesting that we have nothing except later accounts, either very positive or very negative.

Thanks to the Nag Hammadi discoveries in 1945, we now see that the early Christian movement was much wider and much more varied, and that the views of Jesus were much more wide ranging than we ever thought. This applies as well to the classical view of his disciples and, of particular interest at the moment, the later developing view that Mary Magdalene was a prostitute. But in the sources we have now, which include the *Gospels of Mary Magdalene, Thomas,* and *Philip,* we have early evidence that Mary was regarded not only as one of the women associated with the circle around Jesus, but was considered an important follower and disciple by many. We also know there were others.

Is there not a contradiction here? Would not the social and religious belief systems of the Judaic culture at the time militate against women playing an independent role as proselytizers?

In Jewish groups, it would have been very untypical to have women participating and learning and traveling with men. I'm picturing the circle around Jesus as a circle around an itinerant charismatic rabbi, and this group apparently did include women as well as men. That would have been unusual. Most rabbinic sources—which are a little later than this—thought it was not at all appropriate to teach women about the divine scriptures. And even among Greco-Roman circles, only the Epicurean philosophers and a couple of others had women students, but there were few of them. Much more often, it would be only men. Perhaps Mary's reputation of being a prostitute came about because the idea of a woman traveling, or simply spending time in the company of a group of men, would have been very unusual and obviously suspect.

Is it possible that she was closer to Jesus than the other disciples and privy to secret knowledge, as the Gospel of Mary *suggests?*

> We don't know much detail, but yes, she must have had some important relationship to Jesus. There are some hints of that in the *Gospel of Mary*, where it is mentioned that he told her things that he didn't tell the others and that he had a special love for her. As to whether Jesus told her things he didn't tell others, we can't be sure, but there are hints of that. Whether it was a sexual relationship, I don't see the evidence in the sources I know. Dan Brown took a line from the *Gospel of Philip* that suggests Jesus loved Mary more than all the other disciples, and he read it as a sexual relationship. However, if you read the rest of the *Gospel of Philip*, many scholars think the sexual language there suggests a mystical union, not literal. It depicts Mary as a symbol of divine wisdom in some parts of the text and in other sections as the church, which is the bride of Christ. So she's understood to be Jesus' spiritual counterpart.

Might there be more documents waiting to be found that would shed further light on the relationship between Mary and Jesus, and between the orthodox tradition and this lost tradition? And, if so, why were some Gospels preserved and not others?

> There were probably countless people preserving copies of these texts. But because papyrus rots, except in the very driest parts of the world, like the part of Egypt where the Nag Hammadi texts were found, most of the copies would not have survived. As for why some Gospels were handed down through history and others hidden away, I wrote *The Gnostic Gospels* to try to figure that out.
>
> I think as the orthodox tradition progressed and became more popular, some of its leaders felt they had to

sort out what really were the right teachings of Jesus and what weren't. They were trying to consolidate an enormous number of people who were clustered in what is today Turkey, Africa, Spain, France, England, Italy, Egypt—what the Romans thought of as the known world. And some leaders, some bishops for example, were trying to say, well, let's choose the fundamental teachings on which we all agree. And then, let's look at all this other material, the mystical material, and just say this is irrelevant. We don't need it—it's misleading, it leads people to set up their own groups, which we don't want because we're bishops, after all. There's a more serious reason, as well. The Christian movement was also facing persecution and destruction by the Roman state, so it was trying to consolidate and unify. But we really don't have details about that process, so we have to try and reconstruct it. That's a hard thing to do, but that's what I try to do with my books.

What does that process of reconstruction lead you to believe about the differences between the way people worshipped under these discarded texts and those who followed the canonical texts of the New Testament?

I believe that the Nag Hammadi Gospels were written by people who felt that they had visions, revelations, and deeper understanding. A baptized Christian, in the middle of Egypt in the second century, might have needed a spiritual master who went beyond the orthodox, who said, "Yes, I can take you further. I can initiate you into the deeper mysteries, and you can receive the Holy Spirit so that you might have revelations of your own."

So this smaller group, dedicated to ecstatic prayer and visions, could have led people away from allegiance to the local bishops, which the bishops wouldn't have liked because they thought having revelations and visions was threatening to the unity of the church. This problem remains: should a Catholic come forward today, describe a vision of the Virgin Mary, and say, "The Virgin Mary told me that women should be priests," he or she is certainly going to be called a heretic.

Yet Christianity could not have spread without revelation. The New Testament Gospels, particularly Luke, are full of dreams and revelations. The movement explodes in claims about visions and revelations. But later, these become problematic because leaders of the church responded, "Wait a minute, which are the right ones and which are the wrong ones?" And then standards of orthodoxy needed to be established. The texts that were found, like the *Gospel of Philip* and the *Gospel of Mary*, were discovered in Egypt in a monastery library. And it was a bishop who ordered the monks to destroy them.

Can you summarize the Gnostic texts for us?

Although we used to call these texts Gnostic texts, that term is often associated with a negative, dualistic view of the world that isn't found in these texts. So I don't use the term Gnosticism anymore or call the texts Gnostic. I prefer to look at them individually.

The *Gospel of Thomas* presents the idea that if you bring forth what is within you, what is within you will save you, but if you do not bring forth what is within you, what is within you will destroy you. And the idea behind that is, if you can bring forth something from within yourself, something intrinsic to human beings, it allows you to have access to God.

The *Gospel of Mary* says, in effect, seek the Son of Man within yourself; in other words, look within yourself to find the divine source rather than looking to Jesus the God Man. You can find the divine source through your own being, which comes from the same source as Jesus. It's more like a Buddhist teaching. This is heretical to priests, of course. A priest wants to say that the only access to God is to be found through the church. But these Gospels imply that you can go off on your own and discover the divine within yourself. You might not need the church. You might not need a priest. You might just go meditate or have your own vision.

Is it possible that some of Christianity was influenced by mystery cults as Dan Brown suggests?

Yes. Dan Brown is right that some of the mystery cults, like the cult of the mother goddess, involved the mysteries of sexuality, death, and transcending death. But I don't see any evidence of those in the texts that we found. That's quite a different strain. There may well be, in Christian rituals, an influence of mystery cults, but I don't see sexual rituals there. I think it makes a good novel, I just don't know of any evidence.

Was this issue of sexuality central for early church leaders?

Yes, it certainly was an issue for Paul, just twenty years after Jesus' death. He thought it is better to be celibate, as he was, for the sake of evangelizing the movement. Many people think he was widowed and had been married before. Peter was married and had children. That was, of course, normal for followers of Jesus because they were brought up in Jewish customs and that was understood to be a sacred value.

I think what happened is, these followers of Jesus, even the ones who weren't Jews, adopted Jewish attitudes about sexuality: it was meant for procreation, and any sexual relationship between a man and a woman might well end up with children. A sexual relationship between people of the same sex was absolutely regarded as an abomination by many Jews. Abortion was prohibited. So was killing infants, which was commonly done as birth control in the early centuries. So, since Christians were prohibited to kill babies or attempt abortions or even contraception, if they were going to devote themselves to the Kingdom and have a life that was free of the burdens of family and children and making money, then celibacy seemed to be required.

Coming back to today, what do you believe accounts for the widespread fascination with these spiritual issues in what might easily be called the age of rationality and skepticism?

First, I know for myself and for many others there is a tremendous hunger for spiritual understanding and a spiritual path. And that's true whether people are evangelical—I don't like the word *fundamentalists*—or Southern Baptists or Roman Catholic mystics or atheists. Many people really are exploring spiritual issues because, I think, these issues are a deep part of human life and we need them. Whether one believes that the world was created in six days or holds some other philosophic understanding, I think our heart, emotions, and attitudes towards other people are at the center of this tradition.

Do you think these texts and your work allow people who have trouble with their faith to say, "Oh, there is another dimension here?"

To me, that's very important because, I think, if you try to swallow Christian faith as it is often taught, it's indigestible. There is an element in it that, if you must take it all literally, causes most people to raise questions. Was Jesus really born from a virgin? What do we mean by the resurrection of the dead? So, yes, my work and what I try to do in my books is an invitation to say, "We can think about these things." We can look at them historically. We can look at the Bible, not as something that just descended from heaven in a cloud of gold, but a collection, laboriously assembled by countless people, with some very powerful truths in it. But that doesn't mean we have to take it all as if it were literally true and just simply try to swallow it. We can think about it, we can discuss it. As Jesus says, "Let the one who seeks not stop seeking until he finds. When he finds, he'll be troubled. When he's troubled, he'll be astonished." Jesus clearly invites us to a process of exploration—not simply a set of beliefs which we either accept or reject. We can hold to the elements we love about it, and say that for others maybe it's different. And with this new evidence, I think that's a remarkable opportunity.

The Gospel of Thomas

INTRODUCED BY HELMUT KOESTER

Selections from the *Gospel of Thomas*, the *Gospel of Philip*, the *Gospel of Mary*, and the *Sophia of Christ* are excerpted from *The Nag Hammadi Library* in English, 3rd, Complete Revised Edition by James M. Robinson, General Editor. Copyright © 1978, 1988 by E. J. Brill, Leiden, The Netherlands. Reprinted by permission of HarperCollins Publishers, Inc.

The *Gospel of Thomas* is a collection of traditional sayings of Jesus. These sayings or small groups of sayings are introduced in most instances by "Jesus said [to them]," sometimes by a question or a statement of the disciples. Only in one instance is a saying expanded into a longer discourse between Jesus and the disciples. . . .

The authorship of this Gospel is attributed to Didymos Judas Thomas, that is, Judas "the twin." In the Syrian church, (Judas) Thomas was known as the brother of Jesus who founded the churches of the East, particularly of Edessa (in a somewhat later tradition, he even travels to India). Other Christian writings of the Eastern churches have been attributed to the same apostle.

A large number of the sayings of the *Gospel of Thomas* have parallels in the Gospels of the New Testament, in the Synoptic Gospels (Matthew, Mark, and Luke), as well as the *Gospel of John* (parallels with the latter are especially striking).

The theme of recognizing oneself is further elaborated in sayings which speak of the knowledge of one's divine origin which even Adam did not share, although "he came into being from a great power. . . ." The disciples must "pass by" the present corruptible existence. The existence of the ideal Gnostic disciple is characterized by the term *solitary one*, which describes the one who has left behind everything that binds human beings to the world. Even women can obtain this goal, if they achieve the "maleness" of the solitary existence.

The Gospel of Thomas

TRANSLATED BY THOMAS O. LAMBDIN

These are the secret sayings which the living Jesus spoke and which Didymos Judas Thomas wrote down.

(1) And he said, "Whoever finds the interpretation of these sayings will not experience death."

(2) Jesus said, "Let him who seeks continue seeking until he finds. When he finds, he will become troubled. When he

becomes troubled, he will be astonished, and he will rule over the all."

(3) Jesus said, "If those who lead you say to you, 'See, the kingdom is in the sky,' then the birds of the sky will precede you. If they say to you, 'It is in the sea,' then the fish will precede you. Rather, the kingdom is inside of you, and it is outside of you. When you come to know yourselves, then you will become known, and you will realize that it is you who are the sons of the living father. But if you will not know yourselves, you dwell in poverty and it is you who are that poverty."

(5) Jesus said, "Recognize what is in your sight, and that which is hidden from you will become plain to you. For there is nothing hidden which will not become manifest."

(16) Jesus said, "Men think, perhaps, that it is peace which I have come to cast upon the world. They do not know that it is dissension which I have come to cast upon the earth: fire, sword, and war. For there will be five in a house: three will be against two, and two against three, the father against the son, and the son against the father. And they will stand solitary."

(37) His disciples said, "When will you become revealed to us and when shall we see you?"

Jesus said, "When you disrobe without being ashamed and take up your garments and place them under your feet like little children and tread on them, then [will you see] the son of the living one, and you will not be afraid."

(70) Jesus said, "That which you have will save you if you bring it forth from yourselves. That which you do not have within you [will] kill you if you do not have it within you."

(114) Simon Peter said to them, "Let Mary leave us, for women are not worthy of life." Jesus said, "I myself shall lead her in order to make her male, so that she too may become a living spirit resembling you males. For every woman who will make herself male will enter the kingdom of heaven."

The Gospel of Philip

INTRODUCED BY WESLEY W. ISENBERG

The *Gospel of Philip* is a compilation of statements pertaining primarily to the meaning and value of sacraments within the context of a Valentinian conception of the human predicament and life after death [Valentinians rejected the way most of their fellow Christians interpreted the Bible as being overly literal].

Like the Gospels of the New Testament canon these statements employ a variety of literary types: aphorism, analogy, parable, paraenesis, polemic, narrative dialogue, dominical sayings, biblical exegesis, and dogmatic propositions. However, the *Gospel of Philip* is not a Gospel like one of the New Testament Gospels.

To be sure, it does provide the occasional word or deed of Jesus. . . . . [But] these few sayings and stories about Jesus . . . are not set in any kind of narrative framework like one of the New Testament Gospels. In fact, the *Gospel of Philip* is not organized in a way that can be conveniently outlined. Although some continuity is achieved through an association of ideas, a series of contrasts, or by catchwords, the line of thought is rambling and disjointed. Complete changes of subject are common.

The Gospel of Philip

TRANSLATED BY WESLEY W. ISENBERG
[This is the Gospel famed for its passage "He kissed her frequently on her. . . ." which is highlighted in bold type].

The *Gospel of Philip*: Fragments like this one are what remain of the alternative Gospels found in the Egyptian desert at Nag Hammadi in 1945. The fragmentary nature of the *Gospel of Philip* is particularly tantalizing. The passage refers to the apparently well-known fact (in Gnostic circles at the time) that Jesus kissed Mary Magdalene frequently on the m. . . . The first letter of the Coptic word for mouth follows, then the hole in the fragment renders the rest of the word indiscernible.   INSTITUTE FOR ANTIQUITY AND CHRISTIANITY, CLAREMONT, CA

. . . Christ came to ransom some, to save others, to redeem others. He ransomed those who were strangers and made them his own. And he set his own apart, those whom he gave as a pledge according to his plan. It was not only when he appeared that he voluntarily laid down his life, but he voluntarily laid down his life from the very day the world came into being. Then he came first in order to take it, since it had been given as a pledge. It fell into the hands of robbers and was taken captive, but he saved it. He redeemed the good people in the world as well as the evil.

Light and Darkness, life and death, right and left, are brothers of one another. They are inseparable. Because of this neither are the good good, nor evil evil, nor is life life, nor death death. For this reason each one will dissolve into its earliest origin. But those who are exalted above the world are indissoluble, eternal.

Some said, "Mary conceived by the Holy Spirit." They are in error. They do not know what they are saying. When did a woman ever conceive by a woman? Mary is the virgin whom no power defiled. She is a great anathema to the Hebrews, who are the apostles and [the] apostolic men. This virgin whom no power defiled [. . .] the powers defile themselves. And the lord [would] not have said "My [father who is in] heaven" (Mt 16:17), unless [he] had had another father, but he would have said simply "[My father]."

Faith receives, love gives. [No one will be able to receive] without faith. No one will be able to give without love. Because of this, in order that we may indeed receive, we believe, and in order that we may love, we give, since if one gives without love, he has no profit from what he has given. He who has received something other than the lord is still a Hebrew.

As for the Wisdom who is called "the barren," she is the mother [of the] angels. And the companion of the [. . .] Mary Magdalene. [. . . loved] her more than [all] the disciples, [and used to] kiss her [often] on her [. . .]. The rest of [the disciples . . .]. They said to him "Why do you love her more than all of us?" The Savior answered and said to them, "Why do I not love you like her? When a blind man and one who sees are both together in darkness, they are no different from one another. When the light comes, then he who sees will see the light, and he who is blind will remain in darkness."

Great is the mystery of marriage! For [without] it the world would [not exist]. Now the existence of [the world . . .], and the existence of [. . . marriage]. Think of the [. . . relationship], for it possesses [...] power. Its image consists of a [defilement].

The forms of evil spirit include male ones and female ones. The males are they that unite with the souls which inhabit a female form, but the females are they which are mingled with those in a male form, though one who was disobedient. And none shall be able to escape them, since they detain him if he does not receive a male power or a female power, the bridegroom and the bride....

A bridal chamber is not for the animals, nor is it for the slaves, nor for defiled women; but it is for free men and virgins.

The world came about through a mistake. For he who created it wanted to create it imperishable and immortal. He fell short of attaining his desire. For the world never was imperishable, nor, for that matter, was he who made the world. For things are not imperishable, but sons are. Nothing will be able to receive imperishability if it does not first become a son. But he who has not the ability to receive, how much more will he be unable to give?...

The Gospel of Mary

INTRODUCED BY KAREN KING

The extant text of the *Gospel of Mary* can easily be divided into two parts. The first section (7,1–9,24) describes the dialogue between the (risen) Savior and the disciples. He answers their questions concerning matter and sin.... The Savior argues, in effect, that sin is not a moral category, but a cosmological one; it is due to the improper mixing of the material and the spiritual. In the end all things will be resolved into their proper root. After finishing his discourse, the Savior gives them a final greeting, admonishes them to beware of any who may try to lead them astray and commissions them to go and preach the Gospel of the kingdom. After he departs, however, the disciples are grieved and in considerable doubt and consternation. Mary Magdalene comforts them and turns their hearts toward the Good and a consideration of the Savior's words.

The second section of the text . . . contains a description by Mary of special revelation given to her by the Savior. At Peter's request, she tells the disciples about things that were hidden from them. The basis for her knowledge is a vision of the Lord and a private dialogue with him. Unfortunately four pages of the text are missing here so that only the beginning and end of Mary's revelation are extant.

The revelation is in the form of a dialogue. The first question Mary asks the Savior is how one sees a vision. The Savior replies that the soul sees through the mind which is between the soul and the spirit. At this point the text breaks off. When the text resumes . . . Mary is in the midst of describing the Savior's revelation concerning the rise of the soul past the four powers. The four powers are most probably to be identified as essential expressions of the four material elements. The enlightened soul, now free of their bonds, rises past the four powers, overpowering them with her *gnosis*, and attains eternal, silent rest.

After Mary finishes recounting her vision to the disciples, Andrew and then Peter challenge her on two grounds. First of all, Andrew says, these teachings are strange. Secondly, Peter questions, would the Savior really have told such things to a woman and kept them from the male disciples. Levi admonishes Peter for contending with the woman as against the adversaries and acknowledges that the Savior loved her more than the other disciples. He entreats them to be ashamed, to put on the perfect man, and to go forth and preach as the Savior had instructed them to do. They immediately go forth to preach and the text ends.

The confrontation of Mary with Peter, a scenario also found in the *Gospel of Thomas*, *Pistis Sophia*, and the *Gospel of the Egyptians*, reflects some of the tensions in second-century Christianity. Peter and Andrew represent orthodox positions that deny the validity of esoteric revelation and reject the authority of women to teach. The *Gospel of Mary* attacks both of these positions head-on through its portrayal of Mary Magdalene. She is the Savior's beloved, possessed of knowledge and teaching superior to that of the public apostolic tradition. Her superiority is based on vision and private revelation and is demonstrated in her capacity to strengthen the wavering disciples and turn them toward the Good. . . .

The *Gospel of Mary* was originally written in Greek some time in the second century. Unfortunately the two extant copies of the *Gospel of Mary* are extremely fragmentary. . . .

The Gospel of Mary

TRANSLATED BY GEORGE W. MACRAE AND
R. McL. WILSON

. . . Peter said to him, "Since you have explained everything to us, tell us this also: What is the sin of the world?" The Savior said "There is no sin, but it is you who make sin when you do the things that are like the nature of adultery, which is called 'sin.' That is why the Good came into your midst, to the (essence) of every nature, in order to restore it to its root." Then he continued and said, "That is why you [become sick] and die, for [. . . .] of the one who [. . . He who] understands, let him understand. [Matter gave birth to] a passion that has no equal, which proceeded from (something) contrary to nature. Then there arise a disturbance in the whole body. That is why I said to you, 'Be of good courage,' and if you are discouraged [be] encouraged in the presence of the different forms of nature. He who has ears to hear, let him hear." . . .

When he had said this, he departed.

But they were grieved. They wept greatly, saying, "How shall we go to the gentiles and preach the gospel of the kingdom of the Son of Man? If they did not spare him, how will they spare us?" Then Mary stood up, greeted them all, and said to her brethren, "Do not weep and do not grieve nor be irresolute, for his grace will be entirely with you and will protect you. But rather let us praise his greatness, for he has prepared us and made us into men." When Mary said this, she turned their hearts to the Good, and they began to discuss the words of the [Savior].

Peter said to Mary, "Sister, we know that the Savior loved you more than the rest of women. Tell us the words of the Savior which you remember—which you know [but] we do not, nor have we heard them." Mary answered and said, "What is hidden from you I will proclaim to you." And she began to speak to them these words: "I," she said, "I saw the Lord in a vision and I said to Him, 'Lord I saw you today in a vision.' He answered and said to me, 'Blessed are you, that you did not waver at the sight of me. For where the mind is, there is the treasure.' I said to Him, 'Lord, how does he who sees the vision see it, [through] the soul [or] through the spirit?' The Savior answered and said, 'He does not see through the soul nor through the spirit, but the mind which [is] between the two—that is [what] sees the vision and it is [. . .].' "

When Mary had said this, she fell silent, since it was to this point that the Savior had spoken with her. But Andrew answered and said to the brethren, "Say what you [wish to] say about what she has said. I at least do not believe that the Savior said this. For certainly these teachings are strange ideas." Peter answered and spoke concerning these same things. He questioned them about the Savior: "Did he really speak with a woman without our knowledge [and] not openly? Are we to turn about and all listen to her? Did he prefer her to us?"

Then Mary wept and said to Peter, "My brother Peter, what do you think? Do you think that I have thought this up myself in my heart, or that I am lying about the Savior?" Levi answered and said to Peter, "Peter, you have always been hot-tempered. Now I see you contending against the woman like the adversaries. But if the Savior made her worthy, who are you indeed to reject her? Surely the Savior knows her very well. That is why he loved her more than us. Rather let us be ashamed and put on the perfect man, and acquire him for ourselves as he commanded us, and preach the gospel, not laying down any other rule or other law beyond what the Savior said." When [...] and they began to go forth [to] proclaim and to preach.

Introducing the Sophia of Jesus Christ

By Douglas M. Parrott

In form, the *Sophia of Jesus Christ* is a revelation discourse given by the risen Christ in response to the questions of his disciples. This text allows one to see the process by which a non-Christian tractate was modified and transformed into a Christian gnostic one ... It would not be surprising if it has been composed soon after the advent of Christianity in Egypt—the latter half of the first century C.E. That possibility is supported by the tractate's relatively nonpolemical tone.

The *Sophia of Jesus Christ* was directed to an audience for whom Christianity was an added element in their religious environment (i.e., not its primary one). . . . In it, the Savior (Christ) came from the supercelestial region. Sophia is the one responsible for the fall of drops of light from the divine realm into the visible world; and, a god exists who, with his subordinate powers, directly rules this world to the detriment of those who come from the divine realm.

Sex, it is suggested, is the means by which enslavement to the powers is perpetuated. But the Savior (Christ) broke the bonds imposed by the powers, and taught others to do the same . . . In addition, it should be noted that the disciples named in the *Sophia of Jesus Christ*, Philip, Matthew, Thomas, Bartholomew, and Mary, reflect a tradition within Gnosticism of disciples who are distinctively gnostic, and who are contrasted with some regularity, and in various ways, with "orthodox" or "orthodox turned gnostic" disciples (principally, Peter and John).

The Sophia of Jesus Christ

TRANSLATED BY DOUGLAS M. PARROTT

After he rose from the dead, his twelve disciples and seven women continued to be his followers and went to Galilee onto the mountain called "Divination and Joy." When they gathered together and were perplexed about the underlying reality of the universe and the plan and the holy providence and the power of the authorities and about everything the Savior is doing with them in the secret of the holy plan, the Savior appeared—not in his previous form, but in the invisible spirit. And his likeness resembles a great angel of light. But his resemblance I must not describe. No mortal flesh could endure it, but only pure, (and) perfect flesh, like that which he taught us about on the mountain called "Of the Olives" in Galilee. And he said: "Peace be to you! My peace I give you!" And they all marveled and were afraid.

The Savior laughed and said to them: "What are you thinking about? [Why] are you perplexed? What are you searching for?" Philip said: "For the underlying reality of the universe and the plan."

The Savior said to them: "I want you to know that all men born on earth from the foundation of the world until now, being dust, while they have inquired about God, who he is and what he is like, have not found him. Now the wisest among them have speculated from the ordering of the world and [its] movement. But their speculation has not reached the truth. For it is said that the ordering is directed in three ways by all the philosophers, [and] hence they do not agree. For some of them say about the world that it is directed by itself. Others, that it is providence [that directs it]. Others, that it is fate. But it is none of these. Again, of the three voices I have just mentioned, none is close to the truth, and [they are] from man. But I, who came from Infinite Light, I am here—for I know him [Light]—that I might speak to you about the precise nature of the truth. For whatever is from itself is a polluted life; it is self-made. Providence has no wisdom in it. And fate does not discern. . . .

Matthew said to him: "Lord, no one can find the truth except through you. Therefore teach us the truth."

The Savior said: "He Who Is is ineffable. No principle knew him, no authority, no subjection, nor any creature from the foundation of the world until now, except he alone, and anyone to whom he wants to make revelation through him who is from First Light. From now on, I am the Great Savior. For he is immortal and eternal. Now he is eternal, having no birth; for everyone who has birth will perish. He is unbegotten, having no beginning; for everyone who has a beginning has an end. Since no one rules over him, he has no name; for whoever has a name is the creation of another. . . . And he has a semblance of his own—not like what you have seen and received, but a strange semblance that surpasses all things and is better than the universe. It looks to every side and sees itself from itself. Since it is infinite, he is ever incomprehensible. He is imperishable and has no likeness [to anything]. He is unchanging good. He is faultless. He is eternal. He is blessed. While he is not known, he ever knows himself. He is immeasurable. He is untraceable. He is perfect, having no defect. He is imperishability blessed. He is called 'Father of the Universe.' ". . .

Matthew said to him: "Lord, Savior, how was Man revealed?"

The perfect Savior said: "I want you to know that he who appeared before the universe in infinity, Self-grown, Self-constructed Father, being full of shining light and ineffable, in the beginning, when he decided to have his likeness become a great power, immediately the principle [or beginning] of that Light appeared as Immortal Androgynous Man, that through that Immortal Man they might attain their salvation and awake from forgetfulness through the interpreter who was sent, who is with you until the end of the poverty of the robbers.

"And his consort is the Great Sophia, who from the first was destined in him for union by Self-begotten Father, from Immortal Man, 'who appeared as First and divinity and kingdom,' for the Father, who is called 'Man, Self-Father', revealed this. And he created a great aeon, whose name is Ogdoad, for his own majesty. . . .

"All who come into the world, like a drop from the Light, are sent by him to the world of Almighty, that they might be guarded by him. And the bond of his forgetfulness bound him by the will of Sophia, that the matter might be [revealed] through it to the whole world in poverty, concerning his

[Almighty's] arrogance and blindness and the ignorance that he was named. But I came from the places above by the will of the great Light, [I] who escaped from that bond; I have cut off the work of the robbers; I have awakened that drop that was sent from Sophia, that it might bear much fruit through me and be perfected and not again be defective but be [joined] through me, the Great Savior, that his glory might be revealed, so that Sophia might also be justified in regard to that defect, that her sons might not again become defective but might attain honor and glory and go up to their Father and know the words of the masculine Light. And you were sent by the Son, who was sent that you might receive Light and remove yourselves from the forgetfulness of the authorities, and that it might not again come to appearance because of you, namely, the unclean rubbing that is from the fearful fire that came from their fleshly part. Tread upon their malicious intent.". . .

These are the things [the] blessed Savior [said,] [and he disappeared] from them. Then [all the disciples] were in [great, ineffable joy] in [the spirit from] that day on. [And his disciples] began to preach [the] Gospel of God, [the] eternal, imperishable [Spirit]. Amen.

4 The Early Days of Christianities

One form of Christianity . . . emerged as victorious from the conflicts of the second and third centuries. This one form of Christianity decided what was the "correct" Christian perspective; it decided who could exercise authority over Christian belief and practice; and it determined what forms of Christianity would be marginalized, set aside, destroyed. It also decided which books to canonize into Scripture and which books to set aside as "heretical," teaching false ideas . . .

Only twenty-seven of the early Christian books were finally included in the canon, copied by scribes through the ages, eventually translated into English, and now on bookshelves in virtually every home in America. Other books came to be rejected, scorned, maligned, attacked, burned, all but forgotten—lost.

—Bart D. Ehrman

In the beginning, there was not one Christianity, but many. And among them was a well-established tradition of Gnosticism, one of the key "heresies" upon which Dan Brown builds the plot of *The Da Vinci Code.*

Sacred roots and twenty centuries of primacy in the Western world have led to the generally dominant view that modern Christianity evolved more or less linearly and directly from the teachings of Jesus. The snapshot Western civilization has tended to see is a natural progression: starting with Jesus and followed by the preaching of the apostles as depicted in the New Testament, on through the establishment of the church by Peter, brought under the wing of Constantine and the Council of Nicea, and from thence throughout the Roman Empire, Europe, and on into the modern world. If we think about debate, conflict, and heresy in Christian thought, our history and humanities classes tend to emphasize the comparatively recent experience of the Reformation.

Dan Brown's *The Da Vinci Code* wants to acquaint the reader with the lesser known, even "hidden" side of the story, the unanswered questions about the early history of Christianity:

- Who was Jesus?
- Who was Mary Magdalene?
- Why did people accept the notions of a virgin birth or of resurrection?
- Were Jesus and his fellow Jews seeking to define a different path for Judaism, or seeking to create a new religion?
- How credible are the four accepted Gospels, when their accounts are at odds with each other?
- What can one make of all the other accounts that did not find their way into the New Testament?

Early Christian history proceeds to an untidy story punctuated by loose ends, unknowns, intrigues both political and personal, ironies, and considerable doses of what in today's political vernacular might be called "spin." As it turns out, the history of Christianity is primarily one of widely and sometimes wildly differing understandings of what correct Christian belief is, and considerable zeal in the identification and persecution of those thought not to believe correctly. These divergences, diversities, and differences may even go back to the very first moments of the Jesus movement. As we see throughout this book, the differences between Peter and others, the question of Mary Magdalene's role, and the inner questions and doubts of Jesus himself are all becoming far more apparent given today's scholarship, textual analysis, and archaeology, than they were at any time in the last sixteen hundred years or so.

Scholars have long known that there is roughly a forty-year gap (maybe less, but maybe much more) between the death of Jesus and the writing of the first Gospel. During that period the followers of Jesus were consolidating their beliefs through oral tradition, and deciding who Jesus was and what his life and death meant. Each Gospel was an evangelist's telling of the story from a somewhat different point of view, based on the teller's own circumstances and audience. Eventually, four Gospels and twenty-three other texts were canonized (declared to be the Holy Scriptures) into a Bible. This did not occur, however, until the sixth century.

As Deirdre Good points out in her lectures on Mary Magdalene and *The Da Vinci Code*, "Virtually everyone in the New Testament should be thought of as Jewish unless you can produce any evidence to suggest they are not." Most experts agree that Jesus was a Jew. New Testament accounts repeatedly describe his involvements in Jewish temple life—from his precocious understanding of the temple service as a child to his attack on the money changers in the temple during his maturity. In all cases, it is the traditional Jewish temple to which he relates, and which he is trying to induce to change according to his vision.

Indeed, there was so much ferment in Judaism in those days—different cults, sects, clans, tribes, prophets, false prophets, rabbis, teachers, the Greek-influenced, the Roman-influenced—that the Jesus movement may not have appeared as anything shockingly new or different when it first emerged. The Jewish communities scattered across Egypt, Turkey, Greece, Syria, Iraq, and elsewhere all had their own traditions of modified beliefs and influences drawn from their surrounding cultures. Judaism in those days was a big tent—even if under it, things were often unruly, fractious, and bitterly—even fatally—divided.

It would certainly appear that for a long time after the death of Jesus, his followers were not necessarily perceived as believers in a fundamentally different religion. What became Christianity was initially Jews preaching an increasingly different form of Judaism to other Jews. Sometimes called Nazareans by Jews and Christians by gentiles (non-Jews), some of the circles of Jesus' followers required that males be circumcised and that the Jewish ritual and dietary laws be followed, yet they professed belief that Jesus was the Son of God and the sole path to salvation—beliefs inconsistent with Jewish orthodoxy. Ebionites, described recently as "Christians still climbing out of their Jewish shell," insisted that to be part of their movement one had to be Jewish. Yet, as Bart Ehrman, the contemporary expert on lost Christian beliefs and scriptures argues, the Ebionites believed deeply in Jesus, but they saw him as "the Jewish Messiah sent from the Jewish God to the Jewish people in fulfillment of the Jewish scripture." The Ebionites believed that Jesus was a mortal man who was so righteous that God adopted him as His son and allowed his sacrifice to redeem humanity's sins.

Saul, a Greek Jew, was strongly opposed to the Nazareans, but on the road to Damascus he had a vision in which Jesus told him to spend the remainder of his life spreading the gospel to the gentiles. Saul changed his name to Paul. His beliefs differed in significant ways from those of the others of the groups then emerging from the Jewish tradition: Paul felt that male converts should not have to be circumcised, and that following Jewish law was not necessary, thereby setting up one of the earliest Christian conflicts. Paul concentrated his efforts on converting gentiles, while others attempted to convert from within the Jewish community. Paul traveled widely and established Christian churches throughout the eastern Mediterranean. Even more zealous than the Paulines were the Marcionites, who sought to cast off their Jewish heritage completely, even to the point of looking on the Jewish concept of God as a God that had failed.

The apostles, and later their followers, went forth to spread the "good news." The spread of Christianity was a protracted, complicated, and decidedly messy process, that must be viewed within the context of the political world in the early centuries of this era. This was the time of the Roman Empire. As the Empire spread geographically, it incorporated populations whose religious beliefs were primarily pagan and naturalistic, tied to Greek and Egyptian mythology. These existed side by side, with the state taking no side.

It was within this theological stew that Christianity arose. Against the dominant polytheistic religions, Christianity and Judaism were monotheistic, teaching an entirely different relationship of man to God (as opposed to man to gods), and a decidedly different path to salvation. Along the way, many diverse interpretations of the Christian belief system arose, some borrowing elements from the surrounding pagan traditions and others simply having alternate interpretations of key doctrinal beliefs.

Against all the commotion of this backdrop, yet another trend to emerge—and one especially relevant to those interested in the real background of *The Da Vinci Code*'s version of history—was Gnosticism. Gnostics sought knowledge in a mystical, cosmological, and secret sense. They tended to fuse Christianity as a philosophy with more Greek, Egyptian, mythic, and even Eastern elements. Gnostics seem to have been highly literate and to have inherited a mix of the Greek and rabbinic traditions of forming schools to share knowledge and discussion. Bearing in mind that in this time period religion, science, philosophy, politics, poetry, cosmology, and mysticism were all essentially flowing into one primordial soup, the Gnostics created a rich variety of documents, scriptures, and gospels. Representing a variant of Christianity at sharp odds with the increasingly dominant Pauline Christians, the Gnostics were declared to be heretics to be opposed and suppressed.

Some of the Gnostics lived communally in mountaintop or desert communities, far from the madding crowds immersed in other streams of thought. They may have done so out of desire for purity of their pursuit, or out of the fear that their beliefs were anathema to mainstream Christian and Roman trends to such an extent that they needed safe havens for their practice.

Over the first two centuries, Christianity morphed from belief taught by itinerant evangelists to small communities of believers organized in local churches—each with its own leaders, writings, and beliefs—with no overarching authority or hierarchy. Slowly at first, then with increasing rapidity, a formal hierarchy came about, and with it a need for doctrinal uniformity. Bishops met in synods to declare what was doctrinally correct. Other views were heresies to be eradicated.

In 313 Emperor Constantine declared that it was "salutary and most proper" that "complete toleration" should be given by the Roman Empire to anyone who had "given up his mind either to the cult of the Christians" or any other similar cult. With this Edict of Milan, official persecution of Christianity and Christians was supposed to end. It is often said that Constantine converted to Christianity, but most scholars understand that this was not until much later, near his death. Many historians believe Constantine's decision can best be explained as politically astute—a move that took into account the accumulating power of Christianity, and a way to put that power at his disposal. Moreover, it was a decision born of a fascinating mix of mystical, superstitious, military, and philosophical threads, in addition to the political impetus. As the historian Paul Johnson notes, Constantine was a "sun-worshipper, one of a number of late-pagan cults which had observances in common with Christians. Thus, the followers of Isis adored a Madonna nursing her holy child," and the followers of Mithras, many of whom were senior military men, celebrated their deity in much the same way Christians would celebrate Christ. "Constantine was almost certainly a Mithraic . . . Many Christians did not make a clear distinction between this sun cult and their own. They referred to Christ driving his chariot across the sky" and held a feast on December 25, considered the sun's birthday at winter solstice. Whatever the reality, this was a major turning point in Christian history. When the state became at least nominally Christian, the presiding bishops became judicial and administrative as well as scriptural authorities. Constantine and the church both gained power.

A major thorn in Constantine's side was the ongoing controversy with the followers of Arius (Arians) who disputed the notion that Jesus was of the same substance as the Father. Only the Father was God, said Arius and his followers; Christ was not a deity. Constantine wanted the matter settled, and so in 325 convened the Council of Nicea, which declared Arianism a heresy. Heresies from the early church point of view had always been struggled against (see Chapter 5), and would continue to be—from the Sabellian heresy which said that the Father and the Son were different aspects of one Being rather than distinct persons, to the Inquisition and the Salem witch trials. Although the various shades of opinion of Arians and Donatists and other heretical groups are foggy to us today, the historical record is quite clear that Constantine stepped in and personally presided over the Council of Nicea, even crafting some of the language that came out of the meeting as the ultimate statement on the controversies. What did and didn't happen at the Council of Nicea is a subject of debate between Dan Brown in *The Da Vinci Code* and what many religious practitioners and scholars believe. But Dan Brown's version is highly compelling in this key sense: this was a power struggle over the intellectual infrastructure that would rule much of European politics and thought for the following thousand years. Nicea was not about truth or veracity of religious or moral vision. Ruling some ideas in and others out was fundamentally about politics and power. From Constantine at Nicea to Pope Gregory nearly three hundred years later (and much in between) turns out, at least in retrospect, to have been all about developing the intellectual and political infrastructure of Europe for the next thousand years. You might say it was about codification of the code.

This chapter will help the reader better understand the documentation, suppositions, and scenarios upon which Dan Brown built his plot, from the pagan underpinnings of modern theology to the brief flourishing of the Gnostics before they were "forced" underground.

The Pagan Mysteries Behind Early Christianity

BY TIMOTHY FREKE AND PETER GANDY

From *The Jesus Mysteries: Was the "Original Jesus" a Pagan God?* by Timothy Freke and Peter Gandy, copyright © 1999, by Timothy Freke and Peter Gandy. Used by permission of Harmony Books, a division of Random House, Inc.

We had shared an obsession with world mysticism all our lives which recently had led us to explore spirituality in the ancient world. Popular understanding inevitably lags a long way behind the cutting edge of scholarly research and, like most people, we initially had an inaccurate and outdated view of Paganism. We had been taught to imagine a primitive superstition, which indulged in idol worship and bloody sacrifice, and dry philosophers wearing togas stumbling blindly toward what we today call *science*. We were familiar with various Greek myths, which showed the partisan and capricious nature of the Olympian gods and goddesses. All in all, Paganism seemed primitive and fundamentally alien. After many years of study, however, our understanding has been transformed.

Pagan spirituality was actually the sophisticated product of a highly developed culture. The state religions, such as the Greek worship of the Olympian gods, were little more than outer pomp and ceremony. The real spirituality of the people expressed itself through the vibrant and mystical "Mystery religions." At first underground and heretical movements, these Mysteries spread and flourished throughout the ancient Mediterranean, inspiring the greatest minds of the Pagan world, who regarded them as the very source of civilization.

Each Mystery tradition had exoteric Outer Mysteries, consisting of myths, which were common knowledge, and rituals, which were open to anyone who wanted to participate. There were also esoteric Inner Mysteries, which were a sacred secret known only to those who had undergone a powerful process of initiation. Initiates of the Inner Mysteries had the mystical meaning of the rituals and myths of the Outer Mysteries revealed to them, a process that brought about personal transformation and spiritual enlightenment.

The philosophers of the ancient world were the spiritual masters of the Inner Mysteries. They were mystics and miracle workers more comparable to Hindu gurus than dusty academics. The great Greek philosopher Pythagoras, for example, is remembered today for his mathematical theorem, but few people picture him as he actually was: a flamboyant sage—who was believed to be able to miraculously still the winds and raise the dead.

At the heart of the Mysteries were myths concerning a dying and resurrecting godman, who was known by many different names. In Egypt he was Osiris, in Greece Dionysus, in Asia Minor Attis, in Syria Adonis, in Italy Bacchus, in Persia Mithras. Fundamentally all these godmen are the same mythical being. . . . We will use the combined name Osiris-Dionysus to denote his universal and composite nature, and his particular names when referring to a specific Mystery tradition.

From the fifth century B.C.E. philosophers such as Xenophanes and Empedocles had ridiculed taking the stories of the gods and goddesses literally. They viewed them as allegories of human spiritual experience. The myths of Osiris-Dionysus should not be understood as just intriguing tales, therefore, but as a symbolic language, which encodes the mystical teachings of the Inner Mysteries. Because of this, although the details were developed and adapted over time by different cultures, the myth of Osiris-Dionysus has remained essentially the same.

The various myths of the different godmen of the Mysteries share what the great mythologist Joseph Campbell called "the same anatomy." Just as every human is physically unique yet it is possible to talk of the general anatomy of the human body, so with these different myths it is possible to see both their uniqueness and fundamental sameness. A helpful comparison may be the relationship between Shakespeare's *Romeo and Juliet* and Bernstein's *West Side Story*. One is a sixteenth century English tragedy about wealthy Italian families, while the other is a twentieth century American musical about street gangs. On the face of it they look very different, yet they are essentially the same story. Similarly, the tales told about the godmen of the Pagan Mysteries are essentially the same, although they take different forms.

The more we studied the various versions of the myth of Osiris-Dionysus, the more it became obvious that the story of Jesus had all the characteristics of this perennial tale. Event by event, we found we were able to construct Jesus' supposed biography from mythic motifs previously relating to Osiris-Dionysus:

Osiris-Dionysus is God made flesh, the savior and "Son of God."

His father is God and his mother is a mortal virgin.

He is born in a cave or humble cowshed on December 25 before three shepherds.

He offers his followers the chance to be born again through the rites of baptism.

He miraculously turns water into wine at a marriage ceremony.

He rides triumphantly into town on a donkey while people wave palm leaves to honor him.

He dies at Eastertime as a sacrifice for the sins of the world.

After his death he descends to hell, then on the third day he rises from the dead and ascends to heaven in glory.

His followers await his return as the judge during the Last Days.

His death and resurrection are celebrated by a ritual meal of bread and wine, which symbolize his body and blood.

These are just some of the motifs shared between the tales of Osiris-Dionysus and the biography of Jesus. Why are these remarkable similarities not common knowledge? Because, as we were to discover later, the early Roman Church did everything in its power to prevent us perceiving them. It systematically destroyed Pagan sacred literature in a brutal program of eradicating the Mysteries, a task it performed so completely that today Paganism is regarded as a "dead" religion.

Although surprising to us now, to writers of the first few centuries C.E. these similarities between the new Christian religion and the ancient Mysteries were extremely obvious. Pagan critics of Christianity, such as the satirist Celsus, complained that this recent religion was nothing more than a pale reflection of their own ancient teachings. Early "Church fathers," such as Justin Martyr, Tertullian, and Irenaeus, were understandably disturbed and resorted to the desperate claim that these similarities were the result of diabolical mimicry. Using one of the most absurd arguments ever advanced, they accused the Devil of "plagiarism by anticipation," of deviously copying the true story of Jesus before it had actually happened in an attempt to mislead the gullible. These Church fathers struck us as no less devious than the Devil they hoped to incriminate.

Other Christian commentators have claimed that the myths of the Mysteries were like "pre-echoes" of the literal coming of Jesus, somewhat like premonitions or prophecies. This is a more generous version of the diabolical mimicry theory, but seemed no less ridiculous to us. There was nothing other than cultural prejudice to make us see the Jesus story as the literal culmination of its many mythical precursors. Viewed impartially, it appeared to be just another version of the same basic story.

The obvious explanation is that as early Christianity became the dominant power in the previously Pagan world, popular motifs from Pagan mythology became grafted onto the biography of Jesus. This is a possibility that is even put forward by many Christian theologians. The virgin birth, for example, is often regarded as an extraneous later addition that should not be understood literally. Such motifs were "borrowed" from Paganism in the same way that Pagan festivals were adopted as Christian saints' days. This theory is common among those who go looking for the "real" Jesus hidden under the weight of accumulated mythological debris.

Attractive as it appears at first, to us this explanation seemed inadequate. We had collated such a comprehensive body of similarities that there remained hardly any significant elements in the biography of Jesus that we did not find prefigured by the Mysteries. On top of this, we discovered that even Jesus' teachings were not original, but had been anticipated by the Pagan sages! If there was a "real" Jesus somewhere underneath all this, we would have to acknowledge that we could know absolutely nothing about him for all that remained for us was later Pagan accretions! Such a position seemed absurd. Surely there was a more elegant solution to this conundrum?

The Gnostics

While we were puzzling over these discoveries, we began to question the received picture of the early Church and have a look at the evidence for ourselves. We discovered that far from being the united congregation of saints and martyrs that traditional history would have us believe, the early Christian community was actually made up of a whole spectrum of different groups. These can be broadly categorized into two different schools. On the one hand there were those we will call *Literalists*, because what defines them is that they take the Jesus story as a literal account of historical events. It was this school of Christianity that was adopted by the Roman Empire in the fourth century C.E., becoming Roman Catholicism and all its subsequent offshoots. On the other hand, however, there were also radically different Christians known as *Gnostics*.

These forgotten Christians were later persecuted out of existence by the Literalist Roman Church with such thoroughness that until recently we knew little about them except through the writings of their detractors. Only a handful of original Gnostic texts survived, none of which were published before the nineteenth century. This situation changed dramatically, however, with a remarkable discovery in 1945 when an Arab peasant stumbled upon a whole library of Gnostic gospels hidden in a cave near Nag Hammadi in Egypt. This gave scholars access to many texts which were in wide circulation among early Christians, but which were deliberately excluded from the canon of the New Testament-gospels attributed to Thomas and Philip, texts recording the acts of Peter and the twelve disciples, apocalypses attributed to Paul and James, and so on.

It seemed to us extraordinary that a whole library of early Christian documents could be discovered, containing what purport to be the teachings of Christ and his disciples, and yet so few modern followers of Jesus should even know of their existence. Why hasn't every Christian rushed out to read these newly discovered words of the Master? What keeps them confined to the small number of gospels selected for inclusion in the New Testament? It seems that even though two thousand years have passed since the Gnostics were purged, during which time the Roman Church has split into Protestantism and thousands of other alternative groups, the Gnostics are still not regarded as a legitimate voice of Christianity.

Those who do explore the Gnostic gospels discover a form of Christianity quite alien to the religion with which they are familiar. We found ourselves studying strange esoteric tracts with titles such as *Hypostasis of the Archons* and *The Thought of Norea*. It felt as if we were in an episode of *Star Trek*—and in a way we were. The Gnostics truly were "psychonauts" who boldly explored the final frontiers of inner space, searching for the origins and meaning of life. These people were mystics and creative free-thinkers. It was obvious to us why they were so hated by the bishops of the Literalist Church hierarchy.

To Literalists, the Gnostics were dangerous heretics. In volumes of anti-Gnostic works—on unintentional testimony to the power and influence of Gnosticism within early Christianity—they painted them as Christians who had "gone native." They claimed they had become contaminated by the Paganism that surrounded them and had abandoned the purity of the true faith. The Gnostics, on the other hand, saw themselves as the authentic Christian tradition and the orthodox bishops as an "imitation church." They claimed to know the secret Inner Mysteries of Christianity, which the Literalists did not possess.

As we explored the beliefs and practices of the Gnostics we became convinced that the Literalists had at least been right about one thing: the Gnostics were little different from Pagans. Like the philosophers of the Pagan Mysteries, they believed in reincarnation, honored the goddess Sophia, and were immersed in the mystical Greek philosophy of Plato. Gnostics means "Knowers," a name they acquired because, like the initiates of the Pagan Mysteries, they believed that their secret teachings had the power to impart *Gnosis*: direct experiential "Knowledge of God." Just as the goal of a Pagan initiate was to become a god, so for the Gnostics the goal of the Christian initiate was to become a Christ.

What particularly struck us was that the Gnostics were not concerned with the historical Jesus. They viewed the Jesus story in the same way that the Pagan philosophers viewed the myths of Osiris-Dionysus—as an allegory that encoded secret mystical teachings. This insight crystallized for us a remarkable possibility. Perhaps the explanation for the similarities between Pagan myths and the biography of Jesus had been staring us in the face the whole time, but we had been so caught up with traditional ways of thinking that we had been unable to see it. . . .

Early Mainstream Christianity Did Not Mean Simply Following Jesus

BY LANCE S. OWENS

Lance S. Owens is both a physician in clinical practice and an ordained priest. He also maintains the website www.gnosis.org. Copyright © 2004 Lance S. Owens. Reprinted by permission.

In the first century of the Christian era the term 'Gnostic' came to denote a heterodox segment of the diverse new Christian community. Among early followers of Christ it appears there were groups who delineated themselves from the greater household of the church by claiming not simply a belief in Christ and his message, but a "special witness" or revelatory experience of the divine. It was this experience or gnosis that set the true follower of Christ apart, so they asserted. Stephan Hoeller explains that these Christians held a "conviction that direct, personal and absolute knowledge of the authentic truths of existence is accessible to human beings, and, more-over, that the attainment of such knowledge must always con-stitute the supreme achievement of human life."

What the "authentic truths of existence" affirmed by the Gnostics were will be briefly reviewed below, but first a histori-cal overview of the early church might be useful. In the initial century and a half of Christianity—the period when we find first mention of "Gnostic" Christians—no single acceptable format of Christian thought had yet been defined. During this formative period Gnosticism was one of many currents mov-ing within the deep waters of the new religion. The ultimate course Christianity, and Western culture with it, would take was undecided at this early moment. Gnosticism was one of the seminal influences shaping that destiny.

That Gnosticism was, at least briefly, in the mainstream of Christianity is witnessed by the fact that one of its most influential teachers, Valentinus, may have been in consideration during the mid-second century for election as the Bishop of Rome. Born in Alexandria around 100 C.E., Valentinus distinguished himself at an early age as an extraordinary teacher and leader in the highly educated and diverse Alexandrian Christian community. In midlife he migrated from Alexandria to the church's evolving capital, Rome, where he played an active role in the public affairs of the church. A prime characteristic of Gnostics was their claim to be keepers of sacred traditions, gospels, rituals, successions, and other esoteric matters for which many Christians were either not properly prepared or simply not inclined. Valentinus, true to this Gnostic predilection, apparently professed to have received a special apostolic sanction through Theudas, a disciple and initiate of the Apostle Paul, and to be a custodian of doctrines and rituals neglected by what would become Christian orthodoxy. Though an influential member of the Roman church in the mid-second century, by the end of his life Valentinus had been forced from the public eye and branded a heretic by the developing orthodox church.

While the historical and theological details are far too complex for proper explication here, the tide of history can be said to have turned against Gnosticism in the middle of the second century. No Gnostic after Valentinus would ever come so near prominence in the greater church. Gnosticism's emphasis on personal experience, its continuing revelations and production of new scripture, its asceticism and paradoxically contrasting libertine postures, were all met with increasing suspicion. By 180 C.E. Irenaeus, bishop of Lyon, was publishing his first attacks on Gnosticism as heresy, a labor that would be continued with increasing vehemence by the church Fathers throughout the next century.

Orthodox Christianity was deeply and profoundly influenced by its struggles with Gnosticism in the second and third centuries. Formulations of many central traditions in Christian theology came as reflections and shadows of this confrontation with the gnosis. But by the end of the fourth century the struggle was essentially over: the evolving ecclesia had added the force of political correctness to dogmatic denunciation, and with this sword so-called heresy was painfully cut from the Christian body. Gnosticism as a Christian tradition was largely eradicated, its remaining teachers ostracized, and its sacred books destroyed. All that remained for students seeking to understand Gnosticism in later centuries were the denunciations and fragments preserved in the patristic heresiologies. Or at least so it seemed until the mid-twentieth century.

Diverging Views on Mythic Beginnings
Was Genesis History with a Moral, or a Myth with Meaning?

By Stephan A. Hoeller

Excerpt from *Gnosticism: New Light on the Ancient Traditions of Inner Knowing* by Stephan A. Hoeller. Copyright © 2002 by Stephan A. Hoeller. Reprinted by permission of Quest Books/The Theosophical Publishing House, Wheaton, Ill.

Most Westerners assume that Western culture has only one creation myth: the one in the first three chapters of Genesis. Few seem to be aware that there is an alternative: the creation myth of the Gnostics. This myth may strike us as novel and startling, yet it offers views of the creation and of our lives that are well worth considering.

William Blake, the Gnostic poet of the early nineteenth century, wrote: "Both read the Bible day and night, but you read black where I read white." Similar words might have been uttered by early Gnostics about their opponents in the ranks of Judaism and Christianity. The non-Gnostic, or orthodox, view in early Christendom regarded most of the Bible, particularly Genesis, as history with a moral. Adam and Eve were historical personages whose tragic transgression resulted in the Fall, and from their Fall later human beings were to learn portentous moral lessons. One consequence of this reading of Genesis was the ambivalent and worse than ambivalent status of women, who were regarded as Eve's co-conspirators in disobedience in Paradise. Tertullian, one of the church fathers who despised the Gnostics, wrote thus to a group of Christian women:

> You are the devil's gateway ... You are she who persuaded him whom the devil did not dare attack.... Do you know that you are each an Eve? The sentence of God on your sex lives on in this age; the guilt, necessarily, lives on too. (De Cultu Feminarum I. 12)

The Gnostic Christians, whose legacy of sacred literature we find in the splendid Nag Hammadi library, read Genesis not as history with a moral but as a myth with a meaning. They regarded Adam and Eve not as historical figures but as representatives of two intrapsychic principles present within every human being. Adam was the dramatic embodiment of psyche, or "soul": the mind/emotion complex where thinking and feeling originate. Eve stood for *pneuma*, or "spirit," representing the higher, transcendental consciousness.

There are two biblical accounts regarding the creation of

the first woman. One tells us that Eve was created out of Adam's rib (Gen. 2.21); the other, that God created the first human pair, male and female, in his own image (Gen. 1.26–27). The second account suggests that the Creator God himself has a dyadic nature, combining male and female characteristics. The Gnostics generally endorsed this version and developed various interpretations of it. This version accords equality to the woman, while the Adam's rib version makes her subordinate to the man.

For the ancient Gnostics, the conventional image of Eve was not credible. That image presented her as the one who was led astray by the evil serpent and who, with her feminine seductive charm, persuaded Adam to disobey God. In their view, Eve was not a gullible dunce turned persuasive temptress; rather, she was a wise woman, a true daughter of Sophia, the celestial Wisdom. In this capacity, she was the one who awakened the sleeping Adam. Thus in the Apocryphon of John, Eve says:

> I entered into the midst of the dungeon which is the prison of the body. And I spoke thus: "He who hears, let him arise from the deep sleep." And then he [Adam] wept and shed tears. . . . He spoke, asking: "Who is it that calls my name, and whence has this hope come unto me, while I am in the chains of this prison?" And I spoke thus: I am the foreknowledge of pure light; I am the thought of the undefiled spirit. . . . Arise and remember . . . and follow your root which is I . . . and beware of the deep sleep."

In another scripture, On the Origin of the World, Eve is presented as the daughter, and especially the messenger, of the divine Sophia. It is in the capacity of messenger that she comes as an instructor to Adam and raises him up from his sleep of unconsciousness. In most Gnostic scriptures, Eve appears as Adam's superior. The conclusion drawn from these texts is obviously different from that of church fathers such as Tertullian: man is indebted to woman for bringing him to life and to consciousness. One cannot help but wonder how the Western attitude toward women might have developed had the Gnostic view of Eve been the widely accepted view.

Of Snakes and Men

Eve's mistake, the orthodox view tells us, was that she listened to the evil serpent, who persuaded her that the fruit of the tree would make both herself and Adam wise and immortal. A treatise from the Nag Hammadi Gnostic collection, The Testimony of Truth reverses this interpretation. Far from an embodiment of evil, the serpent is considered the wisest creature in Paradise. The text extols the wisdom of the serpent and casts serious aspersions on the Creator, asking: "What sort is he then, this God?" It answers that God's prohibition concerning the fruit of the tree is motivated by envy, because he does not wish humans to awaken to higher knowledge.

Neither are the threats and anger of the Old Testament Creator God left without reproach. The Testimony of Truth tells us that he has shown himself to be "an envious slanderer," a jealous God who inflicts cruel and unjust punishment on those who displease him. The text comments: "But these are the things he said (and did) to those who believe in him and serve him." The clear implication is that with a God like this, one needs no enemies, and perhaps no devil either.

Another scripture from the same collection, The Hypostasis of the Archons, informs us that not only Eve but also the serpent was inspired and guided by the divine Sophia. Sophia allowed her wisdom to enter the serpent, who thereby became a teacher and then taught Adam and Eve about their true source. They came to understand that they were not lowly beings created by the Demiurge (in this case, the Creator in the Genesis story), but rather, that their spiritual selves had originated beyond this world, in the fullness of the ultimate Godhead.

While the mainstream version of Genesis says that after eating the forbidden fruit Adam and Eve fell from paradisiacal grace, the Gnostic version says that "their eyes were opened"—a metaphor for *gnosis*. The first humans could then see for the first time that the deities who had created them were loathsome in appearance, having the faces of animals, and they recoiled in horror at the sight of them. Although cursed by the Demiurge and his archons, the first human pair had acquired the capacity for *gnosis*. They could pass this on to those of their descendants who were inclined to receive it. Eve thus passed on her gift of *gnosis* to her daughter Norea, and Adam gave the same to his third son, Seth. . . .

The Nature of Gnostic Exegesis

What motivated the Gnostic interpreters of Genesis to proclaim such unusual versions of the creation story? Did they wish only to bitterly criticize the God of Israel, as the church fathers would have us believe? The several possible reasons are not necessarily mutually exclusive and in some cases are complementary.

First, the Gnostics, along with some other early Christians, looked upon the Old Testament God as an embarrassment. Members of the more intellectual echelons of early Christendom were people of a certain spiritual sophistication. Those conversant with the teachings of Plato, Philo, Plotinus, and similar teachers would have had a difficult time relating to a God expressing vengefulness, wrath, jealousy, tribal xenophobia, and dictatorial pretensions. . . .

Second, as noted earlier, the Gnostics were inclined to interpret the old scriptures symbolically. Modern theologians, like Paul Tillich, . . . say that the story of the Fall was a symbol for the human existential situation, not a recounting of a historical event. . . .

Third, the Gnostic interpretations of Genesis may have been connected with Gnostic visionary experiences. Through their explorations and experiences of divine mysteries, the Gnostics might have come to understand that the deity spoken of in Genesis was not the true and only God, contrary to what the Bible claimed, and that there must be a God above him. . . .

The Gnostics understood the creation story in Genesis as mythic, and myths are necessarily subject to interpretation. Greek philosophers frequently looked upon their myths as allegories, while the common people saw them as a sort of quasi-history, and the *mystae* (initiates) of the Eleusinian and other mysteries brought the myths to life by way of visionary experiences. There is no reason to believe that the Gnostics approached myths in a manner substantially different from these. . . .

As the child is father to the man, so the creation myths of various cultures leave their imprint on the histories of peoples and nations. The Gnostics apparently made a valiant attempt to free the youthful Western culture of their time from the shadow of the Judeo-Christian creation myth. If the alternative myth they suggested seems radical to us, it is only because we have been accustomed to the Genesis version for so many centuries. Many of the implications of the Gnostic version are in fact potentially useful for the culture of the twenty-first century.

Errors of Religious Omission and Commission in *The Da Vinci Code*

By Bart D. Ehrman

1. Jesus' life was decidedly not "recorded by thousands of followers across the land." He did not have thousands of followers, let alone literate ones.

2. It is not true that eighty Gospels "were considered for the New Testament." This makes it sound like there was a contest, entered by mail.

3. It is absolutely not true that Jesus was not considered divine until the Council of Nicea, that before that he was considered merely as "a mortal prophet." The vast majority of Christians by the early fourth century acknowledged him as divine.

4. Constantine did not commission a "new Bible" that omitted references to Jesus' human traits. For one thing, he did not commission a new Bible at all. For another, the books that were already included are full of references to his human traits (he gets hungry, tired, angry; he gets upset; he bleeds, he dies . . .).

5. The Dead Sea Scrolls were not "found in the 1950s." It was 1947. And the Nag Hammadi documents do not tell the Grail story at all; nor do they emphasize Jesus' human traits. Quite the contrary.

6. "Jewish decorum" in no way forbade "a Jewish man to be unmarried." In fact, most of the community behind the Dead Sea Scrolls were unmarried male celibates.

7. The Dead Sea Scrolls were not among "the earliest Christian records." They are Jewish, with nothing Christian in them.

8. We have no idea about the lineage of Mary Magdalene; nothing connects her with the "house of Benjamin." And even if she were, this would not make her a descendent of David.

9. Mary Magdalene was pregnant at the crucifixion?!? That's a good one.

10. The "Q" document is not a surviving source being hid by the Vatican, nor is it a book allegedly written by Jesus himself. It is a hypothetical document that scholars posit as having been available to Matthew and Luke—principally a collection of the sayings of Jesus. Roman Catholic scholars think the same thing of it as non-Catholics; there's nothing secretive about it.

Bart D. Ehrman is a professor of religion at the University of North Carolina and author of *Lost Christianities: The Battle for Scripture and the Faiths We Never Knew.*

5 Consolidation or Cover-up?

The Establishment of the One True Faith

One of the major players in this cover-up operation was a character called Eusebius who, at the beginning of the fourth century, compiled from legends, fabrications, and his own imagination the only early history of Christianity that still exists today . . . All those with a different perspective . . . were branded as heretics and eradicated. In this way falsehoods compiled in the fourth century have come down to us as established facts . . .

—TIMOTHY FREKE AND PETER GANDY

That modern "philosopher-theologian" Yogi Berra once said, "When you come to the fork in the road, take it." The metaphorical junction of Christian theology and the struggle for control of the church presented itself as a series of forks in the road during the first five or six hundred years after the death of Christ. Where these roads led, how they clashed, and what the overt and covert meaning of the outcome was, is the subject matter for this chapter.

To achieve primacy, the early church fathers believed they needed to turn Christianity into a force to unite and strengthen the empire, consistent with the empire's values, politics, and social and military infrastructure. Those who led the Roman Empire in this pursuit believed that a key task was to distill a core ideology and cosmology out of all the various ideas that made up the Christian message. In doing so, they chose to glorify certain Gospel accounts that reinforced their version of Christendom's message—even to select those to be included in the Bible and in what order—at the same time as they vigorously rejected as heretical anything seen as politically or textually deviating from the mainstream.

The Gnostics—far from the centers in Rome and Constantinople—ended up on the defensive in this battle. As Timothy Freke and Peter Gandy argue, the church was systematically eliminating Gnostic and other "heretical" influences, even those that may have been closer to the beliefs and practices of the original revolution Jesus had started, in favor of those that served the cause of consolidating a standardized, hierarchical, powerful church. Down one path lay mystics having ecstatic experiences in the desert; down the other lay strong popes, central cathedrals, peasants arranging their lives against the backdrop of heaven and hell, and motivated Christian soldiers prepared to march forward.

As Bart Ehrman notes in his interview in this chapter, "Once Constantine converts to Christianity, he converts to an orthodox form of Christianity, and once the state has power, and the state is Christian, then the state starts asserting its influence over Christianity. So by the end of the fourth century, there's actually legislation against heretics. So the empire that used to be completely anti-Christian becomes Christian, and not just becomes Christian, but tries to dictate what shape Christianity ought to be."

This chapter reflects this historical argument. The struggle against the alleged heretics can be found in the excerpts included here from some of the most influential writers of the second and third centuries: Tertullian, Irenaeus, and Eusebius.

These individuals were real, historically well-documented figures of the early church. They played a critical, if sometimes inadvertent, role in selecting which Gospels and which texts would become the New Testament and the modern Christian canon, as well as in destroying—intellectually, ideologically, and physically—the "heretical" Christian movements of those days. Although their names are scarcely known today to the average person of Christian faith, they wielded extraordinary power over determining the ultimate content of modern Christianity. They were the editors, so to speak, of the Bible. Reacting as they were to the severe repression of Christians they had witnessed, these church leaders developed their own biases, and have to be understood in their own context. And when you read some of their original pronouncements in this chapter, you will understand just how dark and fearful the age was in which they lived and worked.

With the benefit of more than sixteen hundred years of hindsight, some experts now see those Gnostic "heretics" denounced by early church officialdom as having been on a more humanist, more meaningful, more feminist, and more "Christian" spiritual path than those who ultimately triumphed. If ever there were a case of the winners getting to write history the way they saw it, this is it. Out of this epoch-defining process came a small number of Gospel truths on one side, and a great many heretical documents on the other.

The extreme extension of the church's arguments against the heresies of sixteen hundred years ago would be recycled a thousand years later in the Inquisition. *Malleus Maleficarum*, written in 1487 as the political platform of the Inquisition, has its roots in the earlier battles against alleged heresies; we reprint some of its chilling words here.

The theological and passionate cry of "foul" put forward by those who took the second road—expressed primarily in Gnosticism—can be found in the writings of Timothy Freke and Peter Gandy, among many other postmodern commentators. Freke and Gandy see the deeply spiritual, mythical, poetic, romantic, Goddess-cult, sacred feminine roots of Christianity being stamped out by these virulent antiheresy campaigns. They go so far as to argue that "there was no evidence that Jesus ever lived." Jesus was another in a long line of mythic god-man figures, who was supposed to exist in harmony with the Goddess. They see the efforts to select the Gospel truths and edit the rich history of Christian origins into an industrial-strength pabulum as the destruction of the feminine side of the continuum, a deracinating break with the collective unconscious and the collective past. "Some of the things that we put in Jesus' Word were actually words that were originally in the goddess's mouth," they say.

Two eminent scholars of religion provide perspective on this struggle of interpretation. Elaine Pagels looks at how the Word of God became the Word of man through the selection of the Gospels to be included in the Bible. Bart Ehrman surveys the "other Christianities" and the religious, political, and cultural implications of the church's victory and the Gnostics' loss.

A variety of other views are presented along the way, as we start to peel the onion skin of time away from what Leigh Teabing tells Sophie Neveu was "the greatest cover-up in human history."

The Jesus Mysteries

By Timothy Freke and Peter Gandy

From *The Jesus Mysteries: Was The "Original Jesus" a Pagan God?* by Timothy Freke and Peter Gandy. Copyright ©1999 by Tim Freke and Peter Gandy. Used by permission of Harmony Books, a division of Random House, Inc.

The traditional version of history bequeathed to us by the authorities of the Roman Church is that Christianity developed from the teachings of a Jewish Messiah and that Gnosticism was a later deviation. What would happen, we wondered, if the picture were reversed and Gnosticism viewed as the authentic Christianity, just as the Gnostics themselves claimed? Could it be that orthodox Christianity was a later deviation from Gnosticism and that Gnosticism was a synthesis of Judaism and the Pagan Mystery religion? This was the beginning of the Jesus Mysteries Thesis.

Boldly stated, the picture that emerged for us was as follows. We knew that most ancient Mediterranean cultures had adopted the ancient Mysteries, adapting them to their own national tastes and creating their own version of the myth of the dying and resurrecting godman. Perhaps some of the Jews had, likewise, adopted the Pagan Mysteries and created their own version of the Mysteries, which we now know as Gnosticism. Perhaps initiates of the Jewish Mysteries had adapted the potent symbolism of the Osiris–Dionysus myths into a myth of their own, the hero of which was the Jewish dying and resurrecting godman Jesus.

If this was so, then the Jesus story was not a biography at all but a consciously crafted vehicle for encoded spiritual teachings created by Jewish Gnostics. As in the Pagan Mysteries, initiation into the Inner Mysteries would reveal the myth's allegorical meaning. Perhaps those uninitiated into the Inner

Mysteries had mistakenly come to regard the Jesus myth as historical fact and in this way Literalist Christianity had been created. Perhaps the Inner Mysteries of Christianity, which the Gnostics taught but which the Literalists denied existed, revealed that the Jesus story was not a factual account of God's one and only visit to planet Earth, but a mystical teaching story designed to help each one of us become a Christ.

The Jesus story does have all the hallmarks of a myth, so could it be that that is exactly what it is? After all, no one has read the newly discovered Gnostic gospels and taken their fantastic stories as literally true; they are readily seen as myths. It is only familiarity and cultural prejudice that prevent us from seeing the New Testament gospels in the same light. If those gospels had also been lost to us and only recently discovered, who would read these tales for the first time and believe they were historical accounts of a man born of a virgin, who had walked on water and returned from the dead? Why should we consider the stories of Osiris, Dionysus, Adonis, Attis, Mithras, and the other Pagan Mystery saviors as fables, yet come across essentially the same story told in a Jewish context and believe it to be the biography of a carpenter from Bethlehem?

We had both been raised as Christians and were surprised to find that, despite years of open-minded spiritual exploration, it still felt somehow dangerous to even dare think such thoughts. Early indoctrination reaches very deep. We were in effect saying that Jesus was a Pagan god and that Christianity was a heretical product of Paganism! It seemed outrageous. Yet this theory explained the similarities between the stories of Osiris, Dionysus, and Jesus Christ in a simple and elegant way. They are parts of one developing mythos.

The Jesus Mysteries Thesis answered many puzzling questions, yet it also opened up new dilemmas. Isn't there indisputable historical evidence for the existence of Jesus the man?

And how could Gnosticism be the original Christianity when St. Paul, the earliest Christian we know about, is so vociferously anti-Gnostic? And is it really credible that such an insular and anti-Pagan people as the Jews could have adopted the Pagan Mysteries? And how could it have happened that a consciously created myth came to be believed as history? And if Gnosticism represents genuine Christianity, why was it Literalist Christianity that came to dominate the world as the most influential religion of all time? All of these difficult questions would have to be satisfactorily answered before we could wholeheartedly accept such a radical theory as the Jesus Mysteries Thesis.

The Great Cover-up

Our new account of the origins of Christianity only seemed improbable because it contradicted the received view. As we pushed farther with our research, the traditional picture began to unravel completely all around us. We found ourselves embroiled in a world of schism and power struggles, of forged documents and false identities, of letters that had been edited and added to, and of the wholesale destruction of historical evidence. We focused forensically on the few facts we could be confident of, as if we were detectives on the verge of cracking a sensational "whodunit," or perhaps more accurately as if we were uncovering an ancient and unacknowledged miscarriage of justice. For, time and again, when we critically examined what genuine evidence remained, we found that the history of Christianity bequeathed to us by the Roman Church was a gross distortion of the truth. Actually the evidence completely endorsed the Jesus Mysteries Thesis. It was becoming increasingly obvious that we had been deliberately deceived, that the Gnostics were indeed the original Christians, and that their anarchic mysticism had been hijacked by an authoritarian institution which had created from it a dogmatic religion and then brutally enforced the greatest cover-up in history.

The Jesus Mysteries

One of the major players in this cover-up operation was a character called Eusebius who, at the beginning of the fourth century, compiled from legends, fabrications, and his own imagination the only early history of Christianity that still exists today. All subsequent histories have been forced to base themselves on Eusebius's dubious claims, because there has been little other information to draw on. All those with a different perspective on Christianity were branded as heretics and eradicated. In this way falsehoods compiled in the fourth century have come down to us as established facts.

Eusebius was employed by the Roman Emperor Constantine, who made Christianity the state religion of the Empire and gave Literalist Christianity the power it needed to begin the final eradication of Paganism and Gnosticism. Constantine wanted "one God, one religion" to consolidate his claim of "one Empire, one Emperor." He oversaw the creation of the Nicene creed, the article of faith repeated in churches to this day and Christians who refused to assent to this creed were banished from the Empire or otherwise silenced.

This "Christian" Emperor then returned home from Nicaea and had his wife suffocated and his son murdered. He deliberately remained un-baptized until his deathbed so that he could continue his atrocities and still receive forgiveness of sins and a guaranteed place in heaven by being baptized at the last moment. Although he had his "spin doctor" Eusebius compose a suitably obsequious biography for him, he was actually a monster just like many Roman Emperors before him. Is it really at all surprising that a "history" of the origins of Christianity created by an employee in the service of a Roman tyrant should turn out to be a pack of lies?

History is indeed written by the victors. The creation of an appropriate history has always been part of the arsenal of political manipulation.

Was Jesus Real?

AN INTERVIEW WITH TIMOTHY FREKE

In Chapter 2, Timothy Freke discussed archetypes of the sacred feminine. Here, in a continuation of that interview, he questions the existence of a historical Jesus.

In your opinion, is there any evidence that Jesus lived?

None at all. The only evidence we have is fake. I would categorically say there is no evidence at all for the historical Jesus, but loads to suggest that the Gospel story is a myth. If someone found the Jesus story in a cave, like the Nag Hammadi texts, and said, "Look I've got this story of a man, he's born of a virgin, walks on water, teaches these amazing spiritual insights, and then dies and comes back from the dead," I think everyone would go, "Well, this is clearly another myth, there's loads of them like this." It's only because we're so familiar with it that we can't see the obvious. One hundred fifty years ago people thought Adam and Eve were true—some people still do. But the educated amongst us know that it's not, it's a myth, a powerful, important allegorical myth about a transformation. It's not history, and the same will be seen probably within a few decades with the Jesus story. It's just at the moment it is so embedded in us, we can't quite see it for what it is. And when the Gnostic Christians were destroyed in the fourth century, these mysteries did survive in underground secret societies—this is where a lot of the secret societies Dan Brown talks about have their roots, for sure. And he's right about that; what I think he's wrong about is that it has nothing to do with the lineage of kings and queens.

You brand the wing of Christianity that survived and thrived Literalist. What has been the result of this Literalist reading of the Jesus story?

The legacy of Literalist Christianity has been horrendous. It has been the holocaust for the sake of God on the one hand, and on the other hand it has been the holocaust of women, the witch trials. It has been what happens through the rejection of the feminine, and the irony is that the church branded the Gnostics as world renouncers— whereas the fact is, it is the church which damned women, which damned sex, which set up monastic communities where men could get away from women and away from the world, and encouraged all these people flagellating themselves in the Middle Ages. All of that comes from Roman Literalism, because you're wanting to suffer as Jesus literally suffered, rather than understanding that it's all metaphorical, it's all allegory. The treatment of women has only changed over the last few hundred years—really dramatically in the last few decades—and that's a great irony because the people who originally created the Jesus story were part of the Pythagorean tradition famous for treating people well. Many early Christian Gnostic works are attributed to women, Gnostic teachers were often women, their leaders were often women. And this tradition was destroyed by this horrendous Roman revolt and we've lost the divine feminine, which is not just bad for women, it's bad for men. As a man, it's very hard to have an erotic relationship with the divine if you haven't got a female image with which to relate.

God's Word or Human Words?

By Elaine Pagels

Excerpted from *Beyond Belief: The Secret Gospel of Thomas* by Elaine Pagels. Copyright © 2003 by Elaine Pagels. Used by permission of Random House, Inc.

Within a century of Jesus' death, some of his most loyal followers had determined to exclude a wide range of Christian sources, to say nothing of borrowing from other religious traditions, although, as we have also seen, this often happened. But why, and in what circumstances, did these early church leaders believe that this was necessary for the movement to survive? And why did those who proclaimed Jesus the "only begotten son of God," as the Gospel of John declares, dominate later tradition, while other Christian visions, like that of Thomas, which encourages disciples to recognize themselves, as well as Jesus, as "children of God," were suppressed?

Traditionally, Christian theologians have declared that "the Holy Spirit guides the church into all truth"—a statement often taken to mean that what has survived must be right. Some historians of religion have rationalized this conviction by implying that in Christian history, as in the history of science, weak, false ideas die off early, while the strong and valid ones survive. The late Raymond Brown, a prominent New Testament scholar and Roman Catholic Sulpician priest, stated this perspective baldly: What orthodox Christians rejected was only "the rubbish of the second century"—and, he added, "it's still rubbish." But such polemics tell us nothing about how and why early church leaders laid down the fundamental principles of Christian teaching. To understand what happened we need to look at the specific challenges—and dangers—that confronted believers during the critical years around

100 to 200 C.E., and how those who became the architects of Christian tradition dealt with these challenges. The African convert Tertullian, living in the port city of Carthage in North Africa about eighty years after the Gospels of John and Thomas were written, around the year 190 (or, as Tertullian and his contemporaries might have said, during the reign of Emperor Commodus), acknowledged that the Christian movement was attracting crowds of new members—and that outsiders were alarmed:

> The outcry is that the State is filled with Christians—that they are in the fields, in the cities, in the islands; and [outsiders] lament, as if for some calamity, that both men and women, of every age and condition, even high rank, are going over to profess Christian faith.

Tertullian ridiculed the non-Christian majority for their wild suspicions and denounced the magistrates for believing them:

> [We are called] monsters of evil, and accused of practicing a sacred ritual in which we kill a little child and eat it; in which, after the feast, we practice incest, while the dogs, our pimps, overturn the lights and give us the shameless darkness to gratify our lusts. *This is what people constantly charge,* yet you take no trouble to find out the truth. . . . Well, *you think the Christian is capable of every crime—an enemy of the gods, of the emperor, of the laws, of good morals, of all nature.*

Tertullian was distressed that throughout the empire, from his native city in Africa to Italy, Spain, Egypt, and Asia Minor, and in the provinces from Germany to Gaul, Christians had become targets of sporadic outbreaks of violence. Roman magistrates often ignored these incidents and sometimes participated in them. In the city of Smyrna on the coast of Asia Minor, for example, crowds shouting "Get the atheists!" lynched the convert Germanicus and demanded—successfully—that the authorities arrest and immediately kill Polycarp, a prominent bishop.

What outsiders saw depended considerably on which Christian groups they happened to encounter. Pliny, governor of Bithynia, in modern Turkey, trying to prevent groups from sheltering subversives, ordered his soldiers to arrest people accused as Christians. To gather information, his soldiers tortured two Christian women, both slaves, who revealed that members of this peculiar cult "met regularly before dawn on a certain day to sing a hymn to Christ as to a god." Though it had been rumored that they were eating human flesh and blood, Pliny found that they were actually eating only "ordinary, harmless food." He reported to the emperor Trajan that, although he found no evidence of actual crime, "I ordered them to be taken away and executed; for, whatever they admit to, I am convinced that their stubbornness and unshakable obstinacy should not go unpunished. But twenty years later in Rome, Rusticus, the city prefect, interrogated a group of five Christians who looked to him less like members of a cult than like a philosophy seminar. Justin Martyr the philosopher, arraigned along with his students, admitted to the prefect that he met with like-minded believers in his Roman apartment "above the baths of Timothy" to discuss "Christian philosophy." Nevertheless Rusticus, like Pliny, suspected treason. When Justin and his pupils refused his order to sacrifice to the gods, he had them beaten, then beheaded.

Thirty years after Justin's death, another philosopher, named Celsus, who detested Christians, wrote a book called *The True Word*, which exposed their movement and accused some of them of acting like wild-eyed devotees of foreign gods such as Attis and Cybele, possessed by spirits. Others, Celsus charged, practiced incantations and spells, like magicians; still others followed what many Greeks and Romans saw as the barbaric, Oriental customs of the Jews. Celsus reported, too, that on large estates throughout the countryside Christian woolworkers, cobblers, and washerwomen, people who, he said, "ordinarily are afraid to speak in the presence of their superiors," nevertheless gathered the gullible—slaves, children, and "stupid women"—from the great houses into their workshops to hear how Jesus worked miracles and, after he died, rose from the grave. Among respectable citizens, Christians aroused the same suspicions of violence, promiscuity, and political extremism with which secretive cults are still regarded, especially by those who fear that their friends or relatives may be lured into them.

Despite the diverse forms of early Christianity—and perhaps because of them—the movement spread rapidly, so that by the end of the second century Christian groups were proliferating throughout the empire, despite attempts to stop them. Tertullian boasted to outsiders that "the more we are mown down by you, the more we multiply; the blood of Christians is seed!" Defiant rhetoric, however, could not solve the problem that he and other Christian leaders faced: How could they strengthen and unify this enormously diverse and widespread movement, so it could survive its enemies?

Tertullian's younger contemporary Irenaeus, often identified as bishop of Lyons, himself had experienced the hostility Tertullian was talking about, first in his native town of Smyrna (Izmir, in today's Turkey) and then in the rough provincial town of Lyons, in Gaul (now France). Irenaeus also witnessed the fractiousness that divided Christian groups. As a boy he had lived in the household of his teacher Polycarp, the venerable bishop of Smyrna, whom even his enemies called the teacher of Asia Minor. Although he knew that they were scattered in many small groups throughout the world, Irenaeus shared Polycarp's hope that Christians everywhere would come to see themselves as members of a single church they called catholic, which means "universal." To unify this worldwide community, Polycarp urged its members to reject all deviants. According to Irenaeus, Polycarp liked to tell how his own mentor, "John, the disciple of the Lord"——the same person whom tradition reveres as the author of the Gospel of John——once went to the public baths in Ephesus, but, seeing Cerinthus, whom he regarded as a heretic, John ran out of the bath house without bathing, exclaiming, "Let us flee, lest the bath house fall down; because Cerinthus, the enemy of the truth, is inside." When Irenaeus repeated this story, he added another to show how Polycarp himself treated heretics. When the influential but controversial Christian teacher Marcion confronted the bishop and asked him, "Do you recognize me?" Polycarp replied, "Yes, I recognize you——firstborn of Satan!"

Irenaeus says that he tells these stories to show "the horror that the apostles and their disciples had against even speaking with those who corrupt the truth." But his stories also show what troubled Irenaeus: that even two generations after the author of the Gospel of John qualified the claims of Peter Christians and confronted Thomas Christians, the movement remained contentious and divided. Polycarp himself denounced people who, he charged, "bear the [Christian] name with evil deceit" because what they teach often differs from what he had learned from his own teachers. Irenaeus, in turn, believed that he practiced true Christianity, for he could link himself directly to the time of Jesus through Polycarp, who personally had heard Jesus' teaching from John himself, "the disciple of the Lord." Convinced that this disciple wrote the Gospel of John, Irenaeus was among the first to champion this gospel and link it forever to Mark, Matthew, and Luke. His contemporary Tatian, a brilliant Syrian student of Justin

Martyr the philosopher, killed by Rusticus, took a different approach: he tried to unify the various gospels by rewriting all of them into a single text. Irenaeus left the texts intact but declared that only Matthew, Mark, Luke, and John *collectively*—and only these gospels *exclusively*—constitute the *whole* gospel, which he called the "four formed gospel." Only these four gospels, Irenaeus believed, were written by eyewitnesses to events through which God has sent salvation to humankind. This four gospel canon was to become a powerful weapon in Irenaeus's campaign to unify and consolidate the Christian movement during his lifetime, and it has remained a basis of orthodox teaching ever since. . . .

When Irenaeus met in Rome a childhood friend from Smyrna named Florinus, who like himself as a young man had studied with Polycarp, he was shocked to learn that his friend now had joined a group headed by Valentinus and Ptolemy—sophisticated theologians who, nevertheless, like the new prophets, often relied on dreams and revelations. Although they called themselves spiritual Christians, Irenaeus regarded them as dangerously deviant. Hoping to persuade his friend to reconsider, Irenaeus wrote a letter to warn him that "these views, Florinus, to put it mildly, are not sound; are not consonant with the church, and involve their devotees in the worst impiety, even heresy." Irenaeus was distressed to learn that an increasing number of educated Christians were moving in the same direction.

When he returned from Rome to Gaul, Irenaeus found his own community devastated; some thirty people had been brutally tortured and killed in the public arena on a day set aside to entertain the townspeople with this spectacle. With Bishop Pothinus dead, the remaining members of his group now looked to Irenaeus for leadership. Aware of the danger, he nevertheless agreed, determined to unify the survivors. But he saw that members of his own "flock" were splintered into various, often fractious groups—all of them claiming to be inspired by the holy spirit.

How could he sort out these conflicting claims and impose some kind of order? The task was enormous and perplexing. Irenaeus believed, certainly, that the holy spirit had initiated the Christian movement. From the time it began, a hundred years earlier, both Jesus and his followers claimed to have experienced outpourings of the holy spirit dreams, visions, stories, sayings, ecstatic speech—many communicated orally, many others written down—reflecting the vitality and diversity of the movement. The New Testament gospels abound in visions, dreams, and revelations, like the one that Mark says initiated Jesus' public activity:

> In those days, Jesus came from Nazareth, and was baptized by John in the Jordan. And just as he was coming up out of the water, *he saw the heavens torn apart and the spirit descending like a dove upon him, and a voice came from heaven:* "You are my beloved son; with you I am well pleased."

Luke adds to his version of this story an account of Jesus' birth, in which a vision precedes every event in the drama, from the moments the angel Gabriel appeared to the aging priest Zacharias and later to Mary, to the night when "an angel of the Lord" appeared to shepherds to tell them of Jesus' birth, terrifying them with a sudden radiance that lighted up the nighttime sky. . . .

Irenaeus says that he tried hard, at a friend's request, to investigate Marcus's teaching in order to expose him as an interloper and a fraud. For by attracting disciples, performing initiations, and offering special teachings to "spiritual" Christians, Marcus's activity threatened Irenaeus's effort to unify all Christians in the area into a homogenous church. Irenaeus charged that Marcus was a magician, "the herald of

Antichrist" a man whose made-up visions and pretense to spiritual power masked his true identity as Satan's own apostle. He ridiculed Marcus's claims to investigate "the deep things of God" and mocked him for urging initiates to seek revelations of their own:

> While they say such things as these about the creation, every one of them generates something new every day, according to his ability; for no one is considered "mature" [or "initiated"] among them who does not develop some enormous lies.

Irenaeus expresses dismay that many other teachers, too, within Christian communities, "introduce an indescribable number of secret and illegitimate writings, which they themselves have forged, to bewilder the minds of foolish people, who are ignorant of the true scriptures." He quotes some of their writings, including part of a well known and influential text called the Secret Book of John (discovered among the so-called gnostic gospels at Nag Hammadi in 1945), and he refers to many others, including a Gospel of Truth (perhaps the one discovered at Nag Hammadi), which he attributes to Marcus's teacher, Valentinus, and even a Gospel of Judas. Irenaeus decided that stemming this flood of "secret writings" would be an essential first step toward limiting the proliferation of "revelations" that he suspected of being only delusional or, worse, demonically inspired.

Yet the discoveries at Nag Hammadi show how widespread was the attempt "to seek God"—not only among those who wrote such "secret writings" but among the many more who read, copied, and revered them, including the Egyptian monks who treasured them in their monastery library even two hundred years after Irenaeus had denounced them. But in 367 c.e., Athanasius, the zealous bishop of Alexandria—an admirer of Irenaeus—issued an Easter letter in which he demanded that Egyptian monks destroy all such writings, except for those he specifically listed as "acceptable," even "canonical"—a list that constitutes virtually all of our present "New Testament." But someone—perhaps monks at the monastery of St. Pachomius—gathered dozens of the books Athanasius wanted to burn, removed them from the monastery library, sealed them in a heavy, six-foot jar, and intending to hide them, buried them on a nearby hillside near Nag Hammadi. There an Egyptian villager named Muhammad 'Alī stumbled upon them sixteen hundred years later.

Now that we can read for ourselves some of the writings that Irenaeus detested and Athanasius banned, we can see that many of them express the hope of receiving revelation, and encourage "those who seek for God." The author of the Secret Book of James, for example, *reinterprets* the opening scene we noted from the New Testament Acts, in which Luke tells how Jesus ascended . . .

But those who criticize such "proof from prophecy" suggest that Christians like Justin argue fallaciously—for example, by mistaking a misleading translation for a miracle. The author of the Gospel of Matthew, for example, apparently reading Isaiah's prophecy in Greek translation, took it to mean that "a virgin [*parthenos* in Greek] shall conceive." Justin himself acknowledges that Jewish interpreters, arguing with Jesus' followers, pointed out that what the prophet had actually written in the original Hebrew was simply that "a *young woman* [*almahl*] shall conceive and bear a son"—apparently predicting immediate events expected in the royal succession.

Yet Justin and Irenaeus, like many Christians to this day, remained unconvinced by such arguments, and believed instead that ancient prophecies predicted Jesus' birth, death, and resurrection, and that their divine inspiration has been proven by actual events. Unbelievers often find these proofs far-fetched, but for believers they demonstrate God's "history of salvation." Justin staked his life on this conviction, and believed that he had given up philosophical speculation for truth as empirically verifiable as that of the scientist whose experiments turn out as predicted.

Since Irenaeus saw the proof from prophecy as one way to resolve the problem of how to tell which prophecies—and which revelations—come from God, he added certain writings of "the apostles" to those of "the prophets," since he, like Justin, believed that together these constitute indispensable witnesses to truth. Like other Christians of their time, Justin and Irenaeus, when they spoke of "the Scriptures," had in mind primarily the Hebrew Bible: what we call the New Testament had not yet been assembled. Their conviction that God's truth is revealed in the events of salvation history provides the essential link between the Hebrew Bible and what Justin called "the apostles' memoirs," which we know as the gospels of the New Testament.

It was Irenaeus, so far as we can tell, who became the principal architect of what we call the four gospel canon, the framework that includes in the New Testament collection the gospels of Matthew, Mark, Luke, and John. First Irenaeus denounces various Christian groups that settle on only one gospel, like the Ebionite Christians, who, he says, use only Matthew, or followers of Marcion, who use only Luke. Equally mistaken, Irenaeus continues, are those who invoke many gospels. Certain Christians, he says, declared that certain Christians "boast that they have more gospels than there really are . . . but really, they have no gospel which is not full of blasphemy." Irenaeus resolved to hack down the forest of "apocryphal and illegitimate" writings—like the Secret Book of James and the Gospel of Mary—and leave only four "pillars"—standing. He boldly declared that "the gospel," which contains all truth, can be supported by only these four "pillars" namely, the gospels attributed to Matthew, Mark, Luke, and John. To defend his choice, he declared that "it is not possible that there can be either more or fewer than four," for "just as there are four regions of the universe, and four principal winds," the church itself requires "only four pillars." Furthermore, just as the prophet Ezekiel envisioned God's throne borne up by four living creatures, so the divine Word of God is supported by this "four formed gospel." (Following his lead, Christians in later generations took the faces of these four "living creatures"—the lion, the bull, the eagle, and the man—as symbols of the four evangelists.) What makes these gospels trustworthy, he claimed, is that these authors, who he believed included Jesus' disciples Matthew and John, actually witnessed the events they related; similarly, he added, Mark and Luke, being followers of Peter and Paul, wrote down only what they had heard from the apostles themselves.

Few New Testament scholars today would agree with Irenaeus; we do not know who actually wrote these gospels, any more than we know who wrote the gospels of Thomas or Mary; all we know is that all of these "gospels" are attributed to disciples of Jesus. Nevertheless, as the next chapters will show, Irenaeus not only welded the Gospel of John to the far more widely quoted gospels of Matthew and Luke but praised John as the greatest gospel. For Irenaeus, John was not the *fourth* gospel, as Christians call it today, but the *first* and *foremost* of the gospels, because he believed that John alone understood who Jesus really is—God in human form. What God revealed in that extraordinary moment when he "became flesh" trumped any revelations received by mere human beings—even prophets and apostles, let alone the rest of us.

Irenaeus could not, of course, stop people from seeking revelation of divine truth—nor, as we have seen, did he intend to do so. After all, religious traditions survive through time only as their adherents relive and re-imagine them and, in the process, continually transform them. But, from his own time to the present, Irenaeus and his successors among church leaders did strive to compel all believers to subject themselves to the "fourfold gospel" and to what he called apostolic tradition. Henceforth all "revelations" endorsed by Christian leaders would have to agree with the gospels set forth in what would become the New Testament. Throughout the centuries, of course, these gospels have given rise to an extraordinary range of Christian art, music, poetry, theology, and legend. But even the church's most gifted saints, like Teresa of Avila and John of the Cross, would be careful not to transgress—much less transcend—these boundaries. To this day, many traditionally minded Christians continue to believe that whatever trespasses canonical guidelines must be "lies and wickedness" that come either from the evil of the human heart or from the devil.

Yet Irenaeus recognized that even banishing all "secret writings" and creating a canon of four gospel accounts could not, by itself, safeguard the Christian movement. What if some who read the "right" gospels read them in the wrong way—or in *many* wrong ways? What if Christians interpreted these same gospels to inspire—or, as the bishop might say, to spawn—new "heresies"? This is what happened in Irenaeus's congregation—and . . . he responded by working to construct what he called orthodox (literally, "straight-thinking") Christianity.

The Battle for Scripture and the Faiths We Didn't Get a Chance to Know

AN INTERVIEW WITH BART D. EHRMAN

Bart D. Ehrman chairs the Department of Religious Studies at the University of North Carolina at Chapel Hill. An authority on the early church and the life of Jesus, his most recent book is *Lost Christianities: The Battle for Scripture and the Faiths We Never Knew.*

A major notion of The Da Vinci Code is that a major alternate tradition to the Catholic Church—a side of the argument over the meaning of Jesus' life—has been lost to us for two thousand years. How do you look at this question?

There were actually a lot of different sides to the alternate tradition in Christianity, but perhaps the best examples can be found by looking at three of the variant forms of early Christianity: the Ebionites, the Marcionites, and the Gnostics. They are all sects within Christianity, but they are very different from each other.

The Ebionites were these Jewish Christians who emphasized the importance of being Jewish as well as Christian. The Marcionites were anti-Jewish, and believed that all things Jewish actually belong to the god of the Old Testament, who was not the true God. The Gnostics held to the belief that there were a number of different gods.

All of these groups claimed to go back to Jesus, which means they probably originated soon after Jesus' death and resurrection, or within a few decades at least. For example, the Ebionites claim that their teachings were derived from James the Just, who was the brother of Jesus, and who better to know what Jesus taught than his own brother? And they may have been right, actually—they may have been propounding beliefs that James taught. Their faith did not spread widely, however, perhaps in part because their belief that people who were Gentiles had to become Jewish to be Christian meant that men had to become circumcised, which means they probably didn't win too many converts.

The Ebionites emphasized the Jewishness of Christianity. How about the Marcionites?

The Marcionites were followers of the mid-second-century Greek philosopher and teacher Marcion, who had spent about five years in Rome working out his theological system. He believed the apostle Paul had the true insight into Christianity because Paul differentiated between the law and the gospel. Marcion pushed that view to an extreme, maintaining that if there is a separation between law and gospel they must have been given to humankind from two different gods—the god who gave the law is the god of the Old testament, whereas the god who saved people from the law is the god of Jesus. Similarly, the wrathful god of the Old Testament is the god who created this world, and chose Israel, and gave them his law, whereas the god of Jesus is the one who saves people from this god by dying for their sins.

Marcion had a huge following even after he was excommunicated (he may have been the first), going to Asia Minor, in modern-day Turkey, to establish churches. In truth, Marcionite Christianity was a real threat to the other forms—it almost took over Christianity as a whole.

How about the Gnostics?

All sorts of groups, very different from each other, are classified today by scholars as Gnostics. They were so different from each other that some scholars like the historian Elaine Pagels wonder whether we should even call them Gnostic anymore. Gnostics as a rule believed that this material world we live in is a cosmic catastrophe and that somehow sparks of the divine have become entrapped in this material world and need to escape, and they can escape when they acquire true knowledge of their situation. And the Gnostic system provides them with the knowledge they need for escape, so salvation comes by getting the true knowledge necessary for salvation.

Where the Gnostics come from intellectually is difficult to determine. They appear to represent a kind of amalgam of a variety of different religions, including Judaism and Christianity and Greek philosophy, especially Platonic philosophy, and they appear to have taken elements of these various religions and philosophies and combined them together into a major religious system. We know that there was a full-blown Gnostic system in the second century, probably early- to mid-second century, which is right around the time of Marcion. It's hard to know if Gnosticism began in Alexandria or if it began in Palestine, or where exactly, but we have evidence of Gnostics in Syria and Egypt. Eventually they make their way to Rome.

So what finished the Gnostics and these other sects? Did they just die out?

Although there were a variety of historical and cultural reasons, most of these groups probably died out because they were attacked—successfully attacked, on theological grounds—and they weren't nearly as effective in their own propaganda campaigns. They failed to recruit new converts even while the orthodox groups created a strong structure, used letter campaigns and other means to propagate their views, and their rhetoric convinced people.

But what really secured the victory was that the Roman emperor Constantine converted to Christianity Naturally, he converted to the kind of Christianity that was dominant at that time. Once Constantine converts to an orthodox form of Christianity, and once the state has power, and the state is Christian, then the state starts asserting its influence over Christianity. So by the end of the fourth century, there's actually legislation against heretics. So the empire that used to be completely anti-Christian becomes Christian, and not just becomes Christian, but also tries to dictate what shape Christianity ought to be.

The ramifications of this change of events are enormous, of course. It changed the entire way the Western world understands itself, and how people understand something. Think of the concept of guilt alone: if some other groups had won, things might have been completely different.

So did the debates stop once the church had unified itself at the Council of Nicea?

The debates didn't end, but shifted. By the time you get to the Council of Nicea, you just don't have large groups of Gnostics anymore, or Marcionites, or Ebionites. They're old history now. But it didn't stop the debates. They just became more refined, and more heated. As an example, the Council of Nicea was about a form of Christianity called Arianism, which by second- or third-century standards was completely orthodox. By the time you get to the fourth century, however, and the theologians have refined their beliefs, Arianism becomes a major heresy. These Arians believed Jesus must have been subservient to the Father; after all, he prays to the Father and does the Father's will. Therefore, he's a subordinate deity. But the

Arians were defeated by the Christians who maintained that Christ is not a subordinate deity, but that he's been divine from eternity past, that he's always existed in relationship to God. And so Christ isn't a divine being who comes into existence—he's always been divine, and of the same substance as God the Father himself.

The shifts in theology weren't as important as another shift that took place when Constantine became a Christian. Now he, an authoritarian political leader, could decide what kind of Christianity was acceptable and what kind wasn't. Suddenly everything related to the Church became a *political* issue as well as a religious one. Some people think that Constantine converted to Christianity precisely because he thought that the Christian church might be able to help unify the empire because unlike paganism, which worshipped lots of different gods in lots of different ways, Christianity insisted on one god, and one way. That is why Constantine may have called the Council of Nicea—if the church was going to play the role of unifying the empire, the church itself must be unified. That is the when, why, and how it became a political issue.

Heretics, Women, Magicians, and Mystics
The Fight to Become the One True Faith

The earliest history of Christianity was oral, rather than written, passed first from apostle to disciple, from person to person, from generation to generation and, in some cases, from one language to another. There were no churches or formal meeting places and the Word could travel only by letters and itinerant believers. There was no one church. There was no church hierarchy. Small groups, in out of the way places, believed to varying degrees in numerous variations of the message delivered by the apostles and disciples of Jesus—or in one of the hundreds of variations of the admixture of paganism, ancient belief systems, and the new teachings.

The lack of consistent doctrine to which all believers could adhere suited many, but not all. Soon the minority got organized. They formed groups, instituted hierarchies, and actively passed the Word along to "nonbelievers" through apostles. By the late part of the first century C.E., there were already those proclaiming that they knew what was right and that everything else was not only wrong, but dangerous and in urgent need of extinction. The Crusades and Inquisition were presaged by these early efforts to rid the church of heresies.

Heresies, loosely speaking, are those views that disagree with the official doctrinal version. One man's fervent belief is another man's heresy, and so it was for Irenaeus, Tertullian, and Eusebius, three of the early ecclesiasts who helped to define what was Christian and to eliminate what was not. Which made it a short leap of faith, through a millennium, to the abyss of the *Malleus Maleficarum*—the book, as Dan Brown puts it, that "indoctrinated the world to 'the dangers of free-thinking women' and instructed the clergy how to locate, torture, and destroy them."

In pursuit of piety, the early writers, as well as those of the *Malleus*, agreed to incremental degrees that it was women who posed the greatest threat to the church. While some women, such as Jesus' mother and later the martyred St. Perpetua, may have been placed on pedestals, many more were seen as harboring inherently dangerous traits, beliefs, and inclinations to consort with evil. While much of paganism and a great deal of Gnosticism revolved around the balance of forces, male and female, in early Christianity, the role of women was very different, more ambivalent, as will be shown in the excerpts below.

The us-versus-them mentality may have gotten its first formal religious underpinnings in the writings of Irenaeus. Irenaeus was a second-century theologian and polemicist who campaigned vociferously against "false knowledge" and, in his *Against Heresies*, written in 187, he helped to produce the first systematic exposition of Catholic Christianity's belief system—creed, canon, and apostolic succession.

Tertullian, an early church father whose life overlapped with Irenaeus's, took the sacredness of the Gospels one step further, declaring that the Gospels were divinely inspired, contained *all* truth and provided that from which the church "drinks her faith." He was even more vociferous against the Gnostics than Irenaeus.

Eusebius (d. 357[?]) systemized this and other knowledge into a great compendium known as the *History of the Church*. He later became so famous and respected that he was called upon to become a leading participant in the Council of Nicea (325). The "confession" he proposed became the basis for the Nicene Creed.

Despite these early attempts at unification and elimination, heresies continued to arise, particularly in the Middle Ages and early Renaissance when, in 1487, the *Malleus Maleficarum* was first published—the summa of us-versus-them. While lumping these three ecclesiasts together greatly oversimplifies the history of a church attempting to achieve unrivaled power and influence through both theological and political means, the selections from their writings that follow demonstrate how the level of discipline and vigilance escalated as the threats to the True Faith seemed to grow ever greater. The prose in the excerpts may seem a difficult hurdle for the modern reader, but they represent the highest learning of the time and a way to truly get "in the heads" of some of the earliest Christians.*

Irenaeus

Irenaeus's magnum opus, *Against Heresies*, achieved such wide circulation and influence that some scholars hold him single-handedly responsible—for good or for ill, depending upon one's belief system—for removing Gnosticism as a serious theological threat to the primacy of Catholic Christianity.

In his book he first warns his readers about the evils that lurk in the hearts of mankind:

> In as much as certain men have set the truth aside, and bring in lying words and vain genealogies, which, as the apostle says, "minister questions rather than godly edifying which is in faith," and by means of their craftily-constructed plausibilities draw away the minds of the inexperienced and take them captive, I have felt constrained, my dear friend, to compose the following treatise in order to expose and counteract their machinations. These men falsify the oracles of God, and prove themselves evil interpreters of the good word of revelation. They also overthrow the faith of many, by drawing them away, under a pretence of [superior] knowledge ... By means of specious and plausible words, they cunningly allure the simple-minded to inquire into their system; but they nevertheless clumsily destroy them, while they initiate them into their blasphemous and impious opinions. (*Against Heresies*, Preface)

*A number of these texts are widely available via the Internet.

He then takes on those who, by their "craftily constructed plausibilities," lead them to believe in the word and not the written documents, thereby willfully committing blaspheme.

> When ... they are confuted from the Scriptures, they turn round and accuse these same Scriptures, as if they were not correct, nor of authority, and [assert] that they are ambiguous, and that the truth cannot be extracted from them by those who are ignorant of tradition. For [they allege] that the truth was not delivered by means of written documents, but by the word. And this wisdom each one of them alleges to be the fiction of his own inventing, forsooth; so that, according to their idea, the truth properly resides at one time in Valentinus, at another in Marcion, at another in Cerinthus, then afterwards in Basilides, or has even been indifferently in any other opponent, who could speak nothing pertaining to salvation. For every one of these men, being altogether of a perverse disposition, depraving the system of truth, is not ashamed to preach himself. ... Such are the adversaries with whom we have to deal ... endeavoring like slippery serpents to escape at all points. (*Against Heresies*, 3:2)

The solution, unsurprisingly, was for Christians to unify under one faith, one God, and one set of apostles:

> The Church, though dispersed throughout the whole world, even to the ends of the earth, has received from the apostles and their disciples this faith: [She believes] in one God, the Father Almighty, Maker of heaven, and earth, and the sea, and all things that are in them; and in one Christ Jesus, the Son of God, who became incarnate for our salvation; and in the Holy Spirit, who proclaimed through the prophets the dispensations of

God, and the advents, and the birth from a virgin, and the passion, and the resurrection from the dead, and the ascension into heaven in the flesh of the beloved Christ Jesus, our Lord, and His [future] manifestation from heaven in the glory of the Father "to gather all things in one." ... (*Against Heresies*, 1:10)

Tertullian

Tertullian, like Irenaeus, was one of the early church fathers who attacked the Gnostics and is singled out by some (see the excerpts from Freke and Gandy that start this chapter) as one of the chief perpetrators of the church's attempt to cover up the existence of a robust counter-tradition. The Gnostics were in many ways the most troubling, for Gnosticism incorporated some distinctly pre-Christian (not to mention pagan) ideas *and* its very name referred to the concept of secret knowledge.

Women carried an even greater burden of sin. "The sentence of God on this sex of yours lives in the age," Tertullian insisted. "The guilt must of necessity live too. Your are the devil's gateway." But he still isn't through. "And it should be noted that there was a defect in the formation of the first woman, since she was formed from a bent rib, that is, a rib of the breast, which is bent as it were in a contrary direction to a man. And since through this defect she is an imperfect animal, she always deceives."

Tertullian was born in Africa (circa A.D. 150–60), the son of a Roman soldier. He wrote three books in Greek and practiced jurisprudence. He was considered a pagan until middle life, "sharing pagan prejudices" and "indulging like others in shameful pleasures," according to the *Catholic Encyclopedia*. Tertullian converted to Christianity in 197, and, to quote the *Catholic Encyclopedia* again, "embraced the Faith with all the ardor of his impetuous nature." A decade later, however, he broke with the Catholic Church and became a leader and passionate advocate of Montanism, which claimed that new revelations were coming via Montius and two women prophets. Nevertheless, Tertullian continued fighting heresy, as he saw it.

As a Christian, he believed that we would know God only through practicing strict discipline and austerity. The force threatening to subvert that impulse in man was woman, who, Tertullian wrote, brought sin into the world. "Do you not know," Tertullian asks rhetorically, "that you are each an Eve?"

> The sentence of God on this sex of yours lives in this age: the guilt must of necessity live too.... You are the un-sealer of that (forbidden) tree: you are the first deserter of the divine law: you are she who persuaded him whom the devil was not valiant enough to attack. You destroyed so easily God's image, man. On account of your desert—that is, death—even the Son of God had to die. And do you think about adorning yourself over and above your tunics of skins? ... (*On the Apparel of Women*, Book I)

Heretics, he believed, were put on earth to test man's Faith. These heresies came about for two reasons. The first was the temptation offered by philosophers, like Plato, who simply want to engage in endless questions rather than simply accept the Word:

> These are "the doctrines" of men and "of demons" produced for itching ears of the spirit of this world's wisdom: this the Lord called "foolishness," and "chose the foolish things of the world" to confound even philosophy itself. For [philosophy] it is which is the material of the world's wisdom, the rash interpreter of the nature

and the dispensation of God. Indeed heresies are themselves instigated by philosophy ... The same subjectmatter is discussed over and over again by the heretics and the philosophers; the same arguments are involved. Whence comes evil? Why is it permitted? What is the origin of man? And in what way does he come? ... Whence comes God? ... [They have a] human wisdom which pretends to know the truth, whilst it only corrupts it, and is itself divided into its own manifold heresies, by the variety of its mutually repugnant sects.

Away with all attempts to produce a mottled Christianity of Stoic, Platonic, and dialectic composition! We want no curious disputation after possessing Christ Jesus, no inquisition after enjoying the gospel! With our faith, we desire no further belief. For this is our palmary faith, that there is nothing which we ought to believe besides. (*The Prescription Against Heretics*, Chapter 7)

Therefore rein in your curiosity, lest you end up like the heretics who are "perverters of Christ's teaching." And, especially, rein in your curiosities about their behavior because it is sinful indeed—especially those women:

I must not omit an account of the conduct also of the heretics—how frivolous it is, how worldly, how merely human, without seriousness, without authority, without discipline, as suits their creed. ... The very women of these heretics, how wanton they are! For they are bold enough to teach, to dispute, to enact exorcisms, to undertake cures—it may be even to baptize. Their ordinations, are carelessly administered, capricious, changeable. At one time they put novices in office; at another time, men who are bound to some secular employment; at another, persons who have apostatized from us, to bind them by vainglory, since they cannot by the truth. (*The Prescription Against Heretics,* Chapter 41)

Eusebius

Eusebius was a bishop of Caesarea in Palestine (where he met Constantine while rewriting the Bible) and is often referred to as the father of church history because of his meticulous recording of the evolution of the Gospels, the role of the apostles, and the heresies to be faced in the early Christian church. He is also supposed to have found in the records of Edessa the letters purporting to be written back and forth by its king Abgar and Jesus Christ.

For Eusebius, doctrine should be inseparable from daily life; the key to faith, therefore, was in knowing which scriptures should be adopted.

To be able to do that required knowing which of the "divine scriptures" were acceptable and which were not. Eusebius set out the many Gospels and other books, which he felt, were valid scripture; this list, with slight variations, was later canonized and became the Bible.

Eusebius also set about to catalogue the heresies of the Gnostics more thoroughly than had been done before and, at the same time, cheered on the growth in power and magnitude of the Catholic Church:

> [There was] another heresy, called the heresy of the Gnostics, who did not wish to transmit any longer the magic arts of Simon in secret, but openly. For they boasted—as of something great—of love potions that were carefully prepared by them, and of certain demons that sent them dreams and lent them their protection, and of other similar agencies; and in accordance with . . . their abominations, to practice all the worst kinds of

wickedness, on the ground that they could escape the cosmic powers, as they called them, in no other way than by discharging their obligations to them all by infamous-conduct.... One new heresy arose after another, and the former ones always passed away, and now at one time, now at another, now in one way, now in other ways, were lost in ideas of various kinds and various forms. But the splendor of the catholic and only true Church, which is always the same, grew in magnitude and power, and reflected its piety and simplicity and freedom, and the modesty and purity of its inspired life and philosophy to every nation both of Greeks and of Barbarians. (*The History of the Church*, 3:25)

Malleus Maleficarum

In years and in location, there is a great separation between the writings of Eusebius and those found in the *Malleus Maleficarum (The Witch's Hammer)*, written by Heinrich Kramer and James Spenger, two monks, in Germany in 1486. Yet theologically, scholars make a case; they have a connection. The argument is that it does not require a great leap to go from intolerance, condemnation, and forced exile to systematic elimination.

Heresies were always springing up, especially in medieval and early Renaissance eras, and as their expression grew ever more powerful, so did the response. Still, even if modern sensibilities might be surprised, even shocked, at the writings of the early church fathers, they are likely to be horrified at the meticulous cataloguing of crimes and punishments of witches to be found in the *Malleus Maleficarum*.

The *Witch's Hammer* was perhaps even more known in its time than *The Da Vinci Code* is in ours (at least proportionately speaking), and on the "bestseller" list far longer. And it was not nearly so benign. The book quickly proliferated into many editions, spreading throughout Europe and England. The impact of the work—used over time by both Catholics and Protestants—was felt in witch trials on the Continent for almost two hundred years. In colonial America it was used as a foundation for the Salem witch trials.

The work is divided into three sections. The first sets out to prove that witchcraft or sorcery existed (and that women were more prone to this lure of Satan than men). The second describes the forms of witchcraft (from the destruction of crops to whether demons could father children from a witch), while the third provides a detailed "how to" of detection, trial, and punishment.

That women were more prone to be witches was certain and, according to the *Malleus Maleficarum*, the reason was clear: "As to why a greater number of witches is found in the fragile feminine sex than among men; it is indeed a fact that it were idle to contradict, since it is accredited by actual experience, apart from the verbal testimony of credibly witnesses."

This view of women as inherently flawed permeates the *Malleus*. Further on it says,

> Others again have propounded other reasons why there are more superstitious women found than men. And the first is, that they are more credulous; and since the chief aim of the devil is to corrupt faith, therefore he rather attacks them. . . . The second reason is that women are naturally more impressionable, and more ready to receive the influence of a disembodied spirit; and that when they use this quality well they are very good, but when they use it ill they are very evil. . . . The third reason is that they have slippery tongues, and are unable to conceal from the fellow-women those things which by evil arts they know; and, since they are weak, they find an

> easy and secret manner of vindicating themselves by witchcraft. . . . (Part I, Question 6)

There *are* good women, of course. The *Malleus* instructs, that "for good women there is so much praise, that we read that they have brought beatitude to men, and have saved nations, lands, and cities; as is clear in the case of Judith, Debbora, and Esther." Christian theology, it seems clear, is filled with the good-bad, good-evil, virgin-whore dichotomy.

Like Tertullian long before, the *Malleus* advocates the notion that it all started to go awry with Eve: "Therefore a wicked woman is by her nature quicker to waver in her faith, and consequently quicker to abjure the faith, which is the root of witchcraft."

The final section of the *Malleus Malleficarum* deals with the way a case can come to trial, the procedure by which the trial is to be carried out (public rumor is enough to bring someone to trial and a vigorous defense means guilt; hot pokers and other tortures can be used to elicit confessions), and, in sixteen chapters, the differing levels of guilt and requisite punishment.

Accusation was easy:

> The first question, then, is what is the suitable method of instituting a process on behalf of the faith against witches. In answer to this it must be said that there are three methods allowed by Canon Law. The first is when someone accuses a person before a judge of the crime of heresy, or of protecting heretics, offering to prove it, and to submit himself to the penalty of talion if he fails to prove it. The second method is when someone denounces a person, but does not offer to prove it and is not willing to embroil himself in the matter; but says that he lays information out of zeal for the faith, or because of a sentence of excommunication inflicted by

the Ordinary or his Vicar; or because of the temporal punishment exacted by the secular Judge upon those who fail to lay information.

The third method involves an inquisition, that is, when there is no accuser or informer, but a general report that there are witches in some town or place; and then the Judge must proceed, not at the instance of any party, but simply by the virtue of his office.... (Part 3, Question I)

Which is not to say there weren't some standards. The rules were that a witch could only be executed if she confessed, "for common justice demands that a witch should not be condemned to death unless she is convicted by her own confession."

Of course, they didn't always confess readily.

And here, because of the great trouble caused by the stubborn silence of witches, there are several points which the Judge must notice. . . . The first is that he must not be too quick to subject a witch to examination, but must pay attention to certain signs which will follow. And he must not be too quick for this reason: unless God, through a holy Angel, compels the devil to withhold his help from the witch, she will be so insensible to the pains of torture that she will sooner be torn limb from limb than confess any of the truth.

But the torture is not to be neglected for this reason, for they are not all equally endowed with this power, and also the devil sometimes of his own will permits them to confess their crimes without being compelled by a holy Angel."

And in the end, it may all come down to tears, for if the Judge, wishes to find out whether she is endowed with a witch's power of preserving silence, let him take note whether she is able to shed tears when standing in his presence, or when being tortured. For we are taught both by the words of worthy men of old and by our own experience that this is a most certain sign, and it has been found that even if she be urged and exhorted by solemn conjurations to shed tears, if she be a witch she will not be able to weep: although she will assume a tearful aspect and smear her cheeks and eyes with spittle to make it appear that she is weeping; wherefore she must be closely watched by the attendants.

In passing sentence the Judge or priest may use some such method as the following in conjuring her to true tears if she be innocent, or in restraining false tears. Let him place his hand on the head of the accused and say: I conjure you by the bitter tears shed on the Cross by our Saviour the Lord Jesus Christ for the salvation of the world, and by the burning tears poured in the evening hour over His wounds by the most glorious Virgin Mary, His Mother, and by all the tears which have been shed here in this world by the Saints and Elect of God, from whose eyes He has now wiped away all tears, that if you be innocent you do now shed tears, but if you be guilty that you shall by no means do so. In the name of the Father, and of the Son, and of the Holy Ghost, Amen. (Part 3, Question 13)

Witches were dangerous, and judges "must not allow themselves to be touched physically by the witch, especially in any contact of their bare arms or hands." Judges, the *Malleus Maleficarum* advises,

must always carry about them some salt consecrated on Palm Sunday and some Blessed Herbs. For these can be enclosed together in Blessed Wax and worn round the neck, as we showed in the Second Part when we discussed the remedies against illnesses and diseases caused by witchcraft; and that these have a wonderful protective virtue is known not only from the testimony of witches, but from the use and practice of the Church, which exorcizes and blesses such objects for this very purpose, as is shown in the ceremony of exorcism when it is said, For the banishing of all the power of the devil, etc.

But let it not be thought that physical contact of the joints or limbs is the only thing to be guarded against; for sometimes, with God's permission, they are able with the help of the devil to bewitch the Judge by the mere sound of the words which they utter, especially at the time when they are exposed to torture. (Part 3, Question 15)

Finally, the *Malleus Maleficarum* cautions that accused witches must be handled with care when brought before the judge.

And if it can conveniently be done, the witch should be led backward into the presence of the Judge and his assessors. . . . the hair should be shaved from every part of her body. The reason for this is the same as that for stripping her of her clothes, which we have already mentioned; for in order to preserve their power of silence they are in the habit of hiding some superstitious object in their clothes or in their hair, or even in the most secret parts of their bodies which must not be named. (Part 3, Question 15)

In *The Da Vinci Code*, Robert Langdon recalls the *Malleus Maleficarum* while standing in the Salles des Etats of the Louvre and staring at the *Mona Lisa*. He thinks of the *Malleus* as "arguably . . . the most blood-soaked publication in human history." Dan Brown places the number of victims at five million; others have placed the death toll from the Inquisition worldwide at between six hundred thousand and nine million. Nearly all, scholars tell us, were women, old, young, midwives, Jews, poets, and gypsies—anyone who didn't fit the contemporary view of what it took to be a pious Christian.

Why Were the Gnostics Seen as Such a Threat?

By Lance S. Owens

Lance S. Owens is both a physician in clinical practice and an ordained priest. He also maintains the website www.gnosis.org. This excerpt is from an essay he wrote for the site. Copyright © 2004 by Lance S. Owens. Reprinted by permission of The Gnostic Archive, www.gnosis.org.

What made Gnostics such dangerous heretics? The complexities of Gnosticism are legion, making any generalizations wisely suspect. While several systems for defining and categorizing Gnosticism have been proposed over the years, none has universal acceptance. Nevertheless, four elements are generally agreed upon as general characteristics of Gnostic thought.

The first essential characteristic is Gnosticism asserts that "direct, personal, and absolute knowledge of the authentic truths of existence is accessible to human beings," and the attainment of such knowledge is the supreme achievement of human life. Gnosis is not a rational, propositional, logical understanding, but a knowing acquired by experience. The Gnostics were not much interested in dogma or coherent, rational theology—a fact that makes the study of Gnosticism particularly difficult for individuals with "bookkeeper mentalities." One simply cannot cipher up Gnosticism into syllogistic dogmatic affirmations. The Gnostics cherished the ongoing force of divine revelation—Gnosis was the creative experience of revelation, a rushing progression of understanding, and not a static creed. . . .

In his study, *The American Religion*, noted literary critic Harold Bloom suggests a second characteristic of Gnosticism that might help us conceptually circumscribe its mysterious heart. Gnosticism, says Bloom, "is a knowing, by and of an uncreated self, or self-within-the self, and [this] knowledge leads to freedom. . . ." Primary among all the revelatory perceptions a Gnostic might reach was the profound awakening that came with knowledge that something within him was uncreated. The Gnostics called this "uncreated self" the divine seed, the pearl, the spark of knowing: consciousness, intelligence, light. And this seed of intellect was the self-same substance of God. It was man's authentic reality, the glory of humankind and divinity alike. . . . By all rational perception, man clearly was not God, and yet in essential truth, was Godly. This conundrum was a Gnostic mystery, and its knowing was their treasure. . . .

This brings us to the third prominent element in our brief summary of Gnosticism: its reverence for texts and scriptures unaccepted by the orthodox fold. Gnostic experience was mythopoetic: in story and metaphor, and perhaps also in ritual enactments, Gnosticism sought expression of subtle, visionary insights inexpressible by rational proposition or dogmatic affirmation. For the Gnostics, revelation was the nature of Gnosis. Irritated by their profusion of "inspired texts" and myths, Irenaeus complains in his classic second-century refutation of Gnosticism that "every one of them generates something new, day by day, according to his ability; for no one is deemed perfect, who does not develop ... some mighty fiction."

The fourth characteristic ... is the most difficult of the four to succinctly untangle, and also one of the most disturbing to subsequent orthodox theology. This is the image of God as a dyad, or duality. While affirming the ultimate unity and integrity of the Divine, Gnosticism noted in its experiential encounter with the numinous, contrasting manifestations and qualities. In many of the Nag Hammadi Gnostic texts God is imaged as a dyad of masculine and feminine elements. ... Several trends within Gnosticism saw in God a union of two disparate natures, a union well imaged with sexual symbolism. Gnostics honored the feminine nature and, in reflection, Elaine Pagels has argued that Christian Gnostic women enjoyed a far greater degree of social and ecclesiastical equality than their orthodox sisters. Jesus himself, taught some Gnostics, had prefigured this mystic relationship: His most beloved disciple had been a woman, Mary Magdalene, his consort. ...

Christ came to rectify the separation ... and join the two components; and to give life unto those who had died by separation and join them together. ... We are left with our poetic imaginations to consider what this might mean. Though Orthodox polemicists frequently accused Gnostics of unorthodox sexual behavior, exactly how these ideas and images played out in human affairs remains historically uncertain. ...

Breaking The Da Vinci Code

So the Divine Jesus and Infallible Word Emerged Out of a Fourth-Century Power-Play? Get Real.

BY COLLIN HANSEN

Dan Brown's *The Da Vinci Code* has achieved coveted bestsellerdom, inspiring an ABC News special along the way, along with debates about the legitimacy of Western and Christian history.

While the ABC News feature focused on Brown's fascination with an alleged marriage between Jesus and Mary Magdalene, *The Da Vinci Code* contains many more (equally dubious) claims about Christianity's historic origins and theological development. The central claim Brown's novel makes about Christianity is that "almost everything our fathers taught us about Christ is false." Why? Because of a single meeting of bishops in 325, at the city of Nicea in modern-day Turkey. There, argues Brown, church leaders who wanted to consolidate their power base (he calls this, anachronistically, "the Vatican" or "the Roman Catholic church") created a divine Christ and an infallible Scripture—both of them novelties that had never before existed among Christians.

Brown is right that in the course of Christian history, few events loom larger than the Council of Nicea in 325. When the newly converted Roman emperor Constantine called bishops from around the world to present-day Turkey, the church had reached a theological crossroads. Led by an Alexandrian theologian named Arius, one school of thought argued that

Jesus had undoubtedly been a remarkable leader, but he was not God in flesh. In *The Da Vinci Code*, Brown apparently adopts Arius as his representative for all pre-Nicene Christianity. Referring to the Council of Nicea, Brown claims that "until that moment in history, Jesus was viewed by His followers as a mortal prophet—a great and powerful man, but a man nonetheless."

In reality, early Christians overwhelmingly worshipped Jesus Christ as their risen Savior and Lord. For example, Christians adopted the Greek word *kyrios*, meaning "divine," and applied it to Jesus from the earliest days of the church.

The Council of Nicea did not entirely end the controversy over Arius's teachings, nor did the gathering impose a foreign doctrine of Christ's divinity on the church. The participating bishops merely affirmed the historic and standard Christian beliefs, erecting a united front against future efforts to dilute Christ's gift of salvation.

With the Bible playing a central role in Christianity, the question of Scripture's historic validity bears tremendous implications. Brown claims that Constantine commissioned and bankrolled a staff to manipulate existing texts and thereby divinize the human Christ. Yet for a number of reasons, Brown's speculations fall flat. Brown correctly points out that "the Bible did not arrive by fax from heaven." Indeed, the Bible's composition and consolidation may appear a bit too human for the comfort of some Christians. But Brown overlooks the fact that the human process of canonization had progressed for centuries before Nicea, resulting in a nearly complete canon of Scripture before Nicea or even Constantine's legalization of Christianity in 313.

Ironically, the process of collecting and consolidating Scripture was launched when a rival sect produced its own quasi-biblical canon. Around 140 a Gnostic leader named Marcion began spreading a theory that the New and Old Testaments didn't share the same God. Marcion argued that the Old Testament's God represented law and wrath while the New Testament's God, represented by Christ, exemplified love. As a result Marcion rejected the Old Testament and the most overtly Jewish New Testament writings, including Matthew, Mark, Acts, and Hebrews. He manipulated other books to downplay their Jewish tendencies. Though in 144 the church in Rome declared his views heretical, Marcion's teaching sparked a new cult. Challenged by Marcion's threat, church leaders began to consider earnestly their own views on a definitive list of Scriptural books including both the Old and New Testaments.

By the time of Nicea, church leaders debated the legitimacy of only a few books that we accept today, chief among them Hebrews and Revelation, because their authorship remained in doubt. In fact, authorship was the most important consideration for those who worked to solidify the canon. Early church leaders considered letters and eyewitness accounts authoritative and binding only if they were written by an apostle or close disciple of an apostle. This way they could be assured of the documents' reliability. As pastors and preachers, they also observed which books did in fact build up the church—a good sign, they felt, that such books were inspired Scripture. The results speak for themselves: the books of today's Bible have allowed Christianity to spread, flourish, and endure worldwide.

6 Secret Societies

The secret things belong to the Lord,
the things revealed are ours and our children's forever ...

—DEUTERONOMY 29:29

Like a good spy thriller, the plot of *The Da Vinci Code* moves from one stunning secret to another, from one coded message to the next, from an ancient conspiracy to a modern one, exploring all the while some of the most fundamental secrets of the archaic past of human culture and even archaic areas of the brain itself where primal myths and Jungian archetypes cavort and secret fears, compulsions, and ancient traumas reside.

Dan Brown has said that Robert Ludlum is among his favorite writers, and you can see in *The Da Vinci Code* a touch of vintage Ludlum: start with incredibly compelling and powerful secrets, throw an ordinary man (and a beautiful woman) into fast-paced, high-stakes action to figure out these secrets against the ticking clock of a threat to civilization, confront the characters with deep, dark, powerful secret societies no one thought still existed, bend their minds around conspiracies so intricate the reader can't ever really diagram the plot, and wrap it all into action fast-paced enough to make the reader forget the cardboard characters and the plot holes.

The role of secret societies in such plots—whether Ludlum, Le Carré, J. K. Rowling, J. R. R. Tolkien, or Dan Brown—is not to be understated.

In this chapter, we look especially at three secret societies at work in the action of *The Da Vinci Code*: the Knights Templar, the Priory of Sion, and Opus Dei. Along the way, we consider various other secret rites and practices from modern-day Gnostics celebrating *hieros gamos* rites in twenty-first-century New York, to the plethora of secret societies that grew out of the Templar massacre in the fourteenth century.

As *The Da Vinci Code* points out, everyone loves a good conspiracy. Everyone finds it interesting to be let in on a mind-boggling secret. In the case of the three most prominent secret societies in *The Da Vinci Code*—the Templars, the Priory, and Opus Dei—each one is a fascinating world unto itself. The novel compresses the essence of these secret cultures into some easy-to-understand background material. But then it goes on to exaggerate greatly each one's power, influence, and history.

The Templars, for example, may have had some cultlike practices in medieval days that could be construed as sacred sex rites. Mary Magdalene may have figured more prominently in their culture than in contemporaneous Christianity. And they may well have found treasure in Jerusalem and built a nexus of power and influence. But it is extremely doubtful that they cared much for the theory of the sacred feminine or that they believed the Holy Grail had anything to do with Mary Magdalene's womb and the royal bloodline of the offspring she may or may not have had.

The Priory of Sion, while interesting to speculate about, may never have really existed as anything more than a minor political arm of the Templars during their heyday. As for the modern era, the idea of the Priory may be a complete canard in its twentieth-century incarnation. Leonardo da Vinci may well have been involved with secret sects, heretical philosophies, and unusual sexual practices—and his paintings may well have sought to pass on secret knowledge (or at least make insider jokes) to future generations. But it is highly unlikely Leonardo served as a "grand master" of a functioning secret organization, while leaving not a single clue or bit of documentary evidence behind amid the tens of thousands of pages of notebooks he left to posterity. The same could be said about the other alleged grand masters. With all we know about the lives of Victor Hugo and Jean Cocteau, Newton and Debussy, don't you think there would be a scrap of corroborating evidence somewhere? And for an organization that is supposed to hold the sacred feminine in such high esteem (at least according to the novel), how come there are no prominent women on the list?

Opus Dei is certainly wealthy, powerful, and secretive. It may well be pledged to a religious philosophy and even a set of political goals that many find anathema. It may have a very interesting history of unexplained involvements with the CIA, the Vatican's finances, and right-wing death squads in Latin America's civil wars. But it is not dispatching albino monks to the streets of Paris to murder people over ancient religious secrets.

That is not to deny the concerns and fears some people may have about this or any other secretive group or conspiracy. Just the opposite is true: Dan Brown, like many novelists, exaggerates even to extremes and lets his imagination run wild for the express purpose of creating the right metaphors and the right thought provocations to rise above the clutter in this information and entertainment saturated world. His approach has had demonstrable success. He got our attention for secret societies and esoteric knowledge, which we had heard of, vaguely, but knew little about.

Welcome to the nether world of *The Da Vinci Code's* secret societies.

Recollections of a Gnostic Mass

By John Castro
John Castro is a New York-based writer.

I stand in a florescent-lit hallway, cold and apprehensive.

I'm not wearing any shoes.

A man dressed in black denim has just asked everyone gathered to remove our shoes to show respect for the temple we are about to enter. We comply. When we are finished, he asks us to wait for the ceremony to begin. While I wait, I listen. There are couples, groups of friends, people who seem to have known each other for years, greeting each other. I focus on a few conversations to pass the time.

An attractive young Hispanic woman, probably twenty-one or twenty-two, chatters on her cell phone: ". . . yeah, yeah, yeah. Three times. No, this is my third time. I'll be going min-erval at the next initiation . . ."

A thin, muscular man with greased-back hair and a small goatee walks up the hall and joins the rest of us. He waits for a moment or two, spies a serious young woman with a pentacle medallion on a chain around her neck, and strikes up a conver-sation with her. "Ninety-three," he says.

"Ninety-three," she replies, smiling.

They begin talking to each other in low voices, heads bent.

"Man, I heard that *Jimmy Page* comes when he's in New York," says a heavy-metal enthusiast with a long ponytail, who appears to be in his thirties. His short, stocky friend nods with a weary nonchalance. I stand silently—I'm all alone here—and wait for admittance.

These are my recollections of a ceremony I attended in late 2002. I was an observer, and a surprisingly nervous partic-ipant, in a ritual hosted by the Ordo Templis Orientalis, an organization led for many years by Aleister Crowley. *The* Aleister Crowley—poet, magician, iconoclast, drug addict, and moral scourge of Great Britain, the esoteric magus who referred to himself as the "Great Beast 666."

Reading *The Da Vinci Code*, many of my memories of the event rose to the surface. These memories are almost two years old. I know that I missed details and may have remembered others incorrectly. Yet, like Sophie Neveu, my impressions of what I saw have remained intense and vivid.

The temple is in a small room. The walls are painted black, the room dimly lit by small scoop lamps hanging from the ceiling and dozens of candles at the base of an altar on the right side of the room. It's a large structure with three steps leading up to it and a stone slab carved with hieroglyphs at its summit. A long frame surrounds the altar, supporting an opened curtain.

Across the room from the altar is an oblong box, the height and width of a tall man, with a small curtain covering its front. Spaced at equal distances between the altar and the casket are two black boxes on the floor, each bearing an incense burner, books, and a mixing bowl.

On either side of this aisle are rows of chairs for the congregation. We all enter slowly, awkwardly, about sixty of us in all, noisily placing our shoes, bags, and coats under our chairs.

I'm no longer cold. In fact, I'm beginning to sweat. By the time we're seated, we are packed in, the room filled to capacity, all of us feeling the heat of the candles and our fellow congregants. I am surprised by the number and variety of the worshippers—all ages, many different ethnicities, in fashions ranging from well-dressed yuppie to Dungeons and Dragons archetype.

A thin bearded man in a loose white robe stands facing the altar. He crosses himself at the forehead, chest, and shoulders; with each touch he speaks a word of what sounds like Hebrew.

He throws his arms forward, places his hands together, and begins slowly circumambulating the room with long steps. He breathes heavily, his face pinched, concentrating, staring past the walls of the temple. At four points in the room, he stops and intones a word or phrase—I can't guess what the language is—and dramatically draws the shape of a pentagram in the air.

When all four points have been inscribed with a pentagram, he faces the altar again. He recites the names of angels: Gabriel, Michael, Rafael, and Uriel ... He crosses himself once more, turns to face the congregants, and spreads his arms wide, taking a deep breath. He holds it in, releases it slowly, then relaxes and smiles. Music, provided by a sitar player, winds its way through the dark air.

The bearded man in the white robe intones: "Do What Thou Wilt shall be the whole of the law."

The congregants respond: "Love is the Law, Love under Will."

The man recites what reminds me of a familiar element of the Catholic Mass—a list of beliefs reminiscent of the Nicene Creed. In the middle of the creed is a line that gives me chills, although I don't know why:

> "And I believe in the Serpent and the Lion, Mystery of Mystery, in His name BAPHOMET."

A woman dressed in blue and white slowly weaves her way down the aisle, eyes focused on the floor, followed by a man in black robes and a woman in white. She carries a sheathed sword at her side. She is a plump, attractive woman in her forties with dark red-brown hair. She stands before the oblong box and parts the curtain with her sword.

A stout young man steps out of the box, dressed in a white robe, bearing a long lance in front of him.

The woman sprinkles him with water that's been handed to her by one of her attendants. She then takes an incense burner on a chain and crosses it over him. They speak the whole time, the man with the lance proclaiming that he is not worthy to administer the rites, the woman enjoining him in a whispery voice to be pure in body and soul. She runs her open hands over his body, not touching him, then stands and drapes him in a red robe and places a crown on his head. He leans the lance forward, staring across at the altar.

She kneels and runs her hands up and down the shaft of the lance about a dozen times with open palms. Her air is reverent, quiet. "The Lord is among us!" She exclaims.

The congregation is now kneeling on the floor, arms in the air, hands clasped with the hands of our neighbors. A young woman with long blond hair is on my right and a balding African-American man with a salt-and-pepper beard to my left. All of the other congregants are in the same position, clasping hands. My arms begin to ache. I wonder if others are thinking of the intense pain in their arms and the ache in their backs. I long for sympathy, but find none—most of the congregants are staring at the altar or have their eyes closed in quiet worship. I try, surreptitiously, to lean against my chair, but it is fruitless; my neighbors will not sway. I try to focus on the altar instead.

The man with the lance is on the first step leading to the altar. The curtain is closed; a moment before the woman with the sword was sitting on the altar, but now she is hidden.

The man with the lance is speaking poetry to the woman behind the curtain; and after a moment, the woman responds in kind from behind the veil.

I can't focus. I'm starting to sweat, and the only thing I can think about besides the fire in my arms and back is that the perspiration from my arm, pressed against the arm of the woman to my right, is starting to dribble down her arm as well.

There's a naked woman on the altar.

We're standing again, staring up at her. The man with the lance has just parted the curtain, and there's the woman with the sword—stark naked, seated on the altar, facing us, with her legs hanging off the side. I try to take in the whole scene, but I keep averting my eyes.

A tiny voice in my head—the remnant of my Catholicism, made up of communion and confession and CCD classes every Wednesday after school—is starting to become louder, more insistent: *There's a naked woman on the altar. What the hell are you doing here?*

The man presents his lance to her. She takes it, kisses it perhaps a dozen times, and then presses it between her breasts. The man falls to his knees before her, throws his arms on the altar along the sides of her legs. Bent in adoration, he begins slowly kissing her knees and thighs.

When I was younger, I was terrified of botching communion. Which hand over which? What were the words I needed to say to the priest? I almost do it again tonight.

The congregants are filing through the rows of chairs and walking up the central aisle to the altar, where they receive the host from the naked priestess. They walk solemnly, slowly, with their arms crossed over their chests. I follow suit.

When I finally reach the altar, I focus on the naked woman's eyes; I don't want to embarrass her by staring. It doesn't matter. It's more my problem than hers, and I almost trip up the steps to the altar. Her eyes lock beatifically on mine, with a sweet look of utterly sincere welcome and comfort. It doesn't really feel like she's looking at me, which makes me feel better somehow. I take the host: sweet, chewy bread about the size of a quarter, and before I eat it, I say the same words that the other congregants have intoned, one by one:

"There is no part of me that is not of the gods."

The last part of the Mass that I remember is a poem, chanted by the congregation. It was written by Crowley, and I only remember a few lines:

MEN: Glory to Thee from Gilded Tomb!
WOMEN: Glory to Thee from Waiting Womb!
MEN: Glory to Thee from earth unploughed!
WOMEN: Glory to Thee from virgin vowed!

It was actually quite moving. The congregants knew it by heart; the semichoral effect was entrancing.

Now I am reflecting in retrospect on the connections to *The Da Vinci Code*.

There were obvious connections of subject matter: the mention of Baphomet; a link to the Knights Templar; ceremonial rituals echoing orthodox practices; deeper hints of a synthesis of many older Egyptian, Hebrew, and Greek traditions; echoes of Freemasonry and Rosicrucianism. Finally and most important, there was a willingness to place a woman at the center of the ceremony, and obvious, frank references to sexuality in the symbology of the event.

The Ordo Templis Orientalis is a secret society (although you can find a Web presence for it, including full texts of the Gnostic Mass). Like so many of the occult or esoteric societies that are mentioned in *The Da Vinci Code*, you have to be on the inside to really understand. While the trappings of the Mass might be related to the subjects in the book, I recognize that the "true" meaning of the Mass—the significance for the members themselves—is not for me to know. And it would never be, unless I joined and became a silent participant myself.

What I do know is that what I saw was a celebration of genuine belief and devotion from the congregation. When I recall my reaction to the event, I wonder: what unsettled reactions, what nervous bouts of laughter or discomfort did the first Christians inspire in Rome? And is this not always the way with every new god?

The Templar Revelation

BY LYNN PICKNETT AND CLIVE PRINCE

Lynn Picknett and Clive Prince are London-based writers, researchers, and lecturers on the paranormal, the occult, and historical and religious mysteries. Their book, *The Templar Revelation*, from which the following passage is excerpted, is one of the key books in *The Da Vinci Code's* bibliography and the original source of a number of the novel's theories about Leonardo, the Templars, and the Priory of Sion. Copyright © 1997 by Lynn Picknett and Clive Prince. Reprinted with the permission of Simon & Schuster Adult Publishing Group from *The Templar Revelation* by Lynn Picknett and Clive Prince.

The names of Leonardo da Vinci and Jean Cocteau appear on the list of the Grand Masters of what claims to be one of Europe's oldest and most influential secret societies—the Prieuré de Sion, the Priory of Sion. Hugely controversial, its very existence has been called into question and therefore any of its alleged activities are frequently the subject of ridicule and their implications ignored. At first we sympathized with this kind of reaction, but our further investigations certainly revealed that the matter was not as simple as that.

The Priory of Sion first came to the attention of the English-speaking world as late as 1982, through the best-selling *The Holy Blood and the Holy Grail* by Michael Baigent, Richard Leigh and Henry Lincoln, although in its homeland of France reports of its existence gradually became public from the early 1960s. It is a quasi-Masonic or chivalric order with certain political ambitions and, it seems, considerable behind-the-scenes power. Having said that, it is notoriously difficult to categorize the Priory, perhaps because there is something essentially chimerical about the whole operation. . . .

The underlying power of the Priory of Sion is at least partly due to the suggestion that its members are, and always have been, guardians of a great secret—one that, if made public, would shake the very foundations of both Church and State. The Priory of Sion, sometimes known as the Order of Sion or the Order of Our Lady of Sion as well as by other subsidiary titles, claims to have been founded in 1099, during the First Crusade—and even then this was just a matter of formalizing a group whose guardianship of this explosive knowledge already went back much further. They claimed to be behind the creation of the Knights Templar—that curious body of medieval soldier-monks of sinister reputation. The Priory and the Templars became, so it is claimed, virtually the same organization, presided over by the same Grand Master until they suffered a schism and went their separate ways in 1188. The Priory continued under the custodianship of a series of Grand Masters, including some of the most illustrious names in history such as Sir Isaac Newton, Sandro Filipepi (known as Botticelli), Robert Fludd, the English occult philosopher—and, of course, Leonardo da Vinci, who, it is alleged, presided over the Priory for the last nine years of his life. Among its more recent leaders were Victor Hugo, Claude Debussy—and the artist, writer, playwright and filmmaker Jean Cocteau. And although they were not Grand Masters, the Priory has, it is claimed, attracted other luminaries over the centuries such as Joan of Arc, Nostradamus (Michel de Notre Dame) and even Pope John XXIII.

Apart from such celebrities, the history of the Priory of Sion allegedly involved some of the greatest royal and aristocratic families of Europe for generation after generation. These include the d'Anjous, the Habsburgs, the Sinclairs and the Montgomeries.

The reported aim of the Priory is to protect the descendants of the old Merovingian dynasty of kings in what is now France—who ruled from the fifth century until the assassination of Dagobert II in the late seventh century. But then, critics claim that the Priory of Sion has only existed since the 1950s and consists of a handful of mythomaniacs with no real power—royalists with unlimited delusions of grandeur.

So on the one hand we have the Priory's own claims for its pedigree and *raison d'être* and on the other the claim of its detractors. . . .

Any mystery connected with the Priory of Sion also involves those warrior-monks [the Templars], and so they are an intrinsic part of this investigation.

A third of all the Templars' European property was once found in the Languedoc, and its ruins only add to the savage beauty of the region. One of the more picturesque local legends has it that whenever 13 October falls on a Friday (the day and date of the Order's sudden and brutal suppression) strange lights appear in the ruins and dark figures can be seen moving among them. Unfortunately on the Fridays when we were in that area, we saw and heard nothing except the alarming snufflings of wild boars; but the story shows how much the Templars have become part of local legend.

The Templars have lived on in the memories of the local people, and those memories are by no means negative. Even in this century, the famous opera singer Emma Calvé, who came from Aveyron in the north of the Languedoc, recorded in her memoirs that the locals would say of an especially good-looking or intelligent boy, "He is a true son of the Temples."

The main facts concerning the Knights Templar are simple. Officially known as The Order of the Poor Knights of the Temple of Solomon, they were formed in 1118 by the

French nobleman Hugues de Payens as knightly escorts for pilgrims to the Holy Land. Initially there were just nine of them, for the first nine years, then the Order opened up and soon it had established itself as a force to be reckoned with, not only in the Middle East, but also throughout Europe.

After the recognition of the Order, Hugues de Payens himself set out on a European trip, soliciting land and money from royalty and nobility. He visited England in 1129, when he founded the first Templar site in that country, on the site of what is now London's Holborn Underground Station.

Like all other monks, the knights were sworn to poverty, chastity and obedience but they were in the world and of it and pledged to use the sword if necessary against the enemies of Christ—and the image of the Templars became inseparably linked with the crusades that were mounted in order to drive the infidel out of Jerusalem, and to keep it Christian.

It was in 1128 that the Council of Troyes officially recognized the Templars as a religious and military order. The main protagonist behind this move was Bernard of Clairvaux, the head of the Cistercian Order, who was later canonized. But as Bamber Gascoigne writes in *The Christians*:

> He was aggressive, he was abusive ... and he was a devious politician who was quite unscrupulous in the methods he used to bring down his enemies.

Bernard actually wrote the Templars' Rule—which was based on that of the Cistercians—and it was one of his protégés who, as Pope Innocent II, declared in 1139 that the Knights would be answerable only to the papacy from that time onwards. As both the Templars and the Cistercian Orders developed in parallel, one can discern a certain amount of deliberate co-ordination between them—for example, Hugues de Payens' lord, the Count of Champagne, donated to

St Bernard the land in Clairvaux on which he built his monastic "empire." And significantly, André de Montbard, one of the nine founding knights, was Bernard's uncle. It has been suggested that the Templars and Cistercians were acting together according to a pre-arranged plan to take over Christendom, but this scheme never succeeded.

It is hard to exaggerate the prestige and financial power of the Templars when they were at the height of their influence in Europe. There was hardly a major centre of civilization where they did not have a preceptory—as, for example, the wide scatter of such place names as Temple Fortune and Temple Bar (London) and Temple Meads (Bristol) in England still shows. But as their empire spread, so their arrogance grew and began to poison their relations with both temporal and secular heads of state.

The Templars' wealth was partly a result of their Rule: all new members had to hand over their property to the Order, and they also gained a considerable fortune through massive donations of land and money from many kings and nobles. Their coffers were soon overflowing, not least because they had also amassed impressive financial astuteness, which had resulted in them becoming the first international bankers, upon whose judgement the credit ratings of others depended. It was a sure way of establishing themselves as a major power. In a short space of time their title of "Poor Knights" became a hollow sham, even though the rank and file might well have remained impecunious.

Besides their staggering wealth, the Templars were renowned for their skill and courage in battle—sometimes to the point of foolhardiness. They had specific rules to govern their conduct as fighters: for example, they were forbidden to surrender unless the odds against them were greater than three to one, and even then had to have their commander's approval. They were the Special Services of their day, an élite force with

God—and money—on their side.

Despite their finest efforts, the Holy Land fell to the Saracens bit by bit until in 1291 the last Christian territory, the city of Acre, was in enemy hands. There was nothing for the Templars to do but to return to Europe and plot their eventual reconquest, but unfortunately by then the motivation for such a campaign had disappeared among the various kings who might have financed it. Their main reason for existing dwindled to nothing. Lacking employment, but still rich and arrogant, they were widely resented because they were exempt from taxation and their allegiance was to the Pope and to him alone.

So in 1307 came their inevitable fall from grace. The supremely powerful French king, Philip the Fair, began to orchestrate the downfall of the Templars with the connivance of the Pope, who was in his pocket anyway. Secret orders were issued to the king's aristocratic representatives and the Templars were rounded up on Friday 13 October 1307, arrested, tortured and burnt.

That, at least, is the story as told in most standard works on the subject. One is left with the idea that the entire Order met its horrible doom on that day long ago, and that the Templars were effectively wiped off the face of the earth forever. Yet that is nowhere near the truth.

For a start, relatively few Templars were actually executed, although most who were captured were "put to the question"—a well-worn euphemism for suffering excruciating torture. Relatively few faced the stake, although notably their Grand Master Jacques de Molay was slowly roasted to death on the Ile de la Cité, in the shadow of Notre-Dame Cathedral, in Paris. Of the thousands of others, only those who refused to confess, or recanted their confession, were killed. . . .

The accounts of Templar confessions are colourful, to say the least. We read of their having worshipped a cat or indulging in homosexual orgies as part of their knightly duties, or venerating a demon known as Baphomet and/or a severed head. They were also said to have trampled and spat upon the cross in an initiatory rite. . . .

This is hardly surprising—not many victims of torture manage to grit their teeth and refuse to agree with the words put in their mouths by their tormenters. But in this case there is more to the story than meets the eye. On the one hand, there have been suggestions that all the charges levelled against the Templars were trumped up by those envious of their wealth and exasperated by their power, and that they provided a good excuse for the French king to extricate himself from his current economic difficulty by seizing their wealth. On the other hand, although the charges may not have been strictly true, there is evidence that the Templars were up to something mysterious and perhaps "dark" in the occult sense. . . .

Much ink has been spilt on the debate over the charges made against the Templars, and their confessions. Had they actually committed the deeds to which they confessed, or did the Inquisitors invent the charges in advance and simply torture the knights until they agreed with them? (Some knights had testified that they had been told that Jesus was a "false prophet," for example.) It is impossible to say one way or the other conclusively. . . .

Certainly the Priory of Sion claims to have been the power behind the creation of the Knights Templar: if so, then this is one of the best-kept secrets of history. Yet it is said that the two Orders were virtually indistinguishable until their schism in 1188—after which they went their separate ways. If nothing else there does seem to have been some kind of conspiracy about the conception of the Templars. Common sense suggests that it would have taken more than just the original nine knights to protect and provide refuge for all the pilgrims who visited the Holy Land, especially for *nine years*, moreover, there is little evidence that they ever made much of a serious attempt to do so. . . .

Another mystery connected with their beginnings centres on the fact that there is evidence that the Order actually existed well before 1118, although why the date was falsified remains unclear. Many commentators have suggested that the first account of their creation—by William of Tyre and written a full fifty years after the event—was simply a cover story. (Although William was deeply hostile to the Templars, he was, presumably, recounting the story as he understood it.) But once again, just what it was covering up is a matter for speculation.

Hugues de Payens and his nine companions all came from either Champagne or the Languedoc . . . and it is quite apparent that they went to the Holy Land with a specific mission in mind. Perhaps, as has been suggested, they were searching for the Ark of the Covenant, or for other ancient treasure or documents that might lead them to it, or for some kind of secret knowledge which would give them mastery of people and their wealth. . . .

Researching Western Civilization's Darkest Secrets

An Interview with Lynn Picknett and Clive Prince

Throughout this volume, the reader can find contributions from Lynn Picknett and Clive Prince, whose work was part of the source material for Dan Brown in writing *The Da Vinci Code*. For our book, we interviewed the two of them by email, to follow-up on some of the questions we thought readers might have after reading their material. Excerpts from the interview follow.

What are the Dossiers Secrets *that are in the Bibliothèque Nationale in Paris, and why does Dan Brown give them such prominence in* The Da Vinci Code?

Dossiers Secrets is a convenient term, coined by Baigent, Leigh, and Lincoln in *Holy Blood, Holy Grail,* for a set of seven related documents of varying lengths—in total, less than fifty pages—deposited in the library between 1964 and 1967.

They deal with subjects such as the Priory of Sion, the Rennes-le-Château mystery, Mary Magdalene, and the Merovingians. The purpose of the documents is to establish the existence of the Priory of Sion and its role as guardian of historical and esoteric secrets, but *Dossiers Secrets* only drops hints as to their nature.

Anyone with a reader's card to the Bibliothèque Nationale can read the originals. There also are more accessible facsimile editions, published by French researcher Pierre Jarnac in the 1990s. They may not still be in print, but they were widely available in France.

In The Templar Revelation, *you say that the* Dossiers Secrets, *which Dan Brown uses as key to establishing links between several of the great secrets in* The Da Vinci Code, *appear to be complete nonsense. Why?*

We say that because, in our view and at first glance, they *do* appear to be complete nonsense. Because so much of what's in them clashes with accepted history, it's tempting to just reject them as pure fantasy. But it's not as simple as that. While some of the information is demonstrably wrong and some deliberately misleading, some—unexpectedly—checks out.

Moreover, the *Dossiers* are mightily disappointing. They are *not*, as Dan Brown claims, romantic old parchments, but in fact, simply typewritten or cheaply typeset. It's hard to imagine great secrets being revealed on such shabby bits of paper.

What is the direct connection between the Knights Templar and the Priory of Sion?

The central paradox of the Priory of Sion is that there's no evidence of its existence before 1956, yet it claims that it's been around since the Middle Ages. In recent years, though, it's changed its story, claiming to have been founded in the eighteenth century.

The conclusion that we've come to since writing *The Templar Revelation* is that the Priory of Sion that declared itself to the world in 1956 *was* invented then, but as a front for a network of related secret societies and esoteric orders that *do* have a genuine pedigree. This front has allowed them to do certain things in a semi-public way without revealing who or what is really behind them.

In the *Dossiers Secrets*, the Priory of Sion claimed it was a brother organization to the Knights Templar, but there is no proof of such a connection. In any case, the Priory of Sion has since retracted the claim (if it was founded in the eighteenth century then obviously there was no connection!).

There was an Order of Our Lady of Mount Sion that belonged to the abbey of the same name in Jerusalem that had some connection with the Templars, and it has claimed that the Priory of Sion is the continuation of that order, but unfortunately that's as far as it goes.

On the other hand, there's a close connection between the *modern* Priory of Sion and secret societies that claim descent from the medieval Templars. These neo-Templar groups can all be traced back to an eighteenth-century society called the Strict Templar Observance, which claimed—with some justification—to be the authentic heirs of the medieval Templars' secrets. And the organization led by Pierre Plantard [reputed grand master of the Priory of Sion in more recent times] acts as a front for these groups.

What made the Templars so famous? What secret information are they supposed to be guarding?

Historically, it is accepted that the Templars were unusually skilled in the fields of medicine, diplomacy, and the military arts—being the elite forces of their day. They acquired much of this knowledge on their travels, especially in the Middle East, and a good deal from their enemies, the Saracens, who were particularly renowned for their scientific knowledge. (One reason why the Saracens were so far ahead of the Europeans is that all scientific experimentation was banned by the church.)

There's no doubt the Templars also sought esoteric and spiritual knowledge—although you won't find much about that aspect of their *raison d'être* in standard history texts. The Templars were so secretive that nothing is known for certain about their hidden agendas: it's a matter for informed speculation. They've been linked to everything from the Ark of the Covenant and the Holy Grail to the Lost Gospels and the Shroud of Turin. Nobody really knows for sure.

However, our research has indicated that the Templars were very much a society within a society: the mass of rank-and-file knights being no more or less than the good Christians they were supposed to be. But the founding knights and the continuing inner circle appeared to follow a different—and very heretical—agenda. It's known there was a big secret about Baphomet, the severed head that the Templar initiates were alleged to have worshipped. Was Baphomet really a head—a bearded, severed head, as some knights claimed? And if so, who or what could it represent?

How are the Freemasons connected with all this?

Freemasonry has undergone so many schisms, evolutions, and reinventions that it's not really correct to talk of "the Freemasons"—there's no such thing, there are so many variations. But we do think that the link between the Templars and the origins of Freemasonry—among Templars who went underground after the order was suppressed—is as conclusively proven as anything in this field. The network of orders behind the Priory of Sion is closely entwined with certain forms of Freemasonry, such as the Rectified Scottish Rite.

What is the main goal or purpose of the Freemasons?

Today it depends on which Masonic order you're talking about. Most would claim to be nothing more than charitable, philosophical, and ethical organizations; while their critics say they're only about mutual commercial and social advancement. Originally, Freemasonry's aim was the acquisition, study, and passing on of knowledge, primarily esoteric (enlightenment). Some orders still maintain that tradition.

Who is Pierre Plantard?

Pierre Plantard (aka Pierre Plantard de Saint Clair) was grand master of the Priory of Sion until his death in 2000. He was their public face. With him, the Priory of Sion emerged into the public domain, mainly through the interviews he gave to Michael Baigent, Richard Leigh, and Henry Lincoln, authors of *Holy Blood, Holy Grail*—which led indirectly to Dan Brown's book. Who the grand master is now, or even if there is one, is a matter of conjecture.

It is important to stress that he [Plantard] never said anything about the bloodline of Jesus and Mary Magdalene. That was Baigent, Leigh, and Lincoln's hypothesis. After their second book, *The Messianic Legacy*, came out [in the United Kingdom in 1986], Plantard explicitly repudiated that idea. [Dan Brown doesn't seem to be aware of this!]

Given the history of famous names said to be Grand Masters of the Priory of Sion, what big names are involved now?

If the Priory of Sion is a cover for other politico-esoteric societies, in a sense, it doesn't have members of its own. Various names have been linked with it, up to and including President François Mitterand. But the problem with a secret society is how can you prove someone is a member? And are they guardians of a great historical secret, as Dan Brown suggests? Or do they have some kind of political goal they don't want us to know about?

What is the Merovingian line and what is its connection to Jesus?

The Merovingians were a dynasty of Frankish kings who reigned over parts of what are now northern France, Germany, and Belgium between the fifth and eighth centuries. They were usurped by the Carolingians in collusion with the church.

The central contention of the *Dossiers Secrets* is that the Merovingian line did not die out, as history records, and that the Priory of Sion has protected its descendants throughout the ages to the present day. There's a suggestion that they are the legitimate kings of France, and that the aim of the Priory of Sion is to restore them to the French throne. This is absolute nonsensical rubbish. Even if the Merovingians survived, which is extremely doubtful, they would have no claim whatsoever to the throne—which no longer exists anyway in the Republic of France.

The central theory of *Holy Blood, Holy Grail* is the secret of the Merovingian bloodline and that it was descended from the children of Jesus and Mary Magdalene. This is the idea that particularly inspired *The Da Vinci Code.* We can't stress too much that this is *entirely* Baigent, Leigh, and Lincoln's hypothesis. It appears *nowhere* in the *Dossiers Secrets,* nor in any other Priory-related documents, and was explicitly repudiated by Pierre Plantard.

What basis is there for thinking that the Holy Grail represents Jesus' bloodline through Mary Magdalene's womb?

Baigent, Leigh, and Lincoln argue that the Holy Grail, the "vessel" that contained Jesus' blood and seed, is a coded reference to the womb in which Mary Magdalene carried his children. It's an intriguing but very debatable hypothesis, especially as the "vessel" idea of the Grail was not its original form. The first tales either didn't describe the mysterious Holy Grail as anything in particular or had it as a *stone.*

We absolutely do not agree with the Grail as Magdalene's womb theory. This was *explicitly* rejected by the Priory of Sion itself and is the central mistake of both *Holy Blood, Holy Grail* and, less seriously, *The Da Vinci Code,* which is, after all, fiction.

Can you talk a bit about Leonardo and his link to a secret society?

Historically, Leonardo is known to have been a heretic and to have been interested in esoteric ideas. The Priory of

Sion claimed him as their ninth Grand Master—but whether this is literally true is impossible to say, although it is very unlikely. There's no contemporary document that makes such a link, but if we're talking secret society, there wouldn't be, would there?

But what is clear is that Leonardo incorporated symbolic elements into his works that fit with the themes in the *Dossiers Secrets,* establishing at least that both adhered to the same tradition.

For us, as we explain in our book *The Templar Revelation: Secret Guardians of the True Identity of Christ,* the key element is Leonardo's elevation of John the Baptist to the point that he seems superior to Jesus—even the "true Christ." Ironically, the chapter of our book that we called "The Secret Code of Leonardo da Vinci" (ring any bells?) was *not* about the alleged bloodline of Jesus, but actually about this "Johannite" heresy.

Holy Blood, Holy Grail

BY MICHAEL BAIGENT, RICHARD LEIGH, AND HENRY LINCOLN

Michael Baigent, Henry Lincoln, and Richard Leigh, authors of *The Messianic Legacy,* spent over ten years on their own kind of quest for the Holy Grail, into the secretive history of early France, in order to write *Holy Blood, Holy Grail,* which was published in the United Kingdom in 1982. Excerpted from *The Holy Blood and the Holy Grail* by Henry Lincoln, Michael Baigent and Richard Leigh, published by Jonathan Cape. Reprinted by permission of The Random House Group Ltd.

Holy Blood, Holy Grail is the book that "started it all," in terms of the late twentieth century's interest in the intersecting secrets and conspiracies of the marriage of Jesus and Mary Magdalene, their supposed bloodline, the lost Gospels, the Templars, the Priory of Sion, Leonardo da Vinci, the *Dossiers Secrets*, the mystery of Rennes-le-Château and Abbé Saunière, etc. Reading *Holy Blood, Holy Grail*, one can almost see the places where Dan Brown might have highlighted something or put a Post-it on it, and said, "Aha! I've got to use that!"

However, as a number of articles in this volume point out, *Holy Blood, Holy Grail* has been seriously questioned in terms of its research, its methods, its conclusions and so forth. Most academics with expertise in the fields the book touches on, find it either noncredible at best, or supportive of the hoax that many experts believe the whole Priory of Sion to be.

Holy Blood, Holy Grail is definitely worth the reader's attention. Whether it is true or not, or how much of it might be true, we will leave to each reader to judge. Let's just say Dan Brown had a good idea in weaving this fascinating material into a work of fiction.

The text that follows is just a sampling of the many fascinations to be found in the book. Much of the material is obscure and hard to follow without all the material that went before. Our aim here is to give readers a taste for this true Ur-text for *The Da Vinci Code*. If it interests you, get *Holy Blood, Holy Grail* and read the whole thing!

Granted, Guillaume [de Tyre] does provide us with certain basic information, and it is this information on which all subsequent accounts of the Templars, all explanation of their foundation, all narratives of their activities have been based. But because of Guillaume's vagueness and sketchiness, because of the time at which he was writing [1175–85], because of the dearth of documented sources, he constitutes a precarious basis on which to build a definitive picture. Guillaume's chronicles are certainly useful. But it is a mistake—and one to which many historians have succumbed—to regard them as unimpugnable and wholly accurate. Even Guillaume's dates, as Sir Steven Runciman stresses, "are confused and at times demonstrably wrong."[1]

According to Guillaume de Tyre the Order of the Poor Knights of Christ and the Temple of Solomon was founded in 1118. Its founder is said to be one Hugues de Payen, a nobleman from Champagne and vassal of the count of Champagne. One day Hugues, unsolicited, presented himself with eight comrades at the palace of Baudouin I, king of Jerusalem, whose elder brother, Godfroi de Bouillon, had captured the Holy City nineteen years earlier. Baudouin seems to have received them most cordially, as did the patriarch of Jerusalem—the religious leader of the new kingdom and special emissary of the Pope.

The declared objective of the Templars, Guillaume de Tyre continues, was, "as far as their strength permitted, they should keep the roads and highways safe ... with especial regard for the protection of pilgrims."[2] So worthy was this objective apparently that the king vacated an entire wing of the royal palace and placed it at the knights' disposal. And despite their declared oath of poverty the knights moved into this lavish accommodation. According to tradition their quarters were built on the foundations of the ancient temple of Solomon, and from this the fledgling order derived its name.

For nine years, Guillaume de Tyre tells us, the nine knights admitted no new candidates to their order. They were still supposed to be living in poverty—such poverty that official seals show two knights riding a single horse, implying not

1. Runciman, *History of the Crusades*, Vol. 2, p. 477.
2. William of Tyre, *History of Deeds Done Beyond the Sea*, Vol. I, p. 525ff.

only brotherhood, but also a penury that precluded separate mounts. This style of seal is often regarded as the most famous and distinctive of Templar devices, descending from the first days of the order. However, it actually dates from a full century later, when the Templars were hardly poor—if, indeed, they ever were.

According to Guillaume de Tyre, writing a half century later, the Templars were established in 1118 and moved into the king's palace—presumably sallying out from there to protect pilgrims on the Holy Land's highways and byways. And yet there was at the time an official royal historian employed by the king. His name was Fulk de Chartres, and he was writing not fifty years after the order's purported foundation, but during the very years in question. Curiously enough, Fulk de Chartres makes no mention whatever of Hugues de Payen, Hugues' companions, or anything even remotely connected with the Knights Templar. Indeed, there is a thunderous silence about Templar activities during the early days of their existence. Certainly there is no record anywhere—not even later—of their doing anything to protect pilgrims. And one cannot but wonder how so few men could hope to fulfill so mammoth a self-imposed task. Nine men to protect the pilgrims on all the thoroughfares of the Holy Land? Only nine? And *all* pilgrims? If this was their objective, one would surely expect them to welcome new recruits. Yet according to Guillaume de Tyre, they admitted no new candidates to the order for nine years.

Nonetheless, within a decade the Templars' fame seems to have spread back to Europe. Ecclesiastical authorities spoke highly of them and extolled their Christian undertaking. By 1128 or shortly thereafter, a tract lauding their virtues and qualities was issued by no less a person than Saint Bernard, abbot of Clairvaux and the age's chief spokesman for Christendom. Bernard's tract, "In Praise of the New Knighthood," declares the Templars to be the epitome and apotheosis of Christian values.

After nine years, in 1127, most of the nine knights returned to Europe and a triumphal welcome, orchestrated in large part by Saint Bernard. In January 1128 a Church council was convened at Troyes—court of the count of Champagne, Hugues de Payen's liege lord—at which Bernard was again the guiding spirit. At this council the Templars were officially recognized and incorporated as a religious-military order. Hugues de Payen was given the title of grand master. He and his subordinates were to be warrior-monks, soldier-mystics, combining the austere discipline of the cloister with a martial zeal tantamount to fanaticism—a "militia of Christ" as they were called at the time. And it was again Saint Bernard who helped to draw up, with an enthusiastic preface, the rule of conduct to which the knights would adhere—a rule based on that of the Cistercian monastic order, in which Bernard himself was a dominant influence.

The Templars were sworn to poverty, chastity, and obedience. They were obliged to cut their hair but forbidden to cut their beards, thus distinguishing themselves in an age when most men were cleanshaven. Diet, dress, and other aspects of daily life were stringently regulated in accordance with both monastic and military routines. All members of the order were obliged to wear white habits of surcoats and cloaks, and these soon evolved into the distinctive white mantle for which the Templars became famous. "It is granted to none to wear white habits, or to have white mantles, excepting the . . . Knights of Christ."[3] So stated the order's rule, which elaborated on the symbolic significance of this apparel: "To all the professed knights, both in winter and summer, we give, if they can be procured, white garments, that those who have cast behind them a dark life may know that they are to commend themselves to their creator by a pure and white life."[4]

In addition to these details the rule established a loose administrative hierarchy and apparatus. And behavior on the battlefield was strictly controlled. If captured, for instance, Templars were not allowed to ask for mercy or to ransom themselves; they were compelled to fight to the death. Nor were they permitted to retreat unless the odds against them exceeded three to one.

In 1139, a papal bull was issued by Pope Innocent II—a former Cistercian monk at Clairvaux and protégé of Saint Bernard. According to this bull the Templars would owe allegiance to no secular or ecclesiastical power other than the Pope himself. In other words, they were rendered totally independent of all kings, princes, and prelates, and of all interference from both political and religious authorities. They had become, in effect, a law unto themselves, an autonomous international empire.

During the two decades following the Council of Troyes the order expanded with extraordinary rapidity and on an extraordinary scale. When Hugues de Payen visited England in late 1128, he was received with "great worship" by King Henry I. Throughout Europe younger sons of noble families flocked to enroll in the order's ranks, and vast donations—in money, goods, and land—were made from every quarter of Christendom. Hugues de Payen donated his own properties, and all new recruits were obliged to do likewise. On admission to the order a man was compelled to sign over all his possessions . . .

. . . Many of their [the Templars'] contemporaries shunned them, believing them to be in league with unclean powers. As early as 1208, at the beginning of the Albigensian

4. Ibid.

Crusade, Pope Innocent III had admonished the Templars for unChristian behavior and referred explicitly to necromancy. On the other hand, there were individuals who praised them with extravagant enthusiasm. In the late twelfth century Wolfram von Eschenbach, greatest of medieval *minnesingers* or *romanciers*, paid a special visit to *Outremer* to witness the order in action. And when, between 1195 and 1220, Wolfram composed his epic romance *Parzival*, he conferred on the Templars a most exalted status. In Wolfram's poem the knights who guard the Holy Grail, the Grail castle, and the Grail family are Templars.[5]

After the Temple's demise, the mystique surrounding it persisted. The final recorded act in the order's history had been the burning of the last grand master, Jacques de Molay, in March 1314. As the smoke from the slow fire choked the life from his body, Jacques de Molay is said to have issued an imprecation from the flames. According to tradition he called his persecutors—Pope Clement and King Philippe—to join him and account for themselves before the court of God within the year. Within a month Pope Clement was dead, supposedly from a sudden onslaught of dysentery. By the end of the year Philippe was dead as well, from causes that remain obscure to this day. There is, of course, no need to look for supernatural explanations. The Templars possessed great expertise in the use of poisons. And there were certainly enough people about—refugee knights traveling incognito, sympathizers of the order, or relatives of persecuted brethren—to exact the appropriate vengeance. Nevertheless, the apparent fulfillment of the grand master's curse lent credence to belief in the order's occult powers. Nor did the curse end there. According to legend it was to cast a pall over the French royal line far into the future. And thus echoes of the Templars'

5. Wolfram von Eschenbach, *Parzival*, p. 251.

supposed mystic power reverberated down the centuries.

By the eighteenth century various secret and semisecret confraternities were lauding the Templars as both precursors and mystical initiates. Many Freemasons of the period appropriated the Templars as their own antecedents. Certain Masonic "rites" or "observances" claimed direct lineal descent from the order as well as authorized custody of its arcane secrets. Some of these claims were patently preposterous. Others—resting, for example, on the order's possible survival in Scotland—may well have a core of validity, even if the attendant trappings are spurious.

By 1789 the legends surrounding the Templars had attained positively mythic proportions and their historical reality was obscured by an aura of obfuscation and romance. Knights Templar were regarded as occult adepts, illumined alchemists, magi and sages, master masons, and high initiates—veritable supermen endowed with an awesome arsenal of arcane power and knowledge. They were also regarded as heroes and martyrs, harbingers of the anticlerical spirit of the age; and many French Freemasons, in conspiring against Louis XVI, felt they were helping to implement Jacques de Molay's dying curse on the French line. When the king's head fell beneath the guillotine, an unknown man is reported to have leaped onto the scaffold. He dipped his hand in the monarch's blood, flung it out over the surrounding throng and cried, "Jacques de Molay, thou art avenged!"

Since the French Revolution the aura surrounding the Templars has not diminished. At least three contemporary organizations today call themselves Templars, claiming to possess a pedigree from 1314 and characters whose authenticity has never been established. Certain Masonic lodges have adopted the grade of "Templar" as well as rituals and appellations supposedly descended from the original order. Toward the end of the nineteenth century a sinister Order of the New

Templars was established in Germany and Austria, employing the swastika as one of its emblems. Figures like H. P. Blavatsky, founder of Theosophy, and Rudolf Steiner, founder of Anthroposophy, spoke of an esoteric "wisdom tradition" running back through the Rosicrucians to the Cathars and Templars—who were purportedly repositories of more ancient secrets still. . . .

Of all the privately published documents deposited in the Bibliothèque Nationale, the most important is a compilation of papers entitled collectively *Dossiers secrets (Secret Dossiers)*. Catalogued under Number 4° lm¹ 249, this compilation is now on microfiche. Until recently, however, it comprised a thin, nondescript volume, a species of folder with stiff covers that contained a loose assemblage of ostensibly unrelated items— news clippings, letters pasted to backing sheets, pamphlets, numerous genealogical trees, and the odd printed page apparently extracted from the body of some other work. Periodically some of the individual pages would be removed. At different times other pages would be freshly inserted. On certain pages additions and corrections would sometimes be made in a minuscule longhand. At a later date these pages would be replaced by new ones, printed and incorporating all previous emendations.

The bulk of the *Dossiers*, which consist of genealogical trees, is ascribed to one Henri Lobineau, whose name appears on the title page. Two additional items in the folder declare that Henri Lobineau is yet another pseudonym—derived perhaps from a street, the rue Lobineau, which runs outside Saint Sulpice in Paris—and that the genealogies are actually the work of a man named Leo Schidlof, an Austrian historian and antiquarian who purportedly lived in Switzerland and died in 1966. On the basis of this information we undertook to learn what we could about Leo Schidlof.

In 1978 we managed to locate Leo Schidlof's daughter,

who was living in England. Her father, she said, was indeed
Austrian. He was not a genealogist, a historian, or an antiquarian, however, but an expert and dealer in miniatures who had
written two works on the subject. In 1948 he had settled in
London, where he lived until his death in Vienna in 1966—the
year and place specified in the *Dossiers secrets.*

Miss Schidlof vehemently maintained that her father had
never had any interest in genealogies, the Merovingian dynasty,
or mysterious goings-on in the south of France. And yet, she
continued, certain people obviously believed he had. During
the 1960s, for example, he had received numerous letters and
telephone calls from unidentified individuals in both Europe
and the United States who wished to meet with him and discuss matters of which he had no knowledge whatever. On his
death in 1966 there was another barrage of messages, most of
them inquiring about his papers.

Whatever the affair in which Miss Schidlof's father had
become unwittingly embroiled, it seemed to have struck a sen-
sitive chord with the American government. In 1946—a
decade before the *Dossiers secrets* are said to have been compiled—Leo Schidlof applied for a visa to enter the United
States. The application was refused on grounds of suspected
espionage or some other form of clandestine activity. Eventually the matter seems to have been sorted out, the visa issued,
and Leo Schidlof was admitted to the States. It may all have
been a typical bureaucratic mix-up. But Miss Schidlof seemed
to suspect that it was somehow connected with the arcane pre-
occupations so perplexingly ascribed to her father.

Miss Schidlof's story gave us pause. The refusal of an
American visa might well have been more than coincidental,
for there were among the papers in the *Dossiers secrets* references
that linked the name Leo Schidlof with some sort of international espionage. In the meantime, however, a new pamphlet
had appeared in Paris—which, during the months that fol-

lowed, was confirmed by other sources. According to this pamphlet the elusive Henri Lobineau was not Leo Schidlof after all, but a French aristocrat of distinguished lineage, Comte Henri de Lénoncourt.

The question of Lobineau's real identity was not the only enigma associated with the *Dossiers secrets*. There was also an item that referred to "Leo Schidlof's leather briefcase." This briefcase supposedly contained a number of secret papers relating to Rennes-le-Château between 1600 and 1800. Shortly after Schidlof's death the briefcase was said to have passed into the hands of a courier, a certain Fakhar ul Islam—who, in February 1967, was to rendezvous in East Germany with an "agent delegated by Geneva" and entrust it to him. Before the transaction could be effected, however, Fakhar ul Islam was reportedly expelled from East Germany and returned to Paris "to await further orders." On February 20, 1967, his body was found on the railway tracks at Melun, having been hurled from the Paris–Geneva express. The briefcase had supposedly vanished.

We set out to check this lurid story as far as we could. A series of articles in French newspapers of February 21 did confirm most of it.[6] A decapitated body had indeed been found on the tracks at Melun. It was identified as that of a young Pakistani named Fakhar al-Islam. For reasons that remained obscure the dead man had been expelled from East Germany and was traveling from Paris to Geneva—engaged, it appeared, in some form of espionage. According to the newspaper reports the authorities suspected foul play and the affair was being investigated by the DST (Directory of Territorial Surveillance, or Counterespionage).

On the other hand, the newspapers made no mention of Leo Schidlof, a leather briefcase, or anything else that might

6. *Le Monde* (Feb. 21, 1967), p. 11. *Le Monde* (Feb. 22, 1967), p. 11, *Paris-Jour* (Feb. 21, 1967), no. 2315, p. 4.

connect the occurrence with the mystery of Rennes-le-Château. As a result we found ourselves confronted with a number of questions. On the one hand, it was possible that Fakhar ul Islam's death was linked with Rennes-le-Château—that the item in the *Dossiers secrets* in fact drew upon "inside information" inaccessible to the newspapers. On the other hand the item in the *Dossiers secrets* might have been deliberate and spurious mystification. One need only find any unexplained or suspicious death and ascribe it, after the fact, to one's own hobby horse. But if this were indeed the case, what was the purpose of the exercise? Why should someone deliberately try to create an atmosphere of sinister intrigue around Rennes-le-Château? What might be gained by the creation of such an atmosphere? And who might gain from it?

These questions perplexed us all the more because Fakhar ul Islam's death was not, apparently, an isolated occurrence. Less than a month later another privately printed work was deposited in the Bibliothèque Nationale. It was called *Le Serpent rouge (The Red Serpent)* and dated, symbolically and significantly enough, January 17. Its title page ascribed it to three authors—Pierre Feugère, Louis Saint-Maxent, and Gaston de Koker.

Le Serpent rouge is a singular work. It contains one Merovingian genealogy and two maps of France in Merovingian times, along with a cursory commentary. It also contains a ground plan of Saint Sulpice in Paris, which delineates the chapels of the church's various saints. But the bulk of the text consists of thirteen short prose poems of impressive literary quality—many of them reminiscent of the work of Rimbaud. Each of these prose poems is no more than a paragraph long, and each corresponds to a sign of the zodiac—a zodiac of thirteen signs, with the thirteenth, Ophiuchus or the Serpent Holder, inserted between Scorpio and Sagittarius.

Narrated in the first person, the thirteen prose poems are a type of symbolic or allegorical pilgrimage, commencing with Aquarius and ending with Capricorn—which, as the text explicitly states, presides over January 17. In the otherwise cryptic text there are familiar references—to the Blanchefort family, to the decorations in the church as Rennes-le-Château, to some of Saunière's inscriptions there, to Poussin and the painting of "Les Bergers d'Arcadie," to the motto on the tomb, "Et in Arcadia Ego." At one point there is mention of a red snake, "cited in the parchments," uncoiling across the centuries—an explicit allusion, it would seem, to a bloodline or a lineage. And for the astrological sign of Leo there is an enigmatic paragraph worth quoting in its entirety:

> From she whom I desire to liberate, there wafts towards me the fragrance of the perfume which impregnates the Sepulchre. Formerly, some named her ISIS, queen of all sources benevolent. COME UNTO ME ALL YE WHO SUFFER AND ARE AFFLICTED AND I SHALL GIVE YE REST. To others, she is MAGDALENE, of the celebrated vase filled with healing balm. The initiated know her true name: NOTRE DAME DES CROSS.[7]

The implications of this paragraph are extremely interesting. Isis, of course, is the Egyptian mother goddess, patroness of mysteries—the "White Queen" in her benevolent aspects, the "Black Queen" in her malevolent ones. Numerous writers on mythology, anthropology, psychology, and theology have traced the cult of the mother goddess from pagan times to the Christian epoch. And according to these writers she is said to have survived under Christianity in the guise of the Virgin Mary—the Queen of Heaven, as Saint Bernard called her, a designation applied in the Old Testament to the mother

7. Feugère, Saint-Maxent, and Koker, *Le Serpent rouge*, p. 4.

goddess Astarte, the Phoenician equivalent of Isis. But according to the text in *Le Serpent rouge* the mother goddess of Christianity would not appear to be the Virgin. On the contrary, she would appear to be the Magdalen—to whom the church at Rennes-le-Château is dedicated and to whom Saunière consecrated his tower. . . .

The Grand Masters and the Underground Stream

In the *Dossiers secrets* the following individuals are listed as successive grand masters of the Prieuré de Sion—or, to use the official term, *Nautonnier*, an old French word that means "navigator" or "helmsman":

Jean de Gisors	1188–1220
Marie de Saint-Clair	1220–1266
Guillaume de Gisors	1266–1307
Edouard de Bar	1307–1336
Jeanne de Bar	1336–1351
Jean de Saint-Clair	1351–1366
Blanche d'Evreux	1366–1398
Nicolas Flamel	1398–1418
René d'Anjou	1418–1480
Iolande de Bar	1480–1483
Sandro Filipepi	1483–1510
Leonardo da Vinci	1510–1519
Connétable de Bourbon	1519–1527
Ferdinand de Gonzague	1527–1575
Louis de Nevers	1575–1595
Robert Fludd	1595–1637
J. Valentin Andrea	1637–1654
Robert Boyle	1654–1691
Isaac Newton	1691–1727

Charles Radclyffe	1727–1746
Charles de Lorraine	1746–1780
Maximilian de Lorraine	1780–1801
Charles Nodier	1801–1844
Victor Hugo	1844–1885
Claude Debussy	1885–1918
Jean Cocteau	1918–[8]

When we first saw this list, it immediately provoked our skepticism. On the one hand it includes a number of names which one would automatically expect to find on such a list—names of famous individuals associated with the "occult" and "esoteric." On the other hand it includes a number of illustrious and improbable names—individuals whom, in certain cases, we could not imagine presiding over a secret society. At the same time many of these latter names are precisely the kind that twentieth-century organizations have often attempted to appropriate for themselves, thus establishing a species of spurious "pedigree." There are, for example, lists published by AMORC, the modern "Rosicrucians" based in California, which include virtually every important figure in Western history and culture whose values, even if only tangentially, happened to coincide with the order's own. An often haphazard overlap or convergence of attitudes is misconstrued as something tantamount to "initiated membership." And thus one is told that Dante, Shakespeare, Goethe, and innumerable others were "Rosicrucians"—implying that they were card-carrying members who paid their dues regularly.

Our initial attitude toward the above list was equally cynical. Again, there are the predictable names—names associated with the "occult" and "esoteric." Nicolas Flamel, for instance, is perhaps the most famous and well-documented of medieval

8. Henri Lobineau, *Dossiers secrets*, planche no. 4., Ordre de Sion.

alchemists. Robert Fludd, seventeenth-century philosopher, was an exponent of Hermetic thought and other arcane subjects. Johann Valentin Andrea, German contemporary of Fludd, composed, among other things, some of the works that spawned the myth of the fabulous Christian Rosenkreuz. And there are also names like Leonardo da Vinci and Sandro Filipepi, who is better known as Botticelli. There are names of distinguished scientists, like Robert Boyle and Sir Issac Newton. During the last two centuries the Prieuré de Sion's grand masters alleged to have included such important literary and cultural figures as Victor Hugo, Claude Debussy, and Jean Cocteau.

By including such names the list in the *Dossiers secrets* could not but appear suspect. It was almost inconceivable that some of the individuals cited had presided over a secret society—still more, a secret society devoted to "occult" and "esoteric" interests. Boyle and Newton, for example, are hardly names that people in the twentieth century associate with the "occult" and "esoteric." And though Hugo, Debussy, and Cocteau were immersed in such matters, they would seem to be too well known, too well researched and documented, to have exercised a "grand mastership" over a secret order. Not, at any rate, without some word of it somehow leaking out.

On the other hand, the distinguished names are not the only names on the list. Most of the other names belong to high-ranking European nobles, many of whom are extremely obscure—unfamiliar not only to the general reader, but even to the professional historian. There is Guillaume de Gisors, for instance, who in 1306 is said to have organized the Prieuré de Sion into an "Hermetic Freemasonry." And there is Guillaume's grandfather, Jean de Gisors, who is said to have been Sion's first independent grand master, assuming his position after the "cutting of the elm" and the separation from the Temple in 1188. There is no question that Jean de Gisors existed historically. He was born in 1133 and died in 1220.

He is mentioned in charters and was at least nominal lord of the famous fortress in Normandy where meetings traditionally convened between English and French kings took place [sic], as did the cutting of the elm in 1188. Jean seems to have been an extremely powerful and wealthy landowner and, until 1193, a vassal of the king of England. He is also known to have possessed property in England, in Sussex, and the manor of Titchfield in Hampshire.[9] According to the *Dossiers secrets*, he met Thomas à Becket at Gisors in 1169—though there is no indication of the purpose of this meeting. We were able to confirm that Becket was indeed at Gisors in 1169,[10] and it is therefore probable that he had some contact with the lord of the fortress; but we could find no record of any actual encounter between the two men.

In short, Jean de Gisors, apart from a few bland details, proved virtually untraceable. He seemed to have left no mark whatever on history, save his existence and his title. We could find no indication of what he did—what might have constituted his claim to fame or have warranted his assumption of Sion's grand mastership. If the list of Sion's purported grand masters was authentic, what, we wondered, did Jean do to earn his place on it? And if the list were a latter-day fabrication, why should someone so obscure be included at all?

There seemed to us only one possible explanation, which did not really explain very much in fact. Like the other aristocratic names on the list of Sion's grand masters, Jean de Gisors appeared in the complicated genealogies that figured elsewhere in the "Prieuré documents." Together with those other elusive nobles he apparently belonged to the same dense forest of family trees—ultimately descended, supposedly, from the Merovingian dynasty. It thus seemed evident to us that the

9. Loyd, *Origins of Anglo-Norman Families*, p. 45ff. And Powicke, *Loss of Normandy*, p. 340.
10. Roger de Hoveden, *Annals*, Vol. I, p. 322.

Prieuré de Sion—to a significant extent at least—was a domestic affair. In some way the order appeared to be intimately associated with a bloodline and a lineage. And it was their connection with this bloodline or lineage that perhaps accounted for the various titled names on the list of grand masters.

From the list quoted above it would seem that Sion's grand mastership has recurrently shifted between two essentially distinct groups of individuals. On the one hand, there are the figures of monumental stature who—through esoterica, the arts, or the sciences—have produced some impact on Western tradition, history, and culture. On the other hand, there are members of a specific and interlinked network of families— noble and sometimes royal. In some degree this curious juxtaposition imparted plausibility to the list. If one merely wished to "concoct a pedigree," there would be no point in including so many unknown or long-forgotten aristocrats. There would be no point, for instance, in including a man like Charles de Lorraine—Austrian field marshal in the eighteenth century, brother-in-law to the Empress Maria Theresa, who proved himself signally inept on the battlefield and was trounced in one engagement after another by Frederick the Great of Prussia.

In this respect, at least, the Prieuré de Sion would seem to be both modest and realistic. It does not claim to have functioned under the auspices of unqualified geniuses, superhuman "masters," illumined "initiates," saints, sages, or immortals. On the contrary, it acknowledges its grand masters to have been fallible human beings, a representative cross section of humanity—a few geniuses, a few notables, a few "average specimens," a few nonentities, even a few fools.

Why, we could not but wonder, would a forged or fabricated list include such a spectrum? If one wishes to contrive a list of grand masters, why not make all the names on it illustrious? If one wishes to concoct a pedigree that includes Leonardo, Newton, and Victor Hugo, why not also include Dante, Michelangelo, Goethe, and Tolstoi—instead of obscure people like Edouard de Bar and Maximilian de Lorraine? Why, moreover, were there so many "lesser lights" on the list? Why a relatively minor writer like Charles Nodier, rather than contemporaries like Byron or Pushkin? Why an apparent "eccentric" like Cocteau rather than men of such international prestige as André Gide or Albert Camus? And why the omission of individuals like Poussin, whose connection with the mystery had already been established? Such questions nagged at us and argued that the list warranted some consideration before we dismissed it as an arrant fraud.

We therefore embarked on a lengthy and detailed study of the grand masters—their biographies, activities, and accomplishments. In conducting this study we tried, as far as we could, to subject each name on the list to certain critical questions:

I) Was there any personal contact, direct or indirect, between each alleged grand master, his immediate predecessor, and his immediate successor?

2) Was there any affiliation, by blood or otherwise, between each alleged grand master and the families who figured in the genealogies of the "Prieuré documents"—with any of the families of purported Merovingian descent, and especially the ducal house of Lorraine?

3) Was each alleged grand master in any way connected with Rennes-le-Château, Gisors, Stenay, Saint Sulpice, or any of the other sites that had recurred in the course of our previous investigation?

4) If Sion defined itself as a "Hermetic Freemasonry," did each alleged grand master display a predisposition toward Hermetic thought or an involvement with secret societies?

Although information on the alleged grand masters before 1400 was difficult, sometimes impossible to obtain, our investigation of the later figures produced some astonishing results and consistency. Many of them were associated, in one way or another, with one or more of the sites that seemed to be relevant—Rennes-le-Château, Gisors, Stenay, or Saint Sulpice. Most of the names on the list were either allied by blood to the house of Lorraine or associated with it in some other fashion; even Robert Fludd, for example, served as tutor to the sons of Henry of Lorraine. From Nicolas Flamel on, every name on the list, without exception, was steeped in Hermetic thought and often also associated with secret societies—even men whom one would not readily associate with such things, like Boyle and Newton. And with only one exception each alleged grand master had some contact—sometimes direct, sometimes through close mutual friends—with those who preceded and succeeded him. . . .

Opus Dei in the United States

BY JAMES MARTIN, S.J.

James Martin, S.J., is an associate editor at the Catholic magazine *America* and a priest at St. Ignatius Loyola Church in Manhattan. *"Opus Dei in the United States"* by James Martin, S.J. was originally published in *America* on February 25, 1995. Although written almost a decade ago, his article remains one of the best and most balanced treatments of Opus Dei, the organization which Silas, the albino monk-assassin in *The Da Vinci Code*, belongs. Martin's article is eye opening. Copyright © 1995 by America Press. All rights reserved. For subscription information, visit www.america-magazine.org.

Opus Dei is the most controversial group in the Catholic Church today. To its members it is nothing less than The Work of God, the inspiration of Blessed Josemaría Escrivá, who advanced the work of Christ by promoting the sanctity of everyday life. To its critics it is a powerful, even dangerous, cult-like organization that uses secrecy and manipulation to advance its agenda. At the same time, many Catholics admit knowing little about this influential group.

This article is a look at Opus Dei's activities in the United States. It is based on material written by Opus Dei and its critics, as well as on interviews with current and former Opus Dei members and with priests, religious laypersons, campus ministers, scholars and journalists who have encountered Opus Dei in the United States.

Some Basics.

Any look at Opus Dei must begin with Msgr. Josemaría Escrivá de Balaguer, the Spanish priest who founded the group on Oct. 2, 1928. On that day, according to Opus Dei's literature, while on a retreat in Madrid, "suddenly, while bells pealed in a nearby church, it became clear: God made him see Opus Dei." Monsignor Escrivá, invariably referred to as the Founder by members, envisioned Opus Dei as a way of encouraging lay people to aspire to sanctity without changing their state of life or occupation. Today Opus Dei sees itself as very much in line with the Second Vatican Council and its renewed emphasis on the laity.

Some of the group's spirituality can be gleaned from Escrivá's numerous writings, most notably his 1939 book, *The Way*. The book is a collection of 999 maxims, ranging from traditional Christian pieties ("The prayer of a Christian is never a monologue") to sayings that could easily have come out of *Poor Richard's Almanac* ("Don't put off your work until tomorrow").

His group grew rapidly, spreading from Spain to other European countries, and in 1950 received recognition by the

Holy See as the first "secular institute." Over the next two decades the Work, as members call it, moved into Latin America and the United States.

In 1982 Pope John Paul II granted Opus Dei the status of "personal prelature," a canonical term meaning that jurisdiction covers the persons in Opus Dei rather than a particular region. In other words, it operates juridically much as religious orders do, without regard for geographical boundaries. This unique recognition—it is the only personal prelature in the church—demonstrated the high regard in which it is held by John Paul II as well as Opus Dei's standing in Vatican circles. But it also prompted critics to ask why a professedly lay organization would need such a status. Today Opus Dei counts 77,000 members (including 1,500 priests and 15 bishops) in over 80 countries.

Further evidence of Vatican favor—and added legitimacy—came in 1992 when Escrivá was beatified in a ceremony attended by 300,000 supporters in St. Peter's Square. But coming only a few years after Escrivá's death in 1975 and leapfrogging over figures like Pope John XXIII, the beatification was, to say the least, controversial. "Is Sainthood Coming Too Quickly for Founder of Influential Catholic Group?" read a January 1992 *New York Times* headline, echoing other critical articles appearing around the same time. An article in the *London Spectator*, for example, included allegations by former close associates about Escrivá's less than saintly behavior. "He had a filthy temper," said one, "and pro-Nazi tendencies, but they never mention that."

Opus Dei in the United States.

There are over 3,000 Opus Dei members in the United States, with 64 centers, or residences for members, in 17 cities.... Each center typically houses 10 to 15 members, with separate centers for women and men. Opus Dei also sponsors other programs, such as retreat houses, programs for married Catholics and outreach programs to the poor, like its education program for children in the South Bronx. . . .

In light of their growing presence in this country, I contacted each of the seven U.S. cardinals and one archbishop requesting comments on Opus Dei for this article. I had hoped in this way to gauge the opinions of the U.S. Catholic leadership. None would comment—either positively or negatively. The majority said they had either no substantial knowledge or no contact with them, though Opus Dei is active in nearly every large archdiocese in the country.

Secrecy and Privacy.

It is difficult to read anything about Opus Dei without running across accounts of its alleged secrecy. ("Pope Beatifies Founder of Secretive, Conservative Group" ran a *New York Times* headline in 1992.) Indeed, while a few members of Opus Dei are well known, like the Vatican press officer Joaquín Navarro-Valls, M.D., most are not. Critics also point out that most of Opus Dei's organizations are not clearly identified as being affiliated with Opus Dei.

Opus Dei denies all this. "It's not secret," says communications director Bill Schmitt, "it's private. Big difference." Mr. Schmitt describes the vocation to Opus Dei as a private matter, a personal relationship with God. The members are known by their friends, their families, their neighbors, their colleagues at work. Even Escrivá in a 1967 interview said, "The members detest secrecy."

But most critics are not concerned about whether members publicly announce their affiliation with Opus Dei. . . . When critics speak of "secrecy," they refer instead to frustration in their efforts to get answers about the basic corporate activities and practices of Opus Dei.

I encountered perhaps one example of this difficulty in the course of my research. Early on, I asked Bill Schmitt for a copy of Opus Dei's constitutions. I thought that by reading them I could better understand Opus Dei and lay to rest some misconceptions. He gave me a copy of the 1982 statutes. But they were in Latin, and a technical "church" Latin at that. Could I have a copy of the English translation? There was none, he said. Why not? First he said that Opus Dei had not had sufficient time to translate them. I replied that this seemed odd, given that the statutes had been around for 12 years and that *The Way* had already been translated into 38 languages.

When I pressed him, he provided a second explanation . . . "It's a church document," he said. "We don't own them. The Holy See wants them in Latin." . . . But how could English-speaking members study their own statutes? The members study them in depth, he explained. "All of it should be clear to them in their formation."

Nevertheless, it still seemed odd, so I asked Mr. Schmitt again. I received the same answer: "The document belongs to the Holy See and the Holy See does not want it translated. I'm sure there's a reason."

I asked three experts in canon law what that reason might be. One canon lawyer said, "Property of the Holy See? I've never heard of such a thing." Another, John Martin, S.J., professor of canon law at Regis College in Toronto, noted that religious orders and lay associations as a matter of course publish their statutes in local languages, and as far as he knew, "there is no general ecclesiastic prohibition against the translation of documents of religious orders." . . . So it appears to be Opus Dei, not the Holy See, that is keeping the statutes from being translated.

Ann Schweninger is a 24-year-old former Opus Dei member now living in Columbus, Ohio, where she works with the

Diocese of Columbus. She was not surprised when I told her of my difficulty in making sense of all this. "Opus Dei plays by its own rules," she said. "If they don't want to have something out in the open, they won't make it accessible." Referring to her own time in Opus Dei, she said: "The statutes were never shown to me nor were they available. They are mentioned but not discussed." According to Ms. Schweninger, the only official document available is the catechism of Opus Dei, which even members can read only with the permission of the house director. "It's kept under lock and key." She also mentioned that during classes on the catechism, she was encouraged to take notes "in code" in case non-members should read them.

A Lay Institution.

To encounter Opus Dei is to encounter dedicated, energetic Catholics engaged in a variety of occupations. It is also to encounter a sometimes bewildering array of priests, numeraries, supernumeraries, cooperators, associates, directors and administrators. Opus Dei describes the various types of membership as different levels of availability for their mission. Critics maintain that Opus Dei, with its emphasis on hierarchy as well as celibacy and obedience, merely replicates religious life while professing lay spirituality. . . .

A few basic terms: Numeraries are single members who pledge a "commitment" of celibacy and normally live in "centers." Numeraries turn over their income and receive a stipend for personal expenses. Numeraries (accounting for roughly 20 percent of the membership) follow the "plan of life," a daily order that includes Mass, devotional reading, private prayer and, depending on the person, physical mortification. Numeraries also attend summer classes on Opus Dei. Every year an oral commitment to Opus Dei is made, and after five years the "fidelity" is made, a lifetime commitment. There are separate centers for men and women, each with a director. Male numeraries are encouraged to consider ordination to the priesthood. After 10 years of training, those who feel called are sent to Opus Dei's seminary in Rome, the Roman College of the Holy Cross.

Most members are supernumeraries, married persons who contribute financially and sometimes serve in corporate works like schools. Associates are single people who are "less available," remaining at home because of other commitments, such as responsibilities toward aging parents. Cooperators, strictly speaking, are not members because "they do not yet have the divine vocation." They cooperate through work, financial help and prayers. . . .

According to two former numeraries, women numeraries are required to clean the men's centers and cook for them. When the women arrive to clean, they explained, the men vacate so as not to come in contact with the women. I asked Bill Schmitt if women had a problem with this. "No. Not at all." It is a paid work of the "family" of Opus Dei and is seen as an apostolate. . . . "That's totally wrong," said Ann Schweninger. . . . "I had no choice. When in Opus Dei you're asked, you're being told." . . .

Casting a Wide Net.

But it is Opus Dei's way of attracting new members that comes under the most vigorous attack by its critics. . . . One man who attended Columbia University in the early 1980's, who asked not to be named, described the process of being recruited by Opus Dei. "They had someone become my friend," he said bluntly. After Mass one day he was approached by another student, with whom he soon became good friends. Eventually he was invited to the Riverside Study Center near Columbia's campus. He was not certain exactly what it was. "I thought it was a group of students that were a think tank or something." After dinner a priest gave a short talk. He was later invited to join a "circle," which he described as a sort of an informal prayer group. Soon afterwards Opus Dei suggested that he take one of the priests at the center as his spiritual director.

After becoming more involved—at this point meeting with the group frequently—he decided to investigate on his own. He spoke with a few priests and professors at Columbia and was surprised at how little he really knew: "I didn't know anything about the secrecy, the numeraries, supernumeraries, any of that. And I didn't know there were people taking vows of celibacy. I felt kind of upset that I didn't know much about them. I didn't think they were honest or straightforward about who they were. I felt very indignant."

At the next circle meeting he raised some questions about issues that troubled him—for example, women and minority presence in Opus Dei. "They really didn't have any answers and asked me not to return." And more disturbing for him: "I never heard from my friend again. I was totally cut off."

According to two former numeraries, if this man had stayed in the circle Opus Dei would have confronted him with a decision to join. Tammy DiNicola talked about her experience. "They staged a vocation crisis for me," she said. "At the time, I didn't realize they had staged it. But it's standard practice. The person that's working on you is consulting with the director, and the two of them decide when is the best time to propose the question of vocation to the recruit."

Why is it a crisis? "Well, they make it a crisis for you!" said Ann Schweninger. "And it's totally orchestrated. They tell you it's a decision you have to make now, that God is knocking on the door, and that you have to have the strength and fortitude to say yes." Tammy DiNicola was told that it was her only chance for a vocation. "Basically it's a one-shot deal—if you don't take it, you're not going to have God's grace for the remainder of your life."

Opus Dei looks at it differently, stressing the fact that any relationships are entered into freely. "There is no recruitment to Opus Dei," said Bill Schmitt.

Still, even Escrivá's writings emphasize at least the idea of recruiting. In the internal magazine, *Cronica,* he wrote in 1971: "This holy coercion is necessary, *compelle intrare* the Lord tells us." And, "You must kill yourselves for proselytism."

Ann Schweninger finds this closer to her experience: "Whenever you're in Opus Dei, you're recruiting."

On Campus.

Opus Dei is an increasingly strong presence on U.S. college campuses. Traditionally, their effort to attract new members has led them to colleges and universities. And it has sometimes led them into conflict with other groups.

Donald R. McCrabb is executive director of the Catholic Campus Ministry Association (C.C.M.A.), an organization of 1,000 of the 1,800 Catholic chaplains in the United States. What was he hearing about Opus Dei from his members? "We are aware that Opus Dei is present at a number of campuses across the country. I'm also aware that some campus ministers find their activities on campus to be counterproductive." One of his concerns was Opus Dei's emphasis on recruiting, supported by an apparently large base of funding. "They are not taking on the broader responsibility that a campus minister has." He had other concerns as well. "I have heard through campus ministers that there's a spiritual director that's assigned to the candidate who basically has to approve every action taken by that person, including reading mail, what classes they take or don't take, what they read or don't read."

The former Columbia student echoed this: "They recommended I not read some books, particularly the Marxist stuff, and instead use their boiled-down versions. I thought this was odd—I was required to do it for class!"

The director of campus ministry at Stanford University from 1984 through 1992, Russell J. Roide, S.J., initially approached Opus Dei with an open mind. However, students began coming to him complaining about Opus Dei's recruiting. "They just didn't let the students alone. Students would come to me and say, 'Please get them off our backs.'" He felt his only recourse was to pass out information to these students about Opus Dei, including critical articles. This prompted Opus Dei numeraries to visit Father Roide to tell him that he was "interfering with their agenda." Eventually, because of continued student complaints about their recruiting, "I decided not to let them anywhere near the campus." He now describes them as "subtle and deceptive."

Opus Dei Awareness Network.

Dianne DiNicola, Tammy DiNicola's mother, knows some things about Opus Dei that she would like to change. In 1991 she started the Opus Dei Awareness Network, a self-described support group concerned with outreach to families with children in Opus Dei.

A few years ago Mrs. DiNicola noticed that Tammy, then an undergraduate at Boston College, "seemed to be going through a personality change." According to Mrs. DiNicola, she became "cold and secretive," not wanting to spend time with the family—which had not been the case before. "I just had the feeling something was wrong."

When Tammy wrote a letter saying that she would no longer return home, Mrs. DiNicola grew more worried. She eventually found out that Tammy had joined Opus Dei as a numerary, living in one of their centers in Boston. "Our daughter," she recalls, "became totally estranged from us. I can't tell you the turmoil that our family went through. We tried to keep in touch with her, but it was like she was a completely different person."

Initially trying to accept her daughter's decision, she met with Opus Dei officials and diocesan officials to obtain more information. "I was just trying to feel good about Opus Dei. I love my religion. I mean, you're not talking about the Moonies. This is something within the Catholic Church." But the situation deteriorated, and Mrs. DiNicola felt that the church either was not in a position to help or did not want to do so.

Finally, Mr. and Mrs. DiNicola enlisted the help of an "exit counselor" and asked Tammy to come home for her graduation in 1990. They later discovered that this would have been the last time she would have come home, since she had already been told to sever contacts with her family. According to both Mrs. DiNicola and Tammy, the counseling enabled Tammy to think about Opus Dei critically for the first time.

After the 24-hour counseling session Tammy decided to leave. . . . "It was pretty tumultuous," recalled Tammy, now 26. She said that since Opus Dei "shut down" all of her emotions, she experienced a flood of emotions after she left. Now Mrs. DiNicola runs the Opus Dei Awareness Network (ODAN), which she says enables her to help to spare others the pain that her family went through.

If ODAN is alarmed by Opus Dei, Opus Dei is alarmed by ODAN. "Let me stress that no one is ever counseled not to speak to their parents." said Bill Schmitt. "Please keep in mind that some parents do not accept the faith or have had 'other' plans for their son or daughter. I do not need to point out to you that the methods these people use are highly objectionable. But we have not pressed this."

Mrs. DiNicola responded that she would have been

powerless had her daughter decided to stay in Opus Dei: "We certainly weren't going to hold her physically."

At Riverside one numerary said his blood boils when he hears about ODAN, "We are approved by the Holy See! We are not cult-like. Those people [who were counseled] were just violated. We do pray for them, of course. But there is a lot of misunderstanding, and parents become irrational."

"It was very difficult for me," recalled Mrs. DiNicola. "I mean, here I am trying to justify all of this. How could this happen in the Catholic Church? Here's this organization with the approval of the Pope, Escrivá beatified, and there's such destruction that's happening to families because of this organization. So how to come to peace with that is so difficult."

Opus Dei Responds to *The Da Vinci Code*

From the Prelature of Opus Dei

Excerpted from *The Da Vinci Code, the Catholic Church and Opus Dei: A Response to The Da Vinci Code from the Prelature of Opus Dei in the United States.* Copyright © 2004 Information Office of Opus Dei on the Internet, www.opusdei.org. Opus Dei's official website in the United States has responded to what the organization believes is an unfair characterization of its beliefs and activities in The Da Vinci Code by publishing an unprecedented lengthy and detailed set of answers to frequently asked questions (FAQs). Calling the depiction of their group "bizarre" and "inaccurate," Opus Dei responds in the FAQs to many of the impressions that were created about them by the novel. Below, we excerpt two responses and interpolate additional material provided by Opus Dei from other religious experts and officials. For the full set of FAQs, you can visit the Opus Dei website at www.opusdei.org.

Is the description of Opus Dei in The Da Vinci Code *as a "Catholic sect" valid?*

The Da Vinci Code falsely describes Opus Dei as a Catholic sect, which makes no sense because Opus Dei has always been fully a part of the Catholic Church. Opus Dei received its first official approval from the Bishop of Madrid in 1941, and in 1947 the Holy See approved it. Then in 1982, the Holy See made it a personal prelature, which is one of the Church's organizational structures. (Dioceses and ordinariates are other examples of organizational structures of the Church). Moreover, one of Opus Dei's hallmarks is fidelity to the Pope and to the Church's teachings. All of Opus Dei's beliefs, practices, and customs are those of the Church. Opus Dei also has excellent relations with all the other institutions of the Catholic Church, and considers the great variety of expressions of the Catholic faith to be a wonderful thing. To call Opus Dei a sect is simply inaccurate.

Cardinal Christoph Schönborn, O.P.: "Nobody needs to have studied theology to recognize the basic contradiction in the slogan 'sects within the Church.' Their presumed existence in the Church is an indirect reproach of the Pope and Bishops who are responsible for investigating whether ecclesiastical groups are in agreement with the faith of the Church in teaching and practice. From a theological and ecclesiastical point of view, a group is considered a sect when it is not recognized by the relevant Church authority. ... It is therefore wrong if communities which are approved by the Church are called sects (by institutions, individuals, or in media reports).... Communities and movements approved by the Church should not be called sects, since their ecclesiastical approbation confirms their belonging to and grounding in the Church." *L'Osservatore*

Romano, 13/20 August 1997. [Cardinal Schönborn is Archbishop of Vienna and Editor of the Catechism of the Catholic Church.]

Pope John Paul II: "With very great hope, the Church directs its attention and maternal care to Opus Dei, which—by divine inspiration—the Servant of God Josemaría Escrivá de Balaguer founded in Madrid on October 2, 1928, so that it may always be an apt and effective instrument of the salvific mission which the Church carries out for the life of the world. From its beginnings, this Institution has in fact striven, not only to illuminate with new lights the mission of the laity in the Church and in society, but also to put it into practice." *Ut Sit,* November 1982.

Does Opus Dei encourage the practice of corporal mortification as described in The Da Vinci Code*?*

As part of the Catholic Church, Opus Dei adheres to all its teachings, including those on penance and sacrifice. The foundation of the Church's teaching on mortification is the fact that Jesus Christ, out of love for mankind, voluntarily accepted suffering and death (his "passion") as the means to redeem the world from sin. Christians are called to emulate Jesus' great love and, among other things, join him in his redemptive suffering. Thus Christians are called to "die to themselves." The Church mandates certain mortifications—fasting and abstinence from meat—as Lenten penances. Some people in the history of the Church have felt called to undertake greater sacrifices, such as frequent fasting or using a hairshirt, cilice, or discipline, as can be seen in the lives of many of those explicitly recognized by the Church as models of holiness, e.g., St. Francis of Assisi, St. Teresa of Avila, St. Ignatius of Loyola, St. Thomas More, St. Francis de Sales, St. John

Vianney, and St. Therese of Lisieux. In any event, the practice of mortification as lived in Opus Dei gives more emphasis to everyday sacrifices than to these greater sacrifices, and is not like the distorted and exaggerated depiction in *The Da Vinci Code*.

New Catholic Encyclopedia (2003): "Mortification. The deliberate restraint that one places on natural impulses in order to make them increasingly subject to sanctification through obedience to reason illumined by faith. Jesus Christ required such renunciation of anyone who wished to come after Him (Lk 9.29). And so mortification, or what St. Paul calls the crucifixion of the flesh with its vices and concupiscences (Gal. 5.24), has become a distinguishing mark of those who are Christ's. All theologians agree that mortification is necessary for salvation because man is so strongly inclined to evil by the threefold concupiscence of the world, the flesh, and the devil, which, if not resisted, must lead to grievous sin. One who wishes to save his soul must, at the very least, flee the proximate occasions of mortal sin. Of itself, such flight involves some mortification.

Pope Paul VI: "True penitence, however, cannot ever prescind from physical ascetism as well. . . . The necessity of mortification of the flesh stands clearly revealed if we consider the fragility of our nature, in which, since Adam's sin, flesh and spirit have contrasting desires. This exercise of bodily mortification—far removed from any form of stoicism—does not imply a condemnation of the flesh which the Son of God deigned to assume. On the contrary, mortification aims at the 'liberation' of man." Apostolic Constitution *Paenitemini*, February 17, 1966

Part III

Keeping the Secrets Secret

7 The Mystery of Codes

Nothing is hidden that shall not be made clear;
nothing is secret that shall not be made manifest.

—LUKE 8:17

In the 1997 movie *Conspiracy Theory*, Mel Gibson plays the part of paranoid New York cabbie and conspiracy buff Jerry Fletcher, who clips articles from the *New York Times* which he believes contain coded information about the secret plans of NASA, the UN—and even Oliver Stone—to destroy America. Unfortunately, he accidentally turns out to be right with one of his conspiracy theories and, as with the boy who cried wolf, the wolves finally do come after him.

The movie illustrates how broadly conspiracy theories in general, and secret codes with hidden meanings in particular, have permeated the zeitgeist of modern society, American society especially. And to be sure, this widespread belief in conspiracy—the sense that "there's a covert force at work keeping things undercover and admitting only certain things to the public," to quote the real-life Mel Gibson and not his character—does have some foundation in reality. (And no, the foregoing is not an encrypted message about what we think of

Mel Gibson's controversial movie, *The Passion of the Christ*; it is just a garden-variety allusion to the world of popular culture.)

After all, the government really did conspire in the Watergate and Iran—Contra scandals, and the church really did suppress evidence of widespread sexual abuse by its priests. The list of proven, true conspiracy tales in politics and in the courtroom uncovered by investigative journalism is frightening indeed.

As for secret codes, one does not need to believe, like Gibson's Jerry Fletcher or the schizophrenic John Nash in *A Beautiful Mind*, that *Life* magazine or the *New York Times* place hidden messages in their articles to recognize how ubiquitous and powerful secret codes have become in everyday affairs. Without them, business and finance would grind to a halt, our military and government could not function effectively or defend the nation against its enemies, and no citizen could shop online or get cash from an ATM. Secrecy of coded messages is now a daily front-page issue, whether as admonishments to keep one's Social Security or PIN number safe from prying eyes, or debates over who may copy the software code that defines digital music and images.

In every shocking event and mass tragedy, someone appears from outside the mainstream box to publicize a secret code and allege a conspiracy. September 11 was just such an example. On the one hand, thousands of people chatted across the Internet about secret signs and codes—everything from the meaning of the "911" date itself (a nearly universal American code for emergency), to the covers of rock albums and scenes from movies that, in our ultraviolent society, had depicted buildings being blown up. Otherwise seemingly intelligent people argued that the Bush administration knew 9/11 was going to happen, but, like FDR at Pearl Harbor, "wanted" it to happen to galvanize the country for war. Or that somehow 9/11 was a "Jewish conspiracy" designed to, designed to . . . well, no one who holds this view can actually articulate anything that makes enough sense to finish the sentence. But the motivations for entering into conspiracies are accepted by conspiracy theorists as irrational or unimportant. Thus, even with all the debate and discussion *The Da Vinci Code* has generated, almost no one has spent any time on how utterly irrational and illogical the motivations of "the Teacher" are for killing Saunière and the other sénéchaux, or how magnificently improbable a plot structure is that relies on an unholy alliance of the most dedicated Holy Grail hunters with those most opposed to allowing the "truth" of the Holy Grail to come out.

"At the end of an exhausting century," wrote *Newsweek* recently, "conspiracy is a comfortable way to make sense of a messy world. One-stop shopping for every explanation. Things don't just fall apart. Somebody *makes* them fall apart."

The public also wants heroes and heroines like Langdon and Neveu (note the two equal halves of the male-female unity they represent, this kind of true equal status being rare in a potboiler of this type). Given all the crazy and conflicting information coming at us in our daily lives, we all wish we could be like these New Age superheroes in figuring out what's really happening and what it all means, and acting intelligently and heroically—mentally and physically—to solve problems and avert disaster. In this extended novel-length exercise in code-breaking, Robert and Sophie retrace the steps of Theseus, Odysseus, Moses, Job, Jesus, Frodo, and Harry Potter—and plenty of others from the world of the hero's journey in myth and archetype. They must crack the code before it is too late!

With that in mind, we offer the following discussions by journalist Michelle Delio and professor Brendan McKay on the role of secret codes in history, as well as in *The Da Vinci Code*.

Da Vinci: Father of Cryptography

BY MICHELLE DELIO

This article is excerpted from *Wired* magazine, April 2003. Michelle Delio is a journalist who has frequently written about encryption, Internet security, hackers, spam, privacy and related topics. Reprinted from Wired News, www.wired.com. Copyright © 2003 Wired Digital Inc., a Lycos Network Company. All rights reserved.

Most of all *The Da Vinci Code* is about the history of encryption—the many methods developed over time to keep private information from prying eyes. The novel begins with Harvard symbologist Robert Langdon receiving an urgent late-night phone call: the elderly curator of the Louvre has been murdered inside the museum.

Near the body, police have found a secret message. With the help of a gifted cryptologist, Langdon solves the enigmatic riddle. But it's only the first signpost along a tangled trail of clues hidden in the works of Leonardo da Vinci. If Langdon doesn't crack the code, an ancient secret will be lost forever.

Brown's characters are fictional, but he swears that "all descriptions of artwork, architecture, documents and secret rituals in this novel are accurate." The author provides detailed background on the novel's historic basis on his website, but he suggests readers finish the book before reviewing the site, which gives away some of the plot's twists.

The book's publicity hints darkly that the story lays bare "the greatest conspiracy of the past 2,000 years." Perhaps, but anyone who is interested in conspiracy theories won't find anything new here.

Where *The Da Vinci Code* does shine—brilliantly—is in its exploration of cryptology, particularly the encoding methods developed by Leonardo da Vinci, whose art and manuscripts are packed with mystifying symbolism and quirky codes.

Brown, who specializes in writing readable books on privacy and technology, cites da Vinci as an unheralded privacy advocate and encryption pioneer. His descriptions of da Vinci's cryptology devices are fascinating.

Throughout history, entrusting a messenger with a private communication has been rife with problems. In da Vinci's time, a major concern was that the messenger might be paid more to sell the information to adversaries than to deliver it as promised.

To address that problem, Brown writes that da Vinci invented one of the first rudimentary forms of public-key encryption centuries ago: a portable container to safeguard documents.

Da Vinci's cryptography invention is a tube with lettered dials. The dials have to be rotated to a proper sequence, spelling out the password, for the cylinder to slide apart. Once a message was "encrypted" inside the container only an individual with the correct password could open it.

This encryption method was physically unhackable: If anyone tried to force the container open, the information inside would self-destruct.

Da Vinci rigged this by writing his message on a papyrus scroll, and rolling it around a delicate glass vial filled with vinegar. If someone attempted to force the container open, the vial would break, and the vinegar would dissolve the papyrus almost instantly.

Brown also brings readers deep into the Cathedral of Codes, a chapel in Great Britain [Rosslyn Chapel, Scotland] with a ceiling from which hundreds of stone blocks protrude. Each block is carved with a symbol that, when combined, is thought to create the world's largest cipher.

"Modern cryptographers have never been able to break this code, and a generous reward is offered to anyone who can decipher the baffling message," Brown writes on his site.

"In recent years, geological ultrasounds have revealed the startling presence of an enormous subterranean vault hidden beneath the chapel. This vault appears to have no entrance and no exit. To this day, the curators of the chapel have permitted no excavation."

Brown specializes in literary excavation. His previous books have all involved secrets—keeping them and breaking them—and how personal privacy slams up against national security or institutional interests.

He's written about the National Reconnaissance Office, the agency that designs, builds and operates the nation's reconnaissance satellites. He's also written about the Vatican and the National Security Agency.

Brown's first novel, *Digital Fortress*, published in 1998, details a hack attack on the NSA's top-secret super computer, Transltr, which monitors and decodes e-mail between terrorists.

But the computer can also covertly intercept e-mail between private citizens. A hacker discovers the computer and takes it down, and demands that the NSA publicly admit Transltr's existence or he'll auction off access to the computer to the highest bidder.

"My interest in secret societies sparks from growing up in New England, surrounded by the clandestine clubs of Ivy League universities, the Masonic lodges of our Founding Fathers and the hidden hallways of early government power," Brown said. "New England has a long tradition of elite private clubs, fraternities and secrecy."

Is God a Mathematician?

AN INTERVIEW WITH BRENDAN MCKAY

Brendan McKay is a professor of computer science at the Australian National University. He achieved notoriety a few years ago by debunking the Bible code theory, most notably espoused by author Michael Drosnin, which claims that the Hebrew text of the Bible contains intentional coincidences of words or phrases (appearing as letters with equal spacing) that predict an impressive array of historical events from assassinations to earthquakes. McKay showed that by applying the same mathematical techniques used by promoters of *The Bible Code* to other books similar "amazing" predictions could be found (indeed, McKay noted that a mathematical "analysis" of *Moby Dick* even found a "prediction" of Michael Drosnin's death). As McKay noted at the time, "The results of our very extensive investigation is that all the alleged scientific evidence for the Bible codes is bunk."

In the 1990s, *The Bible Code* was as big a sensation as *The Da Vinci Code* is today. Although *The Bible Code* does not figure particularly in *The Da Vinci Code*, McKay's experience is a case study in the need for skeptical, critical thinking about hidden messages, symbols, and codes from the Biblical era.

How did you first become interested in analyzing the Bible code?
I'm interested in the study of pseudoscience as a discipline. And because I'm also a mathematician, it was natural for me to examine the Bible code theory as a mathematical example of pseudoscience, which I define as something that has a scientific appearance but, upon closer examination, can be shown to not be based on scientific principles at all. What was intriguing about the Bible code theory was that some of the evidence for it was produced by qualified scientists, whose work—at least superficially—looked very convincing and scientifically solid.

So what did your investigation reveal?

Our finding is that the word patterns and seeming predictions in the Bible are there purely by random chance, and that similar word patterns can be found in every book.

It's also important to realize that over the course of time the Bible has changed a lot. Especially in the early days before Christ, there were probably substantial changes. What's more, the Hebrew spelling practice in the Bible today—which Bible code proponents use as the basis for their supposed discovery of hidden messages—does not follow the practice in use at the time the Bible was supposedly written. It's been rewritten using updated spelling rules. Because of this, any messages that might have been encoded in the very original text have been wiped out. So the whole basis for the Bible code theory is flawed. From the scientific point of view, we can say that no evidence has been found for word patterns or hidden messages in the Bible except those you'd expect by chance. We demonstrated convincingly that you can do the same thing with almost any text.

But of course some people don't want to be convinced! So the debate never quite ends.

Why do you think that is?

It's much the same as any other type of occult belief, or for that matter things like conspiracy theories. There really isn't anything that you can do to stop people from believing in a good conspiracy theory. Because people really like believing things like that, somehow it satisfies some need they have.

But what about the concept of sacred geometry or the divine proportion discussed in The Da Vinci Code, *which describes the curious fact that the design proportions of man-made objects and even nature (the ratio of the length of your hand to your*

forearm) seem to follow a certain universal pattern defined as
Phi, *or 1.61804?*

I think there's a natural explanation for that. The universe
operates according to a set of rules, and if the physicists
are right, these rules are very few and quite simple. This
almost automatically implies that some aspects of nature,
including its design elements, are going to appear repeatedly in different guises. So the fact that something like the
divine proportion appears in many different places—in
the shape of coastlines, in leaves growing on plants and
lots of other things—should not be too surprising. It
does not indicate that there is some guiding hand behind
it. It's just that the universe operates according to a fairly
small set of rules.

What about the Fibonacci sequence, which plays such a big role
in Dan Brown's book?

There are good reasons why the Fibonacci sequence
occurs often in nature. It's a very mathematically simple
sequence. Each number is the sum of the previous two. So
each time you've got a system which evolves—a plant
that's growing and more leaves are coming on it, and each
new growth depends on the previous ones and the ones
before that—you've got this sequence coming out. And
the sequence also satisfies many other mathematical properties which could correspond to the way nature works.

So is God a mathematician?

Let's put it this way. According to modern science, the
whole of nature operates according to mathematical principles. So anyone wishing to promote "divine" or mystical
reasons for why things are the way they are is naturally
going to try to cloak these in mathematical, pseudoscien-
tific garb. Yes, they'll make God a mathematician.

ANAGRAM FUN

Solving and decoding anagrams is a critical task for Robert Langdon and Sophie Neveu in *The Da Vinci Code*. Fortunately, they are both good at it. But if you read the book and wonder what you would have done if put in their position, relax! You could have used anagram software on any conventional laptop while dashing through the Louvre. Using a program called Anagram Genius, we produced thousands of anagram alternatives for each of the following phrases. We are sharing only sharing a random small sample below.

Our heroic couple has to decode the anagram **O, Draconian devil! Oh, lame saint!** (It turns out, of course, to be: **Leonardo da Vinci! The Mona Lisa!**) But it could have been any one of thousands of phrases:

An odd, snootier Machiavellian.
Honored idea man vacillations.
Ovations and dire melancholia.
A dishonored, mean vacillation.
Avid and snootier melancholia.
Sainthood and lovelier maniac.
Vanities or an odd melancholia.
Oh Man! Anti-social and evildoer.
Valiant homicide as a Londoner.
Lame vile, Draconian sainthood.
Homicidal Satan on an evildoer.
Ovational, disharmonic, leaden.
I am a harlot's ideal on connived.
Oh! Innovate cordial ladies' man.
I am a violent, odd, inane scholar.

Just in case you were wondering, rearranging the letters of *Mona Lisa* by themselves yields these code names for the most famous painting in history:

A man's oil.
Somalian.
Lion as am.
Sol mania.

O! Snail am.
I a salmon.
O! Animals.

Later, our cryptographer–symbologist team has to decode the phrase **"So dark the con of man."** Our anagram finder suggests these, among many others:

Shock mad afternoon.
Craft damn hooknose.
Fat 'n' handsome crook.
Fame and shock or not.
Chats of naked moron.
Oh! Comfort and snake.

And then one wonders whether some of the other phrases called out in the book are anagrams for anything. For example, there is the much-mulled-over scrawl, **"P.S. Find Robert Langdon."** If this was intended to be an anagram, some of the results might be:

Forbidden, strong plan.
Finest bold, grand porn.
Finer, top, grand blonds.
Bold, sporting fan nerd.

When Sophie leaves the scene of her grandfather's *hieros gamos* rite, she runs home, packs her things, and leaves a note on the table: **"I was there. Don't try to find me."** Is this an anagram for anything? It could be any one of the following expressions of Sophie's real feelings about her experience:

Now mystified rotten hatred.
Worthy of strident dementia.
Stonyhearted if modern twit.
Tormented if sainted worthy.
Witty and thorniest freedom.
Fiery, hot, tarted disownment.

All anagrams generated using Anagram Genius™ version 9, www.anagram-genius.com.

8 Leonardo and His Secrets

Wisdom is the daughter of experience.

—LEONARDO DA VINCI

Leonardo da Vinci is the disciple of experience.

—LEONARDO DA VINCI

Leonardo da Vinci hovers over *The Da Vinci Code* from the first moment in the Louvre to the last moment in the Louvre. He is everywhere in Dan Brown's novel, looking over the shoulder of the plot with the Mona Lisa eyes that gaze out from the cover. Did he integrate a secret coded message into *The Last Supper*? And if he did, was it about Mary Magdalene and her marriage to Jesus? Was it more generally about women and sexuality? Was it a heretical in-joke? Was it a secret gay message? Or was it something even more obscure to us today about the relative importance of John the Evangelist and Jesus Christ?

Was Leonardo a secret devotee of the Templars and possibly a grand master of the Priory of Sion? Did he know anything about the Holy Grail beyond what other sophisticated Renaissance men knew? Did he believe the Holy Grail was not literally a chalice but the metaphorical or real womb of

Mary Magdalene? Did he believe in the cult of the sacred feminine? (The aphorisms quoted above suggest he ascribed a feminine character to wisdom and knowledge, much as the Gnostics did.)

Why did he write in codes? Who was the Mona Lisa—or was it actually a self-portrait? What happened toward the end of his life when he moved to France? Why did this greatest of all painters paint so few paintings? Where did he get his insights into physics, anatomy, medicine, the theory of evolution, chaos theory, aviation, and other subjects on which his thinking was hundreds of years ahead of the world's leading-edge thinkers and inventors?

There are many mysteries about Leonardo, and food for many more thrillers and flights of postmodern imagination to come long after *The Da Vinci Code* has become an answer to a trivia game question.

In the commentaries presented here, we have tried to illustrate two basic schools of thought. The mainstream view, held by most Leonardo scholars and art historians, suggests that while there are innumerable mysteries and questions in the life and work of Leonardo, there is no evidence to support conclusions as far afield as the thinking that the John character in *The Last Supper* is really Mary Magdalene, or that Leonardo presided over the Priory of Sion, or that he was leaving coded messages behind in his art works to be interpreted in later eras.

The other view—well expressed here by Lynn Picknett and Clive Prince, and documented much more extensively in their books—is certainly much more interesting, even if the evidence is thin. Their view offers fascinating answers to some of what the more-established experts can only point to as a long list of questions. This type of thinking about Leonardo may turn out to have little basis in fact. But it may have a lot to offer metaphorically and conceptually. Reading Picknett and

Prince, you can see the wheels turning in Dan Brown's mind as he says to himself, "Now, what if I took a bit of this thread and a bit of that, and wove a plot together like this . . ."

The Secret Code of Leonardo da Vinci

BY LYNN PICKNETT AND CLIVE PRINCE

Lynn Picknett and Clive Prince are London-based writers. Their several books on topics ranging from Mary Magdalene to Leonardo da Vinci to the Templars figured prominently in Dan Brown's research for *The Da Vinci Code* and are referred to in Brown's bibliography. Although most mainstream academic experts and scholars disagree with Picknett, seeing little or no evidence for her interpretations of the symbols in Leonardo's work, there is no denying she has had some intriguing, unique ideas and made some fascinating connections that have challenged the status quo of academic debate over many of these issues. The excerpt that follows is a perfect example. Reprinted by permission of Simon & Schuster Adult Publishing Group from *The Templar Revelation* by Lynn Picknett and Clive Prince. Copyright © 1997 by Lynn Picknett and Clive Prince.

To begin our story proper we have to return to Leonardo's *Last Supper* and look at it with new eyes. This is not the time to view it in the context of the familiar art-historical assumptions. This is the moment when it is appropriate to see it as a complete newcomer to this most familiar of scenes would see it, to let the scales of preconception fall from one's eyes and, perhaps for the first time, really look at it.

The central figure is, of course, that of Jesus, whom Leonardo referred to as "the Redeemer" in his notes for the work. (Even so, the reader is warned against making any of the obvious assumptions here.) He looks contemplatively downwards and slightly to his left, hands outstretched on the table before him as if presenting some gift to the viewer. As this is the Last Supper at which, so the New Testament tells us, Jesus initiated the sacrament of the bread and wine, urging his followers to partake of them as his "flesh" and "blood," one might reasonably expect some chalice or cup of wine to be set before him, to be encompassed by that gesture. After all, for Christians this meal came immediately before Jesus' "Passion" in the garden of Gethsemane when he fervently prayed that "this cup pass from me"—another allusion to the wine/blood imagery—and also before his death by crucifixion when his holy blood was spilled on behalf of all mankind. Yet there is no wine in front of Jesus (and a mere token amount on the whole table). Could it be that those spread hands are making what, according to the artists, is essentially an empty gesture?

In the light of the missing wine, perhaps it is also no accident that of all the bread on the table very little is actually broken. As Jesus himself identified the bread with his own body which was to be broken in the supreme sacrifice, is some subtle message being conveyed about the true nature of Jesus' suffering?

This, however, is merely the tip of the iceberg of the unorthodoxy depicted in this painting. In the biblical account it is the young St John—known as "the Beloved"—who was physically so close to Jesus on this occasion as to be leaning "on his bosom." Yet Leonardo's representation of this young person does not as required by the biblical "stage directions," so recline, but instead leans exaggeratedly away from the Redeemer, head almost coquettishly tilted to the right. Even where this one character is concerned this is by no means all, for newcomers to the painting might be forgiven for harbouring curious uncertainties about the so-called St John. For while it is true that the artist's own predilections tended to represent the epitome of male beauty as somewhat effeminate, *surely this is a woman we are looking at*. Everything about "him" is startlingly feminine. Aged and weathered though the fresco may be, one can still make out the tiny, graceful hands, the pretty, elfin features, the distinctly female bosom and the gold necklace. This woman, for surely it is such, is also wearing garments that mark her out as being special. They are the mirror image of the Redeemer's: where one wears a blue robe and a red cloak, the other wears a red robe and a blue cloak in the identical style. No-one else at the table wears clothes that mirror those of Jesus in this way. But then no-one else at the table is a woman.

Central to the overall composition is the shape that Jesus and this woman make together—a giant, spreadeagled "M," almost as if they were literally joined at the hip but had suffered a falling out, or even grown apart. To our knowledge no academic has referred to this feminine character as anything other than "St John," and the M shape has also passed them by. Leonardo was, we have discovered in our researches, an excellent psychologist who amused himself by presenting the patrons who had given him standard religious commissions with highly unorthodox images, knowing that people will view the most startling heresy with equanimity because they usually only see what they expect to see. If you are commissioned to paint a standard Christian scene and present the public with something that looks superficially like it, they will never question its dubious symbolism. Yet Leonardo must have hoped that perhaps others who shared his unusual interpretation of the New Testament message would recognize his version, or that someone, somewhere, some objective observer, would one day seize on the image of this mysterious woman linked with the letter "M" and ask the obvious questions. Who was this "M" and why was she so important? Why would Leonardo risk his reputation—even his life in those days of the flaming pyre—to include her in this crucial Christian scene?

Whoever she is, her own fate appears to be less than secure, for a hand cuts across her gracefully bent neck in what seems to be a threatening gesture. The Redeemer, too, is menaced by an upright forefinger positively thrust into his face with obvious vehemence. Both Jesus and "M" appear totally oblivious to these threats, each apparently lost in the world of their own thoughts, each in their own way serene and composed. But it is as if secret symbols are being employed, not only to warn Jesus and his female companion of their separate fates, but also to instruct (or perhaps remind) the observer of some information which it would otherwise be dangerous to make public. Is Leonardo using this painting to convey some private belief which it would have been little short of insane to share with a wider audience in any obvious fashion? And could it be that this belief might have a message for many more than his immediate circle, perhaps even for us today?

Let us look further at this astonishing work. To the observer's right of the fresco a tall bearded man bends almost double to speak to the last disciple at the table. In doing so he has turned his back completely on the Redeemer. It is this disciple—St Thaddeus or St Jude—whose model is acknowledged to be Leonardo himself. Nothing that Renaissance painters ever depicted was accidental or included merely to be pretty, and this particular exemplar of the time and the profession was known to be a stickler for the visual *double entendre*. (His preoccupation with using the right model for the various disciples can be detected in his wry suggestion that the irritating Prior of the Santa Maria Monastery himself sit for the character of Judas!) So why did Leonardo paint himself looking so obviously away from Jesus?

There is more. An anomalous hand points a dagger at a disciple's stomach one person away from "M." By no stretch of the imagination could the hand belong to anyone sitting at that table because it is physically impossible for those near by to have twisted round to get the dagger in that position. How-ever, what is truly amazing about this disembodied hand is not so much that it exists, but that in all our reading about Leonardo we have come across only a couple of references to it, and they show a curious reluctance to find anything unusual about it. Like the St John who is really a woman, nothing could be more obvious—and more bizarre—once it is pointed out, yet usually it is completely blanked out by the observer's eye and mind simply because it is so extraordinary and so outrageous.

We have often heard it said that Leonardo was a pious Christian whose religious paintings reflected the depth of his faith. As we have seen so far, at least one of them includes highly dubious imagery in terms of Christian orthodoxy, and our further research, as we shall see, reveals that nothing could be further from the truth than the idea that Leonardo was a true believer—a believer, that is, in any accepted, or acceptable, form of Christianity. Already, the curious and anomalous fea-tures in just one of his works seem to indicate that he was tying to tell us of another layer of meaning in that familiar biblical scene, of another world of belief beyond the accepted outline of the image frozen on that fifteenth century mural near Milan.

Whatever those heterodox inclusions may mean, they were, it cannot be stressed too much, totally at variance with orthodox Christianity. This itself is hardly news to many of today's materialist/rationalists, for to them Leonardo was the first real scientist, a man who had no time for superstitions or religion in any form, who was the very antithesis of the mystic or the occultist. Yet they, too, have failed to see what is plainly set out before their eyes. To paint the *Last Supper* without signifi-cant amounts of wine is like painting the critical moment of a coronation without the crown: it either misses the point com-pletely or is making quite another one, to the extent that it marks the painter out as nothing less than an out and out heretic, someone who did possess religious beliefs, but ones which were at odds, perhaps even at war, with those of Christian orthodoxy. And Leonardo's other works, we have discovered, underline his own specific heretical obsessions through carefully applied and consistent imagery, something that would not happen if the artist were an atheist merely engaged in earning his living. These uncalled for inclusions and symbols are also much, much more than the skeptic's satirical response to such a commission—they are not just the equivalent of sticking a red nose on St Peter, for example. What we are looking at in the *Last Supper* and his other works is the secret code of Leonardo da Vinci, which we believe has a startling relevance to the world today.

[Picknett and Prince then go on to discuss their thoughts about another painting by Leonardo, the *Madonna of the Rocks*, also sometimes known as *Virgin of the Rocks*. This painting also figures prominently in the plot of *The Da Vinci Code*. After Sophie Neveu deciphers the anagram "So dark the con of man," and realizes its unscrambled letters spell out "Madonna of the Rocks," she finds the key to the Swiss bank's vault hidden behind this painting. This bit of coded message decrypting affords Robert Langdon the opportunity to explain ideas to Sophie about the painting—ideas that are clearly drawn from the writings of Picknett and Prince, such as the passage that follows.]

This apparent reversal of the usual roles of Jesus and John can also be seen on one of the two versions of Leonardo's *Virgin of the Rocks*. Art historians have never satisfactorily explained why there should be two, but one is currently exhibited in the

National Gallery in London, and the other—to us by far the more interesting—is in the Louvre in Paris.

The original commission was from an organization known as the Confraternity of the Immaculate Conception, and was for a single painting to be the centrepiece of a triptych for the altar of their chapel in the church of San Francesco Grand in Milan. (The other two paintings for the triptych were to be by other artists.) The contract, dated 25 April 1483, still exists, and sheds interesting light on the expected work—and on what the members of the confraternity actually received. In it they carefully specified the shape and dimensions of the painting they wanted—a necessity, for the frame for the triptych already existed. Oddly, both of Leonardo's finished versions meet these specifications, although why he did two of them is unknown. We may, however, hazard a guess about these divergent interpretations which has little to do with perfectionism and more with an awareness of their explosive potential.

The contract also specified the theme of the painting. It was to portray an event not found in the Gospels but long present in Christian legend. This was the story of how, during the Flight into Egypt, Joseph, Mary, and the baby Jesus had sheltered in a desert cave, where they met the infant John the Baptist who was protected by the archangel Uriel. The point of this legend is that it allowed an escape from one of the more obvious and embarrassing questions raised by the Gospel story of Jesus' baptism. Why should a supposedly sinless Jesus require baptism at all, given that the ritual is a symbolic gesture of having one's sins washed away and of one's commitment to future godliness? Why should the Son of God himself have submitted to what was clearly an act of authority on the part of the Baptist?

This legend tells how, at this remarkably fortuitous meeting of the two holy infants, Jesus conferred on his cousin John the authority to baptize him when they were both adults. For several reasons this seems to us to be a most ironic commission for the confraternity to give Leonardo, but equally one might suspect that he would have delighted in receiving it—and in making the interpretation, at least in one of the versions, very much his own.

In the style of the day, the members of the confraternity had specified a lavish and ornate painting, complete with lashings of gold leaf and a flurry of cherubs and ghostly Old Testament prophets to fill out the space. What they got in the end was quite different, to such an extent that relations between them and the artist became acrimonious, culminating in a lawsuit that dragged on for twenty years.

Leonardo chose to represent the scene as realistically as possible, with no extraneous characters—there were to be no fat cherubs or shadowy prophets of doom for him. In fact, the *dramatis personae* have been perhaps excessively whittled down, for although this scene supposedly depicts the flight into Egypt of the Holy Family, Joseph does not appear in it at all.

The Louvre version, which was the earlier, shows a blue-robed Virgin with a protective arm around one child, the other infant being grouped with Uriel. Curiously, the two children are identical, but odder still, it is the child with the angel who is blessing the other, and Mary's child who is kneeling in subservience. This has led art historians to assume that, for some reason, Leonardo chose to pose the child John with Mary. After all, there are no labels with which to identify the individuals, and surely the child who has the authority to bless must be Jesus.

There are, however, other ways to interpret this picture, ways that not only suggest strong subliminal and highly unorthodox messages, but also reinforce the codes used in Leonardo's other works. Perhaps the similarity of the two children here suggests that Leonardo was deliberately fudging their identity for his own purposes. And, while Mary is protectively embracing the child generally accepted as being John with her left hand, her right is stretched out above the head of "Jesus" in what seems to be a gesture of downright hostility. This is what Serge Bramly [art historian] describes as "reminiscent of an eagle's talons." Uriel is pointing across to Mary's child, but is also, significantly, looking enigmatically out at the observer—that is, resolutely away from the virgin and child. While it may be easier and more acceptable to interpret this gesture as an indication of the one who is to be the Messiah, there are other possible meanings.

What if the child with Mary, in the Louvre version of *The Virgin of the Rocks*, is Jesus—as one might logically expect— and the youngster with Uriel is John? Remember that in this case it is John who is blessing Jesus with the latter submitting to his authority. Uriel, as John's special protector, is avoiding even looking at Jesus. And Mary, protecting her son, is casting a threatening hand high above the head of the baby John. Several inches directly below her outstretched palm the pointing hand of Uriel cuts straight across, as if the two gestures are encompassing some cryptic clue. It is as if Leonardo is indicating that some object, some significant—but invisible— thing ought to fill the space between them. In the context it is by no means fanciful to understand that Mary's outstretched fingers are meant to look as if they were placed on the crown of an invisible head, while Uriel's pointing forefinger cuts across the space precisely where the neck would be. This phantom head floats just above the child who is with Uriel ... So this child *is* effectively labeled after all, for which of the two of them was to die by beheading? And if this is truly John the Baptist, it is he who is shown to be giving the blessing, to be the superior one.

Yet when we turn to the much later National Gallery version, we find that all the elements needed to make these heretical deductions are missing—but those elements only. The two children are quite different in appearance, and the one with Mary bears the traditional long-stemmed cross of the Baptist (although it is true that this may have been added by a later artist). Here Mary's right hand is still outstretched above the other child, but this time there is no suggestion of a threat. Uriel no longer points, nor looks away from the scene. It is as if Leonardo is inviting us to "spot the difference"—daring us to draw our own conclusions from the anomalous details.

This kind of examination of Leonardo's work reveals a plethora of provocative and disturbing undercurrents. There does seem to be a repetition, using several ingenious subliminal symbols and signals of the John the Baptist theme. Time and time again he, and images denoting him, are elevated above the figure of Jesus. . . .

There is something driven about this insistence, not least in the very intricacy of the images that Leonardo used, and indeed, in the risk he took in presenting even such clever and subliminal heresy to the world. Perhaps, as we have already hinted, the reason he finished so little of his work was not so much that he was a perfectionist, but more that he was only too aware of what might happen to him if anyone of note saw through the thin layer of orthodoxy to the outright "blasphemy" that lay just under the surface. Perhaps even the intellectual and physical giant that was Leonardo was a little wary of falling foul of the authorities—once was quite enough for him.

However, there was surely no need for him to put his head on the block by working such heretical messages into his paintings unless he had a passionate belief in them. As we have already seen, far from being the atheistic materialist beloved of many moderns, Leonardo was deeply, seriously committed to a system of belief that ran totally counter to what was then, and still is now, mainstream Christianity. It was what many would choose to call the "occult."

To most people today that is a word that has immediate, and less than positive connotations. It is taken to mean black magic, or the cavortings of depraved charlatans—or both. In fact the word "occult" simply means "hidden" and is commonly used in astronomy, such as in the description of one heavenly body "occulting," or eclipsing, another. Where Leonardo was concerned, one might agree that while there were indeed elements in his life and beliefs that smacked of sinister rites and magical practices, it is also true that what he sought was, above and beyond anything else, knowledge. Most of what he sought had, however, been effectively "occulted" by society—and by one omnipresent and powerful organization in particular. Throughout most of Europe at that time the Church frowned upon any scientific experimentation and took drastic steps to silence those who made their unorthodox or particularly individual views public.

However, Florence—where Leonardo was born and brought up, and at whose court his career really began—was a flourishing centre for a new wave of knowledge. This, astonishingly enough, was due entirely to this city being a haven for large numbers of influential occultists and magicians. Leonardo's first patrons, the de Medici family who ruled Florence, actively encouraged occult scholarship and even sponsored researchers to look for, and translate, specific lost manuscripts.

This fascination with the arcane was not the Renaissance equivalent of today's newspaper horoscopes. Although there were inevitably areas of investigation that would seem to us naive or downright superstitious, there were also many more which represented a serious attempt to understand the universe and man's place within it. The magician, however, sought to go a little further, and discover how to control the forces of nature. Seen in this light perhaps it is not so remarkable that

Leonardo of all people was, as we believe, an active participant in the occult culture of his time and place. And the distinguished historian Dame Frances Yates has even suggested that the whole key to Leonardo's far-ranging genius might have lain in contemporary ideas of magic.

The details of the precise philosophies so prevalent in this Florentine occult movement can be found in our previous book, but briefly, the lynchpin of all the groups of the day was hermeticism, which takes its name from Hermes Trismegistus, the great, if legendary, Egyptian magus whose books presented a coherent magical system. By far the most important part of hermetic thinking was the idea that man was in some way literally divine—a concept that was in itself so threatening to the Church's hold on the hearts and minds of its flock as to be deemed anathema.

Hermetic principles were certainly demonstrated in Leonardo's life and work but at first glance there would seem to be a glaring discrepancy between these sophisticated philosophical and cosmological ideas and heretical notions which nevertheless upheld the importance of biblical figures. (We must stress that the heterodox beliefs of Leonardo and his circle were not merely the result of a reaction against a corrupt and credulous Church.

As history has shown, there was indeed a strong, and certainly not undercover, reaction to the Church of Rome—the whole Protestant movement. (But had Leonardo been alive today we would not find him worshipping in *that* kind of church either.)

However, there is a great deal of evidence that hermeticists could also be outright heretics. Giordano Bruno (1548–1600), the fanatical preacher of hermeticism, proclaimed that his beliefs came from an ancient Egyptian religion that preceded Christianity—and which eclipsed it in importance.

Part of this flourishing occult world—but still too wary of the Church's disapproval to be anything other than an underground movement—were the alchemists. Again they are a group which suffers from a modern preconception. Today they are derided as fools who wasted their lives trying vainly to turn base metal into gold; in fact this image was a useful smokescreen for the serious alchemists who were more concerned with proper scientific experimentation—but also with personal transformation and its implicit total control of one's own fate. Again, it is not difficult to see that someone as hungry for knowledge as Leonardo would be part of that movement, perhaps even a prime mover in it. While there is no direct evidence for his involvement, he was known to consort with committed occultists of all shades, and our own research into his faking of the Turin Shroud suggests strongly that the image was the direct result of his own "alchemical" experiments.

Put simply: it is highly unlikely that Leonardo would have been unfamiliar with any system of knowledge that was available in his day, but at the same time, given the risks involved in being openly part of them, it is equally unlikely that he would commit any evidence of this to paper. Yet as we have seen, the symbols and images he repeatedly used in his so-called Christian paintings were hardly those which, had they realized their true nature, would have been appreciated by the Church authorities.

Even so, a fascination with hermeticism might seem, superficially at least to be almost at the opposite end of the scale to a preoccupation with John the Baptist—and the putative significance of the woman "M." In fact, it was this discrepancy which puzzled us to such an extent that we delved further. Of course it could be argued that what all this endless raising of forefingers means is that one Renaissance genius was obsessed with John the Baptist. But was it possible that a deeper significance lay behind Leonardo's own personal belief? Was the message that can be read into his paintings in some way actually *true*?

Certainly the Maestro has long been acknowledged in occult circles as being the possessor of secret knowledge. When we began researching his part in the Turin Shroud we came across many rumours among such people to the effect not only that he had a hand in its creation, but also that he was a known magus of some renown. There is even a nineteenth-century Parisian poster advertising the Salon of the Rose + Cross—a meeting-place for artistically minded occultists—that depicts Leonardo as Keeper of the Holy Grail (which in such circles can be taken to be shorthand for Keeper of the Mysteries). Again, rumours and artistic licence do not in themselves add up to much, but, taken together with all the indications listed above, they certainly whetted our appetite to know more about the unknown Leonardo.

So far we had isolated the major strand of what appeared to be Leonardo's obsession: John the Baptist. While it was only natural that he would receive commissions to paint or sculpt that saint while living in Florence—a place that was dedicated to John—it is a fact that when left to himself, Leonardo chose to do so. After all, the last painting he was to work on before his death in 1519—which was not commissioned by anyone, but painted for his own reasons—was of John the Baptist. Perhaps he wanted the image to look at as he lay dying. And even when he had been paid to paint an orthodox Christian scene, he always, if he could get away with it, emphasized the role of the Baptist in it.

As we have seen, his images of John are elaborately concocted to convey a specific message, even if it is grasped imperfectly and subliminally. John is certainly depicted as important—but then he was the forerunner, herald, and blood relative of Jesus, so it is only natural that his role should be recognized in this way. Yet Leonardo is not telling us that the Baptist was, like everyone else, inferior to Jesus. In his *Virgin of the Rocks* the angel is, arguably, pointing to *John*, who is blessing Jesus and not vice versa. In the *Adoration of the Magi* the healthy, normal-looking people are worshipping the elevated roots of the carob tree—John's tree—and not the colourless Virgin and child. And the "John gesture," that upraised righthand forefinger, is thrust into Jesus' face at the *Last Supper* in what is clearly no loving or supportive manner; at the very least, it seems to be saying in a bluntly threatening manner, "Remember John." And that least known of Leonardo's works, the Shroud of Turin, bears the same kind of symbolism, with its image of an apparently severed head being placed "over" a classically crucified body. The overwhelming evidence is that, to Leonardo at least, John the Baptist was actually superior to Jesus.

All this might make Leonardo appear to have been a voice crying in the wilderness. After all, many great minds have been eccentric, to say the least. Perhaps this was yet another area of his life in which he stood outside the conventions of his day, unappreciated and alone. But we were also aware, even at the outset of our research in the late 1980s, that evidence—albeit of a highly controversial nature—had emerged in recent years that linked him with a sinister and powerful secret society. This group, which allegedly existed many centuries before Leonardo, involved some of the most influential individuals and families in European history, and—according to some sources—it still exists today. Not only, it is said, were members of the aristocracy prime movers in this organization, but also some of today's most eminent figures in political and economic life keep it alive for their own particular aims. . . .

Thinking Far Outside the Frame
More Thoughts on Leonardo from Lynn Picknett

THE GAY LEONARDO ... THE SELF-PORTRAITIST OF THE MONA LISA ... THE PHALLUSES AND THE VIRGIN

If you found Lynn Picknett's ideas in the last excerpt about Leonardo, the *Last Supper* and the *Madonna of the Rocks* interesting, you will want to pursue some of her more recent thoughts along these lines as expressed in her 2003 book, *Mary Magdalene*. What follows are a few brief excerpts. From the book *Mary Magdalene* by Lynn Picknett. Copyright © Lynn Picknett 2003. Appears by permission of the publisher, Carroll & Graf Publishers, an imprint of Avalon Publishing Group.

Who was the Mona Lisa? Why is she smiling or smirking? Indeed, *is* she smiling or smirking, or is the impression simply due to the genius of Leonardo's unique brushwork, which creates a subtle effect, almost of shifting light? And if it was a portrait of some Italian or French lady, why was it never claimed by her family?

The answer to all of those questions may be simple, and characteristically—where that particular artist is concerned—little short of outrageous. Although famous for his art and designs for curiously advanced inventions such as the military tank and even the sewing machine, Leonardo da Vinci should perhaps be just as famed for his jokes and hoaxes ...

Leonardo da Vinci was famous in his own day as a wit and practical joker—scaring the ladies of the court with mechanical lions and convincing a terrified Pope that he had a dragon in a box, for example! But sometimes there was a dark, sharp and in some ways vicious edge to his jokes, some of which became major projects, perhaps even eclipsing his commissioned works in the amount of dedication, time and resources he devoted to them . . .

The *Mona Lisa*, it seems, was a self-portrait—just like St Jude in *The Last Supper* [Picknett believes that the Judas character in the *The Last Supper* was also a self-portrait, as was the figure thought to be Jesus in the Shroud of Turin, about which she has written at length] and other characters in his surviving works . . . This startling—and, on the face of it, sensational and unlikely—hypothesis was put forward in the 1980s by two researchers working independently of each other: Dr Digby Quested, of London's Maudsley Hospital, and Lillian Schwartz, of the prestigious Bell Laboratories in the United States . . . Both of them had noticed that the features of the "female" face of the *Mona Lisa* were exactly the same as those of the 1514 self-portrait of the artist as an old man, drawn in red chalk, now in Turin . . .

If, as seems to be the case, Leonardo *was* both the *Mona Lisa* and the face on the Shroud, then he had achieved a unique double coup: he not only became the universally recognized image of the Son of God, but also the "Most Beautiful Woman in the World"—no wonder "she" was smirking mysteriously!

Over the years, it has been suggested, sometimes even seriously, that the *Mona Lisa* was in fact a portrait of Leonardo's unknown female lover, which is considerably more unlikely than the self-portrait theory, on the grounds that he was almost certainly homosexual. . . .

If the elusive image of the enigmatic woman was indeed a self-portrait, why did he do it, and why did he keep it with him until his dying day? Perhaps the answer is simply that he thought he had produced a masterpiece, and wanted to keep his best work close to him. Perhaps he liked the look of himself as a woman, beardless and in drag. Perhaps it never failed to bring a smile to his lips, just like the one in the painting. Yet there are reasons to consider that, like everything else he did, there was also a deeper reason, a more profound and fundamental layer bubbling away like a witch's cauldron under the slick urbanity, that made him the life and soul of the party, composed of shreds of experience and belief, of love and hate and passion and pain.

Like Mary Magdalene, the illegitimate and probably gay Leonardo was an outsider, a tormented genius without benefit of much formal education, humoured and flattered in the courts of the great, but always dependent on patronage, always wary, mostly alone—and never secure. Always the artistic prostitute, being paid to produce the trophy portrait or the famous religious fresco (and then, not always on time), forever on the outside looking in. As an outsider, he reached out across the dark centuries to another: perhaps the dragged-up Leonardo, in his lady's veil and strange, almost stuck-on bust, was supposed to represent the Magdalene herself. Certainly, it would have been very much in character, for—as we will see—he clearly felt strongly about the much maligned saint of long ago ...

Before turning to the question of Leonardo's secret sources, we should take a new look at one of his other "beautiful religious paintings": *The Virgin of the Rocks* ... There is something else to note, although there are good reasons for any author who wishes to be taken seriously not to mention it at all.

A newcomer to these revelations might concede, even politely suspending disbelief, that perhaps there is a Johannite case to be answered in Leonardo's paintings, and even admire his subtlety and audacity in presenting such naughty imagery to the trusting gaze of the masses. But since the publication of *The Templar Revelation*, another example of Leonardo's extraordinary sublimal anti-Christian campaign has become only too apparent to Clive [Prince, Ms. Picknett's collaborator] and myself.

The following revelation is so sensational, so apparently ludicrous, as to appear the product of a Freudian delusion, or an infantile fantasy. Yet it should be remembered that Leonardo was primarily a hoaxer, a joker, and illusionist—and that he hated the Holy Family. . . . In the context of his jokes, it is wisest to forget everything that has ever been written or taught about Leonardo's "serious" works; this is anything but redolent of rarefied art history or the nobler paintings that drew generations on the Grand Tour. Clive and I wrote in *The Templar Revelation* that Leonardo was subtle in presenting his secret heretical code "for those with eyes to see" and did nothing that was "the equivalent of sticking a red nose on Saint Peter." But, as we discovered more recently, we were very wrong.

Do not think of the reverential hush of the great art galleries as the visitors tiptoe close to Leonardo's five-hundred-year-old brushwork. Think more of giggling schoolboys passing naughty scribblings around behind the bike sheds—or the likes of the Britart stars such as Tracey Emin or Damien Hirst, whose own controversial genius lies in the savagery and delight of iconoclasm. Although this feature can be discerned in both the National Gallery and Louvre versions of *The Virgin of the Rocks*, it is far clearer in the latter, the more truly heretical of the two works. A clue lies in the title of the painting: "rocks" was Italian slang for testicles, as in the modern phrase "getting your rocks off"—the equivalent of the crude modern British term "balls." And so it is that the reason for the mass of rocks above the Holy Family becomes shockingly obvious.

Almost growing out of the Virgin's head are two magnificent male "rocks"—topped with a massive phallus that rises to the very skyline, comprising no less than half the painting. The offending article is created out of the mass of rock, yet it is clearly discernible, and is even impudently topped with a small spurt of weeds. Perhaps this is the equivalent of a "Magic Eye" shape that takes time to filter through into the consciousness, depending on one's resistance to the idea—but it bears little resemblance to the common phenomenon of seeing animal shapes in clouds. This does not require an active imagination, simply the ability to see the painting anew, without any preconceptions or expectations. This is Leonardo the hoaxer and the heretic at his most audacious—and vicious. He created the grotesque male appurtenances deliberately, no doubt perversely and savagely inspired by the organization that commissioned him—the Confraternity of the Immaculate Conception. With a giant penis growing out of her head, he is clearly saying "to those with eyes to see" that this is no Virgin.

Trying to Make Sense of Leonardo's "Faded Smudge"

AN INTERVIEW WITH DENISE BUDD

Denise Budd is a Columbia University Ph.D. whose doctoral dissertation on Leonardo da Vinci focused on a reinterpretation of the documentary evidence from the first half of his career.

Is anything known about Leonardo that would suggest he was a member of the Priory of Sion or similar secret society?

There's no real evidence at all that Leonardo da Vinci was a member of the Priory of Sion or any other secret organization. The documents that Dan Brown relied upon heavily were discovered, apparently, in the Bibliothèque Nationale in Paris in the 1960s, and they appear to be twentieth-century forgeries.

Besides sometimes writing backwards, did Leonardo use codes or coding?

There is evidence of codes in some of his writing; one example is the so-called Ligny memorandum, in which he interspersed names and places in scrambled letters. And he may have worked as a spy when he was a military engineer for Cesare Borgia. But the backwards writing is not a particularly difficult code to crack. That was a function of Leonardo's left-handedness.

Leonardo is known for peppering his works with symbolism and, some say, heretical ideas, in his Virgin of the Rocks *paintings, for example. Do you agree?*

No, I don't. The *Virgin of the Rocks* was a religious commission for the Confraternity of the Immaculate Conception for the church of San Francesco Grande in Milan—not for nuns, as Brown says. Leonardo da Vinci got the commission in 1483. There were some complex legal issues regarding it and its copy, including issues of payment for Leonardo and his associate, Ambrogio de Predis. One of the reasons that Dan Brown argues that the painting is heretical is because he misreads the work, confusing the figure of St. John the Baptist with Christ, and vice versa. The composition shows Mary—with her hand suspended over her son, creating a dominant axis—embracing Christ's cousin St. John, who kneels in reverence. The Baptist is the first to recognize Christ's divinity, which he does in the womb, so this composition falls completely within the norms of tradition.

With the added element of the angel Uriel, Leonardo is actually combining two separate moments: this scene from Christ's infancy, with the scene when the Baptist (who is living as a baby hermit with the angel Uriel, according to an apocryphal text) visits the holy family on the flight into Egypt. Leonardo guides us through the composition by the play of hands, which relate the figures to one another. Presumably, the subject would have been worked out with the confraternity, and it would have played an important role in establishing the iconography, which likely refers to the issue of Mary's immaculate conception, which was not yet a matter of settled church doctrine. During the Renaissance, an artist was not generally given free rein on important commissions. There would have been specific guidelines. And presumably, Leonardo worked within that framework.

Can you comment on Leonardo's hypothesized homosexuality? How might his sexuality have played into his style of painting?

While there is rarely evidence for a person's sexuality in this age, here is what we know: he was accused twice, anonymously, of sodomy in Florence in 1476, while he was living with the painter Verrocchio. The same accusation included a member of the Medici clan, which certainly could suggest political motivation. The charges were dropped. Leonardo did not marry, which was the case for a whole litany of Renaissance artists, from Leonardo to Michelangelo, to Donatello, Brunelleschi, della Robbia, and others. Leonardo's presumed homosexuality stems primarily from later sixteenth-century sources, written after his death, as well as from his penchant for young and often not very talented workshop assistants, who, rather than leaving after their traditional period in the workshop, stayed on for many, many years. Was he a homosexual? Probably. But I do not think it had anything to do with his manner of painting. His women, portraits aside, are among the most beautiful of the period.

In one of the drawings in his notebooks, there's an anatomical study of intercourse. His comment is that the members on the page are so unappealing that if people didn't have beautiful faces the human race would die out. However, his works do not really give us any clues about his sexuality, nor would you expect them to.

What Some People See in the Last Supper

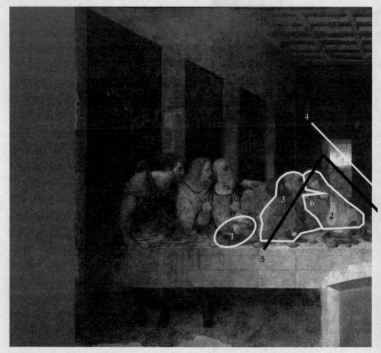

1. A knife hangs in the air seemingly tinged with symbolic meaning as it is disassociated from the rest of the image.

2. *The Da Vinci Code* suggests that the character to Jesus' right, generally thought to be John, is really female, not male, and is Leonardo's vision of Mary Magdalene, sitting in the most important place next to Jesus.

3. Peter's hand, slicing through the air in a menacing way in "Mary Magdalene's" direction, could be a gesture reinforcing Peter's rivalry with Mary Magdalene for control of Jesus' movement after his death and Peter's jealousy over the important place in the movement Jesus may have given to Mary.

4. The 45-degree angled space between Jesus and "Mary Magdalene" suggests a V—said in *The Da Vinci Code* to be the archetypal symbol of the chalice, the vagina, the womb, and female sexuality.

Scala/Art Resources, NY

5. The line that out-
lines Jesus and
"Mary Magdalene"
traces the shape of an
M. According to
another argument
advanced by *The
Da Vinci Code* this M
could connote either
Mary Magdalene or
matrimony.

6. The garments
worn by Jesus and
"Mary" are mirror
images of each
other's red and blue
fabrics.

7. The blue color
denotes spiritual love,
fidelity, and truth.
Red and blue are seen
as the royal colors,
in this case possibly
suggesting the "royal
blood" theme and
the alignment of the
royal House of
Benjamin (from
which Mary is said to
be descended) and
the House of David
(from which Jesus is
said to be
descended).

8. There is no central
chalice or wine goblet
in the *Last Supper*
despite the popular
preconception that
there is. Instead, each
person at the table
has a small glass cup
of his/her own.

What about Dan Brown's thesis about the Last Supper?

There is no disembodied hand as Dan Brown suggests. The hand with the knife—which is the hand Dan Brown says "threatens Mary Magdalene"—that's Peter's hand. And Peter's not threatening Mary Magdalene nor trying to suppress the feminine side of the church. Peter is holding the knife, which is a premonition of the violent reaction he will have during the arrest of Christ, when he cuts off the ear of the Roman soldier. So that is a fairly standard iconographic tool.

Dan Brown uses the absence of a chalice as an introductory point to bring Mary Magdalene into the picture. Yet if you look at the picture, you'll see that Christ's hands are spread out on the table. His right hand is reaching toward a piece of bread, and his left hand is actually, quite clearly, reaching toward a cup of wine. And that's the hand that's pointed down. The institution of the Eucharist is clearly presented in the bread and the wine. Now it's not a chalice per se, like a chalice in your modern church practice, but there's a cup of wine. It's what you would expect to see at the Last Supper.

And what about the idea that the painting depicts Mary
Magdalene instead of John the Baptist?

As far as the Magdalene, clearly there is no dispute. That figure is St. John the Evangelist. St. John is Christ's favorite and he is always shown by Christ's side. The major difference between Leonardo's *Last Supper* and earlier Florentine examples of the scene is that Leonardo put Judas among the disciples, not on the other side of the table. But the figure of John is always by Christ's side, he is always beardless and he's always beautiful. And in some instances, he is so innocent that while Christ is making the announcement that he will be betrayed, John actually sleeps. A perfect example of this "feminine" characterization of John is in Raphael's *Crucifixion* in the London National Gallery, painted around 1500.

A second point that must be mentioned is the atrocious state of the *Last Supper*, which makes it patently unreliable to examine for any reason other than basic composition, which, presumably, it retains. It was called a wreck only twenty years after its completion, while da Vinci was still alive, and has again and again been called barely visible. In the sixteenth century, Vasari called it a "faded smudge." It was restored in 1726, 1770; hung in a room that was used for a barracks for Napoleon's troops in 1799 and as a stable; damaged in a flood of 1800; a door was cut through the bottom of it; there was an attempt to remove it from the wall in 1821; it was restored in 1854–55, 1907–8, 1924, 1947–48, 1951–54, and all throughout the 1980s and 1990s. There is not enough of any of the faces left to make any serious determinations. Christ's face, for example, is a completely modern repainting.

"No, I do not believe there is a woman in the Last Supper . . ."

AN INTERVIEW WITH DIANE APOSTOLOS-CAPPADONA

Diane Apostolos-Cappadona is Adjunct Professor of Religious Art and Cultural History at the Center for Muslim-Christian Understanding and Adjunct Professor and Core Faculty in Art and Culture in the Liberal Studies Program, both at Georgetown University. With Deirdre Good, she has presented a series of workshops and special lectures on the theme of the "Truth of the Da Vinci Code."

*As you know, some people, including Dan Brown, seem to see
all sorts of things in the* Last Supper *that traditional art
historians and scholars do not. What do you see when you look
at this painting?*

What Leonardo presents us with in his painting of the
Last Supper is what he does primarily throughout all of his
art—the humanizing of art. This is one of his biggest
appeals. From my way of reading Christian art, this painting is iconographically important because Leonardo
changes the focus of the iconography. Historically, the
earlier carvings and sculptures on cathedral exteriors and
interiors, on liturgical vestments, and in paintings, sculptures, and manuscript illuminations of the Last Supper,
the artist emphasizes either the identification of the trai-
tor, which is the most important moment for most people,
or the Institution of the Eucharist, which is liturgically the
importance of the Last Supper.

What Leonardo does is portray the announcement,
"I am going to be betrayed," and the aftermath of that
moment. The disciples are in shock. They look at each
other, pointing with exaggerated gestures as if to say, "It
can't be me, it must be you, but who could it be, how could
it be any of us?" And Jesus is saying, not only, "I know I
will be betrayed," but also, "I know which of you is going
to do it."

In the larger context of Leonardo's oeuvre, gestures
are humanizing as well as symbolic. In this particular
painting, the gestures signify surprise, disbelief, accusation, and awe or wonder. This is what is important in this
painting. The Jesus figure is set off in a particular way
because the others are stunned. He is both the announcer
and the betrayed.

What do you think, specifically, about The Da Vinci Code's *supposition that the "John" character is really Mary Magdalene?*

Initially, my response was this is a very interesting interpretation, to say that there was a woman at the table. It fits nicely with feminist theology or the postfeminist era of theology. However that doesn't make it true.

If you look at the history of the Last Supper in Christian art, you see the figure of Jesus, sometimes seated at the center of a table, other times at an end of a table. The table may be round, square, or rectangular depending upon contemporary cultural and social customs as much as for artistic spacing. Simultaneously, you see regularly the figure of John the Evangelist (also known as John the Divine, or John the Beloved Disciple), in closest proximity to Jesus. There is a tradition of John being seen in our eyes—our late-twentieth century/early-twenty-first century eyes—as soft, feminine, and youthful.

However, if you look carefully at the Leonardo painting, you will notice other disciples who do not have beards or who could be construed as possessing feminine features. However from my work in gender studies, I would caution that gender is a culturally and socially conditioned concept. What you and I accept today as being masculine or feminine is most likely not what would have been accepted in Florence or Milan during the fifteenth century. If you look carefully at Christian art, in particular at the depictions of male and female bodies, faces, and gestures, then the *Last Supper* is not such an extraordinary presentation!

Can you be more specific?

If you look at the history of angels in Renaissance art contemporary to Leonardo, or in other Leonardo paintings, these angelic bodies are intended to be masculine. Yet I have students who become quite upset when I project

slides of medieval and Renaissance paintings with depictions of angels. In despair, the students ask, "But why
does he have long hair? Why does he have curls? His face is
sort of preadolescent." We have to stop and to consider
what is our preconception of gender?

No, I do not believe that there is a woman in the *Last
Supper* and I do not believe in any way that it's Mary Magdalene. I think that the *V* that's there—the one Dan Brown
defines as a symbol of femininity—is there, first of all, to
emphasize the Christ figure and to emphasize the reality
of the perspective within that fresco.

What role does artistic form and perspective play in this?

Perspective is extraordinarily important in Renaissance art
generally, and in Leonardo's art in particular. The apostles
are all grouped into triangular formations. For example,
there is the triangle composed of the so-called Mary Magdalene–John figure, the gray-bearded figure behind [who is
Judas], and the foreground figure [who is Peter]. Dan
Brown has omitted any discussion of pyramidal composition in Leonardo's oeuvre, of the four triangular group-
ings which are important to form the compositional
balance for the central triangular figure who is Jesus. Cen-
trally positioned, Jesus is in a pyramidal posture, and it is
this pyramidal composition that is one of Leonardo's
great gifts to Western art.

Today, we see the *Last Supper* within the shrine of a
museum atmosphere, however, the work was created on a
wall, in a refectory where the monks ate. They either looked
up at it or at the painting of the crucifixion on the opposite
wall depending on what was being said and what meal it was,
and what prayers were being recited. So the painting functioned differently, at different days of the liturgical calendar.
Dan Brown ignores totally that original monastic context.

Musings on the Manuscripts of Leonardo da Vinci

By SHERWIN B. NULAND

Sherwin Nuland is the author of the bestselling *How We Die*, winner of the 1994 National Book Award for Nonfiction. He is Clinical Professor of Surgery at Yale University, where he also teaches medical history and bio-ethics. Excerpted from "The Manuscripts" from *Leonardo da Vinci* by Sherwin B. Nuland, copyright © 2000 by Sherwin B. Nuland. Used by permission of Viking Penguin, a division of Penguin Group (USA) Inc.

This is the way I understand Leonardo da Vinci's intent, over the approximately thirty-five years during which he scrawled the more than five thousand manuscript pages of his extant writings, as well as those many undoubtedly lost. Beginning in Milan sometime after his thirtieth year, he began a process that amounts to setting down on paper a long series of notes to himself, some of which were random and brief, and some of which were well-constructed studies of one or another problem of an artistic, scientific, or philosophical nature, usually accompanied by either elaborate or simple drawings. In fact, it would be more correct to say that the drawings—left in various stages of completion—are accompanied by notes, since the former are of far greater significance. The sizes of the manuscript pages vary from quite large, as most of them were, to as small as three and a half by two and a half inches. More than half of the material is on loose sheets and the rest is in notebooks of various kinds. To add to the jumbling, Leonardo sometimes used folded sheets of paper which he later separated and arranged in pages, in such a way that the original juxtaposition was confused.

Almost always, an observation is complete on the page where it appears, although there are a very few instances, in bound volumes of numbered pages, where one finds the instruction "turn over," and "this is the continuation of the previous page." There is no punctuation, no accenting, and a proclivity toward running several short words together into one long one. Just as likely to be encountered is the division of a long word into halves. And once in a while, one comes across words or proper names in which the order of the letters is scrambled, as though in great haste. Some of the letters and numbers are written according to Leonardo's own sometimes inconsistent orthography, and they are at first difficult to decipher until one learns to recognize them, as well as to decipher certain shorthand terminology. In all, these are the personal idiosyncrasies of a personal note taker.

And then there is the so-called mirror writing. Leonardo wrote from right to left, adding considerably to the difficulty of transliterating his manuscripts. It is probably because of the mirror writing that he sometimes turned the pages of his notebooks in the reverse order, so whole sections can be found running back to front. A page of his scrawl is likely to contain a scientific discussion alongside a personal notation concerning daily household doings, and perhaps a sketch without text or text without a sketch or text and sketch all together in a completely lucid arrangement. When seemingly irrelevant notes and drawings are placed on some particular page, they are not infrequently found, when carefully scrutinized by experts, to be not irrelevant at all, but to have either direct or indirect applicability to the rest of the nearby material.

Although there is the volume that has been called since shortly after Leonardo's death the *Treatise on Painting*, its unity is the work of an unknown compiler who brought what he considered to be the appropriate pieces together into a unified form. The codex *On the Flight of Birds* does have something of a completeness about it, but other of the studies on flight are scattered through Leonardo's pages as well. In all of the manuscripts, there is not a single whole work as we conceive of it. What we have been left by Leonardo are the equivalent of thousands of those pieces of paper on which we have all recorded urgent messages to ourselves. Unfortunately, many of them are lost.

Certain of Leonardo's pages were not only never lost, however, but actually were revisited again and again. He might return to a particular sheet at intervals of weeks, months, or even many years in order to add drawings or notes as he learned more about a topic. Most notable in this regard for his anatomical research was his series of drawings of the brachial plexus, a complex bundle of interwoven and branching nerves that supplies the arm from its origin in the spinal cord of the neck. Leonardo's first and final drawings of the perplexing leash of fibers were separated by some twenty years.

Although demanding to read, writing as though seen in a mirror is far less difficult than might be supposed. Left-handed people in general find it quite easy, and it may in fact be more natural to them than standard script. Schooling drills the tendency out of young lefties, but the technique is easily picked up again. Many righties, too, can write right to left in a legible hand. And there is strong, albeit not certain, evidence that Leonardo was left-handed. Luca Pacioli referred to his friend's left-handedness in his own writings, as well as did a man named Saba da Castiglioni, in his *Ricordi*, published in Bologna in 1546. It has also been pointed out that the direction in which Leonardo customarily drew his shading lines is that of a naturally left-handed person, from left to right diagonally downward.

From all of these considerations, it would appear that there is no mystery in Leonardo's motives for writing as he did. He was almost certainly a lefty keeping notes, scribbling them as fast as he could because his hand was unable to keep up with the quickness of his mind. What some have thought a code seems to have been merely the personal scrawl of a man whose stylistic idiosyncrasies were a kind of shorthand to enable him to put things down on paper as quickly as possible. There is plenty of evidence from various of his comments that he intended eventually to collate much of this material, which would have been just as accessible to him as though he had written it in the standard way, even if to no one else.

As convincing as the foregoing might be, it still remains possible that Leonardo did indeed deliberately record his thoughts in such a way that they would be indecipherable to any but those so determined to understand them as to be willing to devote long hours to the process. Vasari wrote that he had been a heretic, and more a philosopher than a Christian; some must have thought him a crypto-atheist; not a few of his notions were far from those of the Church. This is the man, it will be recalled, who wrote, long before Galileo was accused, "The sun does not move." And this is the man also who saw evidence everywhere, whether in the form of fossils, rock formations, or the movements of water, of the great age of the earth and of the constantly changing character of its geologic and living forms. Not until the studies of Charles Lyell early in the nineteenth century would there again be encountered a scholar who theorized with such clarity that the characteristics of the earth's surface are the result of processes taking place over enormously long periods of geological time. "Since things," he wrote, "are far more ancient than letters, it is not to be wondered at if in our day there exists no record of how the aforesaid seas extended over so many countries; and, moreover, such record ever existed, the wars, the conflagrations, the deluges of the waters, the changes in speech and habits, have destroyed every vestige of the past. But sufficient for us is the testimony of things produced in the salt waters and now found again in the high mountains far from the seas."

Leonardo depicted that testimony in some of his paintings, specifically in the *Virgin of the Rocks*, the *St. Anne*, and the *Mona Lisa*. In the background of each can be seen the primeval world as he must have imagined it was before it evolved (I choose the word advisedly—he came close to describing the theory of evolution) into its modern form.

As a man who more than once proclaimed that everything is part of everything else, he surely related the generation of the world to the generation of a human being. His fascination with the one was of a piece with his fascination with the other.

It was unpredictable nature that Leonardo saw as the creator of the ever-changing wonders of the earth, and he did not hesitate to say so: "Nature, being inconstant and taking pleasure in creating and continually producing new forms, because she knows that her terrestrial materials are thereby augmented, is more ready and more swift in her creating than is time in his destruction." There is no mention here of God, and certainly no room for the biblical Creation story. Regardless of my own conviction to the contrary, perhaps considerations like these should be factored into any theory attempting to understand the totality of why Leonardo should have chosen to write so inaccessibly. The dangers of easily discovered heresy in that Church-dominated time cannot be underestimated, as we know all too well from the treatment not only of Galileo, but of others too, who dared to question doctrine.

The Leonardian notes have been mastered by a small band of scholars over the centuries, whose labors provide a precious record of their author's thought for the rest of us to ponder. Even the scattered quotes appearing throughout this book suffice to demonstrate the power of the Vincian's language. To the titles of painter, architect, engineer, scientist, and all the others must be added literary craftsman. What is most remarkable about some of the soaring flights of language and contemplation is the very fact that they seem to have been meant for their author's eyes only, the considerations of heresy notwithstanding.

The aesthete, the observer of man and nature, the moral philosopher who comes forth from the manuscript pages is speaking from the depths of his understanding and the power of his most profound emotion, as though in a constant stream of consciousness extending over a period of more than thirty years. Here there is no inner censor, only the crystal-clear voice of honesty, conviction, and—most remarkably for his era—a refreshingly open-minded curiosity.

Had Leonardo set out to record a volume of the principles by which he lived his life, or a book of aphorisms for which he wished to be remembered, or a compendium of his interpretations of the universe and its relationship to mankind—had any of these been his intention, he could not have accomplished them more effectively than he did in what would appear to be a scattershot miscellany of random thoughts sprayed over the pages of his loose sheets and notebooks, amid sketches, architectural plans, scientific observations, mathematical constructs, quotations from other authors, and records of daily life. He exposes at once his innermost musings and the overt thrust of the message he devoted his life to transmitting: That a human being can be understood only by turning toward nature; that the secrets of nature are discoverable by observation and experiment free of preconception; that there are no bounds to the possibilities of man's understanding, that there is a unity between all elements in the universe; that the study of *form* is essential, but the key to understanding lies in the study of *movement* and *function*, that the investigation of forces and energies will lead to the ultimate comprehension of the dynamics of nature; that scientific knowledge should be reducible to mathematically demonstrable principles; that the ultimate question to be answered about all life and indeed all nature is not *how*, but *why*.

"That a human being can be understood only by turning toward nature." This is a notion far more encompassing than it may at first seem. Leonardo's thought is infused with the ancient thesis that man is a microcosm of the great macrocosm that is the universe. In his thinking, though, this was not a spiritual concept, but a mechanistic one governed by the forces of nature. All arises from all else and all is mirrored in all else. The structure of our planet is like the structure of a man:

> Man has been called by the ancients a lesser world, and indeed, the term is rightly applied, seeing that man is compounded of earth, water, air and fire, this body of the earth is the same. And as man has within himself bones as a stay and framework for the flesh, so the world has the rocks which are the supports of the earth, and as man has within him a pool of blood wherein the lungs as he breathes expand and contract, so the body of the earth has its ocean, which also rises and falls every six hours with the breathing of the world. As from the said pool of blood proceed the veins which spread their branches through the human body, in just the same way the ocean fills the body of the earth with an infinite number of veins of water.

Some of the aphorisms in Leonardo's writings have the soaring quality of biblical verse, and even parallelism, reminiscent of Proverbs, Psalms, or Ecclesiastes. Here is the Leonardo who famously wrote, "Beauty in life perishes, not in art," expressing his certainty that painting is art's highest form: "Thirst will parch your tongue and your body will waste through lack of sleep ere you can describe in words that which painting instantly sets before the eye."

And on his notion of the immortality that we make for ourselves by the way we live our lives and the heritage of accomplishment we leave to posterity: "O you who sleep, what is sleep? Sleep resembles death. Oh, why not let your work be such that after death you acquire immortality, rather than during life you make yourself like unto the hapless dead by sleeping." And elsewhere, a corollary statement: "Avoid that study the resultant work of which dies with the worker."

And this, sounding as though it came whole from the pages of Proverbs: "Call not that riches which may be lost; virtue is our true wealth, and the true reward of its possessor .... As for property and material wealth, these you should ever hold in fear; full often they leave their possessor in ignominy, mocked at for having lost possession of them." All of these thoughts spring from the man some of whose contemporaries accused of being "totally unlettered."

Of course, many of the notations are far from being so lofty. There were lists of books to read or acquire; and there were recordings of the mundane activities involved in caring for a large household and directing a workshop of artists and artisans; and there were letters to various patrons complaining of nonpayment. Thus, in the patched together volume that came to be called the *Codex Atlanticus*, these words are to be found in a fragment of a letter that was to be sent to Ludovico Sforza during the first Milan period. "It vexes me greatly that the fact of having to earn my living [by accepting outside commissions] has forced me to interrupt the prosecution of the work which your Lordship entrusted to me; but I hope in a short time to have earned enough to be able with a calm mind to satisfy your Excellency, to whom I commend myself; and if your Lordship thought that I had money your Lordship was deceived, for I have had six mouths to feed for thirty-six months and I have had fifty ducats."

Never one to hide his talents under a bushel, Leonardo was not averse to lauding himself when the occasion called for it, as in this statement from a letter of the same period, to an unknown recipient. "I can tell you that from this town you will get only makeshift works and unworthy and crude masters:

there is no capable man, believe me, except for Leonardo the Florentine, who is making the bronze horse for Duke Francesco, and who has no need to praise himself, because he has a task which will take him all his life and I doubt that he will ever finish it, because it is such a large work."

Every once in a great while, the reader encounters a statement so prescient that it is necessary to stop and read it again and then yet again, to be certain that it is being interpreted correctly. Leonardo introduced so many new concepts that there is a tendency to credit him with more than he actually deserves, and one must be cautious lest there be overinterpretation of some of his statements. But it is nevertheless not possible to avoid the thought that he is in the following passage elucidating the basis of the evolutionary principles that in numerous other manuscript pages he undoubtedly expresses in his observation of geological formations, waters and fossils. "Necessity is the mistress and the teacher of nature," he writes. "It is the theme and the inspiration of nature, its curb and eternal regulator." The necessity is the need to stay alive—it is the catalyst for the evolutionary process.

In like fashion, he seems to have understood the principles that would in later centuries come to be called inductive reasoning, and the role of experimentation in elucidating the general laws of nature:

First I shall make some experiments before I proceed further, because my intention is to consult experience first and then by means of reasoning show why such experiment is bound to work in such a way. And this is the true rule by which those who analyze natural effects must proceed; and although nature begins with the cause and ends with the experience, we must follow the opposite course, namely (as I said before), begin with the experience and by means of it investigate the cause.

Such a way of proceeding was unheard of in Leonardo's

day. It was seventeenth-century thinking at a time when the great mass of philosophical men were doing just the opposite, namely, expounding overarching theories to explain their experiences and observations. It would be well more than a century before William Harvey, the discoverer of the circulation of the blood, put into a brief sentence the new principle that the "unlettered" Leonardo had brought forth from a virtual scientific vacuum: "We confer with our own eyes, and make our ascent from lesser things to higher."

9 Temples of Symbols, Cathedrals of Codes

The Secret Language of Architectural Symbolism

O brother, had you known our mighty hall, / Which Merlin built for Arthur long ago! /. For all the sacred mount of Camelot, / And all the dim rich city, roof by roof, / Tower after tower, spire beyond spire, / By grove, and garden; lawn, and rushing brook, / Climbs to the mighty hall that Merlin built / And four great zones of sculpture, set betwixt / With many a mystic symbol, gird the hall . . .

—ALFRED TENNYSON

The challenge isn't to find occult links between Debussy and the Templars, Everybody does that. The problem is to find occult links between, for example, cabala and the spark plugs of a car . . . —UMBERTO ECO

Ever since the first artistic renderings of the human sense of the sacred were painted on cave walls, visual signs and symbols have been a key part of the experience and expression of the sacred, the divine, the ritualistic, and the religious.

In *The Da Vinci Code*, we spend a good amount of the twenty-four-hour experience inside churches—Saint-Sulpice, Temple Church, Westminster Abbey, Rosslyn Chapel ... plus the Louvre Museum, arguably a veritable "church" in the opinion of Jacques Saunière. We also hear discussion of Notre Dame and Chartres, King Solomon's Temple in Jerusalem, and more. We also hear Robert Langdon, the symbologist, explain his theories about how the church architecture was designed to reflect the sacred feminine in many architectural and design aspects.

Egyptians, Greeks, and Romans all expressed their religious cosmology in how they designed and constructed their buildings. Certainly, Templars and Masons, master builders, expressed their belief systems in their architectural work.

In this chapter, we take a virtual tour of the main themes of *The Da Vinci Code* as expressed in architecture and visual symbols.

Paris
In the Footsteps of The Da Vinci Code

By David Downie

David Downie is a Paris-based freelance writer, editor, and translator. This article originally appeared in the *San Francisco Chronicle*, January 25, 2004. In this piece, he takes readers on a quick tour of Paris landmarks, symbols, and signposts that have attracted new tourist interest since the publication of *The Da Vinci Code*. Copyright © 2004 by David Downie.

Paris—What do Place Vendôme, the *Mona Lisa*, astronomer Louis Arago and a medieval bishop named Sulpicius have in common? Simple: *The Da Vinci Code*, Dan Brown's breathless, five-hundred-page quest for the Holy Grail, set primarily in Paris.

The thriller's hero, professor Robert Langdon, is a Harvard "symbologist" lucky enough to be lodging at the $1,000-a-night Ritz on elegant Place Vendôme when foul play begins nearby at the Louvre. The museum's director, the Grand Master of a secret society charged with protecting the Grail, is murdered thirty yards from Leonardo da Vinci's enigmatic *Mona Lisa*, one of the tale's keys. An invisible north-south line bisects the Louvre and a church south of the Seine, Saint-Sulpice. The line is the Paris Meridian, first plotted in 1718, then recalculated with precision in the early 1800s by Arago. It predates the Greenwich Meridian and since 1994 has been marked with 135 brass disks.

Other sights scattered around the book's somewhat surreal Paris cityscape include the Palais-Royal, Champs-Elysées, Tuileries Garden, Bois de Boulogne parklands and Gare Saint-Lazare train station.

But it's the blood-soaked Louvre and looming Saint-Sulpice, and the treasure hunt for brass "Arago" disks, that are currently attracting squadrons of Grail seekers, many of whom travel with dog-eared copies of *The Da Vinci Code*.

Until 1645, a Romanesque church and graveyard stood where the imposing, colonnaded pile of Saint-Sulpice rises today, between the Left Bank's Luxembourg Garden and Boulevard Saint-Michel.... Long known for its towering 6,588-pipe organ, and Eugène Delacroix's gloomy *Jacob Fighting an Angel*, Saint-Sulpice has roughly the same footprint (360 feet long by 184 wide and 108 tall) as Notre Dame cathedral. Grail pilgrims now flock here to admire the astronomical gnomon that features prominently in the book. Its significance is twofold, revealing the location of a secret keystone and introducing readers to the Paris Meridian. The author dubs the meridian a "rose line." Apparently roses are symbolic of the Grail and therefore of Mary Magdalene.

Designed to calculate the spring equinox (and from it, Easter), the gnomon's brass strip crosses the transept's floor, then climbs a stone obelisk along the north-south axis. At noon the sun's rays passing through an oculus on the transept's south wall focus on the strip, giving the solar calendar date. Easter (a movable feast with pre-Christian roots) falls on the first Sunday after the equinox, so the gnomon accurately establishes the holiday's date.

In Brown's bestseller, a murderous albino monk named Silas breaks the tiles at the obelisk's base while searching for the keystone, then batters to death a nun assigned to protect it. On a recent visit to the site, Grail pilgrims could be seen prostrate, rapping the floor in front of the obelisk. Others listened to church guides explaining how the gnomon works, or searched for the luckless nun's upstairs rooms.

In reality, the Paris Meridian passes nearby but does not actually correspond to the gnomon's axis. No mention is made in the book of Sulpicius' tomb in the provincial French city of Bourges, which the meridian does traverse.

Church sacristan Paul Roumanet discounts Brown's claim that a temple of Isis lies beneath the sanctuary. On a Sunday afternoon tour of the crypt, attended by a clutch of thriller readers, no ancient temple could be discerned, though Romanesque walls and columns remain.

However, conspiracy theorists may be pleased to learn that a subcrypt containing five tombs is off-limits to the public. Further, according to the *Guide de Paris Mystérieux*, it was in the Romanesque church's graveyard that in 1619 three witches attempted to evoke the devil, and for many years, local residents held "macabre dances" on the toppled tombstones.

The brass Arago disks are a work of installation art titled *Hommage à Arago*, by Dutchman Jan Dibbets. Following an imaginary meridian, they lead north from No. 28 Rue de Vaugirard (near Saint-Sulpice) to Boulevard Saint-Germain, Rue de Seine, Quai Conti and Port des Saints-Pères. Across the river at the Louvre, three disks traverse the museum's Denon Wing (in the Roman Antiquities section, on a staircase and in a corridor). Five others stipple the Cour Carrée behind the main glass pyramid designed by I. M. Pei at the behest of former French president François Mitterrand.

(Warning! If you haven't read *The Da Vinci Code* yet, you might want to stop here. What follows gives away some key plot points.)

In the book's epilogue, Professor Langdon feels the Arago disks pull him south across the Palais Royal into the Passage Richelieu, eventually converging on the pyramid (which, Brown says, has 666 glass panes, a number symbolic of Satan). It's here that the "rose line" turns due west and runs through the Louvre's subterranean Carrousel shopping concourse to an "inverted pyramid" hanging from the ceiling.

In the protagonist's mind, this upside-down pyramid is a metaphorical chalice or grail, symbolizing the "sacred feminine," first venerated here in the Earth goddess rites of antiquity. On the floor beneath the skylight stands a small stone pyramid, symbolic of a blade or phallus. The tips of the pyramids point at each other, hinting that underneath a hidden vault might just contain chests of ancient documents, and the tomb of Mary Magdalene—the Holy Grail.

Ninety percent of the Louvre's annual 6 million visitors make a beeline for the Mona Lisa, making it difficult to spot Grail pilgrims looking for bloodstains or messages near the celebrated painting. But the many budding "symbologists" counting panes in Mitterrand's pyramid, or genuflecting by the inverted skylight, do attract attention.

Were it not for the author's claim that "all descriptions of artwork [and] architecture ... in this novel are accurate," it might be unsporting to reveal that the number 666 can't be divided evenly into four sides of a pyramid. Similarly, pagans never danced around the Carrousel, and there is no chamber beneath the phallus. The miraculous "rose line" capable of a 90-degree turn is none other than the so-called "Triumphal Way," a perspective laid out in 1670 by Louis XIV's royal landscaper Le Nôtre.

However, there may yet be material in Paris for a Grail sequel. The Triumphal Way runs past an ancient Egyptian obelisk in the Place de la Concorde, and Mitterrand might well have belonged to a secret society or two. Who knows what the symbologists will discover when the Louvre's subterranean concourse is remodeled in 2007 to further speed access to museum shops and the *Mona Lisa?*

The "Symbology" of *The Da Vinci Code*

AN INTERVIEW WITH DIANE APOSTOLOS-CAPPADONA

In the previous chapter, Diane Apostolos-Cappadona discussed Brown's references to Leonardo. Here she turns her attention to Brown's use of symbolism. Although, as she points out below, she never heard the word *symbologist* (Robert Langdon's alleged field of expertise at Harvard) until she read Dan Brown's work, she is about as close as one can get to being a real-life professional symbologist.

What is the importance of symbols in Christianity—and in religion in general?

Symbols are a form of communication. However, this is a form of communication that is multileveled, or multilayered, and in that there is no equal, one-for-one exchange. This is what makes them both fascinating and difficult, or confusing. Symbols operate on a variety of levels: they do such "simple things" as teach the ideas or the history of a faith or tradition, teach the stories of religious or societal traditions, teach religious doctrine, and explain how one is to gesture and posture and stand during liturgical services. They tell you about communicating with members of your community, and how to identify yourself within that community. There is the further understanding that symbols—and this principle is at work for all world religions, not specifically Christianity—are a way of communicating an embodied identity of knowledge and an embodied identity of who this community is. So symbolism and symbols are an integral part of the socialization process.

Do the meanings of symbols tend to change over time?

Yes, the meanings of symbols can change because of shifts in theology, doctrine, art styles, politics, and economic situations. For example, enormous changes in symbolism occurred during the Reformation, which was a complex umbrella of economic, political, and social transformations, as well as a religious revolution. This is the problem with symbols, and simultaneously the fascination; it's never as simple as a red light means stop and a green light means go.

What's a Christian symbol that's changed over time?

The fish has had multiple connections and meanings, from the Last Supper to the risen Christ. The fish was found in original depictions of the Last Supper. The fish had many meanings in early Christianity; then, it basically disappeared from the Christian consciousness ... only to return in the late twentieth century when the *ichthyus* was retrieved, or rediscovered, as a symbol. It, not the cross, was the first symbol of Christian identity. The cross didn't become an identifying and visual symbol until the fourth or fifth centuries. The fish, from the Greek *ichthys*, as it is transliterated into English, is related as an anagram of the earliest prayer of the Christian tradition. Taking the first letter of each word from the prayer "Jesus Christ, Son of God and Savior," the Greek letters spell ICHTHYS—that is, the fish. There were several connections in the Hebrew and Christian scriptures between the fish and the Messiah. For example, there was the verbal connection to the "fishers of men," and further connections with relation to water, fish, fishing, and boats in early Christianity.

What symbols historically have been connected to Mary Magdalene?

The most important one is the unguent jar, which relates to her being the anointer and connects her symbolically, if not metaphorically, to the other women anointers in the scripture, including the women who anointed the feet and the head of Jesus before the crucifixion. The female anointer who cared for—that is, washed, anointed, and dressed—the body of the deceased was a common practice in Mediterranean cultures. These anointers were always women. It was taboo for men to wash and anoint the dead. Women were considered "unclean," so for them to wash and anoint the dead was not inappropriate; this may be a negative reading for women. However, you could relate this activity to a Jungian reading—that every man has three women in his life: his mother, his wife, and his daughter. Each woman initiates him into a different part of his life—and one of the functions of the daughter, ultimately, was to purify and anoint her parents' bodies after death. Then again, there are all of those wonderful legends about the Magdalene's unguent jar over the centuries. My favorite story related to the unguent jar is from the *Arabic Gospel of the Infancy of the Savior* (Chapter 5). Mary of Magdala buys a jar of unguents to anoint the body of Jesus of Nazareth. Her purchase turns out to be the jar that was put on the shelf after the birth of this child named Jesus, and which contained within the nard his umbilical cord. So that the anointing of his body becomes profoundly symbolic: making him whole again and reconnecting him to his mother at the end of his life.

What about the pentacle, which is used as an important symbol in The Da Vinci Code?

The pentacle has five sides. The symbolic meaning is related to numbering, numerology, and the significance of the number five. In Christianity, five is the number of the wounds of the crucified Jesus (his two hands, his two feet, and his pierced side). Five relates fundamentally to the concept of "the human"—two arms, two legs, and a head. Numbers have meanings. There are mystical numbers, normally odd numbers, and therefore indivisible. Seven, for example, is the number of fulfillment; there are seven days in the creation story. Three is a mystical number and so forth: three, five, and seven.

What about the rose, another important symbol in The Da Vinci Code?

I have problems with the descriptions of the rose as a symbol in *The Da Vinci Code*. I don't interpret the rose the same way that Dan Brown does, especially with relation to his discussions of genitalia. He suggests that the rose has always been a premier symbol of female sexuality. My guess is that he learned this from reading a series of symbol dictionaries. However, I don't think this is the meaning of the rose in Western Christianity. In classical

Mediterranean cultures, the rose was the flower sacred to Venus or Aphrodite, which is how Brown may have made a connection to female sexuality. Venus or Aphrodite signified much more, however, than simple sex and sexuality. She was about romantic love, and love on a variety of levels, not just sexual intercourse. As a sign of romantic love, the color of the rose becomes important. The early color symbolism of the rose was simpler than it is today with such an array of hues available at florists. For early and medieval Christians, there were only four colors for roses: white signified innocent love or pure love; pink, first love; red, true love; and yellow, which meant "forget it, it's over."

However, what is important about the rose and its relationship to Mary is the thorn. The popular understanding—and it's a legendary, not a scriptural, understanding— is that the roses, and rosebushes, had no thorns in the Garden of Eden. Thereby, whenever you saw a rosebush positioned near Mary, and especially a presentation of Mary and the Child, it was a sign of Paradise, for it was Mary who began the process of our reentry into Paradise, the place where the roses had no thorns. The rose, then, became a symbol and a signifier, if you will, of Mary's role in human salvation. Her rose was a sign of grace; so the rose window was created to glorify Mary the Mother, not Mary Magdalene. Roses were related to a variety of female saints, but Mary Magdalene was not one of them.

Then there's the fleur-de-lis, which plays a prominent role in Dan Brown's book . . .

The fleur-de-lis is both a symbol of France and the city of Florence. It's a lily—a flower that in Christianity signifies the trinity. According to tradition, King Clovis—whose baptism made him the first Christian king of France—initiated the use of the fleur-de-lis as the sign of purification for both his own personal spirituality (that is, when he was baptized) and the purification of France. It became the emblem of French royalty, and later an attribute of many French saints, including Charlemagne. It's important in *The Da Vinci Code* because the key shaped in a fleur-de-lis would connect to the purification of France.

In some instances, like this one, Dan Brown uses symbols very well. Those are the elements that make *The Da Vinci Code* both believable to someone who has symbolic knowledge and absolutely fascinating to those who don't have any idea what these signs were about. The fleur-de-lis connects visually to the lily, which in turn has multiple meanings in Christianity, particularly in relation to women, from purity to innocence to royalty. The beauty of the lily's fragrance pleases the senses. It was sacred traditionally to the virgin and mother goddesses throughout the Mediterranean world prior to Christianity. Then, it became a significant symbol for Mary. There was a popular tradition that the lily sprang up from the tears Eve shed as she was expelled from the Garden of Eden. Weave all of those meanings together, add the relevance of this symbol to French history, and Brown has a powerful symbol to use. Although I suspect he uses it because the fleur-de-lis is the symbol of France.

That raises the question of Mary Magdalene's alleged French connection.

There are several legends and traditions about the Magdalene being the missionary to France, the patroness of France, saving France, Christianizing France, spending her last days in France, and being buried in France. You have your choice; you can go to the Dominicans or the Benedictines, to Vézelay or Aix-en-Provence. You have that whole tradition, even down to the making of madeleine cookies, which used to be served only on the twenty-second of July—that is, her feast day on the Roman calendar. These lemon-flavored, fan-shaped cookies signify both her geographic location in the south of France and the pious legends of her penitence in the desert. For if Mary Magdalene did live in Sainte Baume for thirty years (or fifty years, depending on which legend you're reading), she was reputed to have eaten no food. Rather, she survived on the fragrance of the lemon trees and the sacred food that she received every day when she was elevated for communion. Now, why any person in her right mind would go to the south of France for thirty or fifty years and not eat anything has always escaped me. . . .

Do you believe that the Holy Grail is a metaphor or a real object . . . or both?

I believe that there has been—and always will be—a perpetual mythology about the Holy Grail. Further, there is a history of an understanding that the Grail was a true object, a physical object that could be touched, to which Christians would have had great devotion, and which for some reason disappeared. According to certain legends and popular traditions, the Grail disappears and then reappears in England, reputedly brought there by Joseph of Arimathea. The place in England where the Grail reappears is at the site we would identify as Camelot. Of course, the important principle is that the concept of the Grail is a metaphor for the spiritual quest. So to be honest, I suppose my answer is that it's both—both a metaphor and a real object.

There was a *Newsweek* article [*The Bible's Lost Stories*, 12/08/03] with a small sidebar, "Decoding *The Da Vinci*

Code," which included images of the Last Supper and one of the Chalice of the Abbé Suger now in the National Gallery of Art in Washington, DC. The alabaster part of that chalice was believed to be the Holy Grail. Abbé Suger had it encased in the gold and bejeweled fashion that we have today, and it was used at the first mass that he celebrated at the Cathedral of Saint-Denis in Paris, the first Gothic cathedral. The building of this cathedral was, of course, during the period of the Crusades and the pilgrimages to the Holy Land, when devout Christians brought back as many major relics as possible. The chalice has been tested—carbon-dated—and it's from the appropriate time period. However, I think of the Holy Grail more as a metaphor because the reality of history is that when Jesus of Nazareth and his followers had this meal together, they were not in a position, financially or otherwise, to have had this very elaborate tableware and other objects. If they were, would they have used a chalice? Or would they have used something that was more like a glass or a pitcher or a small urn?

The *San Graal* is a very important metaphor in nineteenth-century pre-Raphaelite painting and literature, with the revival of Dante and the Arthurian romances. The Grail is found in variety of literary, musical, and dramatic productions, from the Ring Cycle by Wagner to *The Lord of the Rings*, in both book and movie formats. It is the same story over and over again: this quest for spiritual salvation. The tangible object being sought takes a variety of shapes, so that in these operas and the Tolkien works, it is a ring rather than a cup. In that way it's a metaphor.

What about the idea put forth in The Da Vinci Code *that the Holy Grail is actually Mary Magdalene?*

That's a very Jungian reading of Mary Magdalene—women as receivers and containers, women as vessels. But historically this is a connection that is older than Jung. You find this symbolism in classical mythologies. There are a variety of metaphors here. The mysterious connection in terms of sexual intercourse is the one that matters most. Women receive the male during sexual intercourse. They thereby conceive a child and hold that child in their sacred vessel, and then expel the child from their sacred vessel. I suppose one can make an argument for Mary Magdalene as the *San Graal* if one is a Jungian. However, I have my own way of reading symbols, so for me it doesn't work. I think Mary Magdalene has sacramental importance, but that's not her primary importance. Who she is is a mystery, and that's what makes her great to write about. I think in the year 3000 people will argue just as much about who she is or who she was as they do right now. By that I don't mean arguing about a prostitute or a woman of means or a poor woman or a sexual woman; I mean how she is in Christianity perhaps the one mirror of all aspects of humanity. The one thing she isn't is a mother or a wife, as far as we know.

What is the significance of Jesus appearing first to Mary Magdalene after the resurrection?

Well, I don't think it was because they were lovers or, for that matter, possibly married as Dan Brown suggests. Rather, I think it was because she signified the witness—the one for whom seeing is enough to believe. This is as a parallel to Thomas, who had to touch the wounds and physically feel the body of Jesus—that is, the empirical evidence—before he would believe that Jesus had been resurrected. I think there are ways of reading scripture that argue for Jesus being very feminist. One way is that it is the women who continue to believe in him, who are faithful to him unto his death and provide the rituals of his death, his dying, his mourning, his burial; and it is the women who still come and who are not afraid. To me, the principle is that they represent that part of humanity that never loses faith, that never loses hope, the people for whom to see is enough to understand. To me it is empowering of women and of the feminine. Intuition is more important to me than reason. The Mary Magdalenes of this world trust their intuition, the Thomases do not.

How accurate do you find Dan Brown's portrayal of Saint-Sulpice church in Paris—where a pivotal scene of the novel takes place—and its iconography?

There is a reality that Christianity built churches, basilicas, and cathedrals on the sites of earlier religious buildings. There are churches throughout Rome, Athens, and France built on the sites of temples to Mithras, Athena, and other prior gods and goddesses. The most obvious is the church in Rome called Santa Maria Sopra Minerva—Mary over Minerva. However, the connection usually is more than architectural; that is, Mary's church is built over the church of Minerva because there is a connection between Mary and Minerva as goddesses of wisdom.

For me, to propose that Saint-Sulpice is built over a temple or shrine to Isis makes no sense, because Isis connects to Mary the Mother more than she connects to Mary Magdalene. If parts of *The Da Vinci Code* were more about Mary the Mother, I might recognize the connection with Isis. For example, the Black Madonna cult relates Mary the Mother and Isis; so that the majority of the churches with black Madonnas were built on sites of earlier Isis shrines. So, yes, there is this whole tradition in Christianity.

In The Da Vinci Code, *Dan Brown's hero is a so-called* symbologist. *Is there such a thing, or such an academic discipline?*

The study of religious symbols is usually identified as iconography or religious art, not symbology. The first time I ever saw the word *symbology*, in fact, was in Dan Brown's *Angels & Demons*; I read his first book in this series of "Robert Langdon mysteries" first.

If such a term, *symbology*, were used as an academic or disciplinary title, it is part of what I do. I'm not a pure-bred academic in the sense that I research and study in an interdisciplinary or multidisciplinary fashion. I work with the arts, with art history, with cultural history, with the history of religion, with theology, with gender studies, and with world religions, so I don't have a pure academic discipline. However, I don't know of anybody who identifies him- or herself as a symbologist, and there is no formal academic study by that name that I know of. There may well be now because Brown's book has taken off.

Rosslyn Chapel: The Cathedral of Codes and Symbols

Saunière's clues lead Robert Langdon and Sophie Neveu to the Rosslyn Chapel in Scotland near the end of *The Da Vinci Code*. When the pair arrives at the chapel to search for the Grail, they discover that the meaning of the legend is more complicated than they previously imagined.

Rosslyn Chapel is a real place, with a fascinating history. Work on the chapel—also known as the Cathedral of Codes—began in 1446 at the behest of Sir William St. Clair, or Sinclair, a hereditary grand master of the Scottish Masons and a reputed descendent of the Merovingian bloodline. Sir William exercised personal control over the chapel's construction, which halted shortly after his death in 1484. Only the choir—the part of the church occupied by the choir and the clergy, where services are performed—is completed.

The chapel is replete with religious imagery that has become a touchstone for endless speculation by esoteric writers, Grail enthusiasts, and conspiracy theorists. It is no wonder Dan Brown set the next to the last scene in *The Da Vinci Code* in this chapel, much worshipped by occultists the world over.

Rosslyn is reputed to be an approximate copy of the design of the ancient Temple of Solomon and is adorned with innumerable carvings, including Judaic, Celtic, Norse, Templar, and Masonic symbols, in addition to mainstream Christian images. The many different signs and symbols from many cultures, certainly a unique architectural rendering for its time, gives Rosslyn Chapel its nickname as the "Cathedral of Codes."

Curators at Rosslyn Chapel are fond of pointing out a code scrawled on the walls of the crypt, a code supposedly left by the masons. Legend has it that the code indicates the presence of a great secret or a hidden treasure within the chapel walls, but so far no one has been able to decipher its meaning.

Technology may, in the end, solve many of the chapel's mysteries. In January 2003, the grand herald of the local branch of the Scottish Knights Templar—the self-proclaimed successors to the warrior monks who fled to Scotland in the fourteenth century to avoid religious persecution— announced that the Knights were using new scanning technology "capable of taking readings from the ground up to a mile deep." They hope to discover ancient vaults beneath the chapel that contain the reputed Rosslyn treasure.

BOOK II

The Da Vinci
Code Revealed

Part I

---

24 Hours, Two Cities, and the Future of Western Civilization

10 Apocrypha and Revelations

The above statement from Dan Brown has wielded an enormous power of suggestion over readers. *The Da Vinci Code*, after all, is a novel. In other words, it is a work of fiction. Every detail is not supposed to be factual and accurate in fiction. Indeed, fiction is supposed to be the province of the authorial imagination. Everyone who buys the book knows this. And yet, somehow, the combination of the extremely well-sculpted and detailed realism of many passages, the big events and issues from history that every reader feels he or she should know more about but doesn't, and the compelling logic of conspiracy theory (i.e., the reason you don't know something is that powerful forces have intentionally kept you in the dark about it), have all worked together to cause readers to take this particular work of fiction very seriously—as seriously as if it were a work of . . . nonfiction.

The reader's fascination with trying to separate fact and fiction has turned deciphering *The Da Vinci Code* into its own Holy Grail hunt. To add value to the hunt, *Secrets of the Code* made up a list of typical reader questions about *The Da Vinci Code* and turned the list over to investigative journalist David Shugarts, a writer with an extremely keen eye for detail, who was fascinated by *The Da Vinci Code*, but troubled here and there by annoying plot details that didn't seem quite right to him. Shugarts combined the search for answers to readers' questions with his own questions, and set off like a bloodhound to track down answers.

Let us make the caveat at the outset: we know that *The Da Vinci Code* is a work of fiction. We fully appreciate the creative mind of Dan Brown that has woven so many interesting facts and historical concepts into the murder mystery–action thriller–potboiler genre. But given the author's opening claim about the factual nature of the material, and given how seriously the debate generated by the novel has been taken by some, we thought it would be fun to share with our readers the many plot holes and flaws that Shugarts has uncovered. It is also interesting to see some of the intriguing details in the text he discovered that are accurate or thought provoking, but which the casual reader might have missed on first encounter. For more of Shugarts's findings beyond what is presented here, visit our website at www.secretsofthecode.com.

One note: The page numbers in this commentary refer to the U.S. English-language hardcover edition of *The Da Vinci Code*, published in 2003, although Shugarts's scrutiny starts before the numbered pages begin—with the dust jacket of the book. We have noticed a few subtle differences in various U.S. hardcover editions, details of which are covered in Shugarts's piece. So every reader should be able to follow along with any edition.

The Plot Holes and Intriguing Details of *The Da Vinci Code*

By DAVID A. SHUGARTS

DUST JACKET: *Is there a secret code on the book's dust jacket and does it indicate what Dan Brown's next book will be about?*

Yes, and here's our take on it. If you look closely you will see that some characters are in slightly bolder face than others on the dust jacket copy. If you find all of these and string them together, they spell out "Is there no help for the widow's son?"

It only takes a moment to search and find out that this sentence refers to the *Book of Enoch*, where a favorite Dan Brown theme arises, about the lost treasure of the Temple of Solomon. There are many allusions to Enoch. Genesis implies that he was a mortal who walked with God and was seen no more because God took him. The mystery surrounding Enoch was a subject for writers in Hebrew apocrypha even before the time of Christ.

"Is there no help for the widow's son?" was the title of a talk given before the Mormons in 1974 which purportedly established a connection between Freemasonry and the founder of the Church of Latter Day Saints, Joseph Smith.

It is said that Smith not only used lots of Mason symbology, but also wore a talisman containing mysterious

symbols. Further, that there are Mormon-identified locations in the United States that lie due west of the Temple
of Solomon (by no coincidence, of course).

The talk goes on to describe the Illuminees, who are
female Masons of two types—the righteous and the
voluptuous. So another Dan Brown theme, of the male
hierarchy's suppression of the sacred feminine is suggested.

Some of this territory has been covered already
by the veteran sci-fi/fantasy novelist Robert Anton
Wilson, including a novel in his Illuminati trilogy called
Widow's Son. Many Masonic lodges have "widow's son"
events and rites to this day. The content of the *Book of
Enoch* has multiple aspects that would attract Dan Brown's
attention. These range from references to the angel Uriel
(who Brown shows interest in with regard to analyzing
Leonardo's *Virgin of the Rocks*) to material said to be from
the lost *Book of Noah* (might we hunt for the lost Ark?).

We're just guessing, but we believe the new Dan
Brown book will not be called *Widow's Son*, but something
like it, and will be a Mormon-Mason treasure hunt
throughout America, starring, of course, Robert Langdon. But will Sophie Neveu be back, now that Langdon
has met her? Stay tuned.

PAGE 3: *Silas has "ghost-pale skin and thinning white hair. His
irises are pink with dark red pupils." Does this describe an
albino?*

Albinism is a pigmentation deficiency affecting about one
in seventeen thousand Americans. Although this can take
many forms (and skin colors), society tends to label people, so albinos are often portrayed with white skin and
hair, and pink eyes.

According to the National Organization for
Albinism and Hyperpigmentation (NOAH), "A common

myth is that by definition people with albinism have red eyes. In fact there are different types of albinism, and the amount of pigment in the eyes varies. Although some individuals with albinism have reddish or violet eyes, most have blue eyes. Some have hazel or brown eyes."

Almost universally, the disorder causes poor eyesight or even legal blindness. "In less pigmented types of albinism, hair and skin are cream-colored, and vision is often in the range of 20/200. In types with slight pigmentation, hair appears more yellow or red-tinged, and vision often corrects to 20/60," according to NOAH. Thus, Silas perhaps ought to be portrayed as having difficulty with vision, perhaps wearing thick glasses.

NOAH has been steadily calling attention to the stereotypical Hollywood portrayal of albinos as nonhuman, evil, or deranged. *The Da Vinci Code*'s Silas is a perfect example. Incidentally, one of the reasons the organization uses the acronym NOAH is that the Noah character of the Bible is believed by some to have been an albino.

PAGE 3: *Silas shoots Saunière in the dark at fifteen feet. Is this likely, given Silas's visual acuity?*

It would be extremely lucky for anyone to shoot someone in the dark with a pistol, but Silas is not likely to be able to do it without his glasses, which are never mentioned. It is extremely rare for an albino to have good vision.

PAGE 4: *Silas fired once and hit Saunière in the stomach. He took dead aim at Saunière's head and pulled the trigger again but "the click of an empty chamber echoed through the corridor." Silas "glanced down at his weapon, looking almost amused. He reached for a second clip, but then seemed to reconsider, smirking calmly at Saunière's gut."*

Silas has killed three people earlier this evening. All were presumably surprised by their assassin. His gun is a thirteen-shot Heckler and Koch USP 40 (see *DVC*, p. 73). The company name is actually Heckler & Koch. But the real question is, how come the clip is empty? Does it take twelve rounds to kill three old men, or did he begin the evening with a weapon only half loaded?

No explanation is given by Dan Brown. But perhaps Silas is making up for his poor eyesight by firing more rounds.

PAGE 4: *Saunière is shot several inches below the breastbone. Because he is "a veteran of la Guerre d'Algérie," he knows "for fifteen minutes, he would survive as his stomach acids seeped into his chest cavity, slowly poisoning him from within."*
Is this really how people die with gunshot wounds in the stomach? Could a man this age survive for fifteen or twenty minutes with this injury?

We consulted medical literature. The overall mortality rate from gunshot wounds to the abdomen is approximately 12 percent. However, in the absence of vascular injury, the mortality rate is less than 5 percent. This includes a wide range of organs that could be injured. The most frequently injured organs from anterior abdominal gunshot wounds are small bowel, colon, liver/biliary system, spleen, vascular system, stomach.

Death is very dependent on which organ might be struck by the bullet. If, for instance, an artery is struck or the spleen damaged, rapid loss of blood can cause shock and death.

But perforation of the stomach alone does not kill a person quickly. It could take many hours. If Saunière is a fit person and has no other injuries, there would be no reason why he should not live until the security guards could open the gate. By the same token, he probably does have sufficient time (and not just fifteen minutes, which seems improbable) to stagger around the Louvre and leave secret messages.

PAGE 4: *Saunière is "a veteran of la Guerre d'Algérie." At age seventy-six, could he have served in the Algerian War?*

Yes. The war for Algerian independence lasted from 1954 to 1962. If *The Da Vinci Code* takes place in 2001 or 2002, Saunière would have been born in the mid-twenties. He would have been in his late twenties to late thirties during the course of the war.

PAGE 15: *The crisp April air is whipping through the window of Citroën as Langdon is taken from his hotel to the Louvre. What day in April does the action take place on and what year is it supposed to be?*

The clues are contradictory. One hint lies in Dan Brown's previous book, *Angels & Demons*. That book also takes place in a twenty-four-hour time period in a month said to be April—in this case, in Rome. Robert Langdon, whose life as a Dan Brown character began with *Angels & Demons*, recalls in *The Da Vinci Code* that the prior experience was "a little over a year ago" (page 11). That would place the action in *The Da Vinci Code later* in the month of April than *Angels & Demons* since it is "a little over" a year ago. We also assumed that the action is in the latter part of April because Easter arrived in early April of 2001 and would have affected any mentions of crowds, traffic, and the like.

April 2001 looks good for a number of reasons. We will learn later that it has to be substantially past the turn of the millennium—probably by a year. This is because the plot instigated by Teabing and carried out through manipulation of Opus Dei and the Vatican, as we will come to find out, arose in a meeting of Aringarosa and churchmen at Castel Gandolfo during the previous November (page 149). The motivating reason for Teabing's actions was that the Priory of Sion, expected to reveal the Grail secret around the turn of the millennium, had failed to do so.

September 11, 2001, was a worldwide shock, and it had a profound effect on security arrangements throughout Europe. Dan Brown would have had to treat the subjects of terrorism, religious fundamentalism, religious tensions in the Middle East, and all the many complexities of September 11 had he consciously been trying to set the action of the book in April 2002, when the memory of September 11 was still so fresh all over the world. Certainly, we would not have seen the same permissive attitude by customs officials allowing Teabing into England, for instance. Many other aspects of the plot, from how Swiss bank vaults are treated to security precautions in public buildings, would undoubtedly have been affected.

But the book has contradictory evidence as well. Langdon has euros in his pocket. This monetary unit was not released as currency and coin until January 1, 2002, which would argue for April 2002. Another item: the article in the *New York Times Magazine* about the art diagnostician Maurizio Seracini (mentioned in *DVC* on page 169) was a real-life article about the secret meanings of some of Leonardo da Vinci's works—and it was published on April 21, 2002. So Langdon could not have known about it the year before. So does the action take place in April 2002, with the noted symbologist simply ignoring the signs and symbols of the September 11 tragedy that has happened so recently (there is not one direct reference to it in the book)? Or is *DVC* set in April 2001 with the noted symbologist having premonitions of the euro coins and the *New York Times Magazine* article to come a year in the future?

PAGE 15: *The night breeze is scented with jasmine blossoms. Does jasmine grow in the area and does it bloom in April?*

There are jasmine shrubs in the nearby Tuileries, but jasmine is a summer-blooming plant, starting around July and reaching a peak of fragrance around August.

PAGE 15: *The Citroën "skimmed south past the Opera House and crossed Place Vendôme." Is this possible?*

No, to leave the Ritz Hotel on place Vendôme and pass the Opera House, you must go north, not south.

PAGE 15: *The Citroën goes south on rue de Castiglione and turns toward the Louvre. It "swerved left now, angling west down the park's central boulevard." Is this possible?*

No, you would be going east after turning left to go to the Louvre.

PAGE 18: *It would take a visitor an estimated five weeks to "properly appreciate the 65,300 pieces of art in this building" (the Louvre museum).*

Think about it. If you spent an average of one minute per piece of art, and did not sleep, it would still take forty-five days of twenty-four hours each. This would hardly be called "properly appreciating" the artwork. Luckily, not all 65,000 pieces are on display, so you don't have to try. The number on display is nonetheless formidable— approximately 24,400 works. If you put in six eight-hour days a week looking at one piece of art per minute, this would still be more than eight weeks.

PAGE 21: *Langdon says that "at President Mitterrand's explicit demand" the new Pyramid monument at the entrance to the Louvre had been constructed of exactly 666 panes of glass." It was a "bizarre request that had always been a hot topic among conspiracy buffs who claimed 666 was the number of Satan." How many panes are actually in the Pyramid?*

For this answer, we contacted the offices of the architect, the renowned I. M. Pei. A spokeswoman said the Pyramid actually contains 698 pieces of glass, as counted by one of the architects who worked on the project. She said the notion that President Mitterrand had specified the number of panes is "not based in fact."

She also said the 666 rumor was published as fact by some French newspapers in the mid-1980s, commenting: "If you only found those old articles and didn't do any deeper fact checking, and were extremely credulous, you might believe the 666 story."

We also contacted Carter Wiseman, whose biography of I. M. Pei is among the works cited on Dan Brown's bibliography. Wiseman points out that I. M. Pei is an architect interested almost exclusively in geometric patterns and abstractions. To think he was concealing symbolic content in his work would be to miss the whole point of his aesthetic, says Wiseman.

PAGE 25: *Fache wears a crux gemmata. What is the origin of this term?*

It is a cross with thirteen gems, described by Brown as "a Christian ideogram for Christ and his twelve apostles." In many places, orthodox Christianity calls for a plain wooden cross, or a cross with the body of Christ depicted. Gem-encrusted crosses arose in some medieval churches and were interpreted as signs of the resurrection. However, a crux gemmata can be seen as a sign of pride, power, and wealth as much as devotion.

PAGE 26: *Brown says the Louvre security cameras are all fake, and most large museums use "containment security." True?*

False. The concept of the gates that drop down and trap a thief comes from *Pink Panther* or *The Thomas Crown Affair*-type movies, not from reality. The Louvre not only believes in security cameras, but, in fact, it recently made a major upgrade of its security system using the French conglomerate Thales, and video cameras are a big part of the system. Thales Security & Supervision is managing "a total of 1,500 proximity access control readers, 10,000 contactless secure badges, 800 video surveillance cameras, including 195 with digital recording systems, and more than 1,500 intrusion alarm points," according to the company.

PAGE 27: *Langdon notices that the security barricade "was raised about two feet . . . Placing his palms flat on the polished parquet, he lay on his stomach and pulled himself forward. As he slid underneath, the nape of his Harris tweed snagged on the bottom of the grate and he cracked the back of his head on the iron." Is this likely?*

No. In *Angels & Demons*, Langdon is said to have "the body of a swimmer, a toned, six-foot physique that he vigilantly maintained with fifty laps a day in the university pool." A fit individual would be only about nine or ten inches thick, back to front. If he puts his stomach on the floor and slithered, it is unlikely his jacket or head would be touching the bottom of a grate that was a full two feet off the ground.

PAGE 28: *Brown says Opus Dei has its world headquarters at Murray Hill Place, 243 Lexington Avenue, New York City. Built for $47 million, 133,000 square feet, redbrick and Indiana limestone. Designed by May & Pinska, with over a hundred bedrooms, six dining rooms, and chapels on the second, eighth, and sixteenth floors. Seventeenth floor entirely residential. Men enter through the main doors on Lexington Avenue. Women enter through a side street and are "acoustically and visually separated" from the men at all times within the building. True?*

> Close enough. According to another source, Opus Dei "had just 84,000 members worldwide—three thousand in the U.S.—but its new $55 million, seventeen-story building in midtown Manhattan reflected a power far beyond its numbers."

PAGE 29: *Brown says Opus Dei founder Escrivá published* The Way *in 1934, with 999 points of meditation for doing God's work in one's life. He says there are now over four million copies in circulation in forty-two languages.*

> Generally accurate. Actually, the original title in 1934 was *Spiritual Considerations*. It was revised a number of times. According to an Opus Dei website (www.josemariae-scriva.info), the book "has been translated into forty-five different languages and has sold more than 4.5 million copies worldwide." *The Way* does indeed have 999 points.

PAGE 30: *Brown writes about an organization that monitors Opus Dei's activities called the Opus Dei Awareness Network [www.odan.org]. Does this group exist?*

> Yes. ODAN exists and that is their website.

PAGE 30: *Brown says FBI turncoat Robert Hanssen was a prominent member of Opus Dei.*

> True. Bonnie Hanssen's brother is an Opus Dei priest in

Rome whose office is mere steps away from the pope. One of Bob and Bonnie's daughters is an Opus Dei numerary, a woman who has taken a vow of celibacy while remaining a layperson.

Bob Hanssen befriended bestselling espionage author James Bamford and, after pumping him for information about interviews he had had with Soviet leaders, would invite him to join him at Opus Dei meetings. "He was a little obsessed about it. Bob would rant about the evil in organizations like Planned Parenthood and how abortion was immoral," Bamford recalled.

PAGE 32: *Fache and Langdon begin at the east end of the Grand Galerie and pass the fallen Caravaggio painting nearby. Is this where the Caravaggios hang?*

No. They are hundreds of feet down the Grand Galerie, not far from Saunière's corpse.

PAGE 35: *Saunière used his left index finger to draw the pentangle on himself. Is he left-handed?*

Yes. Throughout the book there are clues that Saunière is left-handed. This supports a supposed affinity with Leonardo da Vinci, whom some experts think was left-handed. (see *Secrets of the Code*, Chapter 8).

PAGE 35: *Brown says, "A white Ku Klux Klan headpiece conjured images of hatred and racism in the United States, and yet the same costume carried a meaning of religious faith in Spain." True?*

Long dark robes and hoods are worn by penitents during Holy Week throughout Spain, but nowhere so spectacularly as in Seville. Thousands of penitents representing some fifty-seven fraternities form a candlelight procession in honor of the Virgin Mary and in recognition of the suffering of Christ. They are hooded because no one is meant to be able to guess the identity of sinners who are seeking forgiveness. Each of the fraternities chooses their distinctive colors of hoods and robes. Ku Klux Klansmen typically have white hoods, but not quite as pointy as the Spanish penitents. It is unclear whether there is any connection between the two.

Interestingly, the KKK was founded in Polaski, Tennessee, in 1866, by six Confederate officers. One of them, the first imperial wizard of the KKK, was a former Confederate general and Freemason, Nathan Bedford Forrest. Oddly, Forrest was written into the book, *Forrest Gump,* by Winston Groom, which was made into an Oscar-winning movie in 1994. The book's hero is said to be a namesake of Forrest, a distant relative.

PAGE 36: *Langdon says the pentacle is "representative of the female half of all things—a concept religious historians call the "sacred feminine" or the "divine goddess." True?*

No. The pentacle represents both male and female, exactly as does yang and yin.

PAGE 36: *"As a tribute to Venus, the Greeks used her four-year cycle to organize their Olympic Games. Nowadays, few people realized that the four-year schedule of the modern Olympics still followed the half-cycles of Venus. Even fewer people knew that the five-pointed star had almost become the official Olympic seal but was modified at the last moment—its five points exchanged for five intersecting rings to better reflect the game's spirit of inclusion and harmony." True?*

Partially true, partially false, and much more complicated. The Greeks did not use their Olympics to pay tribute to Venus. The Olympics were dedicated to Zeus.

Instead of a decade, the Greeks had calendar cycles of

eight years. Each cycle was called an *octaeteris*, and this was later divided into four-year periods called olympiads.

The primary reason for the eight-year cycle was that the Greeks observed a close fit between ninety-nine lunar cycles and eight earth cycles. More than any other heavenly body, the moon is likely to govern what a month is in any ancient culture. (However, they also did know that Venus completes five synodic cycles in the same eight-year period.) The ninety-nine/eight coincidence allowed them to make five years of twelve months and three years of thirteen months—the added months coming in the third, fifth, and eighth years. As the Greeks improved their calendar, they could divide the *octaeteris* into two parts, of fifty and forty-nine lunar cycles, which became known as olympiads. It wasn't perfect, but it was a calendar!

The average Greek would not have been able to detect it, but a patient astronomer would be able to take note of the five nodes of Venus's travel in the sky. From the latitude of Greece, this would have made a very irregular pentacle.

The five rings are a modern symbol. They were invented in 1913 by Pierre de Coubertin, president of the International Olympic Committee. He originally intended them to signify the first five games, but the interpretation was later amended to have the rings represent the five original continents.

The five-ring symbol was mistakenly ascribed to ancient origins when a Nazi propaganda filmmaker for the famous 1936 games (attended by Hitler), had a five-ring stone carving made and filmed it against the backdrop of Delphi.

PAGE 37: *Langdon says, "Symbols are very resilient, but the pentacle was altered by the early Roman Catholic Church. As part of the Vatican's campaign to eradicate pagan religions and convert the masses to Christianity, the church launched a smear campaign against the pagan gods and goddesses, recasting their divine symbols as evil."*

Brown conveniently disregards the fact that Christian emperor Constantine, who elsewhere in the book is treated as the enemy most responsible for wiping out Gnostic, goddess, and pagan traditions, used the pentagram, together with the Chi-Rho symbol [formed from the first two letters, *X* and *P*, of the Greek word for Christ] in his seal and amulet.

PAGE 45: *Brown says Leonardo had an "enormous output of breathtaking Christian art . . . accepting hundreds of lucrative Vatican commissions, Da Vinci painted Christian themes not as an expression of his own beliefs but rather as a commercial venture—a means of funding a lavish lifestyle." True?*

Not true. Leonardo's output was not enormous. He characteristically had trouble finishing works and they would drag on for long periods. The number of paintings he finished is extremely small compared to most great figures in the history of art.

PAGE 52: *Sophie's personal code for her answering machine is 454. Is this number significant to Dan Brown or a random number?*

We don't know, but the hardcover book does end on page 454.

PAGE 55: *Silas leaves home at the age of seven after his father kills his mother and he kills his father. He is imprisoned at age eighteen and freed by an earthquake at thirty. Aringarosa dubs* him "Silas." According to Dan Brown, he has forgotten "the name his parents had given him."

Hard to believe that he has truly forgotten his name. Anyway, what did he call himself for twenty-three years? What did the authorities call him when they decided he was too dangerous to remain in Marseilles and when they imprisoned him? What did his jailors call him for twelve years?

PAGE 58: *Brown says chapter 16 of Acts speaks of Silas as a prisoner, naked and beaten, laying in his cell, singing hymns to God, when an earthquake frees him. By coincidence, the albino has been freed by an earthquake, so the bishop names him Silas. To what does this refer?*

In the Book of Acts, both Paul and Silas were imprisoned together, by false accusations. The earthquake freed all the prisoners, but Paul and Silas did not leave. Instead, they first converted their jailer to Christianity and baptized him, then they refused to leave until their accusers came and apologized and led them out of the prison.

PAGE 60: *Sophie decrypts the numerical series and comes up with 1-1-2-3-5-8-13-21, which she says is the Fibonacci sequence, "one of the most famous mathematical progressions in history." Is she accurate?*

No. Mathematicians agree that the Fibonacci sequence includes 0, making the full sequence 0-1-1-2-3-5-8-13-21... Note that a math sequence is properly written with an ellipsis at the end, indicating that the series continues indefinitely.

PAGE 65: *Sophie tells Langdon about the "GPS tracking dot." It is described as "a metallic, button-shaped disk, about the size of a watch battery." Sophie explains that it "continuously transmits its location to a Global Positioning System [GPS] satellite that*

DCPJ can monitor. It's accurate within two feet anywhere on the globe." Does such a system exist?

Yes, but it's much larger than the unit that Sophie describes. For instance, units that help in tracking wild animals have been fashioned into somewhat bulky dog collars (or bird or fish collars). They recognize their position via GPS, and transmit to satellites—but these are not GPS satellites. Rather, they are Argos or GlobalStar satellites. [GPS satellites do not receive signals from GPS receivers.] Unfortunately, you cannot use an Argos satellite continuously at any one point on earth, since it orbits and goes out of sight.

But smaller units for continuous tracking can be constructed, if you accept that they do not need to transmit to satellites. These have small radio transmitters, good up to fifteen miles, and if you stay within range, you can track them 24/7. The smallest of these units is still about ten times the size of the so-called GPS dot that Sophie describes.

All of these units require antennas, and there is a relationship of antenna size to receiving sensitivity or transmitting power. So you might require a two- or three-inch antenna even if you could make the transmitter into a dot.

PAGE 78: *The men's room window looks out of the "westernmost tip of the Denon Wing" of the Louvre. Sophie looks out and sees that "Place du Carrousel ran almost flush with the building with only a narrow sidewalk separating it from the Louvre's outer wall. Far below, the usual caravan of the city's nighttime delivery trucks sat idling, waiting for the signals to change." Is the view correct?*

The men's room is not located at the western tip of the Denon Wing and this part of the building is not open to the public, but let's assume it was. The Place du Carrousel is not almost flush with the outer wall. Nor is it a major truck route with caravans of trucks idling in line.

PAGE 79: *Sophie says the U.S. embassy is "only about a mile from here." True?*

Close. It's about 4,100 feet, and you can see it from the posited location of the men's room window, but Sophie will still miss it when she goes to drive there!

PAGE 82: *Fache has a Manurhin MR-93 pistol. Is this used by French authorities?*

Yes, this is the weapon of the French police. It is an extremely rugged revolver with distinctive styling.

PAGE 85: *Brown says, "The last sixty seconds had been a blur." He then describes action beginning with Sophie throwing the GPS dot out the window. Since this includes Fache sprinting the length of the Grand Galerie, how fast was Fache as a runner?*

Sign him up for the French Olympic team! He could be a sub-four-minute miler!

PAGE 85: *Brown says that the "twin-bed Trailor delivery truck" traveled from the Louvre, south on the pont du Carrousel (crossing the Seine) and then turned right onto pont des Saints-Pères. Can this be done?*

No. If you cross the pont du Carrousel southward, you must turn right onto quai Voltaire, a one-way street going west. This takes you away from pont des Saints-Pères, not toward it. Also, pont des Saints-Pères is one-way going north.

PAGE 86: *Brown says the trailer truck drove to within ten feet of the end of the building (the west end of the Louvre's Denon*

Wing). It heads south across the Seine. By tossing the GPS dot into the truck, they make the French police believe that Langdon has jumped out the window into the truck. Is this possible?

No. First of all, the public restrooms of the Louvre's Grand Galerie are not at the end wall of the building. But even if we pencil in a men's room there, the Place du Carrousel is more than fifty feet away from the building's wall. No one could jump and reach the street, even its nearest edge. By law, they drive on the right side of the street in Paris, so the southbound traffic would be farthest from the Louvre, adding another twenty feet or so. We doubt that Fache is going to believe Langdon jumped.

PAGE 92: *Brown says tarot cards come in a deck of twenty-two and have a suit called Pentacles, as well as three cards named the Female Pope, the Empress, and the Star. Does this accurately describe a Tarot deck?*

Yes and no. For a guy who is supposed to be into the occult, Brown misses key facts here. There are actually seventy-eight cards in the most common tarot decks. There are the twenty-two cards of the Major Arcana, and then the fifty-six cards of the Minor Arcana. The Major Arcana can be thought of as Trumps, but literally, the divisions are Major Secrets and Minor Secrets.

The four suits are Wands, Cups, Pentacles, Swords. The suit called Cups, unmentioned by Brown until later in the book, is a clear reference to chalices.

The complete tale of tarot, which can be embellished at will by anyone, will include (at least) Freemasonry, Gnostics, the Female Pope, the Holy Grail and much more, but not always interconnected in the way *The Da Vinci Code* portrays. The card in the Major Arcana now commonly known as the High Priestess stems from an early deck and the legend of the Female Pope, or Pope Joan.

According to a widely told medieval legend, a woman named Joan disguised herself as a man, rose in the priesthood, and actually became pope. But she became pregnant by another priest and not only could not hide it, but came to give birth in the streets, whereupon a crowd recognized her deception and tore her to pieces. There is another story suggesting an Italian female pope closer to the era of the renaissance.

In any event, around 1450, several decks of *tarocchi* (tarot) cards were commissioned by the great Visconti family, including one widely recognized as one of the earliest extant decks, the Visconti-Sforza deck. An early Female Pope card is found in this deck.

PAGE 93: *Brown uses a classroom setting to talk about the Divine Proportion. He congratulates a student who recognizes the number 1.618 as PHI (pronouncing it "fee"). Is this correct?*

Somebody must have told Dan Brown that there are two numbers, one uppercase and the other lower, and he took them to mean Phi and phi. In fact, the numbers are written out as Phi to mean the Divine Proportion, and phi to mean its reciprocal. In English, it is pronounced "fye" to rhyme with "pie."

But we are astounded that a famous symbologist such as Robert Langdon would not use the symbols for this number pair, the Greek uppercase Ø and lowercase ø. With all the other symbols in the book, couldn't Doubleday have gotten the Greek letters set into type?

The true statements are that the number Phi can be derived from the Fibonacci sequence, is found often in nature, math, and architecture and has names like Golden Mean, Golden Ratio, etc.

Phi is an irrational number (goes on forever after the

decimal point). If you want it longer, just do the math—1.618033988 is Phi at nine decimal places, for instance, and some people have calculated it out to thousands of decimal places.

PAGE 94: *"Hold on," said a young woman in the front row. "I'm a bio major and I've never seen this Divine Proportion in nature."*

"No?" Langdon grinned. "Ever study the relationship between females and males in a honeybee community?"

"Sure. The female bees always outnumber the male bees."

"Correct. And did you know that if you divide the number of female bees by the number of male bees in any beehive in the world, you always get the same number?"

"You do?"

"Yup. Phi."

Honey is golden, but do the bees follow the Golden Ratio? Brown bumbles badly. The population of a hive changes throughout the seasons, and the seasons change throughout the world, so there can be no time when all the beehives in the world have the same ratio of male-female population. Bad news for the guys: in the fall, practically all the drones (males) are driven out of the hive to die, so the male population approaches zero.

In the spring and summer, there will be drones. But bee experts have counted hive populations and the numbers they use are nothing like a Divine Proportion. For instance, an average active hive will have one queen, about three hundred to one thousand drones (males), and fifty thousand workers (females). If you do what Langdon says and divide the female number (50,001) by the male number (we'll use one thousand), you get fifty—not even close to 1.618.

PAGE 98: *Brown says, "French kings throughout the Renaissance were so convinced that anagrams held magic power that they appointed royal anagrammatists to help them make better decisions by analyzing words in important documents."*

We don't think there were French kings that were gung-ho for anagrams "throughout the Renaissance," a period that lasted from around 1483 to 1610. But one king, Louis XIII, who reigned from 1610 to 1643, was famous because he appointed a royal anagrammist, Thomas Billon. But there's not much evidence to suggest Billion had a big role in decision making. It was said Billon's function was "to entertain the court with amusing anagrams of people's names."

This citation is found everywhere that anagram aficionados refer to their history. Louis XIII ascended to his throne at the age of nine, but we don't know when the appointment of Billon occurred. The young king was initially governed by his mother, then later heavily influenced by advisors such as Cardinal Richelieu.

PAGE 98: *Brown says, "The Romans actually referred to the study of anagrams as ars magna——'the great art.'"*

Did the Romans speak English? *Anagrams* is the English word that can be rearranged to make ars magna. The Latin word for anagram is *anagrammat* or *anagramma*, modified from earlier Greek terms.

PAGE 99: *Saunière once wrote the word* planets *and told Sophie "that an astonishing ninety-two other English words of varying lengths could be formed using those same letters." True?*

It's astonishing that Saunière did not pose a higher number. We can think of 101 words and we're not that smart.

PAGE 106: *Brown says, "To this day, the fundamental navigational tool was still known as a Compass Rose, its northernmost direction still marked by an arrowhead . . . or, more commonly, the symbol of the fleur-de-lis." Is this factual?*

Perhaps you've seen a movie where the compass rose has a big fleur-de-lis at the top on a treasure map. You'll want to believe it's on modern maps, but no, it's not. It's hard to say which of the compass roses in use on today's charts and maps is the most common. But we can answer for the standard U.S. aviation and marine charts. They don't have a fleur-de-lis.

The air charts have a simple arrow for north, and they are already oriented for magnetic north. The nautical charts have a prominent marker for true north on the outer ring, and a smaller simple arrow for magnetic north on the inner ring. The true north marker? A five-pointed star, oddly enough. Mariners readily recognize its symbology to mean the north star, Polaris.

Since most people don't use a compass for navigating on road maps, which are perhaps the most common maps, they don't have compass roses. They usually just have north arrows. Old charts and maps—particularly charts drawn by those master cartographers, the Portuguese—commonly do have a fleur-de-lis for north. Interestingly, they also often have a cross—typically a Maltese cross—for east. This is because east was thought of as being "toward Jerusalem." So Dan Brown missed his chance to remark on yet another usage of the Knights Templar symbol.

PAGE 106: *Brown says, "Long before the establishment of Greenwich as the prime meridian, the zero longitude of the entire world had passed directly through Paris, and through the Church of Saint-Sulpice. The brass marker in Saint-Sulpice was a memorial to the world's first prime meridian, and although Greenwich had stripped Paris of the honor in 1888, the original Rose Line was still visible today."*

Paris was not the site of the world's first prime meridian. Not by about fourteen hundred years. The first known attempt to establish a prime meridian came in the second century B.C., when Hipparchus of Rhodes proposed that all distances be measured from a meridian running through the island of Rhodes, just off the southern coast of Turkey. But perhaps a stronger attempt was made by the Greek Ptolemy, writing between A.D. 127 and 141. His prime meridian went through the Canary Islands. Ptolemy's works, as revived by the German Benedictine monk Nicholas Germanus around 1470, were hugely influential and became the inspiration for Christopher Columbus.

As many countries established claims throughout the world through voyages of exploration, they often attempted to establish their own prime meridians. There were hundreds of years of confusion on this point, but England emerged as the world's technical leader in cartography and navigation. What it came down to is, if you printed the best charts, you got to say where the zero lines began.

The hubbub came to a head in 1884 when President Chester A. Arthur called a conference in Washington to get international agreement on a prime meridian and a universal twenty-four-hour day. At the time, ships attempting to get their bearings at sea were confronted with a total of eleven national prime meridians: Greenwich, Paris, Berlin, Cadiz, Copenhagen, Lisbon, Rio, Rome, St. Petersburg, Stockholm, and Tokyo. But by then, some 72 percent of commercial shipping recognized Greenwich, while only 8 percent used Paris.

The twenty-five nations voted twenty-two to one to make it Greenwich. Abstaining were Brazil and—you guessed it—France. France clung to the Paris meridian as a rival to Greenwich until 1911 for timekeeping purposes and 1914 for navigational purposes.

PAGE 120: *Professor Langdon refers to the artist as "Da Vinci." Is this correct?*

No. It grates on the nerves of everyone who is knowledgeable about art. His actual name is Leonardo di ser Piero and he was from the town of Vinci, so he was thus, Leonardo di ser Piero da Vinci (from Vinci). Throughout the art world his shortened name is Leonardo.

PAGE 121: *Professor Langdon "reveals" Leonardo's secret joining of male and female in the* Mona Lisa *by rearranging the name to become* Amon L'Isa, *a putative androgynous union. Could Leonardo have intended such a pun?*

This all relies on the painting being called *Mona Lisa*. Since Leonardo never called it *Mona Lisa*, this is completely absurd. In Leonardo's lifetime, the painting had no title. It was referred to by a variety of names, including "a courtesan with a gauze veil."

PAGE 121: *Brown says, "At first Langdon saw nothing. Then, as he knelt beside her, he saw a tiny droplet of dried liquid that was luminescing. Ink? Suddenly he recalled what black lights were actually used for. Blood." Plausible?*

Dan Brown, if you're going to watch *CSI*, ya gotta pay attention! Blood doesn't luminesce in black light without some chemical help. If you use Luminol (a *CSI* favorite) you don't need special light, just a darkened room. That's because the reagent triggers chemiluminescence, giving off its own somewhat eerie glow.

If you use Fluorescein (an alternative preferred for faint latent blood traces), you do need an ultraviolet light. But first, you spray the area of interest with a freshly made batch of Fluorescein solution, and then with a hydrogen peroxide solution. Sophie didn't have the time or materials to do this.

PAGE 124: *The message scrawled in front of the* Mona Lisa *says, "So dark the con of man." Langdon sees this as a perfect expression of a fundamental Priory of Sion philosophy, that the powerful men of the early Christian church conned the world with a bunch of lies.*

As a classical scholar, Langdon should not jump to the meaning of *con* as in confidence game or confidence man, involving cheating and swindling. This term came into use around 1886, relatively late. The Shakespearean-era term *con* meant "to know or learn" or "to commit to memory." To a scholar, the most likely meaning of the phrase would be "So dark the knowledge of man."

PAGE 128: *Dan Brown has Silas look up Job 38:11 in the Bible at the altar in Saint-Sulpice. "Finding verse number eleven, Silas read the text. It was only seven words. Confused, he read it again, sensing something had gone terribly wrong. The verse simply read: 'Hitherto shalt thou come, but no further.' "*

There are more than seven words in the verse. The King James Version gives these seventeen words as the complete verse 11: "And said, Hitherto shalt thou come, but no further: and here shall thy proud waves be stayed?"

It is also highly doubtful that Silas would be reading an English-language Bible at the altar of a venerable French cathedral in the heart of Paris.

PAGE 131: *Sophie gets the key from the back of the painting* Madonna of the Rocks *by Leonardo. Brown's description: "The masterpiece she was examining was a five-foot-tall canvas." Later, he says that Sophie "had actually lifted the large painting off its cables and propped it on the floor in front of her. At five feet tall, the canvas almost entirely hid her body. . . . The canvas started to bulge in the middle . . . The woman was pushing her knee into the center of the canvas from behind!"*

This painting is not five feet tall. It is about six feet six inches tall, not including the frame. Also, it is four feet wide. Sophie would have to be a giant to be visible behind it, and she would have to be unbelievably strong to pull it off the wall and set it down without wrecking it.

PAGE 137: *"The vehicle was easily the smallest car Langdon had ever seen.*

" 'SmartCar,' [Sophie] said. 'A hundred kilometers to the liter.' "

Sorry. The SmartCar is nifty and thrifty. It gets great gas mileage, but not a hundred kilometers to the liter—not even close! Your mileage may vary, but perhaps a typical figure is nineteen kilometers per liter. For several years, SmartCar has been the rage in Europe, built in Germany and France and now owned by DaimlerChrysler under the Mercedes-Benz brand. To see some examples, go to daimlerchrysler.com.

There are a series of two-seat versions of the Smart-Car with hip styling (originally provided by Swatch). At eight feet long, two can fit in a normal parking space. You can't buy these two-seaters in America. The new four-seater versions will be brought to the U.S. market sometime in 2006.

PAGE 138: *The destination is the American embassy. Sophie drives north to the rue de Rivoli, and west on Rivoli a quarter*

mile to a "wide rotary." Coming out the other side of the "wide
rotary," she is heading out the wide Champs Elysées. and now
the embassy is "only about a mile away," according to Brown.
Sophie turns hard right, "cutting sharply past the luxurious
Hôtel de Crillon" and into the diplomatic neighborhood.
Suddenly, they discover themselves one hundred yards short of
the police blockade at the avenue Gabriel.

> Sophie needs a better map. When she was headed west on
> Rivoli and reached the area of the "wide rotary," she had
> found place de la Concorde, a huge open square that is the
> centerpiece of Paris. On the north side of this square is
> the Hôtel de Crillon. Nearby is the American embassy,
> where rue de Rivoli becomes avenue Gabriel. If you have
> found one, you have found the other. (One attraction of
> rooms at the Crillon is the view of the embassy.)

PAGE 147: *The destination is the Gare Saint-Lazare. As Sophie
leaves the area of the rue Gabriel, stymied by the police blockade,
she heads back west onto the Champs Elysées, going to the Arc de
Triomphe and taking a street going north from the rotary there
(most likely, the avenue de Wagram). She goes north a few
blocks, then turns hard right onto the boulevard Malesherbes.
Eventually, with another turn or two, she ends up at the train
station.*

> Once again, Sophie needs a better map. As she leaves the
> rue Gabriel, she is only about a quarter-mile away from the
> Gare Saint-Lazare, if she would only head north. Instead
> she goes a long way west, then north, then back south and
> east, to reach the same point after a trip that is roughly one
> and a half miles longer than it needs to be. Maybe she just
> wants to get to know Langdon a little better?

PAGE 148: *Dan Brown says, "Architectural Digest had
called Opus Dei's building 'a shining beacon of Catholicism*

sublimely integrated with the modern landscape.' " Is this an accurate quote?

We queried *Architectural Digest* about this. They replied tersely, "*Architectural Digest* has never featured the headquarters of Opus Dei."

PAGE 153: *Aiming to leave Paris, Sophie directs the taxi driver and they head north on rue de Clichy. Out the window to his right, Langdon sees Montmartre and Sacré-Coeur.*

Yes. This is a plausible view.

PAGE 154: *While going north on rue de Clichy, Sophie discovers that the address on the key is 24 rue Haxo. The taxi driver tells Sophie that rue Haxo is "out near the [Roland Garros] tennis stadium on the western outskirts of Paris."... "Fastest route is through Bois de Boulogne," the driver says.*

The taxi driver, too, needs a better map. You do not have to meander through the park called the Bois de Boulogne in order to get to the tennis stadium. There is a high-speed, limited-access artery, the boulevard Périphérique, which will take you right to the stadium.

But there is a big discrepancy here, because the rue Haxo is not in this region of Paris. In fact, it is on the east side of the city.

PAGE 155: *Fache learns that Langdon bought train tickets. "What was the destination?" he asks. "Lille," says Collet. "Probably a decoy," says Fache.*

How can he be so sure?

Perhaps because he knows that trains for Lille do not depart the Gare Saint-Lazare. The Lille train departs the Gare du Nord. On page 152 in some earlier editions of *The Da Vinci Code*, Langdon and Neveu buy tickets for the 3:06 A.M. train from the Gare Saint-Lazare to Lyon. In later editions, it is from the same station and at the same time, but to Lille. In general, one would not use Gare Saint-Lazare for either route.

PAGE 157: *Sophie asked Langdon to tell her about the Priory of Sion. " 'The brotherhood's history spanned more than a millennium,' he mused . . ." " 'The Priory of Sion,' he began, 'was founded in Jerusalem in 1099 by a French king named Godefroi de Bouillon.' "*

Well, if it was founded in 1099, how could its history span "more than a millennium"?

PAGE 157: *Dan Brown says the park called Bois de Boulogne was known by Paris cognoscenti as "the Garden of Earthly Delights" because of its "hundreds of glistening bodies for hire, earthly delights to satisfy one's deepest unspoken desires—male, female, and everything in between."*

Our French friends don't call it the Garden of Earthly Delights; maybe that was just an excuse for Brown to introduce an allusion to Hieronymus Bosch and his painting of the same name. It is, however, a fact that the park is teeming with male and female prostitutes and transvestites at night.

PAGE 160: *Langdon describes the plot formulated by Pope Clement V and King Philippe IV of France to arrest and execute the Knights Templar in a coordinated effort starting at dawn on Friday, October 13, 1307. This is said to be the actual, direct source of the modern superstition about Friday the thirteenth.*

This is only one of a variety of explanations for the superstition about Friday the thirteenth being unlucky.

PAGE 166: *Bishop Aringarosa asks Silas, "Were you not aware that Noah himself was an albino?" Does it make sense for the bishop to say this?*

The Bible does not say Noah was an albino, but the *Book of Enoch*—one of the apocryphal books that was omitted from the Bible—does have this description of the birth of Noah:

"Unto Lamech my son there hath been born a son, the like of whom there is none, and his nature is not like man's nature, and the colour of his body is whiter than snow and redder than the bloom of a rose, and the hair of his head is whiter than white wool, and his eyes are like the rays of the sun, and he opened his eyes and thereupon lighted up the whole house."

But this is actually a kind of glued-on appendix to the *Book of Enoch*. And in any case, it is hard to imagine that a mainstream Opus Dei supernumerary such as Aringarosa would subscribe to scriptures from the alternative camp.

PAGE 168: *Sophie takes over the driving and soon has the car "humming smoothly westward along Allée de Longchamp, leaving the Garden of Earthly Delights behind."*
Sophie says the taxi driver had said the destination, rue Haxo, is "adjacent to the Roland Garros tennis stadium" and she is confident of finding it. "I know that area," she says.

Sophie needs a better map. Allée de Longchamp runs north-south and is one-way going north. The tennis stadium is not west of the park, but south of it. As we said before, rue Haxo is on the east side of Paris, miles away.

PAGE 169: *Leonardo's famed Adoration of the Magi was sketched by the master, but filled in by some rogue artist who* modified the composition. This was revealed by X-rays and infrared reflectography. Italian art diagnostician Maurizio Seracini discovered the secrets of the painting and the story was published in the New York Times Magazine.

All true. Seracini is a genuine, renowned art diagnostician. The article was written by Melinda Henneberger and published April 21, 2002. Ms. Henneberger is researching a book on Seracini's main quest, to find the lost Leonardo fresco, *Battle of Anghiari*.

PAGE 172: *The Zurich bank signage reminds Langdon that the Swiss national flag contains an equal-armed cross.*

Not only is the cross equal-armed, but the official flag of Switzerland is unusual in being a perfect square (not a rectangle), further accentuating the symmetry.

PAGE 176: *Is there really a Depository Bank of Zurich?*

If you Google it, you will find a website that looks for half a second like it could be real. Then you will discover it is part of the Dan Brown–Random House treasure hunt. It is a fun site to visit with a lot of inside jokes for readers of the book. Also try Googling Robert Langdon, and you may find a similarly amusing faux site.

PAGE 181: *Collet is at the Gare du Nord when Fache calls him. Why is he there?*

Fache had told Collet to "alert the next station, have the train stopped and searched." He sent Collet off to supervise. Fache has apparently forgotten that Lille trains don't depart the Gare Saint-Lazare, so Gare du Nord is not the "next station." It is even more implausible for Collet to have gone to the Gare du Nord in the earlier editions of the book, where Sophie and Robert have bought tickets for Lyon, far south of Paris.

PAGE 184: *Vernet tells Sophie she needs to know her ten-digit account number. "Ten digits. Sophie reluctantly calculated the cryptographic odds. Ten billion possible choices. Even if she could bring in DCPJ's most powerful parallel processing computers, she still would need weeks to break the code."*

There are at least a couple of things wrong with Sophie's assessment. First, the basic task of getting a computer to run through all ten billion possible numbers isn't at all difficult and any of today's ordinary computers can do it in minutes. You don't need parallel processing or huge computers. Admittedly, if you insist on printing out all the possible numbers, you will be in for a long wait at the laser printer and will face a huge bill for paper and toner.

But it has been a long time since a professional security system was built that would allow the user to make endless attempts to guess the passcode. Recognizing that people often slip on the keyboard, some systems allow up to three attempts, but the Depository Bank of Zurich has a stricter policy—you only get one try, as Sophie learns on page 188.

PAGE 201: *Sophie muses about the cryptex: "If someone attempted to force open the cryptex, the glass vial would break, and the vinegar would quickly dissolve the papyrus. By the time anyone extracted the secret message, it would be a glob of meaningless pulp."*

This isn't plausible to us. Papyrus itself is made from matted strips of the papyrus plant, layered with a flour paste (to which a dash of vinegar was added during manufacture). The fibers are mostly cellulose, an extremely durable material that doesn't instantly dissolve in vinegar. If we were told that the message on the papyrus is written in ink that dissolves with vinegar, we would be much more inclined to believe it. Note that the cryptex would probably contain papyrus that Saunière had obtained, manufactured during his lifetime, not five hundred years earlier.

PAGE 201: *The cryptex has five dials with twenty-six letters each. Sophie does the math:*

"That's 26 to the fifth power ... approximately twelve million possibilities."

Yes, it's 11,881,376, to be exact.

PAGE 218: *Langdon begins to speak of Sir Leigh Teabing's estate, which he says is "near Versailles." Later (page 220), Dan Brown describes it as follows: "The sprawling 185-acre estate of Château Villette was located twenty-five minutes northwest of Paris in the environs of Versailles. . . . The estate fondly had become known as la Petite Versailles." Is the Château Villette real and is it near Versailles?*

The real-life Villette is up for rent to any tourist who can pay five thousand dollars a night, and has been kicking around the Web for some time as a kind of vacation rental listing. The California-based rental agent's ad copy says Villette is "near Versailles, northwest of Paris." The history of the house told in *The Da Vinci Code* matches the history on the rental agent's site, including the seventeenth-century involvement of Le Nôtre (designer of many of the gardens at Versailles) and Mansart. This is clearly a beautiful and historic house. However, we would not call it near Versailles, except in real estate business jargon. Versailles is about ten miles west of the center of Paris and three miles south. Villette is about twenty miles west of Paris and ten miles north. The road distance between them is about nineteen miles.

PAGE 224: *Vernet phones and instructs the bank's night manager to activate the armored truck's "emergency transponder." The manager goes over to the bank's LoJack panel and does so, warning that it will also alert the police. Vernet remains on the phone in order to hear the location of the truck. Is this how LoJack works?*

Not exactly. In France, LoJack is called Traqueur. It requires a call to the police in order to activate the vehicle transmitter. Once this is done, it is the police, in their cars and helicopters, who use tracking gear to find the vehicle. You do not get an instant position report unless the police are ready to spring into action and coordinate their tracking efforts. It may take hours. (If you wanted instant results, you would need a system that reports its own GPS coordinates—like the "GPS dot" on *DVC* page 65, for instance.)

Traqueur has a number of advantages, however. First, it is thoroughly entrenched in France, which has more or less blanket coverage with over twenty-three thousand police cars and forty-two helicopters (far more comprehensive coverage than in the United States, in fact). Second, its discreet, coded signal allows the police to prepare quietly to make the arrest, rather than issuing a signal that can be decoded by anyone.

PAGE 227: *Gargoyles! Flashback to Saunière taking young Sophie to Notre Dame in a rainstorm. The gargoyle rainspouts are gurgling. "They're gargling," her grandfather told her. "Gargariser! And that's where they get the silly name 'gargoyles.'"*

No. *Gargariser* is current French for "gargle." The term that both gargle and gargoyle stem from is not *gargariser* but *gargouille*, an old French word meaning "gullet" or "throat." But the etymology is much more interesting than that! According to myth, in the seventh century a dragon rose up out of the River Seine. But rather than breathing fire, this dragon gushed forth water. His name was Gargouille, or Throat. He proceeded to drown the towns around Paris, until he was confronted and tamed by St. Romain, the archbishop of Rouen, who made the sign of the cross with his two index fingers. Throat was led tamely back to Paris, slain and burned, but not before they cut off his head and mounted it on a building.

Many buildings, old and new, have scary creatures adorning them. Strictly speaking, only those creatures that are part of the gutter systems, spouting water, are called gargoyles in honor of Gargouille. All the other creatures are called grotesques.

PAGE 227: *Sophie says she "studied at the Royal Holloway." Is that a place to learn cryptology?*

Yes, the Royal Holloway is a part of the University of London and has respected undergraduate degree programs in mathematics and computer science. It offers M.Sc. and Ph.D. degrees and is host to the Information Security Group, a graduate-level conclave of scholars known for cryptology work.

PAGE 233: *"Hold on," says Sophie. "You're saying Jesus' divinity was the result of a vote?""A relatively close vote at that," Teabing added.*

Holy hanging St. Chad, Batman, let's see the Supreme Court settle this one!

The vote was 316 to 2. Teabing calls this close? By the way, there really was a St. Chad. He humbly stepped aside in A.D. 669 when a dispute arose as to who was properly ordained as the Bishop of York.

PAGE 234: *Dan Brown says, "The Dead Sea Scrolls were found in the 1950s hidden in a cave near Qumran in the Judean desert."*

The year was 1947. Some Bedouin herders were searching for a lost goat and found the cave with jars containing ancient scrolls. Initially, seven scrolls were brought out, but further searches yielded thousands of scroll fragments over the next decade or so.

PAGE 234: *"Because Constantine upgraded Jesus' status almost four centuries after Jesus' death, thousands of documents already existed,"Teabing says (referring to the Council of Nicea).*

Fuzzy math again: If Jesus died around A.D. 30 and the Council of Nicea met in A.D. 325, how many centuries elapsed in between? We think it rounds off to three centuries, not four.

PAGE 243: *"Our preconceived notions of this scene are so powerful that our mind blocks out the incongruity and overrides our eyes," said Teabing.*

"It is known as scotoma," Langdon added.

Interesting syndrome, but not quite right. What Teabing has said does not correctly describe scotoma, which is a real visual defect or disease, not a mere perceptual quirk.

The definition of scotoma is "a blind spot or dark spot in the visual field." Medically speaking, "Scotomas may be central, if caused by macular or optic nerve disease, or peripheral if the result of chorioretinal lesions or retinal holes." There is even a phenomenon associated with migraine headaches called scintillating scotoma, where the blind spot pulsates and has ragged edges.

True lacunae buffs take note: in the first hardcover edition of *The Da Vinci Code*, this word is misspelled as skitoma.

PAGE 246: *Sophie recalls that "the French government, under pressure from priests, had agreed to ban an American movie called* The Last Temptation of Christ."

The French government did not ban the movie. The 1988 film, directed by Martin Scorsese, was based on a 1955 novel by Nikos Kazantzakis, who is also known for writing *Zorba the Greek*. It did indeed portray Jesus (Willem Dafoe) as lusting after Mary Magdalene (Barbara Hershey).

When the novel was published, it triggered protests and some bannings (the Vatican, most notably), but not in France. The Greek Orthodox Church excommunicated Kazantzakis, who was nominally a member. When Scorsese's movie opened, there were protests practically everywhere, including the firebombing of a theater in Paris, as well as attacks on movie houses elsewhere in France. There were incidents of violence throughout the world. In the United States, a protester crashed a bus into a theater lobby. At least two governments did ban the film—Chile and Israel—but not France.

By the way, if Saunière is supposed to be keeping a low profile, why is he writing such a letter? And if Sophie is supposed to be thirty-two at the time of the novel, making her born around 1969–70, why is she talking to her grandfather about the 1988 movie in the discussion represented on page 247, with childlike naiveté, wondering if Jesus had a girlfriend?

PAGE 251: *Aringarosa "had a chartered turbo prop awaiting him" at Ciampino Airport [page 251]. But on page 272, he is found in a "chartered Beechcraft Baron 58."*

The Beech Baron 58 is not a turboprop. It has piston engines and burns gasoline. A turboprop has turbine engines that drive propellers and it burns jet fuel.

PAGE 271: *The police find Silas's Audi. "It had rental plates. Collet felt the hood. Still warm. Hot even." What are rental plates?*

There isn't a special plate for rental cars, but there is a coding system that sometimes gives away the information that thieves, for instance, might be seeking. Each region (department) of France has a code assigned to the last two digits of a license plate. Taxes vary with different departments, so the rental companies became known for plates ending with ninety-two, fifty-one or twenty-six, where they registered their cars because taxes were lowest. The rental car companies have been phasing out this practice. Insiders can still readily identify a plate as nonlocal, however.

PAGE 272: *Aringarosa is racing "northward" over the Tyrrhenian Sea on a flight from Rome-Ciampini to Paris.*

If you go due north from Rome, you will not reach the sea. You must go northwest or west.

PAGE 279: *On page 220, Langdon brought the armored truck to a shuddering stop at the foot of the mile-long driveway. Now, on page 279, "a sea of blue police lights and sirens erupted at the bottom of the hill and began snaking up the half-mile driveway."*

Leigh Teabing has a long driveway. But is it a mile or half a mile?

PAGE 280: *Here, we learn that "Collet and his agents burst through the front door . . . They found a bullet hole in the drawing room floor, signs of a struggle . . ." But a few pages later, on page 296, we find out that "Collet was grateful that PTS had located a bullet hole in the floor, which at least corroborated Collet's claims . . ."*

Gee, you would think that Collet would have told the PTS people that he had found the bullet hole, but maybe he let them discover it on their own.

PAGE 281: *Here we read this description: "Collet ran to the door, trying to see out into the darkness. All he could make out was the faint shadow of a forest in the distance." But two pages later, on page 283, Rémy "was doing an impressive job of maneuvering the vehicle across the moonlit fields."*

Perhaps the moonlight was different at one end of the field than at the other?

PAGE 293: *"The Hawker 731's twin Garrett TFE-731 engines thundered."*

We understand what airplane Dan Brown is probably talking about, but practically no one would call it a "Hawker 731." It is a Hawker-Siddeley HS-125 with Garrett 731 jet engines, a representative model being an HS-125-400-731. This was originally built by de Havilland, then British Aerospace, and now is under the Raytheon banner.

PAGE 300: *Dan Brown describes the $30.8 million purchase by Bill Gates of "eighteen sheets of paper" comprising the Leonardo notebook known as the Leicester Codex.*

The eighteen sheets are two-sided and fold in half, creating a seventy-two-page booklet. The wealthy Armand Hammer bought the codex in 1980 for $5.2 million and renamed it the Hammer Codex, but Gates restored its name to Leicester Codex. Its home is the Seattle Art Museum, but it has toured the world and has been made into an interactive CD.

PAGE 332: *The police were "awaiting the moment when the plane's engines powered down. The instant this happened, a runway attendant would place safety wedges under the tires so the plane could no longer move."*

Practically the whole world over, the "safety wedges" are called "chocks." In England, Dan Brown's "runway attendant" would be called a "marshaller."

PAGE 332: *"The Hawker's engines were still roaring as the jet finished its usual rotation inside the hangar, positioning itself nose-out in preparation for later departure. As the plane completed its 180-degree turn and rolled toward the front of the hangar . . ."*

No jet pilot would attempt this maneuver. Pilots simply do not operate planes inside hangars. The jet vortices would make lethal projectiles out of anything not bolted down in the hangar, and the thrust would very likely blow the hangar's walls out. A Biggin Hill pilot told us this would be "a sackable offense."

PAGE 343: *The Temple Church survived "only to be heavily damaged by Luftwaffe incendiary bombs in 1940," according to Dan Brown.*

The incendiary bombs actually fell on the night of May 10, 1941.

PAGE 343: *As Teabing and company arrive at Temple Church, "the rough-hewn stone shimmered in the rain." A minute or two later, inside, "Teabing pointed toward a stained-glass window where the breaking sun was refracting through a white-clad knight riding a rose-colored horse."*

We guess that this was the only ray of sun on an otherwise cloudy, rainy morning. Throughout the book's

activities in London during the morning, it is raining—
sometimes heavily.

PAGE 346: *Teabing once had to lie on stage for half and hour
"with my todger hanging out." What's a todger?*

British slang for penis.

PAGE 347: *Teabing has spoken of Temple Church as housing
"ten of the most frightening tombs you will ever see" a few pages
earlier. Now, on page 347, inside Temple Church, Langdon sees
"ten stone knights. Five on the left. Five on the right. Lying
supine on the floor, the carved, life-sized figures rested in
peaceful poses. The knights were depicted wearing full armor,
shields and swords . . . All of the figures were deeply weathered,
and yet each was clearly unique."*

*But they are all surprised to find that "one of the knights is
missing."*

There isn't a knight missing. There are just nine carved
knights in effigy. This should be no surprise to anyone
who knows the Temple Church.

One of the main reasons for the weathered look of
the knights is the damage caused by falling debris in the
incendiary bombing by the Germans on May 10, 1941.
The roof of the Round Church burned first, followed
eventually by all the wood throughout the church.

PAGE 360: *Legaludec's pistol is a "small-caliber, J-frame
Medusa." What is this?*

This appears to be a confusion of two weapons. The
J-frame is commonly associated with a series of snubby
revolvers in the Smith-Wesson lineup, such as the Model
60, a five-shot .357.

The Medusa is a very special weapon made by
Phillips & Rodgers that does not confine itself to one

caliber. Instead, it accepts a wide range of ammo from the same approximate caliber, such as .357, 9 mm and .38 rounds. It is a small six-shot revolver. Interestingly, at the request of forensic scientists, the gun is made with nine rifling lands and grooves, making it probably unique among handguns.

PAGE 365: *In the barn loft at Villette are examples of a listening system that the French police consider "very advanced . . . as sophisticated as our own equipment. Miniature microphones, photoelectric recharging cells, high-capacity RAM chips. He's even got some of those new nano drives." They discover a radio receiving system and they agree that the remote bugs are "voice-activated to save hard disk space, and [they] recorded snippets of conversation during the day, transmitting compressed audio files at night to avoid detection. After transmitting, the hard drive erased itself and prepared to do it all over again the next day." Collet now looks at a shelf containing "several hundred audio cassettes, all labelled with dates and numbers." What's wrong with this picture?*

Quick! Find any ten-year-old kid and ask him or her whether it would make sense to store MP3 files on audio cassette tapes! (Just to be fair, first explain to the kid what a cassette tape was and what the player used to look like!)

For those who can't get the story from a kid, the compressed audio files can be played right on the computer and stored right on the computer's hard drive, or transferred to a CD or DVD for safekeeping. It would be time-prohibitive and unnecessary to make audio tapes. By the way, what are nanodrives? We are students of nanotechnology developments, and can imagine many things there may be in the future, but we're not sure what Dan Brown is talking about here, except to sound futuristic.

PAGE 367: *Langdon and Sophie "hurdled the turnstile at the Temple tube station" on their way from Temple Church to the library of the Institute of Systematic Theology. Does a Tube ride make sense for this trip?*

No. There are two problems with this trip. If you wish to find the Institute of Systematic Theology, you will need to go to Room 2E of the Cresham Building on Surrey Lane (on the day when the institute's scholars meet). If you run to the Temple Tube station, you are only half a block from the Cresham Building and there is no need to go into any station.

But, the octagonal room that is described as the library of the institute won't be found in the Cresham Building. In all likelihood, this is really the Round Room, which is in the Maugham Library of Kings College. To get there from Temple Church, you just go north, cross the Strand, and go up Chancery Lane. It's only a block. If you ran to the Tube station, you would be going the wrong way.

PAGE 377: *Dan Brown says there is a "Research Institute in Systematic Theology" at King's College in London. Is this real?*

Yes. The respected institute is run by the college's Department of Theology and Religious Studies. However, it is really just a conclave of scholars who meet regularly in a seminar room and often host conferences on theology.

PAGE 377: *Dan Brown says the Kings College Research Institute in Systematic Theology has a primary research room that is a "dramatic octagonal chamber." Sophie and Langdon arrive just as the librarian is making tea and settling in for the day. Does that sound right?*

The room he describes does exist as part of Kings College, but it is in the Maugham Library on Chancery Lane.

It doesn't belong to the Research Institute. It does not open until 9:30 a.m. on Saturday, and we estimate that Sophie and Langdon would reach it sometime around 8:30 at the latest (even after getting lost a bit).

PAGE 379: *Dan Brown says the Kings College Research Institute on Systematic Theology for two decades had used "optical character recognition software in unison with linguistic translation devices to digitize and catalogue an enormous collection of texts—encyclopedias of religion, religious biographies, sacred scriptures in dozens of languages, histories, Vatican letters, diaries of clerics, anything at all that qualified as writings on human spirituality." The data is said to be accessible via a "massive mainframe" computer that can search at five hundred Mb/sec through a "few hundred terabytes" of information. Does this exist?*

No. We contacted the faculty of the Research Institute. They were surprised and amused to learn about their putative huge computer and database.

One professor told us, "Our computing facilities are the staff desktops [currently G3 iMacs]." He said, "We do not, unfortunately, have any computing resources devoted to assembling 'a huge [or even modest] database of theological works.'" He added, "I once tried using optical recognition software, but it was such a disaster that I typed the piece in myself instead."

PAGE 392: *In seeking "a knight A. Pope interred," Langdon obtains this "hit" on the Research Institute computer: "Sir Isaac Newton's burial, attended by kings and nobles, was presided over by Alexander Pope, friend and colleague, who gave a stirring eulogy before sprinkling dirt on the tomb." Did Pope really preside and read a eulogy?*

No. Newton's funeral on March 28, 1727, was remarkable

in the lofty honor afforded Sir Isaac. He was considered almost a deity. According to a chronicle of the time, his body was brought from the Jerusalem Chamber of Westminster Abbey by pallbearers that included a lord, two dukes and three earls. The chief mourner was Sir Michael Newton, and the Bishop of Rochester read the service.

Although Alexander Pope was probably the preeminent poet of the time, his role came later, when a number of people decided to erect a monument to Newton about four years after his death. Because Pope had a reputation for writing outstanding epitaphs (and earned a good income from it), he was selected to write the epitaph that appears on the monument. It became one of the most famous of all time:

ISAACUS NEWTONUS:
Quem Immortalem
Testantur, Tempus, Natura, Caelum:
Mortalem
Hoc marmor fatetur.

Nature and Nature's Laws lay hid in Night.
God said, Let Newton be! and All was Light.

PAGE 393: *Sophie and Langdon seemed to have arrived at the King's College institute library around 8:00 a.m. on a Saturday morning, yet they find it open and staffed by the friendly and efficient Pamela Gettum. This seems improbable. What time do these early birds get to Westminster Abbey and is it open?*

Our calculations show that they probably arrive at Westminster Abbey at about 8:45 a.m.. Although they move right into the abbey without problem, the fact is that it doesn't really open until 9:30 a.m. This is just one of several problems we have identified with the timeline of *The Da Vinci Code's* action. Another is with the air travel of Bishop Aringarosa. The bishop's travels are inconsistent with the rest of the timeline, in our opinion. In the extreme possibility, it seems he could be airborne about six hours from Rome to Biggin Hill, with intermediate points that do not fit the trip. But further, if events were taken in sequential order in the book, he would instantly arrive at 5 Orme Court to be shot by Silas, when it should require about fifty minutes to get from Biggin Hill to London center.

We have worked out a detailed timeline of *The Da Vinci Code*—and determined that, improbable as it seems, it is at least technically plausible to pack all the action of the book into a single twenty-four-hour day. If you would like more information on this subject, contact us at www.secretsofthecode.com.

Following the Rose Line from Rosslyn to ... Florence?
Thoughts about the Last Act of The Da Vinci Code

By Dan Burstein

Our extremely able tour guide, David Shugarts, has brought us to this juncture. He has led us through four hundred pages of *Da Vinci Code* plot details and plot flaws. An amazingly jam-packed eight hours has passed from 12:32 a.m., the time the phone awakened Robert Langdon from his reveries (no doubt of the sacred feminine) in his comfortable bed at the Ritz Hotel in Paris, to this moment, at approximately 8:45 a.m., when Robert and Sophie are arriving at Westminster Abbey. At this point, some of the biggest plot mysteries jump out from behind their gargoyles. The story of the Teacher falls apart. His motives for setting this whole plot in motion prove irrational and implausible. The Priory of Sion appears to wimp out on the legacy that has occupied so much of the book. And the fearsome Opus Dei seems humbled and unlikely to launch new conspiracies and intrigues. The strong allusion that is made to the ultimate resting place of the Holy Grail seems silly to many readers.

With a lot to choose from, however, what follows is my personal favorite example of a plot flaw: everything has led us to believe that Sophie, aka Princesse Sophie, the hothouse grandchild of Grand Master and Grand-Père Saunière, is the twenty-first-century descendant of the royal bloodline flowing from the union of Jesus Christ and Mary Magdalene. We were thrown off the scent briefly in the middle of the book when Sophie begins to get the inkling that she might be the modern-day bearer of the bloodline of Jesus. But Langdon tells her that since Saunière is not a Merovingian name, and since no one in her family is named Plantard or Saint-Clair, "it's impossible" that the auburn-haired Sophie is the modern-day descendant of Mary Magdalene and Jesus Christ.

Yet by the end of the book, Dan Brown will let us know he was just tossing us a red herring. Marie Chauvel, Saunière's wife and Sophie's grandmother, is explicit when she tells Sophie the truth: her parents were both descended from Merovingian families—"direct descendants of Mary Magdalene and Jesus Christ." Sophie's parents had changed their names from Plantard and Saint-Clair long before, for protection. "Their children represented the most direct surviving royal bloodline and therefore were carefully guarded by the Priory."

Powerful dark forces (presumably of the church) conspire to kill Sophie's family and to eradicate this sacred bloodline once and for all. But Sophie and her brother survive the car accident that was intended to wipe out the entire family. The parents are dead, and Saunière must act precipitously in the face of great danger. He separates the survivors, moves Sophie in with him, sends his wife and Sophie's brother to live secret, separate lives in Scotland (at the Rosslyn Chapel) and cuts off virtually all communication between the Paris grandfather-granddaughter pair and the Scotland grandmother-grandson pair. After taking all these elaborate precautions to keep the future bright for these last descendants of the royal bloodline, Saunière sets about raising Sophie and training her for her future role.

Then, the unfortunate primal scene takes place when Sophie visits Saunière's country house on an unannounced early return from college. She is so traumatized by the *hieros gamos* rite she briefly witnesses that she refuses to speak to Grand-Père ever again, she refuses to read the letters he sends her, and she refuses every effort he makes to explain. But how can the brilliant Saunivère, a modern-day Leonardo da Vinci and grand master of the great Priory of Sion, not be able to get through at all to the granddaughter he loves? Crusades have happened, wars have been fought, people have been massacred, believers have been tortured to death, all to protect the secrets of the Priory of Sion. Now Saunière can't find a way to communicate these secrets to his granddaughter?

Moreover, if bloodline is so important, and if *sang real*—royal blood—is what the Holy Grail is really all about, as we are told so often in the novel, how is it that both Sophie and her brother—the two last descendants on earth of Jesus Christ and Mary Magdalene, whose families and secret society protectors have withstood every effort to extinguish their line for two millennia—are so blithely unmarried, unengaged, and without even a hint of a girlfriend or boyfriend? Sophie is said to be thirty-two when the action of the book takes place. Her biological clock is definitely ticking. And yet, she is childless. This, to me, is a massively glaring plot hole. Does it all come to an end here?

Well, not exactly. Langdon invites Sophie to join him next month in Florence, where he will be lecturing. They can spend a week in a luxury hotel that Langdon calls the Brunelleschi. (Dan Brown presumably gives the hotel this name as an allusion to Brunelleschi's dome, the centerpiece of Florence, and arguably the ultimate architectural metaphor for the female breast). Sophie wants no museums, no churches, no tombs, art, or relics. Langdon wonders what else they will do? At which point they kiss—on the mouth—and he is reminded of what else one can do in Florence for a week. Thus, we leave Sophie and Langdon dreaming of Florence, the city of Leonardo da Vinci, and the hotel room that awaits them.

Assuming Langdon is not overcome by performance anxiety at the thought of making love to a woman descended directly from Jesus Christ—and there's no reason to believe that he would be, given his belief in the sacred feminine—there may be progeny yet. We'll have to wait for the sequel.

Part II

Reviews and Commentaries on The Da Vinci Code

11 Commentary, Criticism, and Observations

Code Hot, Critics Hotter

—*New York Daily News* HEADLINE,
SEPTEMBER 4, 2003

The spectacular publishing success of *The Da Vinci Code* has generated millions of satisfied readers, fans, and enthusiasts, on the one hand, and a wide variety of critics on the other.

Usually, when you talk about critical reactions to novels, you are talking about what literary critics and book reviewers say in the media that covers books. In the case of *The Da Vinci Code*, these critics were mostly very enthusiastic.

Calling it a "gleefully erudite suspense novel" and a "riddle-filled, code-breaking, exhilaratingly brainy thriller," Janet Maslin of the *New York Times* said she could sum up her reaction in one word: "WOW." (Although in Dan Brown fashion, she got a twofer for her one-word commentary, pointing out that if you rotated WOW upside down, you would get a word critically related to the maternal essence.) "Even if he had not contrived this entire story as a hunt for the Lost Sacred Feminine essence, women in particular would love Mr. Brown."

Patrick Anderson, writing in the *Washington Post*, called it a "considerable achievement" to write "a theological thriller that is both fascinating and fun."

Even many religious groups responded positively—if not to everything in the book, then to the opportunity it afforded them to introduce their own commentary on the same subjects that Dan Brown was addressing. Churches held retreats and convened book groups; experts on formerly esoteric issues (like the biography of Mary Magdalene or the ideas contained within the Gnostic Gospels) were suddenly in great demand for church-sponsored lecture series.

On the website explorefaith.org John Tintera wrote, "Despite being somewhat simplistic, if not outright false, I think the religious content of *The Da Vinci Code* offers a timely wake up call to the Christian church. In doing so, it invites Christians to take a fresh look at our origins and our history, both the good and the bad, which is something we don't do often enough."

Soon, however, even as the reading public continued to lap up the adventures of Robert Langdon and Sophie Neveu, critics who don't usually write book reviews started to comment. Religious groups that took deep offense at what they believed was Dan Brown's desire to attack or defame Catholicism or Christianity began to be heard from. They wrote long commentaries on websites and in religious publications, responding to every idea in the book that they believed to be erroneous. In some cases, they were right about their facts, and Dan Brown was wrong—on matters like when the Dead Sea Scrolls were discovered or some of the details of what happened at the Council of Nicea. But in many ways, the religious critics were proving Dan Brown's point: they were so frightened by the novel's popularity and the possibility that it might supercede church dogma in winning hearts and minds to an alternative view of Christianity, they felt they had to engage in polemics with a writer of popular fiction.

The notion of Brown doing meticulous research also began to come under attack a few months after the publication of the book. Some saw *The Da Vinci Code* as highly derivative of books like *Holy Blood, Holy Grail* and *The Templar Revelation*—books Brown cited by name in the text of *The Da Vinci Code* and credited on his website as important to his research. As several pieces of commentary in this chapter point out, *Holy Blood, Holy Grail*, which has been circulating widely since its publication more than twenty years ago, is generally considered to be an occult stew of myth, legend, and outright hoax, mixed in with some very intriguing historical details.

Then another thriller writer came to the fore, Lewis Perdue, who had written an earlier book called *The Da Vinci Legacy* in 1983, and another called *Daughter of God*. These books featured plot elements and characters that Perdue asserted were remarkably close to *The Da Vinci Code*. Among the similarities: a deep, dark secret from early Christian history involving a Gnostic female messiah named Sophia, dead art curators, Swiss banks, Leonardo da Vinci, Mary Magdalene, discussions of goddess cults, and much more. A drama may play out in the courts over these similarities. But in the meantime, it looks like another battle is looming in Hollywood, where Ron Howard is working on a film version of *The Da Vinci Code* for Sony Pictures, while the creator of *Survivor*, Mark Burnett, has optioned the Perdue novels.

In the rest of this chapter, we offer a variety of commentaries on *The Da Vinci Code*, critical essays, and interesting observations. We welcome our readers to join in the dialogue and post their own views on our website, www.secretsofthecode.com.

The Real Da Vinci Code

By Lynn Picknett and Clive Prince

Lynn Picknett and Clive Prince, the London-based coauthors of *The Templar Revelation* (which figures by name in *The Da Vinci Code*), contributed this commentary to *Secrets of the Code*. Copyright © 2004 by Lynn Picknett and Clive Prince.

We must say that *The Da Vinci Code* was an intriguing 2003 birthday present for one of us. From its opening sequence in the Louvre, like millions of others, we were hooked, breathlessly turning pages, riding high on the sheer fun of it all.

But unlike those other page-turning fans, we had an extra reason for being intrigued: it's not every day that we see the title of our 1997 book, *The Templar Revelation*, embedded in the pages of an international bestselling thriller as one of its four major sources. So we weren't just more or less happy to be whirled along with the action. However, because of our involvement, there in black and white on the page, from the very beginning, we were also *critics*.

Certainly Brown fleshes out the whole concept of the underground society, the Priory of Sion, with its alleged secrets about the bloodline of Jesus and Mary Magdalene, into a dark and turbulent story. Laudably, he's brought these very alternative ideas, which first saw the light of day in *Holy Blood, Holy Grail* back in 1982, to a whole new, excited audience who would probably never have picked up the original. However, it must be remembered that Brown's book is *fiction* and that it draws heavily on other works—not only our own, but also, primarily, *Holy Blood, Holy Grail* by Michael Baigent, Richard Leigh, and Henry Lincoln. This drew on material issued by the enigmatic secret society, the Priory of Sion, indicating that it was the guardian of some great mystery connected with the

Merovingian dynasty of Frankish kings and Mary Magdalene. The authors claim that this secret is that Jesus and Mary Magdalene were married and had children who grew up in France and whose descendants founded the Merovingian line.

Although most people believe this is what the Priory of Sion claims, in fact, it is Baigent, Leigh, and Lincoln's own interpretation. The idea was explicitly disavowed by the Grand Master of the Priory of Sion, Pierre Plantard, to whom the importance of the Merovingians is that they are the rightful heirs to the throne of France (assuming that France ever decides to have kings again).

We are far from convinced about the holy bloodline theory. While we accept that there is abundant evidence that Jesus and Mary Magdalene had a physical relationship, which may or may not have resulted in offspring, there's too much ingenuity involved in crowbarring them into the Merovingians' history. But, in any case, even if there were descendants of Jesus around today, why should they be special? Theologically, Jesus was unique, the one and only Son of God. Therefore, his children and their children throughout the generations could have nothing divine about them.

Many people, caught up in the excitement and romance of all this, have assumed that if there were descendants of Jesus around today, there must be something intrinsically special about them. In fact, this *isn't* what Baigent, Leigh, and Lincoln ever claimed. For them, it was the fact that these descendants would be legal heirs to certain titles and powers, such as the throne of Jerusalem, which was important. And the reason these descendants have had to be kept secret from the church is because their very existence would prove that Jesus was nothing more than a mortal man.

A great many people have missed this point, and this has led to theories that there is something inherently, perhaps even genetically, different about this bloodline. Indeed, we regard the notion as potentially dangerous, just like any elitist system that upholds certain people for their physical characteristics over all others. This may take the form of Hitler's master race or white supremacists or those who believe some carry the Jesus bloodline gene, making them automatically superior to the rest of us.

The holy bloodline aspect of Dan Brown's book may be founded on sandy ground, but we agree that the "great heretical secret," so loathed and feared by the church, is indeed sexuality as a sacrament, the sacred feminine. That *was* a secret that had to be protected by the church and it *did* involve Mary Magdalene and Jesus. Her true role as priestess is the key that, if known, would have allowed people to deconstruct the church's teaching, particularly about the place and worth of women. There is even a case for the Magdalene being the most important woman who ever lived, simply because, out of hatred and fear of her real power, as evidenced in the lost, Gnostic Gospels, the church repressed generations of women and degraded the whole of sexuality in her name.

But *The Da Vinci Code* centers on the paintings of Leonardo da Vinci, another area, in our view, in which Dan Brown misses the mark. By trying to combine our discoveries about da Vinci's "code" and the central theory of *Holy Blood, Holy Grail*, Brown has allowed a much more amazing and even shocking revelation to fall between the cracks. The *real* da Vinci code takes us into a much darker and intensely challenging world.

Brown summarizes our discovery of the weird symbolism in Leonardo's *Virgin of the Rocks* (the Paris version; there is another, less interesting one in London's National Gallery) whereby, instead of the infant Jesus being with his mother and young John the Baptist being with his traditional protector, the archangel Uriel, the children, apparently, are with the wrong guardians. This is particularly interesting because the scene is taken from a story the church invented to circumvent the embarrassment of the fact that when John baptized Jesus, he must have had the authority to do so. This scene depicts the moment, or so we are led to believe, that little Jesus bestows this authority on little John for later life. Indeed, the child with Uriel raises his hand in blessing on the other baby, who kneels submissively. However, what happens if the children are with their *correct* guardians? As Brown points out, John would be blessing Jesus, and Jesus would be kneeling submissively to John. Indeed, there are many other elements in the painting that confirm this interpretation. But how would this Johannite (pro John the Baptist) interpretation gel with Brown's basic thesis about the holy bloodline? It doesn't. It stands out like a sore thumb. That's what comes of trying to lever undigested Leonardo secrets into the wrong context.

In over a decade of research, we have found, time after time, evidence that wherever he could, Leonardo da Vinci elevated John the Baptist over Jesus, showing that he regarded the Baptist as superior to Christ. For example, in Leonardo's famous preliminary work of *The Virgin and Child with St. Anne* (ca. 1499–1500) in London's National Gallery, the group consists of the Virgin Mary, Jesus, St. Anne, and a young John the Baptist. But when Leonardo painted the final version, *St. Anne with the Virgin and Child* (1501–07), we find the Baptist's place taken by a lamb, which Jesus seizes so roughly by the ears that we used to joke it should be called *Pulling the Ears Off a Lamb*. In fact, Jesus also has one chubby leg locked around the lamb's neck, visually *severing* it. But as Jesus is called the "Lamb of God" by the Baptist in the New Testament, why has Leonardo represented John himself as a lamb? Perhaps the secret lies in the tradition among the Knights Templar of honoring the Baptist and representing him as a lamb (as in the Templar seal of the knights in southern France, for example). It must be stressed that this is extremely telling: few non-Templars would dream of representing John as the lamb. So, was Leonardo some kind of Knight Templar, even around two hundred years after the order was brutally suppressed?

Perhaps he was. Certainly we know that the inner circle of the Templars maintained an enormous—many said heretical—reverence for the Baptist, which is reflected in many more of Leonardo's works. The last thing he ever did, for his own bene-fit entirely and not as any commission, was his darkly strange *St. John the Baptist*, which—together with the *Mona Lisa*—adorned the walls of his death chamber in France in 1519. And his only surviving sculpture, a joint work with Giovanni Francesco Rustici (a known and somewhat sinister alchemist and necromancer), is of John the Baptist, which now stands above an entrance to the baptistery in Florence. The Baptist was everywhere in Leonardo's life, by accident or design. Even if his commissions did not require John to be included, some-how Leonardo always managed to sneak in some Baptist sym-bolism, such as the carob tree—a traditional association with John—in his unfinished *Adoration of the Magi* (ca. 1481), which is being worshipped by bright, healthy young people, while the holy family is being clawed at by a group of hideous ancient figures like the undead. And the young man standing radiantly close to the roots of John's carob tree is making what we have come to call the "John gesture"—raising the right forefinger heavenward. Leonardo's sculpture is also making this gesture, as is his last painting, *St. John the Baptist* (1513–16)—clearly it is used to represent or symbolize the Baptist, who may or may be not be present in the work himself. One of the figures in his world-famous wall-painting the *Last Supper* (1495–97) is also making the John gesture almost threateningly right into Jesus' face. (This may be at least partly a reference to a relic that is said to be possessed by the Templars, allegedly of the forefinger of John the Baptist himself, which was kept at the temple in Paris. But the gesture here could well have at least a double meaning.)

Leonardo, we discovered, was not alone in his Johannitism. In fact, rather than being basically Christian, the Priory of Sion, however much their beliefs are embroidered with the Magdalene romance, also reveal a similar fascination with the Baptist. Indeed, as the Priory claims Leonardo as one of their own, this struck us as being too much of a coincidence. Their fascination with the Baptist was drawn to our attention by our first Priory contact, known only as Giovanni (John!) in 1991. We even managed to trace this belief in their documents, the most obvious example being the fact that their Grand Masters always take the name John (or Jean or Giovanni)—Leonardo was, according to their own list, John IX. (And is it merely a coincidence that "Sion" itself is Welsh for John?) More intriguingly, the Priory started the count from John II; John I, as Pierre Plantard said, "being symbolically reserved for Christ." But why should Christ be called John? Could it be that to Johannites, John the Baptist is the true Christ—which, after all, means simply an anointed or chosen one?

There is more of this deeply disturbing Johannitism embedded in a Priory-backed publication of 1982, in which the Templars are described as the "Swordbearers of the Church of John," while declaring that they and the Priory were once more or less the same organization.

Thanks to dangerously heretical Leonardo—not to mention the Priory of Sion, whatever they may really be—we found ourselves drawn into some very deep water indeed. Soon we were faced with the extraordinary revelation that there was an ancient tradition in which John the Baptist was revered—and Jesus was regarded as a lesser being, sometimes even reviled.

This Johannite Church, with branches not only in heretical Europe but also in a Middle Eastern tribe, has been largely ignored both by academics and alternative researchers alike. Yet it has always been there, under the surface, its secrets finding form in perhaps many ways, but certainly in the works of the great Renaissance maestro, Leonardo da Vinci. And whatever one's reaction to such irredeemable heresy, his true "secret code" is considerably more exciting and challenging than even the idea that Jesus and the Magdalene had children.

Why does the baby Jesus' leg apparently sever the lamb's neck? *Why* is he pulling the ears off the lamb? *Why* is a disciple raising the John gesture threateningly into Jesus' face in the *Last Supper*? *Why* are the worshippers of the holy family in *The Adoration of the Magi* evil-looking half-dead wrecks, while those worshipping John's carob tree are bursting with health and youth? Is there any connection with the somewhat different interpretation of Jesus and John's relationship that many modern theologians are now quietly admitting?

Religious Fiction

By David Klinghoffer

David Klinghoffer's new book is *The Discovery of God: Abraham and the Birth of Monotheism* (Doubleday). This article originally appeared in the *National Review*, December 8, 2003. It is reprinted by permission of National Review, 215 Lexington Avenue, New York, NY 10016.

When a novel has stuck around the top of the *New York Times* bestseller list for half a year, there is something interesting going on. Such a book has set off a pretty loud pealing of the electric chimes at the front door of the culture. In the case of Dan Brown's *The Da Vinci Code*, what's so special exactly? That depends on what makes conspiracy theories so fascinating.

The conspiracy theory at the heart of Dan Brown's huge bestseller was not invented by him (it has been kicking around for years), but it's a juicy one and he's made the most of it, creating a story with a very effective cliffhanger at the end of almost every one of his 105 chapters. You are pulled along relentlessly—a feat of narrative art that really does deserve to be called art, no matter what Yale literary critic Harold Bloom said recently in mocking the "immensely inadequate" Stephen King (a similarly gifted writer) when the latter won a lifetime achievement literary prize. If you don't believe writing in this vein merits appreciation, try thinking up a plot like the one in *The Da Vinci Code* yourself. Since Brown's novel is a novel, it can more forthrightly take advantage of the tension inherent in unlocking ancient doors that perhaps should never be opened. He's witty, succinct, and smart—though the reader will have to be prepared to encounter the phrase "the sacred feminine" more than once, and if that makes you extremely queasy, you had better leave this book alone.

But the best thing about *The Da Vinci Code* is that the conspiracy is just an awfully neat one. What makes for an outstanding conspiracy? It doesn't have to be real, as this one is surely not, despite Brown's inclusion of a preface boldly headlined "FACT." One requirement is a complex array of lore. Brown has that: he provides many fascinating historical and quasi-historical tidbits—like the symbolic significance of the figure of a rose, the mathematical phenomenon called the Fibonacci sequence, the ancient Hebrew coding sequence called *atbash*, and much more, with an emphasis on the cryptic meanings of the paintings and drawings of Leonardo da Vinci, all artfully woven into the plot.

Above all, a worthwhile conspiracy needs to explain something that previously you didn't know needed explaining, something also that links to a truth, or at least a pseudotruth, of deep significance. Again, pseudodepth will do fine—we're talking about entertainment, after all. *The Da Vinci Code* has this.

But this book is certainly not for everyone, for the following reason. In this sort of thriller, there has to be something urgently important at stake should the conspiracy be revealed. What's at stake in *The Da Vinci Code* is nothing less than traditional Christianity itself. The Holy Grail, we are told, is not a holy cup but rather holy blood, the lineage of Jesus of Nazareth: the founder of Christianity had a daughter, Sarah, by Mary Magdalene. If true, this theory would overturn some of the central beliefs of Christians.

As a believing Jew, I certainly can't be accused of special pleading on behalf of Christian dogma. This should give me credibility when I say that this "holy blood" theory—of Jesus having descendants—is too nutty to merit serious consideration; any suggestion that such a fact could have been kept secret for two millennia is absurd. Brown does acknowledge that there is some merit—some truth and beauty—in Christianity; but such merit as he sees is very far from the faith of actual Christian believers. Any Christian who is offended by fiction that directly contradicts his faith should certainly avoid this book.

If I were a Christian, though, I think I would find it a little disturbing that some fellow Christians do in fact view this novel as a threat to their faith. Some Catholic magazines have published detailed refutations of *The Da Vinci Code*; that they believe this is necessary indicates that many Catholics, and many in the general reading public, are taking this book far more seriously than they ought to. This also suggests that the problems in Catholic religious education are every bit as severe as Catholic conservatives have been alleging for some time now. If the professional educators were doing their job, any believing Catholic past elementary-school age would know that Brown's book is a total falsehood.

What about the book's influence in the broader culture? Here, I am calmed by the reflection that there's something profoundly religious about conspiracies in the first place, even fictitious ones. Think about this next time you are at the beach in chilly weather. Though the sky is cloudy and a cold wind is up, you'll see people sitting on blankets in the sand just staring out to sea. Why? Because when you look at the ocean you get the intuition that just under the surface resides a vast hidden world of exotic, usually unseen creatures. The realization that there's all that life underneath—in some ways a mirror of our own world on dry land but in others dramatically different—is simply thrilling. It's what keeps people's eyes glued to the ocean even when there is ostensibly nothing going on out there.

This, too, is what makes a conspiracy thrilling, the revelation of concealed complexity all around. Likewise, it's what attracts many of us to thinking about spiritual matters—the gut-level perception, powerful if unproven, of an existence beyond the one of our mundane daily lives. *The Da Vinci Code* may be silly, but in its fashion, it's also thrilling. If its popularity means people are thinking about invisible realities, that's good news.

[In *The Da Vinci Code*, Sophie Neveu is surprised to discover that the book *Holy Blood, Holy Grail*, another of the many real-life works on Leigh Teabing's library shelves, was an "international bestseller," yet she had never heard of it.

"You were young," Teabing tells her. "This caused quite a stir back in the nineteen eighties. To my taste, the authors made some dubious leaps of faith in their analysis, but their fundamental premise is sound, and to their credit, they finally brought the idea of Christ's bloodline into the mainstream."

It is an ironic statement for many reasons. First, Teabing himself is a composite character modeled on the real life trio of authors who wrote *Holy Blood, Holy Grail*. Indeed, his first name derives from Richard Leigh and his surname is an anagram of Michael Baigent. By openly declaring that "to my taste, the authors made some dubious leaps of faith in their analysis," Teabing (and his creator, Dan Brown) seem to be signaling that they know about the issues of questionable research in *Holy Blood, Holy Grail*, as well as all the allegations of hoax and fraud that have surrounded the modern-day desire of Pierre Plantard and several other French citizens to declare themselves to be the Priory of Sion and that of a number of writers to conjure up a Priory of Sion directly descended from the Templars and the Merovingian kings.

Despite Teabing's expressed concern about dubious leaps of faith, there is no doubt that *Holy Blood, Holy Grail* figured prominently in Dan Brown's thinking as he wove the plot for *The Da Vinci Code*. To help readers of *Secrets of the Code* better understand the arguments of *Holy Blood, Holy Grail*, we have excerpted a section from it, which appears in Chapter 6. Below, however, Laura Miller, of the *New York Times Book Review*, takes issue with *Holy Blood, Holy Grail* and the role of its arguments at the center of *The Da Vinci Code*'s plot.]

The Da Vinci Con

By Laura Miller

Reprinted by permission from the *New York Times Book Review*, February 22, 2004. From the *New York Times on the Web.* Copyright © The New York Times Company. Reprinted with permission.

The ever-rising tide of sales of *The Da Vinci Code* has lifted some pretty odd boats, and none odder than the dodgy yet magisterial *Holy Blood, Holy Grail*, by Michael Baigent, Richard Leigh, and Henry Lincoln. A bestseller in the 1980s, *Grail* is climbing the paperback charts again on the strength of its relationship to Dan Brown's thriller (which has, in turn, inspired a crop of new nonfiction books coming out this spring, from *Breaking the Da Vinci Code* to *Secrets of the Code: The Unauthorized Guide to the Mysteries Behind The Da Vinci Code*). *The Da Vinci Code* is one long chase scene in which the main characters flee a sinister Parisian policeman and an albino monk assassin, but its rudimentary suspense alone couldn't have made it a hit. At regular intervals, the book brings its pell-mell plot to a screeching halt and emits a pellet of information concerning a centuries-old conspiracy that purports to have preserved a tremendous secret about the roots of Christianity itself. This "nonfiction" material gives *The Da Vinci Code* its frisson of authenticity, and it's lifted from *Holy Blood, Holy Grail*, one of the all-time great works of pop pseudohistory. But what seems increasingly clear (to cop a favorite phrase from the authors of *Grail*) is that *The Da Vinci Code*, like *Holy Blood, Holy Grail*, is based on a notorious hoax.

The back story to both books, like most conspiracy theories, is devilishly hard to summarize. Both narratives begin with a mystery that leads sleuths to vaster and more sinister intrigues. In Brown's novel, it's the murder of a curator at the Louvre; in *Grail*, it's the unusual affluence of a priest in a village in the south of France. In the late 1960s, Henry Lincoln, a British TV writer, became interested in Rennes-le-Château, a town that had become the French equivalent of Roswell or Loch Ness as a result of popular books by Gérard de Sède. De Sède promulgated a story about parchments supposedly found in a hollowed-out pillar by the town priest in the 1890s, parchments containing coded messages that the priest somehow parlayed into oodles of cash. Lincoln worked on several *Unsolved Mysteries*-style documentaries about Rennes-le-Château, then enlisted Baigent and Leigh for a more in-depth investigation.

What eventually emerges from the welter of names, dates, maps, and genealogical tables crammed into *Holy Blood, Holy*

Grail is a yarn about a secret and hugely influential society called the Priory of Sion, founded in Jerusalem in 1099. This cabal is said to have guarded documents and other proof that Mary Magdalene was the wife of Jesus (who may or may not have died on the Cross) and that she carried his child with her when she fled to what is now France after the Crucifixion, becoming, figuratively, the Holy Grail in whom Jesus' blood was preserved. Their progeny intermarried with the locals, eventually founding the Merovingian dynasty of Frankish monarchs. Although deposed in the eighth century, the Merovingian lineage has not been lost; the Priory has kept watch over its descendants, awaiting an auspicious moment when it will reveal the astonishing truth and return the rightful monarch to the throne of France, or perhaps even a restored Holy Roman Empire.

All the usual suspects and accouterments of paranoid history get caught up in this thousand-year jaunt. The Cathar heretics, the Knights Templar, the Rosicrucians, the Vatican, the Freemasons, Nazis, the Dead Sea Scrolls, the Protocols of the Elders of Zion, the Order of the Golden Dawn—everyone but the Abominable Snowman seems to be in on the game. *Holy Blood, Holy Grail* is a masterpiece of insinuation and supposition, employing all the techniques of pseudohistory to symphonic effect, justifying this sleight of hand as an innovative scholarly technique called "synthesis," previously considered too "speculative" by those whose thinking has been unduly shaped by the "so-called Enlightenment of the 18th century." Comparing themselves to the reporters who uncovered the Watergate scandal, the authors maintain that "only by such synthesis can one discern the underlying continuity, the unified and coherent fabric, which lies at the core of any historical problem." To do so, one must realize that "it is not sufficient to confine oneself exclusively to facts."

Thus liberated, Lincoln et al concoct an argument that is

not so much factual as factish. Dozens of credible details are heaped up in order to provide a legitimizing cushion for rank nonsense. Unremarkable legends (that Merovingian kings were thought to have a healing touch, for example) are characterized as suggestive clues or puzzles demanding solution. Highly contested interpretations (that, say, an early Grail romance depicts the sacred object as being guarded by Templars) are presented as established truth. Sources—such as the New Testament—are qualified as "questionable" and derivative when they contradict the conspiracy theory, then microscopically scrutinized for inconsistencies that might support it. The authors spin one gossamer strand of conjecture over another, forming a web dense enough to create the illusion of solidity. Though bogus, it's an impressive piece of work.

Finally, though, the legitimacy of the Priory of Sion history rests on a cache of clippings and pseudonymous documents that even the authors of *Holy Blood, Holy Grail* suggest were planted in the Bibliothèque Nationale by a man named Pierre Plantard. As early as the 1970s, one of Plantard's confederates had admitted to helping him fabricate the materials, including genealogical tables portraying Plantard as a descendant of the Merovingians (and, presumably, of Jesus Christ) and a list of the Priory's past "grand masters." This patently silly catalog of intellectual celebrities stars Botticelli, Isaac Newton, Jean Cocteau, and, of course, Leonardo da Vinci— and it's the same list Dan Brown trumpets, along with the alleged nine-century pedigree of the Priory, in the front matter for *The Da Vinci Code*, under the heading of "Fact." Plantard, it eventually came out, was an inveterate rascal with a criminal record for fraud and affiliations with wartime anti-Semitic and right-wing groups. The actual Priory of Sion was a tiny, harmless group of like-minded friends formed in 1956.

Plantard's hoax was debunked by a series of (as yet

untranslated) French books and a 1996 BBC documentary, but curiously enough this set of shocking revelations hasn't proved as popular as the fantasia of *Holy Blood, Holy Grail*, or, for that matter, as *The Da Vinci Code*. The only thing more powerful than a worldwide conspiracy, it seems, is our desire to believe in one.

The French Confection
Trying to Sort Out Fact and Fiction in the Strange Tale of Rennes-le-Château

BY AMY BERNSTEIN

Amy Bernstein is an expert on French Renaissance poetry. For *Secrets of the Code*, she reviewed the recent French literature and public discussion about the debate over whether the Priory of Sion, the secretive organization that underlies so much of *The Da Vinci Code's* plot, is a real organization or a twentieth-century hoax. Her report is below.

Like a perfect *île flottante*, which upon tasting reveals itself to be mostly air, the Rennes-le-Château–Prieuré de Sion (Priory of Sion) story is a magnificent French confection of pseudo history built on a delicately thin substructure of truth. Many people have analyzed the set of facts and legends involved in this story. My conclusion from reviewing the most credible among them is that beginning in the 1950s, a small group of men with neo-chivalric, nationalist, and sometimes anti-Semitic leanings was able to perpetrate what is almost certainly a marvelously intricate hoax that still draws people in today.

The history of this hoax is better than any bestselling thriller. It is no surprise then, that *The Da Vinci Code*—set for the most part in present-day France—draws heavily from details of the Priory of Sion–Rennes-le-Château affair described in the 1982 bestseller *Holy Blood, Holy Grail*. By introducing murdered museum director Jacques Saunière in the first chapter of *The Da Vinci Code*—a character who shares the same surname as the central figure in the Rennes-le-Château enigma—Dan Brown picks up where the original tale leaves off. In doing so, he is just one more of the many in France and England who have made a cottage industry out of an obscure provincial drama that took place over a hundred years ago. Here are the basic outlines of the original Rennes-le-Château–Prieuré de Sion story.

In 1885, the abbé Bérenger Saunière, an educated young man from a local bourgeois family, became the parish priest of the church of Saint Mary Magdalene in Rennes-le-Château, an isolated town in the department of Aude in southwestern France, not far from Le Bezu, a local mountain peak (from which was undoubtedly derived the name of the judicial police chief, Bezu Fache, in *The Da Vinci Code*).

The year of Abbé Saunière's appointment as parish priest was also marked by national political elections, with candidates taking an obligatory position on whether France should return to a pro-Catholic monarchy or remain a republic with a constitutional separation of church and state. During the election period, Bérenger Saunière became embroiled in this debate, earning a reputation as a fiery preacher supporting the return to a pro-Catholic monarchy. As a result, he gained the protection of the Countess of Chambord (widow of the pretender to the throne of France), who is said to have given him 3,000 livres to renovate his church.

In the late 1880s, during the course of the renovation of his dilapidated church, Saunière is said to have discovered some coded parchments hidden in a hollow pillar supporting the church's altarpiece. Advised by his bishop, Félix-Arsène Billiard, Saunière reportedly brought the parchments to Paris to show them to experts. While in Paris, he is reported to have made the acquaintance of a circle of occultists and esoterics, among them Emma Calvé (with whom he supposedly had an affair). Upon his return from Paris, he suddenly—and for no apparent reason—gained access to large sums of money with which he financed a number of building projects. These included the renovation of his ancient parish church and the construction of a large house (the Villa Bethania) and a tower (the Tour Magdala) which he used as his study and library for his increasingly large collection of books. He was able to maintain a lavish living style, despite the meagerness of his priestly income. He is said to have conducted numerous nightly excavations in and around his church. It was rumored, but never proven, that he had found treasure hidden in various spots within the church precincts.

Eventually it came out that the abbé Saunière was selling mass indulgences by mail all over Europe, which offered a plausible explanation for his wealth. He was removed from his position as parish priest and prohibited from saying Mass, and later tried and convicted for trafficking in masses by the diocesan authorities in Carcassonne. He died on 22 January 1917, leaving his house and tower to Marie Dénardaud, his lifelong housekeeper and companion (and, some say, his mistress). Interest in the local legend of the buried treasure endured, however, and an article about it appeared in the newspaper daily, *La Dépêche du Midi* in 1956.

Enter the Priory of Sion.

In that same year, in another part of France, a small group of friends formed a recreational club on 25 June 1956, in Annemasse, Haute-Savoie, which called itself the Priory of Sion—apparently after a nearby mountain, the Col du Mont Sion. It was disbanded the following year, but soon morphed into a second, politicized incarnation under the direction of Pierre Plantard. Drawing on the neo-chivalric, utopian, nationalist, and anti-Semitic principles of Paul Le Cour, who had exercised a major influence on Pierre Plantard in the 1930s and '40s, the Priory of Sion began publishing a periodical called *Circuit*, which appeared on and off during the 1950s and 1960s.

Plantard had a history of involvement since the 1930s with anti-Masonic and anti-Semitic nationalist organizations. He first attempted to establish an association called The French Union in 1937 "to engage in purifying and renewing France." This group was conceived in opposition to the leftist Popular Front government of Leon Blum, the first Jewish prime minister of France. In 1941 Plantard attempted to start another organization under the name of "French National Renewal," but was again denied official permission by French authorities. By this time, Plantard was already deeply involved with the Grand Order of the Alpha Galates. According to H. R. Kedward, professor of history at Sussex University, the Alpha Galates were part of "a fringe right-wing society with an emphasis on tradition, chivalry, Catholicism, spiritualism and what can only be called a kind of occult nationalism ... one of the very many 'Occident' movements which pitted what they saw as authentic French history and culture against the 'Freemasonic and Jewish Orient' ... They all flowered in the spring of Vichy (1940–41), began to lose momentum in 1942 and mostly lost all political significance in the declining years of 1943–44."

Plantard's shadowy activities with right-wing and nationalist organizations continued after the war up to the founding of the Priory. During all that time, he did not seem to have had any means of employment. He served four months in Fresnes prison in the early 1950s, convicted of fraud and embezzlement. In 1958, during the political crisis in France over the war for independence in Algeria, Plantard claims to have been a member of the Committees of Public Safety, using the pseudonym "Colonel Way."

At the beginning of the 1960s, Plantard launched a concerted effort to forge a trail of documentation to support his bogus claim of being a descendant of the Merovingian royal line, and to establish the bona fides and pedigree of the Priory of Sion. The story of Rennes-le-Château was little known at that time but it dovetailed conveniently with his own fictions, given the abbé Saunière's right-wing political leanings and his links with an occult circle in Paris. In fact, it served as a convenient point of departure for Plantard's fertile imagination.

During the 1960s, a number of fake documents were deposited at different times in the Bibliothèque Nationale in Paris by Pierre Plantard and his associates under various pseudonyms. The first set, composed in 1965 and fabricated by his accomplice, Philippe de Chérisey, included parchments supposedly found by Bérenger Saunière in Rennes-le Château, as well as other documents concerning the Priory of Sion and genealogical documents of the Merovingian kings. Members of the Priory of Sion were listed, including figures such as Leonardo da Vinci, Isaac Newton, and Jean Cocteau. The next part of the hoax was to spin and disseminate the fairy tale.

One of the authors whose services were enlisted to tell the fabulous story was named Gérard de Sède, who, it seems, was a willing pawn of the Priory. He published two books concerning the *dossiers secrets* and the tales of Rennes-le-Château: *L'Or de Rennes ou la vie insolite de Bérenger Saunière, curé de Rennes-le Château*, (René Juilliard, Paris, 1967), and in expanded form, *Le Trésor maudit* (Editions J'ai Lu, Paris, 1968). In his first book, de Sède reproduced the two coded parchments found by Bérenger Saunière, one of which was signed "PS," linking them to the Priory of Sion. As the journalist Jean-Luc Chaumeil later remarked, "The books of Gérard de Sède were, generally speaking, only the text, the basic tools of Pierre Plantard."

After these books were published, however, Plantard and de Sède had a fight over royalties from *L'Or de Rennes*, and Plantard and de Chérisey began to tell people quietly that the parchments had been faked. But the word leaked out very slowly. About this time, Robert Charroux participated in the filming of a documentary for ORTF (the French National Film Organization), and in 1972 published a book about Rennes-le-Château, entitled *Le Trésor de Rennes-le-Château*, which continued the fiction about the parchments. By 1973, however, Jean-Luc Chaumeil, the journalist who had become deeply involved with Pierre Plantard, wrote a story claiming that the secret dossiers were a hoax.

As interest in Rennes-le-Château deepened—replete with secret symbolic codes in the paintings of Poussin and Teniers and clues to the location of the Holy Grail—historians and journalists began to dispute other parts of the story as well. In 1974, René Descadeillas, a bona fide historian, began the debunking of the story of the treasure of Rennes-le-Château in a book entitled *Mythologie du trésor de Rennes, ou l'histoire véritable de l'abbé Saunière curé de Rennes le Château*, saying that Saunière had amassed his wealth through trafficking in mass indulgences. The following year, Gérard de Sède responded with *Le vrai dossier de l'énigme de Rennes: Réponse à M. Descadeillas*, in which he made the point that the cost of saying a mass was so little, and the time it took to say a mass so long, that the abbé Saunière could never have amassed much money, adding, "Descadeillas's fairytale of trafficking in masses, as we can see, is nothing more than the most fantastic nonsense."

A British film producer, Henry Lincoln, became interested in Rennes-le-Château story and did a series of three documentaries for BBC-TV: *The Lost Treasure of Jerusalem* (1972), *The Priest, the Painter, and the Devil* (1974), and *The Shadow of the Templars* (1979). None of these dealt seriously with the possibility that the Priory of Sion documents were an elaborate hoax, even though by then, their authenticity was subject to widespread questioning as well as allegations of out-and-out fraud. As a result of the enormous interest engendered by the BBC programs, Henry Lincoln and two others involved in the documentaries (Michael Baigent and Richard Leigh) came out with their book, *Holy Blood, Holy Grail*, which discussed not only the mysteries surrounding Rennes-le-Château, but also the claim that the Merovingian kings of France were the descendants of Jesus and Mary Magdalene. The book went on to become a bestseller, an enduring international sensation after it was first published in 1982 in England, and of course, one of Dan Brown's basic texts for developing the storyline of *The Da Vinci Code*. The British bestseller was translated and appeared in France as *L'énigme sacrée*, (Editions Pygmalion, Gérard Watelet, Paris 1983).

Back in France during the late 1970s and '80s, the early debunkers of the authenticity of the parchments came out with their own clarifications on the subject. Jean-Luc Chaumeil, in *Le Trésor du Triangle d'Or* (A. Lefeuvre, Nice, 1979, p. 80), included de Chérisey's confession that his parchment forgeries were copied from an ancient text found in the *Dictionnaire d'archéologie chrétienne et de liturgie* (15 vols., ed. Fernand Cabrol, Paris, Letouzey et Ane, 1907–53). Similarly, Pierre Jarnac in his *Histoire du Trésor de Rennes-le Château* (Cabestany, 1985, pp. 268–69) includes a copy of a letter from de Chérisey from Liège, Belgium, dated 29 January 1974, confessing that he had indeed forged the parchments.

Long after the unmasking of the hoax, Gérard de Sède finally came out with his book, *Rennes-le-Château: Le dossier, les impostures, les phantasmes, les hypothèses* (Les Enigmes de l'univers, Robert Laffont, 1988), in which he essentially admitted that the dossiers were forged and that the Merovingian line does not exist today. In 1997, BBC-TV also produced another program admitting that the story was not true. But the myth lives on, mostly because people want it to; and the list of French books on Rennes-le-Château and related subjects—not to mention the burgeoning bookshelf and Internet world of English-language commentaries—continues to grow. Back in 1974, René Descadeillas summed it up well, when he commented in his above-mentioned book as follows:

> The legend of the treasure of Rennes derives—no more and no less—from something that happened one day, in this poor, half-ruined village, to a priest whose calling was not very much in line with his natural inclinations.
>
> And so, because of all this, we've been regaled in turn with the treasure of Queen Blanche of Spain, of the Cathars, of the Temple and of Dagobert, all jumbled up with the secret archives of goodness knows how many different sects. After assembling and confusing all these different treasures, people then ask us to believe that the soil of Rennes hides the evidence of a conspiracy aimed at regenerating the government and the political life of France! Countless men and women have visited Rennes. Some have even brought expensive equipment with them. . . . They've torn tiles off walls, sounded out rocks with electronic probes, dug holes in the streets and squares, and excavated tunnels.
>
> The church has been turned inside out no fewer than four times and the cemetery has been desecrated. Graves have been opened, corpses have been exhumed. Reams and reams of paper have been covered in scribbles. Newspapers and magazines have been inundated, tracts and leaflets printed, two films made and three books written . . . Hordes of journalists have gathered—from France, England, Germany, Belgium, Switzerland and elsewhere . . . People have gone all the way back to Benjamin, the Jews and the Scriptures, passing by Titus

and Dagobert, the sack of Rome, the Visigoths and Blanche of Castile on the way to Peter the Cruel, Nicolas Poussin and Surintendant Fouquet. They've tried to drag in emperors, kings, archdukes, princes, archbishops, the Grandmasters of every conceivable Order, magi and alchemists, philosophers, historians, magistrates, and humble monks and priests . . . They've brought into existence people whose existence is far from certain and have given birth to others who never existed in the first place. They've touted magicians, paraded mediums in front of us, conjured up spirits and interrogated clairvoyants. They've fabricated books of magic spells, family trees and wills, and have uncovered illegitimacies, murders and assassinations. They've lied to the point of absurdity and have even—surely the ultimate in ridiculousness— invoked the name of the Devil!

And what for may we ask? For absolutely and precisely nothing!*

What the French Are Saying about *the Da Vinci Code*

By DAVID DOWNIE

David Downie is an American journalist based in Paris. Copyright © 2004 by David Downie.

It looks like French readers may soon join American *Da Vinci Code* devotees who genuflect by the Louvre museum's inverted pyramid. Within a week of the thriller's March 2004 release, it

*Translation from Paul Smith's Priory of Sion Archives, priory-of-sion.com/psp/id129.html.

was the country's number-three bestseller, and the prestigious Left Bank publisher, JC Lattès, had shipped some 70,000 copies. The alluring French cover shows the Mona Lisa peering from behind a torn scarlet background.

Frenchmen and women expecting critics to dismiss the book outright or lambaste its fanciful interpretation of Parisian topography, French culture and linguistics, must have been surprised by the generally positive reviews and skyrocketing sales.

The highbrow *Lire*, while scolding Brown for sounding like a high school lecturer on pre-Christian symbols, called him a "virtuoso at staging" who has produced an "intelligent entertainment and not a pure marketing ploy."

The leading weekly magazine, *Le Point*, declared that France would be able to judge for itself now, having watched the book's phenomenal rise abroad. Anne Berthod of the influential weekly, *L'Express*, applauded the "Machiavellian plot and infernal pacing," calling the book an "erudite crime novel" that entices you to take another look at da Vinci's *Last Supper*.

But few French reviewers consider Dan Brown's thriller a work of literature, preferring to class it as genre fiction. Delphine Peras, writing in the daily *France Soir*, had faint praise: "I'm not saying it's a bad book, it's the perfect vacation read ... a vending-machine book." Clichés and "tricks" to keep the reader breathlessly turning pages, she noted, "risk ruining the pleasure of a well-balanced plot." Peras quotes Montpellier bookseller François Huet, saying he put down the book, finding it "heavy handed" and written "with a spatula"—meaning in a slapdash manner.

While most French readers appear to share Peras' judgment, the book's literary merits are a secondary consideration.

Public interest in Opus Dei, the Knights Templar, Priory of Sion and the marital status of Jesus and Mary Magdalene has proved remarkably widespread, giving rise to earnest discussions on street corners and in so-called "philosophy cafés." What appears to fascinate French readers most is the tantalizing prospect put forward in the book that former president François Mitterrand and surrealist poet-playwright Jean Cocteau might have been entwined with secret societies.

The importance to the French of the Louvre as a historic royal residence and the country's first and foremost museum of fine art can't be exaggerated. Mitterrand's glass pyramid remains controversial. Questions regarding the political influence of the Vatican and Opus Dei and the power of religious symbols are highly topical.

A secular Republic of about sixty million inhabitants, France is home, nonetheless, to large numbers of Catholics and Protestants and some five million Moslems, and is struggling with church-versus-state issues, particularly those involving the freedom to display religious symbols in public schools and workplaces. And then along comes Robert Langdon ...

A Philosopher Looks at *The Da Vinci Code*

By GLENN W. ERICKSON

Glenn W. Erickson, Ph.D., is the author of a dozen works in the areas of philosophy, literary criticism, art history, and the history of mathematics.

I must admit to having finished Dan Brown's novel, like some quick-sketch artist, in a single sitting, and, not presuming to have lost the common touch, feel obliged to portray *The Da Vinci Code* in a favorable light. Not having been able to put it down while dandling it on my knee, I would not the cad be who puts it down now in public.

The novel is, in the first place, politically correct insofar as its moral is that world religions, especially the Western religions of the world, have tended and intended to suppress the Woman-God or women-gods, and hence the life values that such divinities might be supposed to manifest or embody. At first, a kind of ideological battle cry for the feminist movement, such a view is now conventional in occidental intellectual circles. It has even been perhaps the majoritarian opinion among scholars of comparative religion for upward to half a century that observation of the relative oblivion of autonomous female deities in at least the last two millennia, of deities who seem to have been prominent in Paleo- and Neolithic contexts, proves valuable in reconstruction of the emergence of our institutionalized world visions. The spin on this story adopted in the novel is that, in the formation of the cannon of the New Testament during the reign of Constantine the Great, edited out was the marriage of Jesus to Mary Magdalene, who is rightfully his divine consort, the luminous bearer of the eternal feminine. And the MM girl was no whore either, as spiteful patriarchal gossips would have it, but the scion of a royal line, an important and powerful person in her own right. The ratio runs: Mary Magdalene : Jesus :: Bathsheba : David.

The premise of the novel is that a supersecretive society, the Priory of Sion, originally the antiquary arm of the Knights Templar, has been closely guarding three items for nearly a thousand years, things which comprise the legendary Holy Grail: first, a plethora of scrolls, including a treasure trove of apocryphal Gospels, which document the role of Mary Magdalene; second, her relics; and finally, her contemporary bloodline, whose most prominent members include the Grand Master of the Priory of Sion and curator of the

Louvre, murdered at the onset of the novel; his wife and his grandson, who have spent ten years hiding in rural Scotland; and his granddaughter Sophie Neveu, the female protagonist of the novel, employed as a code breaker for the French clone of the FBI.

The mechanism of the novel is a series of ciphers that must be decoded in order to preserve the secret of the Holy Grail. Since his three chief subordinates, who together with him alone knew the secret of the Holy Grail, have been slain by a fanatical albino monk of the Opus Dei (an organization which, somehow and somewhat notoriously, really exists within the Roman Catholic Church), the Grand Master is obliged, in his dying hour, to pass on the secret of the Holy Grail. He leaves this secret to his heir and ward, Sophie, in such a manner that she becomes introduced to the male protagonist of the story, a Harvard professor of Religious Symbology [sic], Robert Langdon. Together they decipher an initial riddle, which discovers a painting (*La Giaconda*), which indicates a key and the location of a safe-deposit box, where lies a wooden box containing a marble vessel, with a further marble vessel inside, which contains a conundrum that discovers a tomb which contains a puzzle that points to a temple, where they encounter a third of the Holy Grail (Sophie's brother and grandmother, whom she thought dead), and a further riddle that gives away the whereabouts of the rest of the Grail (back where the whole thing started).

The Da Vinci Code is evidently a detective story, which is to keep the best sort of company, *The Brothers Karamazov*, say, or, *Oedipus the Tyrant*, even *Hamlet, Prince of Denmark*. The reader gets his (or hers, to be sure) chance to break each of the ciphers in turn: the Louvre crime scene, the *Mona Lisa* and environs, the bank vault, the wooden box, the first and second marble containers, Isaac Newton's tomb in Westminster Abbey, Rosslyn Chapel in Scotland, and back to the Louvre. Apart from the hell-for-high-leather manner of telling the tale, which is to say, the technique of cutting back and forth to simultaneous scenes of action and hence following the courses of several characters at once (as familiar today from stage, screen, and tube, as from prose fiction), the fascination of the work lies in the wit of the ciphers and the wisdom of their deciphering. We get an especially enjoyable lesson in the occult symbolism of Leonardo da Vinci's painting and graphics: I think I can see Mary Magdalene close by Christ at the *Last Supper*.

At a deeper level, Brown is casting Mary Magdalene in the role which Nietzsche, in his last spirochetal wits, assigned to Ariadne: the gynogoddess also necessary to deny our nothingness and negate the nattering nabobs of nihilism. Runs the ratio: Ariadne : Dionysus :: Magdalene : Jesus. And in the skein of ciphers, Ariadne is the antitype of Sophia, whose thread leads Bob "Theseus" Langdon out of the Labyrinth.

The Aristotelian unities can be observed in the novel. Except for the recognition scene in Scotland, the action transpires chiefly as a Tale of Two Cities, the Megapolis stretching from Paris to London, and in the course of the twenty-four hours, from the murder of the grand master to the arrest of the murder's intellectual author, Sir Leigh Teabing.

Nevertheless, the occult aspect of the novel comes a cropper. Its pastiche of New Age lore is (I dare not say "lite," for New Age brand is *always* sold in the health foods section of your local supermarket) but silly-all-too-supercilious. There are several, sometimes alternative, explanations for this circumstance.

First is the Platonic: the artist makes copies of things which are in turn copies of the forms, and whether these copies are wrought well or badly, they are yet only copies of copies. And D. Brown gives us bad copy on occult science. It is nearly enough to make us homesick for, say, *Foucault's Pendulum*, when we remember that U. Eco made his occultist plot up out of whole cloth, trying not for historical relevance, but rather for a sublimely paranoiac fugue à la *Pale Fire*. We say "nearly enough" because *Foucault's Pendulum* woefully lacks *The Da Vinci Code*'s narrative flair.

Second is the Sam Waltonesque: Mr. Brown may know his stuff, after all, but he knows his target market better still. In order not to throw the rider in the first gallop of learning, as Harold Bloom did in his novel of the occult (and his only novel not occulted), Dan Brown feels, for example, compelled to reduce what is commonly regarded as one of the two greatest discoveries of ancient mathematics to a *decimal approximation*, 1.618, which, for its part, is observed in the *average proportions* of myriad organic and aesthetic forms. Phi on such treatment of the Golden Mean!

A third is Horatian: Here Brown gives his projected reader more than enough credit to deprecate or despise neopaganism, and never seeks to produce the bona fides of fictive verisimilitude in his intermittent glosses on the occult sciences. He's sending up astrologers, heckling hierophants, prodding I Ching casters, discarding cartomancers knocking numerologists, and, in brief, funning all charlatans and night-crawlers. 'Tis all tongue in cheek, that's to say, the Roman genre, namely, satire ("the reason we are underlings, Horatio, is not in our stars . . ."). Thus, since Walt Disney paid dues at the local Masonic lodge (like any other fellow who expected to get favorable hearing at the Anaheim Savings and Loan (if not in the Appellate Court), Bambi's mother's really Astarte on the high hoof, Snow White's Isis in Lilliput, and Cinderella's Ashtoreth at her Sweet Sixteen. If they do this in the dry wood, what will they do in the holly? It is enough to make the White Goddess grave in her turn.

To be sure, the novel plays the up paranoia angle inherent in the conspiracy theories of the occult tradition—for somebody has been hiding this stuff and probably for no good reason—in a good-natured, mock dramatic, even comic spirit. Here the point of the Priory of Sion is never to reveal it, yet to struggle through the ages to preserve it.

Finally there's the Heideggerian: although both the premise of the novel concerning the rivalry of Priory of Sion and the Opus Dei, and the mechanism of ciphers to be solved, require a grab bag of occultist speculation, neither pagan magic nor pious miracle portends. The point of view of the novel is consistently realistic, doctrinal questions being of mere psychological import, even when a mass disillusionment consequent on an anticipated revelation of the Holy Grail might well spell institutional trouble. In such wise, what turns on the issue is the Gift of Being to Man. As the wise old grandame explains in the unraveling of the novel, our New Dawn of comprehension brings the Mother Goddess to light again in the Work of Art and hence of Culture. And so the cogency of occult explanation is not important in the end, but rather only what works for you, what works for me. Even dumb answers work for lots of folk, or indeed most of them, and a tip of the Duns cap to you, everyone.

Begin the Beguine of forlorn hope and unaddressed question. The Harvard don, Doc Langdon, in his solidarity with the Templar cause, seems more *langue d'oc* than *langue d'oil*, more Cathar yes than Catholic aye. Given their female goddess and the possibility that Sir Steven Runciman might have been an inspiration for Sir Leigh Teabing, why does Brown never push the Grail legend in the traditional direction of the Beghards and the Bogomils?

Insofar as there is some small effort on the part of the author to suggest parallels between his work and John's, the occult text of the novel is surely Revelation; and one leaves it to the reader to identify Saint Michael, the Woman clothed by the Sun, the False Prophet, the Antichrist, and several main personages of the Apocalypse in *The Da Vinci Code*. Perhaps some such program is obligatory given the theme of the novel; you can't tell the players without a program.

What is more, once they are ultimately the flashcard version of Revelation, Brown seems to give short shrift to the Tarot cards. The Tarot is, as I have maintained in a number of books and articles, a series of miniature paintings, secreting a series of graphic images, each composed of a pair of regular polygons, which polygons are determined by the proportions of a series of Pythagorean triangles. These graphic images, which constitute the Angelic Language, are the centerpiece of the Christian cabala, grown out of its Neoplatonic counterpart. Although Joachim de Fiore, Giotto, the original Tarot artists, Fernando de Rojas, and Shakespeare understood the gist of this language, and its place in John's Logos theology; Brown does not. At least the comment in the novel that the Tarot serves as a means for perpetrating pagan symbolism strikes one as especially wrong-headed.

Finally, there is a reasonable possibility that, like numerous contemporary novelists and poets, such as T. S. Eliot, Sylvia Plath, Mario Vargas Llosa, and innumerable lesser lights, Dan Brown has secreted the Major Arcana successively in his work. In the scope of this commentary, these identifications cannot be developed. Yet in any case, were Mr. Brown to have mined this robust central vein of occult tradition, and not hacked gingerly about the edges, he might have produced not only a preeminently readable, but also a more significant, novel.

A Collision of Indiana Jones and Joseph Campbell

WEB INTERVIEWER CRAIG McDONALD INTERVIEWS DAN BROWN

Craig McDonald hosts a website devoted to interviews with interesting authors. As *Secrets of the Code* was researched, we found this to be one of the most interesting interviews with Dan Brown, author of *The Da Vinci Code*, that we came across. Excerpts from it are reprinted here by permission of Craig M. McDonald. Copyright © 2003 by Craig M. McDonald.

You taught English at Exeter. What were some of the books you used in your teaching?

I taught both [literature and writing]. We'd teach books like *The Iliad* and *The Odyssey*, *Of Mice and Men*. You know, anything by Shakespeare. Anything by Dostoyevsky. The classics.

How long did it take you to sell your first novel?

You know, I got exceptionally lucky. My book sold in twenty days. The first editor who saw it bought it. Part of it had to do with the fact that it was an exceptionally commercial topic at that time. That being national security and civilian privacy. Electronic code-breaking. E-mail . . . National Security Agency [NSA]. It was a piece of fiction that had actual ties to the real world.

Would you write Digital Fortress *differently if you were doing it in a post-9/11 world and with some of the controversies stemming from Homeland Security?*

I don't think so. You know what's funny is when I first started writing that book and I learned about NSA, I thought, "Oh my God, this is a *huge* invasion of privacy." I contacted a former NSA cryptographer and said, "You know what you guys are doing? This scanning e-mail and cell phones—this is an invasion of privacy." This guy responded in a brilliant way. He faxed me the transcript of a Senate Judiciary hearing where the then-director of the FBI, Louis Freeh, testified that in one year alone—I believe the year was 1994—the NSA's ability to infiltrate civilian communication had thwarted the downing of two US commercial airliners and a chemical weapons attack on US soil. What was funny, was, I must have done 150 different radio interviews after *Digital Fortress* came out and we'd get these callers who would call in and say, "I can't believe you're supporting the National Security Agency— it's basically *Brave New World*." And then, after September 11, people would call in and say, "I don't care what NSA needs. If they want to put a streaming video camera in my bedroom, that's fine. Whatever they need to stop this, it's fine." The entire feeling about national security, as a priority, shifted. Now, the question is, "Have we gone too far?" and we'll just bounce back and forth, I'm sure.

Given the subject matter, and its potential to offend some on a religious level, how do you account for The Da Vinci Code *selling in such vast quantities?*

I did a lot of research for this novel, and I really got the sense that people were ready for this story. It was the type of thing that people were just ready to hear. As far as my surprise with the success: I'm surprised with the level of success—the fact that this book is just breaking all records and we just found out it went back to number one on every list in the country, next week. I should say that when the book came out, I was a little bit nervous about the response. The response from priests, nuns—all sorts of people in the church—for the most part, has been overwhelmingly positive. There have been a few people for whom the book was shocking and was upsetting, but less than one percent.

Robert Langdon appears in your second and fourth novels. There have been some statements issued that you intend to focus on him as a series characters. A number of crime and thriller writers launch a series, then rue the fact that they can no longer follow their muse in other directions. Why are you moving the other way?

Langdon is a character who has my own interests. I am fascinated with ancient mysteries. Art history. Codes. You spend a year, a year and a half writing a book, you better be darn sure your hero is involved in subject matter you are excited about. As excited as I was about NASA and meteors or the National Security Agency, my passions really do lie with ancient mysteries and codes and that sort of thing.

Have you always had that interest in the covert?

I have. I grew up on the East Coast, right in New England, sort of in the heart of prep schools and Ivy League colleges with all of their little fraternities and eating clubs and secret societies and all of that. I had associations early on with people from the National Security Agency. Secrets, I think, interest everybody and the concept of secret societies—especially after I visited the Vatican— just really captured my imagination.

Ah yes, your famously touted "audience with the Pope."

A lot of people have had an audience with the Pope. It basically means that you are in his presence and that's just a very sort of arcane and silly way to put it. I was in a room with a group of other people and that's about the extent of it.

You were also purportedly afforded some unusual access to the Vatican grounds. . . .

That's true. I have a very good friend who has a connection, extremely high, in the Vatican. The parts of the Vatican that we saw—such as the Necropolis . . . currently, something like eleven people a day are allowed in to see the Necropolis. That was probably the most secure area that we saw that was absolutely really really memorable and special. The Vatican archives—only three Americans in history have been allowed inside. I was not one of them. Two were cardinals and one was a professor of religious studies, I think, at the University of Florida. All of the descriptions were accurate. But I was not allowed inside the secret archives myself. I was allowed inside the Vatican library and the Vatican archives, but not the Vatican secret archives.

Think you might still be afforded that access after Angels & Demons *and* The Da Vinci Code?

Chances are slim.

There was a statement somewhere to the effect that you're in possession of something like a dozen rough outlines for future Robert Langdon novels.

I am. Chances are I won't get to write them all.

Given the plot complexity of the novels, I assume you must write to a pretty structured outline.

Oh my, yeah. The outline to *The Da Vinci Code* was over one hundred pages. The stories are very intricate and plot-driven. They have a lot of twists, a lot of codes. A lot of surprises. You can't write those freehand—those come from careful planning.

You've indicated you spend about a year and a half on a book's composition. How much of that time is committed to research?

About half.

You've taken on some fairly powerful entities in your books—the Catholic Church ... the Masons ... various alleged secret societies and government agencies. Are you starting to have any fears for your own safety?

I really am not. I work very hard to portray these organizations in a fair and even light and I think I've succeeded. Certainly, with respect to Opus Dei, as I say in the book, there are those for whom Opus Dei has been a wonderful addition to their lives. And there are those for whom Opus Dei has been a nightmare, and I talk about both.

Do you think these Langdon books would have been written if you weren't married to an art historian?

My wife is an enormous influence—her knowledge and her passion for the subject matter certainly buoys the process when it bogs down. Writing a book is incredibly hard. I would not wish it on my worst enemy. There are definitely days when it helps to have somebody around—especially in the case of *The Da Vinci Code*—who understands art and da Vinci and is passionate about it and can say, "You know, let's go take a walk and talk about why we got into this in the first place—what's so exciting about da Vinci and what he believed." So I'm very fortunate on that front.

Returning a little bit to September 11, 2001, I read an interview that you gave in 1998 and it's particularly prescient, now, looking back on it. You were commenting on projects that were under way to monitor U.S. citizens for the reason specifically of preventing terrorist attacks, and you said, "The threat is very real. ... Americans hate to admit it, but we have a lot of enemies; we are a ripe target for terrorism and yet have one of the lowest rates of successful domestic terrorist attacks on earth." Such an attack was on your radar a bit before it was on most peoples' radar. Why?

I think because of my shock, well, you probably read the story about the guys who showed up at the campus of Phillips Exeter from the Secret Service.

Yes, you had a student who had written something in an e-mail and they came to investigate the student.

Right. That really was my first encounter with the National Security Agency. The more I read about them, the more upset I got. And I couldn't believe that essentially highly trained American civilians would be working on projects to snoop other civilians. It made no sense to me, until I started to dig deeper and realized why it's happening and why no matter what we say and what we want, it will continue to happen. And ending up getting lists of terrorist attacks that never happened because of NSA. I started to sense, "*Oh my God,* we are under attack, almost daily, and just never hear about it." It's important to remember about terrorists that their job is not necessarily to kill people, it's to create terror. In the event that there is a bomb under the White House, or, say, a bomb in New York City that NSA is able to stop with three seconds left, they will make that bomb disappear and hope nobody ever found out about it, because whether or not the bomb goes off, the second you know it almost went off, it's *almost just as scary.* So there is a lot of protecting our ignorance/innocence.

Looking at the dates, you were touring immediately after September 11 for Deception Point, *I take it?*

Yes.

What was that like?

It was awful. It was a tough time. I was working on *Da Vinci Code* on the morning of September 11. I have an office where I have no telephone, no e-mail, no nothing, where I go just to be totally alone. My wife walked over and just said, "Something terrible is happening" and I instantly knew that it had finally happened. For a couple of months after that, it was very hard to be motivated to write fiction. It felt totally unimportant. With so much going on in the world, how can you afford to allow yourself the luxury of moving fictional characters around in a fictional landscape—you know, how are you helping your country doing that? As it turns out, you *are*—at some point you're giving people release from the pain of reality and some recreation. It's just hard to remember that.

You have a background in music. Have you thought of using any musical themes or elements in your novels?

I have. One of my future novels focuses on a famous composer and his associations with a secret society, all factual.

There have been some mentions that your next book after Da Vinci Code *is going to be set in Washington, D.C.*

That's correct.

And, something about Freemasons . . . ?

Yep . . . Are you hoping I will say more? [laughing]

I thought I would leave some ellipses dangling there and maybe you would fill 'em in . . . but I guess not.

That's about all I'm allowed to say.

You do get a sense of readership through your readings and signings?

You know, that has been the most *gratifying* aspect of tour—to look out at these bookstores and see men, women, and *a lot* of teenagers. Kids have really reacted—especially to *Da Vinci Code* and *Angels & Demons*. It's sort of like a more mature Harry Potter, I guess, is what a lot of kids are feeling. It has some of those ancient mystery elements that people like in Harry Potter.

That comparison is made in some of the press materials from your publisher.

The first time I heard the analogy was Janet Maslin in the *New York Times*, who wrote an absolutely glowing review. People called and said, "Is Janet Maslin your mother, because she never says stuff like that." She invoked the holy name of Harry Potter and I believe she was first. I don't read fiction, except occasionally to blurb somebody's novel if I'm asked by my editor. That's the other thing—I'll get novels almost daily saying, "Wouldn't you love to read this and put a blurb on it?" I have not read Harry Potter, but in my mind, anything that gets kids that excited about reading has got to be really good. I think it's just fantastic.

Any of the books been optioned for film yet?

All kinds of interest. Because Langdon is a series character, I'm hesitant to sell the film rights. One of the beauties of the reading experience is that everybody pictures Langdon in his or her perfect way. The second you slap a character [in a script]—no matter how you describe Langdon or any other character—they picture Ben Affleck or Hugh Jackman or whoever it happens to be, you know? So, I'm hesitant. Also, Hollywood has a way of taking a story like this and turning it into a car chase through Paris with machineguns and karate chops. So, I'm very hesitant, and yet I'm talking to a few specific individuals who are the kinds of people who could make this a *smart* movie, and that's the only way I would sell, is if I had exceptional amounts of control.

The Latin Etymology of *The Da Vinci Code*

BY DAVID BURSTEIN
David Burstein is a high school Latin student and playwright.

Popular modern works of epic fiction ranging from the Harry Potter series to *The Da Vinci Code* often feature a rich use of language, including references to ancient languages and interesting word play. Dan Brown has a few special interests in using some real Latin words into the *The Da Vinci Code*. First, he obviously loves words and wordplay and he knows very well how much of our English language is based on Latin. Second, he is a former teacher at Exeter, one of the country's top private high schools. And third, since *The Da Vinci Code* itself is centered on debates within and without of the Catholic Church, Latin words and allusions are particularly relevant.

Latin is considered a dead language. But Brown makes it very much alive and present in his contemporary novel (along with bits of Greek, French, and smatterings of other languages). For some items, the reader needs only an ordinary Latin dictionary: Opus Dei ("God's Work"), or *crux gemmata* ("jeweled cross"). However, other words and phrases are more subject to interpretation.

Everyone's favorite Albino assassin-monk, Silas, is a devout Catholic and member of Opus Dei. He can be remembered by his skin color (as a character in Homer who is consistently recalled by the same epithet, Brown often refers to Silas as "the Albino monk"). But his more significant character trait is as a penitent. The word *penitent* (*paenitit* in Latin) comes from *paeān*, referring to "praise from the gods." Like the real-life members of Opus Dei, Silas believes the way to praise God is to suffer pain himself. Interestingly, the word for *cloak* in Latin, *paenula*, comes from the same root as *penitent*. This seems to suggest the characteristic cloak that a monk wears comes from this root as well. The painful self-discipline belt that Silas wears is called a cilice, which may come from the Latin word *cicātrīx* which means "scar." And of course the intention of the belt is to cause physical pain (likely leaving a scar) to repent for sins. But the more interesting connection is how close *cilice* and *chalice* are. Chalice, of course, is another word for the Holy Grail—a key concept in a book that is all about defining the Holy Grail and searching for it. Chalice ... cilice ... Silas: although the "Teacher" is the mastermind, Silas is doing all the murdering and other grunt work on this hunt for the Holy Grail.

Silas is the character in the book who invokes the most Latin in the course of the day. When he is flagellating himself he says, "*castīgo corpus meum*." In Latin, this means "castigate" (or "correct" or "punish") my body. This is a logical, ritualistic comment for a religious penitent. However, it's intriguing that *castīgo*, which means "punish" or "correct," is the root of *castitās*, which means "chastity" or "virginity." This of course ties into the purity of Jesus and the Virgin Mary. It also connects to another of the central dramas of the book: whether Jesus Christ and Mary Magdalene had a sexual relationship and, if they did, how it was viewed by their contemporaries and should be viewed in retrospect by following generations. If Brown's theory is true, Jesus was not as pure as is historically imagined and *castīgo corpus meum* could be another wink at this issue.

"O Draconian Devil! Oh Lame Saint!" is one of the clues

a dying and bleeding old man can come up with in the last fifteen minutes of his life to point Robert Langdon and Sophie Neveu on the first step of their hunt for the Holy Grail. These exclamations are an anagram for *Leonardo da Vinci! The Mona Lisa!*, where the next clue turns out to be hidden. An interesting part of this anagram is the word *draconian*, used to mean measures that are very strict or severe. Actually, Draco was no ruthless barbarian. He was, in fact, an early Athenian lawmaker. He emphasized creating laws and writing them down—along with the consequences for breaking them. But the law came first and it is Draco's real contribution to Greco-Roman civilization. Although he did enforce laws strictly, it is interesting that this word has become so associated with evil and ruthlessness. Langdon even suggests that these words are Saunière's violent attack on the church, emphasizing both *Draconian* and *devil*.

When Langdon and Sophie mull over the mysterious key they now possess and assume it is related to the Priory of Sion, Landgon is intrigued that the cross is the equal-armed square type of cross. As a symbologist, this object in his hand gives him an opportunity to discuss the history and etymology of the Christian cross. Langdon points out that *cross* and *crucifix* are derived from the Latin word *cruciāre*, which means "to torture." A word with a similar root, *cruor*, means "blood."

The Da Vinci Code is full of anagrams, several of which come to light through Saunière's last messages to Sophie Neveu and Robert Langdon. Brown, who is obviously an anagram devotee, refers to *ars magna*, which in Latin means "great art" and is considered part of the sacred symbolism of Roman culture. In fact, it is from rearranging the letters of *ars magna* that we get the English word *anagrams*.

Through the years, *heretic* has always been thought to mean something very negative. In fact, the word *heretic*, which Dan Brown relates to the Latin *haereticus*, means "choice." Those who chose not to believe in the standardized set of Gospels—the documents and principles that the Roman emperor Constantine sought to enforce at the Council of Nicea and afterward—became known as heretics, meaning they had made a "choice" to take a different road. Soon, they would be abused, attacked, and tortured for having made this choice, but at the outset, to call them heretics might have been like calling them *choosers* or *pro-choice*.

Brown also includes a meditation on the meaning of the word *pagan*. Some people today assume the word *pagan* was always a religious word, referring to a devil-worshipping deviant opposed to Christianity. Brown suggests that "Pagans were literally unindoctrinated country folk who clung to the old, rural religions of nature worship." The word comes from the Latin *pāgānus*, which means "country dwellers." The peasants of the Roman Empire's countryside would prove to be late converts to Christianity, continuing to practice their old Greco-Roman rites and worship their many gods and goddesses. Over time *pagan*, originally a benign word like *heretic*, became tinged with connotations of evil and devil worship.

The same association with the evil nature of country dwellers arises in the word *villain*, according to yet another etymological discussion in *The Da Vinci Code*. The word *villa* is Latin for "country house." These country houses were the homes of country dwellers or pagans. According to Brown, the church feared those who lived in the rural *villes*. As a result, "the word for a villager—'vilain'—came to mean a wicked soul." But Dan Brown's interpretation is questioned in a *New York Times Magazine* article by the "On Language" columnist, William Safire. He writes, "Villagers did not become villains because the church feared them; more likely, it was just that the lords of the manor looked down on the lower classes and equated their coarse manners with loose mortals." There is a definite class distinction here. The feudal lords who lived in the countryside were not known as villains. The first form of the word *vilein*, French, refers to the serfs in the medieval feudal system.

Brown also does a short riff on the linguistic history of the word *venereal*, suggesting it has something to do with the goddess of love, Venus. Sounds logical, but according to the *Oxford English Dictionary (OED)*, this heritage may be incorrect. The *OED* cites the word as coming from the Latin word *venerābilis*, meaning "honored." Although, there may be a possible connection between the worship of Venus and the Latin word for honor, the *OED* does not make the leap.

Brown makes an interesting point about the history of the English word *sinister*. In Latin, *sinistra* originally meant left-handedness. Left-handedness was often considered unlucky. As Brown states, this had much to do with the church's early decision to associate left with female. In the alleged effort by the church to cover up the role of the sacred feminine in the origins of the early church and to emerge as a more patriarchal culture, the word for *sinister* became very negatively charged. (A number of experts believe Leonardo da Vinci was left-handed. Several clues in the novel emphasize the impression that Jacques Saunière was left-handed, as well.)

The phrase *sub rosa* also figures prominently in *The Da Vinci Code*. Sophie tells Langdon about the meetings that her grandfather used to have under the sign of the rose, which Saunière (and Latin language evolution) suggested meant in secrecy. As William Safire points out, however, Dan Brown may not be correct when he tells readers that the expression *sub rosa* and the technique of using the sign of the rose to signify a confidential meeting originated in ancient times. Safire says, "The earliest citation is in Henry VIII's 1546 State Papers, which in modern English reads, 'The said questions were asked with license, and should remain under the rose ... no more to be rehearsed.'" However, in a subsequent article, Safire seemed to reverse himself, declaring that millions of Dan Brown's readers knew that *sub rosa* was an allusion to Roman secret meeting practices.

Like other aspects of *The Da Vinci Code*, the Latin derivations are not always a hundred percent correct, but the story gets people talking about ideas, philosophy, religion, history—and even Latin—in an unusually compelling way.

Part III

Underneath
the Pyramid

12 Sophie's Library

As we toy with the names of characters in *The Da Vinci Code*, we encounter a variety of interesting concealed meanings that Dan Brown has left for the reader to find.

We start with a person who doesn't appear in *The Da Vinci Code* except as a memory, and very briefly at that (page 16 of the hardcover edition). But she forms a pillar of Robert Langdon's temple: Vittoria Vetra, one of the two women in Langdon's life, and the only one we know of—at least by explicit references—who went beyond a platonic relationship. The story of Vittoria, and of Robert Langdon's adventure in *Angels & Demons*, will have so many resonances for *Da Vinci Code* readers that it is worth pausing for a minute on this character who only appears as a quickly passing memory in the new book.

A Rose by Any Other Name
A Guide to Who's Who in The Da Vinci Code

By David A. Shugarts

Vittoria Vetra

Vittoria is Italian for Victoria, the Roman goddess of victory and the equivalent of the Greek goddess Nike. *Vetra* is a public square (piazza) in Milan—the site where Maifreda, the proffered female pope of the Guglielmites, was burned by inquisitors in the year 1300. Milan is where Leonardo da Vinci's the *Last Supper* resides.

In Dan Brown's prior *Angels & Demons*, Vittoria Vetra is the adopted daughter of Leonardo Vetra, brilliant physicist at CERN (Conseil Européen pour la Recherche Nucléaire). She is also a physicist, and her father's partner in their private lab. In *Angels & Demons*, which, like *The Da Vinci Code*, takes place in April, she and Robert Langdon race around Rome chasing clues and defeating the enemies of the Vatican. In *The Da Vinci Code*, which takes place a little over a year later, Langdon still remembers her scent and kiss—before he meets Sophie Neveu.

Leonardo Vetra is a week shy of his fifty-eighth birthday when he is tortured and killed at the outset of *Angels & Demons*. He considered himself a theo-physicist. He had found a proof that all molecules are connected by a single force. He and Vittoria discovered how to make and store antimatter. Vittoria was called back from biological research in the Balearic Sea. In her own career, she disproved one of Einstein's theories by using atomically synchronized cameras to observe a school of tuna.

She is described as lithe and graceful, tall, with chestnut skin and long black hair. "Her face was unmistakably Italian—not overly beautiful, but possessing full, earthy features that even at twenty yards seemed to exude a raw sensuality." She has "deep sable eyes." Robert Langdon also takes stock of her "slender torso and small breasts." She is a strict vegetarian and CERN's resident guru of hatha-yoga.

At the age of eight she had met her adoptive father, Leonardo Vetra, then a young priest who had been an award-winning physics student at university. Vittoria was at the Organotrofio di Siena, a Catholic orphanage near Florence, "deserted by parents she never knew."

Vetra received a grant to study at the University of Geneva and adopted Vittoria just shy of her ninth birthday. She attended Geneva International School. Three years later, Vetra was hired by CERN, so she has been there since age twelve.

At the close of *Angels & Demons*, Vittoria and Robert fall into bed together—finally—with Vittoria saying, "You've never been to bed with a yoga master, have you?" In *The Da Vinci Code*, Robert Langdon recalls that he and Vittoria had promised each other to meet every six months—but it had already been a year.

The name Vetra is unique, stemming as it does from *vetraschi*, the tanners of Milan, who had their shops on the public square. In the thirteenth century, when the Gnostics and others had female clergy, a woman known as Guglielma of Bohemia came to Milan and began to preach. After her death in 1281, as was not uncommon, a cult sprang up around her relics. Fanatics among Guglielma's followers believed she was an incarnation of the Holy Spirit, and would return to depose the male pope, installing the first of a line of female popes and launching the Age of the Spirit.

The fanatics eventually picked a young Milanese woman, Maifreda di Pirovano, and set the date of Guglielma's return as the Pentecost in the year 1300. When this date arrived, the forces of Pope Boniface VIII seized Maifreda di Pirovano and others, and burned them at the stake on the Piazza Vetra.

Jacques Saunière

According to fanciful legend (or hoax), the Abbé Bérenger Saunière, a poor parish priest, was doing some repairs in 1891 in the village church at Rennes-le-Château, a southern French town. He found some parchments that he took to the abbé of the church of Saint Sulpice in Paris to be deciphered.

Abbé Saunière subsequently became wealthy, and it was supposed that the parchments had contained valuable secrets. A Frenchman, Pierre Plantard, was at the heart of what is now seen by most experts as almost certainly a hoax involving connections between documents he created and the legends surrounding Saunière, as well as the Priory of Sion. Plantard's documents were eventually a source for reporting by Henry Lincoln, who made a documentary on the story for the BBC.

In 1981, Lincoln teamed with two other authors to write *Holy Blood, Holy Grail*, in which speculations originated that the secrets protected by the Priory of Sion were the relics of Mary Magdalene, who had been the wife of Christ and the matriarch of a line of Merovingian kings of France. Dan Brown drew heavily on *Holy Blood, Holy Grail* in writing *The Da Vinci Code*.

Abbé Saunière's village, Rennes-le-Château, lies in the southeastern quadrant of France, home of the Merovingians as well as the later Cathars.

Robert Langdon

On the acknowledgments page of *Angels & Demons*, Dan Brown pays homage to John Langdon, who created the stunning ambigrams for that book. He also shows off work by John Langdon on the website for *The Da Vinci Code*.

Ambigrams are word-images that read the same upside down or right side up. While Dan Brown describes them as an "ancient" and "mythical" symbology, John Langdon apparently believes that the particular art form he is executing is one he invented or discovered. Another artist, Scott Kim, independently began drawing ambigrams at about the same time. Kim credits Langdon with the earliest use, however—and Kim says that it was Douglas Hofstadter who coined the word *ambigram*.

John Langdon has his own website, www.johnlangdon.net, where some of his outstanding works can be seen.

The Languedoc, the French region where so much of the history of Mary Magdalene and of Templars resides, is also suggested by the name Langdon. Finally, Langdon is also a don—a Harvard professor. There are a variety of other connotations to ponder as well.

Bezu Fache

Mount Bezu is a mountain very near Rennes-le-Château; it has at least two aspects of significance. One is that a Templar stronghold was rumored to have been built there. It is also one of five mountaintops said to form a perfect pentacle in the area. Grande Fache is a mountain in the Pyrenees, not far from Andorra (where Aringarosa found Silas) and not far from Rennes-le-Château, the village where the story of Abbé Saunière arises.

Fache, with the appropriate accent, also means angry in French—a characteristic that certainly defines this particular police official.

Sophie Neveu

As is explained in *The Da Vinci Code, sofia* means wisdom in Greek, and has a female avatar in Greek and other mythologies. Various reporters have suggested that "Neveu," in addition to approaching the word for "new" in French, may also suggest "new eve"—with all the resonances to the Eve character in the Bible and in myth. A second coming of Eve, the rebirth of the sacred feminine, the female goddess of wisdom—all fitting distinctions for Sophie Neveu. Indeed, she anagrams as, "Oh! Supine Eve."

Sophia, portrayed as a mystical consort of Christ, is found

in a Nag Hammadi book considered as scripture by the Gnostics. It is called the *Sophia (Wisdom) of Jesus Christ*. In this document, Sophia is the female half of an androgynous Christ, and known as "First Begettress Sophia, Mother of the Universe. Some call her 'Love.'"

Sophie Neveu could herself be considered a Holy Grail under the definitions of *The Da Vinci Code*, as the vessel carrying the bloodline of Christ. At different times the book seems to lean strongly in the direction of suggesting that Sophie, as well as her brother in Scotland, are actually descended from the union of Jesus and Mary Magdalene. But then there is some fairly explicit prose suggesting that is not the case, just for balance. Like many other things, it's a mystery.

Bishop Manuel Aringarosa

Aringa rosa is Italian for "red herring." If the ultimate mastermind of the conspiracy is Teabing, then the work of Aringarosa and his minion, Silas, is the red herring of the plot. The name contains the "rose" phoneme in it as well. The bishop anagrams into "nausea" or "alarming"—two likely reactions one could have to his plot.

Sir Leigh Teabing

Dan Brown owes a lot of *The Da Vinci Code* to a book he cites, *Holy Blood, Holy Grail*, by Michael Baigent, Richard Leigh, and Henry Lincoln. *Leigh* comes from Richard Leigh and *Teabing* is an anagram of Baigent. Teabing has made documentaries for the BBC like the third author of *Holy Blood, Holy Grail*. There are numerous other similarities.

André Vernet

André Vernet, the name of the Swiss bank manager, is apparently a real person, listed amid a long string of names in the acknowledgments page of *The Da Vinci Code*. According to one report, Vernet is a former faculty member at Phillips-Exeter Academy, from which Dan Brown was graduated in 1982 and where he later taught English.

Rémy Legaludec

Rémy is a common French name. Legaludec is likely a kind of wordplay on Languedoc, a region in southern France where many names of significance in *The Da Vinci Code* can be found. We also find the words *legal* and *duce* within his name, which can also be anagrammed into "a glad clue."

Jonas Faukman

Jonas Faukman is Robert Langdon's editor in *The Da Vinci Code*. Jason Kaufman is Dan Brown's real-life editor. Kaufman was with Pocket Books until 2001—the publisher of two of Dan Brown's earlier books, *Digital Fortress* and *Angels & Demons*. Kaufman moved to Doubleday (a division of Random House), and his first acquisition was *The Da Vinci Code*, reportedly the first of a two-book deal for $500,000.

The fictional Faukman gets one of the great lines of *The Da Vinci Code* when he says to Robert Langdon about his desire to write a book on the subject of the sacred feminine, "You're a Harvard historian, for God's sake, not a pop schlockmeister looking for a quick buck." Faukman's words may be the voice of the real-life Dan Brown's conscience, knowing the extent to which he is taking the serious ideas that underlie *The Da Vinci Code* down the primrose path of New Age, occult pop culture.

Random notes:

- Pamela Gettum, a librarian. In addition to the can-do attitude suggested by her name, Pamela Gettum may be to Robert Langdon what Pussy Galore is to James Bond.

- Edouard Desrochers is a name in passing on a list of people whose conversations were regarded by Teabing; there is also a former faculty member from Phillips-Exeter Academy named Edouard Desrochers.

- Colbert Sostaque, another name on that list, yields the anagram "cobalt rose quest." The mysterious parchments discovered by Bérenger Saunière at Rennes-le-Château included a line that refers to "blue apples at noon." Deciphering this nonsensical phrase has become one of the great quests of the Priory-Grail legend. We think Dan Brown may be playing with this a bit. Notably, one of the greatest quests of all time for plant breeders is the development of a blue rose. This has been likened to the "quest for the Holy Grail" among horticulturalists. A team in Australia has been working on it for more than seventeen years.

- Silas, in addition to being a near homonym for the cilice discipline belt he wears, kills silently and is named for the biblical character who also escaped from prison during an earthquake.

Glossary

Adonai One of the names for God in Hebrew. The original name of God—formed by the Hebrew letters *YHWH*—was so sacred that it was believed it should never be pronounced out loud. Over time, *Adonai* became one of the replacements, and the vowel notations for Adonai were added to *YHWH* to remind people to say Adonai instead. This combination of consonants and vowels created the English transliteration, Jehovah. The book of Genesis begins calling God by the name Elohim (interesting itself, because it is a Hebrew word with an ending that implies it is a plural). Later in Genesis, and then in other books of the Torah, Adonai is introduced. There is some argument that Elohim represents the concept of God before man arises and that Adonai is the right name for the God of the postcreation world. Some scholars who have made their life's work the forensic effort to analyze how the Bible was written, believe that Elohim is an older word for God than Adonai, and identify certain documents from the scriptures as belonging to the *E* (for Elohim) editor, others as being the work of the *J* (Jehovah) editor.

Adoration of the Magi Leonardo da Vinci's masterpiece *The Adoration of the Magi* was commissioned during his early career, while he was working in Florence. Dated 1481, the *Adoration* is a work in progress. Portions of the panel are still an "underdrawing"—the sketch over which the artist applies the paint. This seems to indicate that Leonardo abandoned the work before having a chance to finish it. However, in 2001 the "art diagnostician" Maurizio Seracini used ultrasound scans which revealed that "none of the paint we see on the *Adoration* was put there by Leonardo." It was put there, Seracini speculates, by a far inferior artist who deliberately effaced certain compositional elements and added others.

Dan Brown hints darkly in *The Da Vinci Code* that the anonymous painter who added the brushwork to Leonardo's underdrawing was deliberately trying to hide some sort of message in the original. Seracini's *New York Times Magazine* article of April 21, 2002, is mentioned by Robert Langdon in *The Da Vinci Code*.

Albino Silas, the dutiful Opus Dei supernumerary in *The Da Vinci Code*, is an albino. Albinos are either deficient or entirely lacking in pigment in their hair, eyes, and skin. People with albinism generally suffer from severe vision deficits; many are legally blind. Silas seems to have no such impairment; indeed, Bishop Aringarosa insists that albinism makes Silas unique, even holy: "Do you not understand how special this makes you? Were you not aware that Noah himself was an Albino?" The national organization that defends the rights of albinos in the United States goes by the acronym NOAH.

Altar *Altar* means "high" in Latin. The altar originated in pre-Christian religious practices as a platform for sacrificial offerings. In early Christianity it was used to embody the Last Supper.

Amon While Amon is seen in *The Da Vinci Code* as "the Egyptian god of fertility," he has a far bigger portfolio, including a period as the supreme deity. Since Egypt in its early history was far from united politically, there were actually many ruling houses that would later lay claim to the throne. When they did, they brought in their own sets of gods. In later centuries, the stories of these gods were modified and interwoven. Amon (or Amen or Amun) was mentioned in early texts immediately after the pair of gods Nau and Nen, equivalents of the watery abyss from which all things sprang. This association puts Amon and his consort Amaunet among the handful of gods that self-created or, alternatively, was made by Thoth as one of the eight original gods of creation. Until around the Twelfth Dynasty, Amon was a local Theban god, but then the princes of Thebes conquered their rivals and made their city a new capital of Upper Egypt. It was probably then that he began to be called "King of the Gods."

The word *amon* means "what is hidden." This alludes to the unseen spirit. Amon was also known as a keeper of justice, a protector of the poor, and was known as the god of the wind and fertility. He was portrayed as a human, typically with two tall feathers in a red headdress. He also might be found as a man with the head of a frog, as a man with the head of a uraeus (cobra), as an ape, and as a lion crouching upon a pedestal.

Anagrams, which are words or phrases created by transposing the letters of another word or phrase, are important to *The Da Vinci Code*. For example, what Saunière scrawls on the Plexiglas protecting the *Mona Lisa*—"So Dark the Con of Man"—are an anagram for Leonardo's painting, the *Madonna of the Rocks*. Saunière uses several anagrams to lead Sophie's search, including an anagram made up of numbers—the jumbled **Fibonacci sequence.**

Androgyny A combination of the Greek root words *andr* (male) and *gyn* (female), the word signifies indeterminate gender. Toward the end of *The Da Vinci Code*, while flying across the English Channel, Langdon engages Sophie in a conversation about the ritual she viewed decades before that traumatized her and drove her apart from her grandfather. " 'Masks?' he asked, keeping his voice calm. 'Androgynous masks?' 'Yes. Everyone. [...] the women. Black on the men.'" Androgyny is conside[...] on archetypes and myths to be a concept suggesting [...] nature of the human species and psyche, gods and goddes[...]

Apostles The roots of the word *apostle* go back to the Greek [...] sent out." They were to spread the news of the Christian mes[...] [...]e fact that Jesus encountered **Mary Magdalene** first upon his resurrec[...] (according to several Gospel accounts) and specifically asked her to go tell the others the Good News, confirms her role as the "Apostle to the Apostles," a title she has been known by in history. Some scholars theorize that the twelve apostles correspond to the twelve tribes of Israel.

Apple Cut open an apple horizontally and it generally reveals five carpels, forming the richly symbolic **pentagram**. In *The Da Vinci Code*, a line from the poem that leads Sophie and Robert to **Newton**'s tomb reads: "In London lies a knight a Pope interred/ His labor's fruit a Holy wrath incurred." It was a falling apple that reputedly taught Newton about gravity.

The apple is a richly symbolic fruit, from a tree in the same genus as the **rose**, another plant with extensive symbological importance in the Christian tradition. The apple is, of course, a symbol of temptation and evil. In the Garden of Eden, Adam and Eve eat the forbidden fruit of the tree of knowledge of good and evil; legend identifies this fruit as an apple (although the scriptures do not). The apple turns up in many other religious paradises, including the Greek gardens of the Hesperides and the sacred groves of the Celts. Hera, the wife of the Greek god Zeus, received an apple as an engagement gift.

Pommes bleues (blue apples) play an interesting role in a controversial bit of Catholic Church history which is a source for much of *The Da Vinci Code*: one of the encoded parchments claimed to have been found in **Rennes-le-Château** ends with a reference to *pommes bleues*.

Near the end of *The Da Vinci Code*, Teabing finally understands the solution to Jacques Saunière's last puzzle, the poem that provides the word that opens the second cryptex. The orb that "ought be" on the tomb of the famous physicist isn't a star or a planet, but an apple. "Bewildered, Teabing looked back at the keystone and saw it. The dials were no longer at random. They spelled a five-letter word: *APPLE*." Dumbstruck, the defeated Teabing recalls the final line of Saunière's poem, and understands why he has been led to Newton's tomb: "His labor's fruit! The Rosy flesh with a seeded womb!"

Arius Arius is the most familiar figure associated with a powerfully contested heresy, Arianism. At the center of Arianism was a debate about the nature of Christ: was he of the same substance as the Father, or was he inferior to Him, a created being that came into existence at His behest, and therefore unable to his divinity? Arius argued that Christ was not of the same substance of the Father. After years of theological dispute, he presented a creed of his belief at the **Council of Nicea**. His heresy was rejected, and opposition to Arianism was enshrined in the **Nicene Creed**. Arianism however, continued to flare up; in fact, thirty years into **Constantine**'s reign, two new church councils were held to decide the same issue. Both failed to put an end to it. In *The Da Vinci Code* the Visigoths, a medieval Arian tribe, are mentioned as the progenitors of the **Merovingian** dynasty. The village of **Rennes-le-Château** was historically a stronghold of the Visigoths.

Atbash cipher The Atbash cipher is used by Robert Langdon, Sophie Neveu, and Leigh Teabing to open Saunière's first cryptex in Chapter 72 of *The Da Vinci Code*, revealing a further mystery—the second cryptex containing the "map" to the Holy Grail.

Atbash is an early and extremely simple cipher that originated with Hebrew scribes who were transcribing the books of the Old Testament. In the cipher, the alphabet's sequence is reversed, so that the last letter of the alphabet stands in for the first, the second letter replaces the second to last, and so on. In English, the cipher would make *a* equivalent to *z* (and vice versa), *b* equivalent to *y*, *c* to *x*, and so on. Thus, wz ermxr xlwv is an Atbash-ciphered rendering of "da Vinci code." The name Atbash is derived from the first two letters of the Hebrew alphabet (aleph, beth, or *a* and *b* in English) and their equivalents in the cipher (tav, shin, or *t* and *s* in English). Atbash, and other ciphers that use similar methods, are known as substitutions.

בפומת

[tav] [mem] [vav] [pei] [beit]

שופיא

[alef] [yud] [pei] [vav] [shin]

Langdon daydreams about the most famous example of the Atbash cipher while waiting for the cryptex code to be deciphered by Sophie: the reference to "sheshach" in Jeremiah 25:26 and 51:41. The word *sheshach* caused considerable difficulty for biblical scholars, but application of the Atbash cipher revealed the hidden meaning: Babel, equated by many scholars with Babylon, the capital city of the Babylonian empire, and home to many captive Jews after that empire sacked Jerusalem in 600 B.C.

Baphomet An idol said to have the head of a goat; in some descriptions the **pentagram** symbol is said to appear on its head. Although often said to be the idol of the **Knights Templar**, this attribution is a result of confessions obtained under torture by the Inquisition, and thus somewhat suspect. Many Knights Templar members, when tortured by the Inquisition, confessed (truly or otherwise) to worshipping this idol, most frequently described as having "the head of a goat and the body of an ass." Some contemporary followers of paganism retain a belief in Baphomet, feeling it was the god of the witches and came from Pan, the god of nature.

Boaz and Jachin Boaz and Jachin are the names of two pillars supporting the ancient Temple of Solomon. In *The Da Vinci Code*, Langdon and Sophie notice copies of these pillars in the Rosslyn Chapel. Sophie feels that she has seen the pillars before. Langdon notes that the pillars are the "most dupli-cated architectural structures in history," and are twins of the two pillars set inside every Masonic temple on earth. The names are derived from biblical accounts of Solomon's construction of his Temple. Solomon wrote to Hiram of Tyre, asking him to send someone "with skill in engraving, in working gold, silver, bronze, and iron, and in making blue, purple and red cloth." Among this artisan's contributions are two elaborately decorated pil-lars. The pillar on the right side was named Jachin ("to establish"; "stabil-ity"), and the pillar on the left, Boaz ("strength" or "in him there is strength"). Legend has it Boaz was the name of one of Solomon's ancestors; the origin of Jachin is not as clear. Boaz and Jachin became important sym-bols in the practice of Masonry. Masons trace their ancient origins to a sym-bolical representation of the might of the divine and frequently adapt the symbol of the **fleur-de-lis** in their buildings—in this case as bronze capitals at the top of both columns. Others identify the pillars with the great pillars that were thought to hold up the ancient world—one at Gibraltar, one at Cueta. Some see them as representative of many ancient dualities, light and dark, feminine and masculine, active and negative, and elementally, fire and water.

Bois de Boulogne Langdon and Sophie speed through the Bois de Boulogne on their way to 24 rue Haxo, the address left by Sophie's grandfather on a mysterious laser-cut key. Langdon tries to gather his thoughts to tell Sophie about the **Priory of Sion**, but is distracted by bizarre nocturnal inhabitants of the park—sex workers and prostitutes of every stripe.

The Bois de Boulogne is a large (more than two thousand acres), lushly forested park in Paris, containing many recreational areas including horse courses, bike and walking trails, and charming gardens. At night the forest becomes a notorious red-light district. Bois de Boulogne is just a small rem-nant of a considerably larger forest, the Forêt de Rouvray, woods that extended miles to the north of the current park at the time of the invasion of Gaul in the first century B.C. King Childeric II (a seventh-century **Merovin-gian** monarch) bequeathed the land to the Abbey of Saint-Denis, which planned to build monasteries and abbeys in the forest. During the Hundred Years War, the forest—already quite unsafe—became the haunt of robbers before being pillaged by the Parisians. Under Louis XI, the estate was refor-ested and two roads were opened.

Brown mentions that certain Parisians referred to this area as "the

Garden of Earthly Delights," an allusion to a triptych by Hieronymus Bosch known for its bawdy content and mysterious symbolism. The triptych itself depicts Eden before the fall on the left panel, the Garden of Earthly Delights on the larger, central panel, and a portrait of hell on the right panel. Even though each of the panels represents a theologically different place, there is a common element running through the triptych. All three realms, from the inviolate to the damned, are scenes of disquieting surrealism.

Hell is depicted as a realm of bizarre creatures and flamboyantly unusual punishments, where human bodies with animal heads devour sinners. A huge body serves as a cave for the punishment of the damned, and strange symbols (a pair of ears mounted by a knife) abound. However, the surrealism extends into both the Garden of Earthly Delights in the central panel, and the Garden of Eden in the left panel. These mythical places seem free of the bizarre, tortuous imagery of hell, but the surrealism is still there: naked men and women cavort inside fantastic, living structures in the garden, and even the inviolate Eden is infested with strange chimerical animals.

Bosch (1450–1516), a Flemish master painter, is nearly an exact contemporary of **Leonardo da Vinci**. He's also known for having a deep interest in alchemy and secret societies. Most of his paintings were loaded with symbols and coded messages of all types, as well as far more exotic references to sexuality and the **sacred feminine** than anything in the work of Leonardo. Like Leonardo, it is hard to discern if Bosch was a devout believer, a radical freethinker, or a heretical cultist. Some art historians and biographers believe Bosch was involved with the Adamites, a secret society that may have incorporated *hieros gamos*-type activities into their practices.

While argument rages over the meaning of Bosch's symbols, one thing is clear. For Bosch, there is a deep ambiguity and a lurking danger in the places we consider paradise; and this makes the Bois de Boulogne an apt namesake for the painting and a place worthy of mention in *The Da Vinci Code*.

Botticelli In Dan Brown's book, the Italian painter is mentioned as a **Priory of Sion** member according to the *Dossiers Secrets*. Botticelli is perhaps most noted for his *Birth of Venus*, with its obvious connection to the **sacred feminine**. The painter was persecuted by Florentine inquisitors and fundamentalists led by Savanarola, and eventually gave in to them. This, plus his artistic rivalry with Leonardo, makes it hard to see him as a member of the same ultrasecret society, even though it is true his works, including *The Birth of Venus*, introduce a strong element of eros into Renaissance painting.

Caesar cipher A substitution cipher (similar to the Atbash cipher) developed by Julius Caesar to communicate with his generals in wartime. Using the English alphabet the Caesar cipher substitutes the third letter following in the alphabet for the first, thus *d* replaces *a*, *e* replaces *b*, *f* replaces *c*, and so on. Dan Brown would be written as "Gdq Eurzq."

Caravaggio In a desperate ploy to seal himself off from his attacker, Jacques Saunière pulls a painting by Caravaggio off the wall of the **Louvre**. This desperate act sets off the museum's alarms and drops a security gate between Saunière and his attacker. The plan works, but not in the way that Saunière had hoped.

Caravaggio was one of the foremost Italian painters of the Baroque period. Born Michelangelo Marisi in 1573 in a town in Lombardy called Caravaggio (from which he assumed his professional name), he led a hardscrabble life. When he finally achieved success and notoriety, he was unable to fully suppress the anger and violent temper he had honed during his poverty; a series of brawls and fights culminated in his murdering a partner in a tennis match. Thereafter, he fled from city to city, often narrowly escaping imprisonment. During one of his sojourns as a fugitive, he stopped in Malta, where he became a **Knight of Malta**. He died in 1610, awaiting a papal pardon that arrived three days after his death.

Caravaggio used intense lighting to create dramatic scenes, scenes that conveyed a sense of an arrested moment in time—in particular, an amazing flash of light into a dark space, especially good for communicating moments of conversion, epiphany, shock, or violence. Not surprisingly, some of Caravaggio's most famous paintings include scenes that are simultaneously violent and spiritual, such as *The Crucifixion of St. Peter*, *The Conversion of St. Paul*, *The Calling of St. Matthew*, and *The Deposition of Christ*. He painted religious and mythological figures in a "vulgar" way—as if they were laborers or prostitutes; indeed, early in his career, such workers were often the only models that he had.

Castel Gandolfo The Castel Gandolfo appears in *The Da Vinci Code* as the location for both of Bishop Aringarosa's meetings with Vatican officials. The Castel is famous for serving two functions: the summer residence of the pope, and the center of the Vatican's astronomy program. It was once the site of the summer residence of the Roman emperor Domitian (ruled A.D. 81–96). Domitian built a sumptuous palace, with its own aqueduct, a theater for the performance of plays and poetry contests, and a cryptoporticus—a long tunnel-like structure built into one of the surrounding hills, designed especially to shield the emperor from the sun during long walks.

The palace fell into ruin after his death, and was destroyed and rebuilt several times over the next four centuries, a victim of a tug-of-war between various noble families and the church. The Vatican finally bought it from its last owners in the early 1600s. Urban VIII (pope from 1623 to 1644) launched major renovations, and it became the official papal summer residence in 1626. It is known for its simple and tasteful style and its beautiful gardens.

One of the oldest centers for astronomy in the world, the Vatican Observatory—the *Specola Vaticana*—was relocated to the Castel Gandolfo in the 1930s. When the glow of Rome began to outshine the stars for the far-removed Castel Gandolfo observatory, the Vatican created a second astronomical center, where the bright lights of Italy's capital could not reach: Tucson, Arizona. The original Castel Gandolfo, however, is still used as the pope's summer residence.

Cathars The Cathars were a heretical Christian religious sect that flourished in the twelfth and thirteenth centuries A.D. The word comes from the Greek *katharos*, meaning "pure." The Cathars could be found throughout southern Europe—especially in the areas where the control of the Catholic Church was weakest—but they were especially strong in the Languedoc region of **Provence**, a wealthy section in the south of France, which was always known for its political and religious independence.

The origins of the Cathar heresy are obscure, but some scholars believe that the dualism which lay at the heart of their faith was introduced by heretics from the Byzantine empire on the eastern fringes of the Christian world. In any case, the Cathars subscribed to a common **Gnostic** idea—the world was created by an evil god, a god of the material world, who corrupted his creation from the start. Thus, all material things, including the human body itself, were evil; transcending and escaping the prison of flesh was salvation. The Cathars believed that the soul or spirit was trapped between spiritual good and material evil, and if the individual decided to embrace the gross impositions of the material world through self-denial, they would be reincarnated, again and again, until they made the right decision.

The Cathars were also protofeminists. Women could rise to the status of prefect just as easily as men could. The soul was sexless, the material body merely its prison. Spiritually, there was no natural superiority of either sex over the other.

The heretical beliefs of the Cathars frightened the orthodox church, which slandered the Cathars with rumors very similar to those leveled against the **Templars**—that they were devil worshippers, that they ate the ashes of burned babies, that they were inveterate homosexuals. When these slanders didn't reduce the spreading popularity of the Cathar faith, Rome organized a crusade named for the small town of Albi, a focal point of Cathar strength. The Albigensian Crusade, from A.D. 1209 to 1229, used military might to crush the nascent faith. Whole towns and cities thought to harbor the heretical communities were sacked and destroyed.

Cathedral of the Codes The informal name of the **Rosslyn Chapel**.

Chalice In Christian art the chalice signifies the Last Supper, the sacrifice of Jesus, and Christian faith. Langdon explains the nature of the chalice to Sophie during their brief stay at Leigh Teabing's château. The chalice is the simplest symbol for the feminine known to man, the symbol of the womb and femininity. The **Holy Grail** is a more elaborate symbological variant of the chalice, associated with **Mary Magdalene** in her role as the preserver of the holy bloodline.

The opposite but complementary symbol, with which it is sometimes paired, is called the blade (the chalice and the blade). The blade is represented as a phallus, or a knife or spear. It is the symbol of masculinity and aggression. The blade and chalice, when united, form the Star of David, which Langdon identifies with the perfect union of male and female, and the highest principle of the divine.

The chalice and blade symbols have never left us, but exist in various forms throughout Western culture.

Château Villette Leigh Teabing's sumptuous French home, Château Villette, is the safe haven that Sophie and Robert flee to after escaping from the Swiss bank with the priory **keystone**. The château Villette is a real-life architectural landmark outside Paris. It was designed by François Mansart in 1668 for Jean Dyel, the Comte d'Aufflay and French ambassador to Venice. Another Mansart, Jules Hardouin-Mansart, the nephew of François and a great architect in his own right, finished Villette in 1696. Versailles was designed at the same time by Hardouin-Mansart, and the influence of the design of the famous French royal residence is apparent in its smaller cousin. The château is luxury set in stone—eleven bedrooms and baths, a chapel, guest house, stables, gardens, tennis courts, and two lakes. Aspiring modern-day nobility can rent Villette for vacations, meetings, or weddings.

Cilice This French word is defined by the dictionary as "a coarse cloth, or haircloth." As referred to in *The Da Vinci Code*, however, a *cilice* is the spiked chain worn around the upper thigh of Silas, the **Opus Dei** follower who has been sent to murder Saunière and his colleagues. Wearing of the cilice is practiced by some men and women adherents (called numeraries) of Opus Dei. The cilice is an extension of a traditional Catholic Church practice of "corporal mortification": punishing one's self to be able to identify with Jesus' suffering and thereby resist temptation and grow spiritually. Josemaría Escrivá, the founder of Opus Dei, believed only direct pain would allow the sinner to repent. In his text *The Way*, fundamental to Opus Dei followers, he wrote, "Blessed be pain. Loved be pain. Sanctified be pain ... Glorified be pain," and, "What has been lost through the flesh, the flesh should pay back: be generous in your penance." More traditional examples of mortification include practices such as fasting and celibacy.

Clef de voûte *Clef de voûte* is a French term for the architectural device called a "**keystone**," used as the top, central stone in a series of stones (called *voussoir*) that comprise an arch. As the central stone, it receives the weight of the others and holds the arch in place. In the vaulted ceilings of cathedrals, the keystone is the central stone that receives the weight of the ribs of the arch (see illustration). Keystones are often covered with designs (called the "boss"). In *The Da Vinci Code* the keystone is the legendary "map of stone" created by the **Priory of Sion** that—supposedly—leads to the **Holy Grail**. Langdon queries Sophie about whether her grandfather confided in her about the keystone, and when she is confused by the term, gives her a short lecture on the subject, telling her the keystone was a major architectural advancement and is deeply embedded in the symbolism of the Masonic orders. Some interpreters find the "royal arch" of the Masons a graphic representation of the zodiac, laid against an archway, with a prominent keystone at its summit.

Clement V, Pope Pope Clement V is mentioned in Langdon's brief summary of the **Templar** persecution while he and Sophie drive through the **Bois de Boulogne**. Langdon avers that the pope devised a plan to take down the Templars, because they had amassed so much power and wealth. **Philip the Fair** (Langdon calls him King Philipe IV) was acting in concert with the pope, and on an appointed day—Friday the thirteenth, October 1307—the Templars were arrested en masse and subjected to a trial infamous for its sensational charges of heresy and blasphemy, the brutality of its execution, and its fundamental unfairness.

While Langdon seems to have the general story correct, some of the details are disputed. While King Philip is usually recognized as the prime mover of the persecution of the Templars, some scholars believe the initial arrests occurred without Clement's knowledge; indeed, Clement was shocked and angered by the arrests which were made against a group that was legally accountable only to the pope. "Your hasty act is seen by all," he wrote to Philip, "and rightly so, as an act of contempt towards ourselves and the Roman church." Clement eventually came to see the arrests as necessary, particularly, it is said, after the torture-induced confession of Jacques de Molay, the last Templar grand master. With this justification in hand, Clement publicly assented to the propriety of Philip's action.

Cocteau, Jean Famed French artist, writer, poet, novelist (*Les Enfants Terribles*) and filmmaker (*Beauty and the Beast*). Jean Cocteau is cited as a "Grand Master of the **Priory of Sion**" based on a set of documents probably concocted by **Pierre Plantard** and Philippe de Chérisey, the so-called **Dossiers Secrets**. Cocteau had wide-ranging interests; whether he was a twentieth-century neo-**Templar** or *hieros gamos* practitioner remains unknown. He appears in *The Da Vinci Code* as the last Priory of Sion grand master; his name also appears on the list the examiner finds as he searches **Château Villette**.

Codex The word *codex*, which many associate with the word *code* and the puzzles that word evokes, actually has to do with a genuine revolution in record keeping created in Roman times: it is a book made of individual leaves of paper, as distinguished from the previous tradition of writing on rolls or scrolls. Two of these ancient codices have direct relevance to the plot of *The Da Vinci Code*.

The *Berlin Codex*, known formally as "Papyrus Berolinens 8502," contains the most complete surviving copy of the *Gospel of Mary* and was acquired in the Egyptian antiquities market in 1896 by the German scholar Carl Reinhardt. It was not published until 1955, when it was discovered that two duplicate texts were also found at **Nag Hammadi**. Two other small fragments of the *Gospel of Mary* from separate Greek editions were later unearthed in northern Egypt.

Codex Leicester reflects not a religious record, but the fertile artistic genius and technological curiosity of **Leonardo da Vinci**, written between 1506 and 1510 in medieval Italian and rendered in his inventive mirror-image script. It derives its name from its first owner, the Earl of Leicester, who acquired it in 1717. Its current owner, Bill Gates, bought it at auction for $30.8 million.

While trying to decipher Saunière's illegible cursive script on the flight from France to England, Langdon recalls seeing this Codex Leicester at Harvard's Fogg Museum. He remembers being let down by the text of the codex. It was, at first sight, entirely illegible. But a docent with a hand mirror helps him to read the pages, which were written in a mirror-image text Leonardo used to disguise his words.

Constantine I Known as "the Great," Constantine is widely acknowledged to be the first Christian emperor of the Roman Empire (reigned A.D. 306–37). Although historians dispute the details, by convening the **Council of Nicea**, he is largely responsible for legitimizing and enthroning the church as the pre-eminent authority over what was left of the Roman Empire.

Whether Constantine wholeheartedly accepted Christianity as his own one true faith remains a subject of debate. Crediting him for supporting the unification of the disparate strains of early Christianity, thereby assuring the church of a supporter and sympathetic emperor is unquestioned. But did he have his heart in it? He continued stamping pagan symbols onto his coins, for example, and he was also a devotee of Sol Invictus, the **pagan** "Unconquered Sun" deity derived from Syria but imposed on the Roman people a hundred years before Constantine's time. Many scholars believe he may have been straddling the fence, paying attention to both to assure the greatest support.

The Da Vinci Code goes even further. Leigh Teabing tells Sophie and Langdon that Constantine "was a life-long pagan who was baptized on his deathbed, too weak to protest." He only chose, and then imposed, Christianity as the official religion of Rome because he was, in Teabing's words, "a very good businessman." Teabing argues, in effect, that the great cover-up by the church began with Constantine. Mainstream scholars stress Constantine's role in adjudicating specific religious issues—the divinity versus humanity of Christ, for example. In *The Da Vinci Code*, Constantine is seen as covering up the role of the sacred feminine, the marriage of Jesus and **Mary Magdalene**, dealing a body blow to the **Gnostic** tradition, and defining opponents of the mainstream church as heretics.

Coptic The Coptic language is a direct descendant of the ancient Egyptian language, but is also a hybrid. It began to appear in the third century B.C., following the Greek conquest of Egypt, and was used by Christianized Egyptians to translate the Bible and liturgical works. The *Gospel of Mary* and most of the so-called **Gnostic Gospels** were originally in Greek, but most of them only survive in the Coptic translation discovered at **Nag Hammadi**. The Coptic language is still used today among the Copts, a Christian sect in Egypt.

Council of Nicea The first ecumenical council ever held by the Christian church, the Council of Nicea was called by Emperor **Constantine** in A.D. 325 to settle various theological disputes, from the mundane to the highly theoretical. At this time in Christian history, church practice and doctrine was not uniform; the Nicene council was an attempt to settle these disputes once and for all. The council worked out most conflicts, from the dates to be set aside to celebrate Easter and other holidays to the most important question of the time—was Christ of the same substance as the Father, or was he inferior to Him, a created being that came into existence at God's behest, and was therefore unable to share His divinity, as the **Arians** believed? At one point, legend has it, the debate became so heated that Saint Nicholas—the historical personality behind our modern Santa Claus—physically attacked Arius for his heresies.

　　Regardless, unity prevailed and all but three of the bishops present signed the **Nicene Creed**, a statement of church orthodoxy and a rejection of Arianism. Scholar Stringfellow Barr, in his book *The Mask of Jove*, maintains, "Constantine . . . instinctively knew that the Christian *polis*, around which he had planned to rebuild [the Roman empire] must achieve a unity of spirit if his plans were to succeed."

Cross The art historian Diane Apostolos-Cappadone puts its succinctly: "An ancient, universal symbol of the conjunction of opposites with the vertical bar representing the positive forces of life and spirituality, and the horizontal bar the negative forces of death and materialism. There are well over four hundred varieties of this symbol." *The Da Vinci Code* points out that the cross existed as a key symbol long before the crucifixon, and also highlights the differences between the "square" cross (used by the **Templars**) and the traditional elongated Christian cross.

Crux gemmata "Cross of gems," containing thirteen gems, a Christian ideogram for Christ and his twelve apostles. The plain **cross** symbolizes the crucifixion (it often is displayed with Jesus' body on it), while the *crux gemmata* symbolizes the resurrection. Langdon sees it on the tie clasp of Bezu Fache as they meet each other in the **Louvre** following Saunière's untimely death, thus signaling the police captain's pride in his religion.

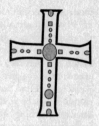

Dagobert II The last of **Merovingian** priest-kings, mentioned in *The Da Vinci Code* because Dagobert's name was raised in the four parchments discovered by **Saunière** known collectively as the *Dossiers Secrets*. One parchment is supposed to contain a ciphered message which, when decoded, states, "To Dagobert II, and to Sion belong this treasure and is there dead." This connection to the **Priory of Sion** is explored in the novel, as is Dagobert's murder, "stabbed in the eye while sleeping," according to Sophie. The act ended the Merovingian dynasty and a bloodline associated more with heresy than papal fidelity (Dagobert's son, Sigisbert, is said by Brown to have escaped and carried on the lineage, which later included **Godefroi de Bouillon**—the presumed founder of the **Templars** and the Priory of Sion.) The interconnection behind these various conspiratorial tales goes even further. When Dagobert married, he moved with his new wife into **Rennes-le-Château**.

Legend has it that Dagobert's assassination by Pepin the Fat was ordered by the Vatican as a way to allow the Carolingians to take over—a dynasty closely allied with the interests of the church. Pepin is also rendered as Pippin, the name of a type of **apple**, a protagonist in a Steinbeck novel, and a 1972 Broadway musical and later a film directed by Bob Fosse. To create even more mystery—or confusion—**Walt Disney** has a cartoon character named Uncle Dagobert, a duck from Scotland, the location of the **Rosslyn Chapel**. Langdon even goes so far as to suggest that "it is no mistake that Disney retold tales like *Cinderella, Sleeping Beauty,* and *Snow White*— all of which dealt with the incarnation of the **sacred feminine**." Proof that Walt Disney was indeed a member of the Priory of Sion, while rumored, has never been found.

DCPJ: Direction Centrale Police Judiciare The French law enforcement organization which in the book employs Captain Bezu Fache and Lieutenant Jerome Collet. Langdon calls the DCPJ the rough equivalent of the FBI. The DCPJ is the French law enforcement institution dedicated to the coordination of technical and scientific police organizations. In the words of the Franco-British Council, "It is responsible for countering theft, terrorism, organized crime, trafficking of human beings, drug trafficking, theft and resale of works of art, and currency counterfeiting and distribution." Given its status, it seems unlikely that Bezu Fache, a high-ranking official within the DCPJ, would actually have been leading a hands-on investigation, let alone the chase, with gun drawn as he runs into the men's room at the **Louvre**.

Dead Sea Scrolls *Dead Sea Scrolls* is a collective term for the remnants of approximately eight hundred manuscripts discovered in limestone caves flanking the Dead Sea at Qumran. Bedouins exploring the site in 1947 first stumbled on the scrolls and sold a few of them to antiquities dealers and scholars, touching off a race to see who could recover the most documents from the same cave-pocked cliffs the fastest. Between 1948 and 1956, ten more caves were discovered and excavated, producing the trove of scrolls and fragments. The Dead Sea Scrolls are a baffling variety, including scriptures and writings relating to community life—scriptural commentaries, laws for community living, etc. One manuscript—called the "Copper Scroll" because unlike the other, mainly parchment manuscripts, the text was inscribed on thin copper—provides instructions on how to find vast quantities of hidden treasure.

Along with the **Nag Hammadi** texts, the Dead Sea Scrolls were one of the most important discoveries related to the modern understanding of both Judaism and Christianity. Much as the Nag Hammadi texts shed light on the many different faces of the early Christian movement, the Dead Sea Scrolls contain priceless information about an unorthodox Jewish group living at the height of Roman power and at the dawn of Christianity. Many scholars believe the ascetic sect known as Essenes wrote the Dead Sea Scrolls, but there is a debate about this. Deviations in the scrolls from the traditional Jewish scriptural texts, and similarities between the teachings of Christ and the edicts of the scrolls, created a challenge for scholars and theologians of both faiths. The controversy over the identity of the authors, their immediate sources both political and theological, and the reason for their being hidden in the first place, rage on to this day.

Didache *Didache*, or Doctrine of the Twelve Apostles, is considered the oldest surviving piece of noncanonical literature, dating from about A.D. 70 to 110. Didache is an instructional guide for new Christian converts, and though ultimately not included as one of the twenty-seven books of the New Testament, Didache was highly regarded as being the wisdom and teachings of the twelve apostles, though the direct authorship was unlikely to have been theirs. There is much practical advice in the Didache, including an extensive section on itinerant ministers. Such ministers are to be received as the Lord. They may stay one day or two. If they stay three days, they are false prophets or charlatans. If, upon leaving, the minister takes anything but bread, he is likewise a false prophet.

Disney, Walt Langdon states as fact the famed cartoonist "made it his quiet life's work to pass on the **Grail** story," and compares him to **Leonardo** in the way he "loved infusing hidden messages in his art," many related to the subjugation of the Goddess. Among those listed by Brown/Langdon are *Cinderella, Sleeping Beauty, Snow White, the Lion King,* and *The Little Mermaid* which, Langdon notices, has a replica of George de la Tour's seventeenth-century painting *The Penitent Magdalene* in Ariel's underwater home, with its "blatant symbolic references to the lost sanctity of **Isis**, Eve, Pisces the fish goddess, and, repeatedly, **Mary Magdalene** (de la Tour is noted for having depicted Mary Magdalene as pregnant, and figures prominently in the mysterious legends surrounding **Rennes-le-Château**). No doubt to honor Disney, Robert Langdon, the Harvard don in Harris tweed, doesn't wear a Rolex, but a Mickey Mouse watch. A recent real-world book, *The Gospel in Disney,* purports to teach the major lessons of Christianity through the plots of Disney animated movies. One problem this analysis raises is the distinction between Walt Disney, the person, and his namesake studio. By the time *The Lion King* and *Little Mermaid* came out, the famed cartoonist had been dead for many years. Are his successors supposed to be consciously following his religious ways as well as his professional ways? Was that one of the recent issues turning the board against CEO Michael Eisner? Is it merely coincidental that Langdon's reverie about Disney gets interrupted by the cold reality of the clicking of Teabing's crutches in a big hallway?

Divine Proportion Also known as the Golden Section, Golden Ratio, and Golden Mean, the term refers to the geometric proportion produced by dividing any line so that the smaller part stands in relation to the greater part as the greater part is to the whole line (see **Phi**). While mathematicians debate the origins of the rigorous application of the Golden Section as a geometric element, there is evidence suggesting that it was first used in the fourth century B.C. Some ancient sources credit its discovery to the secret society of mathematicians, the Pythagoreans, who used the **pentagram** as a symbol of their order.

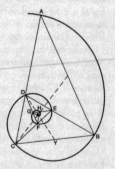

 Areas within objects using the concept of the Golden Section/Phi appear throughout art and nature. Whether that is literally true or not, the mystical associations with geometry and the Golden Section have not faded, but remain as codified aspects of modern secret societies and brotherhoods.

Dossiers Secrets Descriptions of the *Dossiers Secrets* in *The Da Vinci Code* as well as in *Holy Blood, Holy Grail,* the book by Michael Baigent, Richard Leigh, and Henry Lincoln (from which Dan Brown got much of the inspiration for his plot), would have readers believe they form an impressive literary pastiche, from tables of genealogy to complicated maps and works of allegorical poetry. The documents are said to cover the **Merovingian** dynasty, the **Priory of Sion**, and the **Knights Templar**. While some documents were deposited into the national library of France during the 1950s and 1960s, those who have researched them are generally disappointed to find they are twentieth-century typewritten materials, filled with odd details and occult references. Most experts believe the *Dossiers Secrets*, as well as the Priory of Sion itself, are all part of an elaborate hoax dreamed up by **Pierre Plantard**, who billed himself as the mid–twentieth-century Grand Master of the Priory.

Eglise de Saint-Sulpice One of the most exciting early episodes in *The Da Vinci Code* centers on the Eglise de Saint-Sulpice, originally the parish church of the domain of the St. Germain des Prés Abbey. Silas, convinced that he has discovered the hiding place of the priory keystone, enters the church hopefully but finds himself the victim of a cruel hoax.

Some authorities believe there has always been a church on the site of the Eglise. Nonetheless, the current structure was erected in 1646, with the first stone laid by Anne of Austria, Louis XIII's wife, who appears as a central character in *The Three Musketeers*. The building was completed fitfully over the next seventy years, although at the close of construction in 1721 one tower was sixteen or seventeen feet lower than the other. Objects of interest in the Eglise are the meridian line (the **rose** line) that Silas follows to find the **key-stone**; eight statues of the apostles, arranged around the choir, and the Lady Chapel, a beautiful chapel dedicated to Our Lady of Loreto.

Saint-Sulpice has numerous historical connections with the Priory of Sion. **Bérenger Saunière** apparently visited Abbé Bieil, director of the seminary at Saint-Sulpice, with the documents he recovered from the church in **Rennes-le-Château**. Francis Ducaud-Bourget, reputed Sion grand master (after **Jean Cocteau**) was trained in the same seminary. The seminary was a focus point, at the end of the nineteenth century, for the Catholic modernist movement, a school of thought that centered on bringing Catholic religious scholarship up to date with modern critical methods.

Ephesus A city of great importance in New Testament times, Ephesus was situated in what is today Turkey. Ephesus was the second largest city in the Roman Empire and the gateway to Asia. Ephesus was home to the spectacular Temple of Artemis (aka the goddess Diana), the Greek symbol of fertility. Artemis was often depicted with multiple breasts or other exaggerations of her femininity. The temple, built of 127 pillars sixty feet high, was one of the Seven Wonders of the Ancient World. Some scholars believe the Virgin Mary went to Ephesus at the end of her life, accompanied by St. Peter (A.D. 37–45), and you can see her "house" there today. A few legends also exist about Mary going to Ephesus after the crucifixion.

Escrivá, Father Josemaría The founder of **Opus Dei**, whom Silas calls the "Teacher of Teachers." Escrivá (1902–75) was a Spanish priest who, on October 28, 1928, founded Opus Dei—a Catholic organization recognized as a "personal prelature" of the Catholic Church, dedicated to bringing the reality of Jesus Christ into even the most mundane moments of ordinary life. Some have criticized the organization as so authoritarian that it borders on being a cult; Opus Dei rejects the cult label. Along with papal fidelity and a lively devotion to the Virgin Mary, Escrivá especially preached raising one's work up to God each day—and to do so with a great deal of self-sacrifice. That sacrifice includes a recommendation of self-mortification. Some reports say he practiced what he preached, including self-flagellation. The exact relationship of Opus Dei to the Vatican is unclear. It appears Opus Dei was helpful to the Vatican during the financial scandals of the 1980s that threatened to bankrupt the church, and that this particular personal prelature has enjoyed high standing with Pope John Paul II. After Escrivá's death, sainthood was established extremely rapidly.

Female Pope In a discussion with Sophie about the **tarot** deck Langdon explains that the medieval card game was "replete with hidden heretical symbolism," including a reference to a card named the Female Pope. In the tarot, she is supposed to represent hidden or esoteric knowledge and is usually portrayed as a seated woman wearing clerical dress and a triple crown, and holding an open book on her lap.

The primary source for what little we know about the female pope is a Dominican friar, Martin Polonus, who claimed that a certain thirteenth-century Pope John was really Pope Joan, who was only discovered to be female when she gave birth in the middle of a papal procession from St. Peter's to Lateran. Polonus says church historians later eradicated her name "both because of her female sex and on account of the foulness of the matter." In other accounts, she was stoned to death by the crowd on the spot when the deception was discovered. In some stories she was an Englishwoman educated in Germany who dressed as a man so as to become monk; in other stories she hailed from Athens where she had demonstrated extensive knowledge of languages and theology. No historical records have ever been found to fully confirm the story of Pope Joan and it seems to have been discredited in the mid-seventeenth century by a Protestant historian. This legend may also have originated as an antipapal satire centering on the church's fears about deceptions, women having too much authority, and the possibility of a sexually active pope. In any event, Pope Joan still has a tarot card in her honor. A book-length study is available by Rosemary and Darroll Pardoe.

Fibonacci sequence The Fibonacci sequence is used by Saunière in the coded message he scrawls down as he is dying. The scrambled sequence alerts his cryptologist granddaughter, Sophie, to contact Robert Langdon.

The Fibonacci series begins with 0 and 1, and then produces more numbers by adding the last two numbers in the sequence. So the sequence progresses 0, 1, 1, 2, 3, 5, 8, 13, 21, 34 ... Langdon, in a lecture to his Harvard students, explains the ratio **Phi** is derived from the Fibonacci sequence: dividing any number in the sequence by the preceding smaller number produces a ratio that slowly approaches 1.618. The Fibonacci series and the ratio Phi appear, seemingly spontaneously, throughout natural and man-made designs (see **Phi**). But they are not the only numbers that recur in nature. Lucas numbers, for instance, are generated using the same addition as the Fibonacci sequence, except the first two numbers are 1 and 3; so the sequence is 1, 3, 4, 7, 11, 18, 29, 47, 76, 123.

There is a real question, however, as to whether Phi is universally applicable. As H. S. M. Coxeter, in his *Introduction to Geometry*, states: "It should be frankly admitted that in [the growth patterns of] some plants the numbers do not belong to the sequence of Fibonacci numbers but to the sequence of Lucas numbers, or even to the still more anomalous sequences: 3, 1, 4, 5, 9 ... or 5, 2, 7, 9, 16.... Thus we must face the fact that [the Fibonacci sequence] is really not a universal law but only a fascinatingly prevalent tendency."

Flamel, Nicholas *The Da Vinci Code* places Flamel as the head of the **Priory of Sion** from 1398 to 1418. Flamel was a leading alchemist, whose name has returned to fame in recent years. There is a reference to him in the *Harry Potter* series, a biotechnology company uses his name, and a growing number of tourists stop in at the Paris bar that was his former home.

Fleur-de-lis, fleur-de-lys In the political realm, the symbol represents both France (the French monarchy in particular) and the city of Florence. In Christian symbolism it signifies the Trinity. Experts debate whether it is supposed to represent a lily or an iris, each of which has special symbolic connotations. It is invoked in *The Da Vinci Code* in several contexts: translated, Dan Brown says (stretching), the phrase means "flower of Lisa," a reference he says, that points to the *Mona Lisa*. The fleur-de-lis as a symbol also appears on the key given to Sophia by her grandfather with the words, "It opens a box ... where I keep many secrets."

The literal translation is "flower of the lily," but the *lys* is actually an iris flower. Traditionally in French heraldry, the fleur-de-lys is yellow, and yellow is a common color for the iris flower, while the lily is traditionally white, especially in heraldry. As a widely used symbol in heraldry, the fleur-de-lys consists of three petal-like shapes, gathered by a horizontal bar. Sometimes the lower part is cut off, or represented by a mere triangle.

The fleur-de-lys became strongly associated with French kings from about 1200 onward. It can also be seen as strongly symbolic of the Trinity among Christians. There is a legend that an early French king, Clovis, picked an iris and wore it on his helmet in a victorious battle in 507. (A competing legend is that when King Clovis was baptized he offered it as a symbol of purification for both himself and the country as a whole.)

The symbol itself can be found in a wide array of ancient and modern cultures, and in many forms of expression: Mesopotamian cylinders, Egyptian bas-reliefs, Mycenean potteries, Gaulish coins, Japanese emblems, etc. Thus, this stylized figure, probably a flower, was used as ornament or emblem by almost all civilizations of the Old and New Worlds.

Friday the thirteenth In *the Da Vinci Code*, Dan Brown cites an incident involving the **Knights Templar** as the origin of the widespread superstition about Friday the thirteenth being unlucky. On Friday the thirteenth, October 1307, **Pope Clement** "issued secret, sealed orders to be opened simultaneously by his soldiers all across Europe," Brown writes. The fateful and fatal orders said God had visited the pope in a vision and told him that the Knights Templar were all heretics, guilty of homosexuality, sodomy, defiling the **cross**, and all other manner of sins. The soldiers, who were in fact soldiers of the French king **Philip IV**, were directed to take the Knights into custody and torture them to learn the true dimensions of their crimes against God. Although Brown describes the Knights' capture, torture, and burning at the stake in a way that makes it sound as though everything happened in one very hectic twenty-four-hour period, these events took place over the next several years rather than "on that day."

The Knights' real crime, it appears, was power. The Knights had grown both wealthy and influential because of their combination of papal protection and financial activities and they reputedly had secrets related to the **Holy Grail**. The pope felt the Knights were a threat to his power and had to go, so most—but not all—were rounded up on that Friday the thirteenth. The survivors presumably continued to guard the secrets of the Holy Grail.

While Brown cites this incident as *the* reason for continuing superstition surrounding this ominous day and date, Friday the thirteenth has had a lot going against it for a very long time, some of it predating the pope's order by hundreds of years. In Norse mythology there were thirteen present at a banquet in Valhalla when Balder (son of Odin) was slain, which led to the downfall of the gods. Around 1000 B.C., Hesiod wrote in *Works and Days* that the thirteenth day is unlucky for sowing, but favorable for planting. Friday is the unluckiest day of the week for Christians, some of whom believe that Christ was crucified on this day. They also believe the number 13 to be unlucky because there were thirteen present at the Last Supper, including the thirteenth, betraying apostle.

Gnosis *Gnosis* is a Greek term meaning, in English, a combination of "knowledge," "insight," and "wisdom." Gnosis is understood as being a divinely inspired, intuitive, and intimate knowledge as opposed to intellectual knowledge of a specific area or discipline. Gnosis, as an experience, is generally the ultimate aim of a spiritual discipline that seeks union with God, the infinite, or the absolute—the reality beyond perception, or, for that matter, religious doctrine. Gnosis is almost always described as a personal revelation or exploration.

Some of the groups now identified as Gnostics may have believed that one way to achieve gnosis was through the ritual of *hieros gamos,* a celebration of the sacred marriage. As Langdon explains it to Sophie during their flight across the English Channel, "Physical union remained the sole means through which man could become spiritually complete and ultimately achieve *gnosis*—knowledge of the divine."

The scholar and historian Elaine Pagels in her book *The Origin of Satan* has this to say about the meaning of the word: "The secret of gnosis is that when one comes to know oneself at the deepest level, one comes to know god as the source of one's being." The experience of gnosis and other mystical communications with the divine have been seen as a threat by established religious institutions—institutions that prefer to see themselves as the sole conduit to the divine.

The Gnostic Gospels The popularized name given the documents found in **Nag Hammadi,** Egypt, in 1947. The best known texts include:

The *Gospel of Mary* is invoked by Sir Leigh Teabing as one link in a chain of arguments meant to persuade Sophie that the grail is more than just a holy cup: The Gospel, Teabing says, proves Jesus founded his church on Mary, and not on Peter.

The conclusions that Teabing draws from the *Gospel of Mary*—if this is his primary source—seem somewhat misleading. Contrary to what he says, Jesus never gives **Mary Magdalene** specific instructions on how to carry on his church after he is gone, at least not in this gospel. The more traditional view of the Gospel is that although Mary did have a "special relationship" with Jesus, and the other apostles were jealous of it at times, there is no indication that Jesus chose Mary to carry on his church, or that he gave her any special instructions about how to do it.

The *Gospel of Philip* also makes an appearance during Leigh Teabing's discourse on the nature of the **Holy Grail.** Teabing uses it as his source for the claim that Jesus and Mary Magdalene were married, based on the translation that mentions Mary as Jesus' "companion" and that the phrase "he kissed her on the m . . . [text missing]" proved they had a great deal of intimacy. As seen in earlier chapters of this book, there are several scholars and commentators who agree with this interpretation, although others see the kiss as more metaphoric than romantic.

The *Gospel of Thomas* contains many parallels with the orthodox Gospels of the New Testament, including directly parallel sayings and proverbs. Yet they have remarkably enigmatic twists on the familiar canonical texts.

Thomas says, for instance, "If two make peace with each other in this one house, they will say to the mountain, 'Move away,' and it will move away." Another mysterious example is, "Simon Peter said to them, 'Let Mary leave us, for women are not worthy of life.' Jesus [then] said, 'I myself shall lead her in order to make her male, so that she too may become a living spirit resembling you males. For every woman who will make herself male will enter the kingdom of heaven.'" This *Gospel of Thomas* also emphasizes self-knowledge, self-exploration, and self-actualization in passages that are slightly reminiscent of Buddhist analects.

The *Gospel of Sophia of Jesus Christ* Highly mystical, this text concerns the creation of gods, angels, and the universe with an emphasis on infinite and mystical truth. Some scholars believe it may reflect a conversation between Jesus Christ and his disciples after the resurrection; others argue against it. The fulcrum of that debate relates to the date it might have been written. If it was written as far back as the first century it could reflect the true sayings of Jesus. If after that, this assemblage of sayings and proverbs might simply come from post-Jesus philosophers and Gnostics.

Elaine Pagels, the Princeton scholar whose book *Gnostic Gospels* introduced much of this subject matter to the American public more than twenty years ago, now says she no longer refers to these documents as Gnostic Gospels, owing to negative connotations associated with Gnosticism today. Pagels, as well as other scholars, including James Robinson and Bart Ehrman, emphasize that the Nag Hammadi finds do offer specific, documentable facts about early Christian history, as much as they suggest the diversity of thought about religion and philosophy that prevailed in the first few centuries of the Common Era. The suppression of these "alternative scriptures" represented the triumph of what we now know mainstream church doctrine to be over a rich variety of other ways of thinking.

Gnosticism *Gnosticism* is a term used to describe various sects and religious groups, mainly Christian but also Jewish and Egyptian, that hold *gnosis* at the core of their beliefs and practices. Gnosticism as a religious force probably predates Christianity. James Robinson, an expert on the **Nag Hammadi Library** states, "Gnostics were more ecumenical and syncretic with regard to religious traditions than were orthodox Christians, so long as they found in them a stance congenial to their own."

Gnosticism comes into focus early in the Christian era as a major rival to the influence of apostolic Christianity. Gnosticism's personal communion with the divine, its often loose church structure, its secret explication of a higher, hidden knowledge that faith could not reveal: all of these traits made Gnostic streams of worship highly problematic for the coalescing Catholic orthodoxy. The result was a steadily increasing stream of denunciation and accusations of heresy so effective that Gnosticism became marginalized as a movement by fifth century A.D.

A few of the major strands within Gnosticism are that the direct, intimate, and absolute knowledge of the divine and of truth itself (gnosis) is necessary for spiritual fulfillment; the belief in a union with, or a discovery of, a "higher self" that is identified with or identical to the divine; and, that the world was created by a lesser god, a demiurge, who is responsible for the evil inherent in it; the only escape from the evils of material existence was contemplation, self-knowledge, and gnosis with the uncorrupted spiritual. The belief system continues forward to this day; there is a Gnosis Society, for example.

Godefroi de Bouillon French king, leader of the first Crusade, and founder of the **Priory of Sion** in Jerusalem in 1099. According to the genealogies allegedly collected as part of the *Dossiers Secrets*, de Bouillon was a descendent of the **Merovingian** kings. As Langdon further explains to Sophie while they pass through the **Bois de Boulogne** in a taxi, "King Godefroi was allegedly the possessor of a powerful secret that had been in his family since the time of Christ." To protect it he formed a secret brotherhood, the Priory of Sion, that had a military wing to it as well—the **Knights Templar**. After a detailed exposition of the ins and outs of this history, Langdon reveals that de Bouillon dispatched the Knights Templar to find corroborating evidence of his "powerful secret" beneath the ruins of the former **Temple of Solomon** in Jerusalem—and that they did find something very compelling there. The implication is that the secret is the information about the **Sangreal**, better known as the **Holy Grail**, and that the Templars found the Grail—documents, records, relics, the bones of **Mary Magdalene**, etc.—and then brought these items back to France.

Gregory IX Born in 1145 as Count Ugolino of Segni, Gregory IX spent his time as pontiff presiding over a turbulent conflict between the church and the secular Holy Roman emperor, Frederick II of Hohenstaufen. Gregory IX was well known for his fierce opposition to all heresies and partook in the last years of the Albigensian Crusade which nearly wiped out the **Cathars**, who were centered in the area of France known as the **Languedoc**.

Hanssen, Robert Former FBI agent turned Russian spy. For almost twenty-two years during the Cold War period, Hanssen sold crucial intelligence information to the Russians. Hanssen was a member of **Opus Dei** and turned out to be not only an embarrassment to the country but to that organization. He engaged in some unusual sexual practices that came to light during his trial, including photographing himself and his wife having sex to show to his friends. In May of 2002, Hanssen was sentenced to life in prison without possibility of parole, the judge saying, as quoted by Dan Brown, "Hardly the pastime of a devout Catholic."

Hieros gamos The *hieros gamos* appears in *The Da Vinci Code* as an ancient sexual rite that Sophie remembers traumatically witnessing her grandfather practicing in secret. Deep in a chamber below his home, **Saunière** and a female member of the **Priory of Sion** are having sex while the other members, masked and robed, chant prayers to the sacred union. Sophie watches, unseen, then flees the house and cuts off all contact with her grandfather for some time.

He was likely to have been involved in the rite of *hieros gamos*, sometimes referred to as theogamy or hierogamy, a term loosely meaning "sacred marriage" or "divine marriage." This marriage, in the words of scholar David H. Garrison, is "the holy marriage, the union of goddess and god that provides the paradigm for all human unions." This holy marriage was reenacted, in various levels of realism, throughout the early religious history of mankind; remnants of the practice still remain with us today—as depicted in the recent movie *Eyes Wide Shut*. Some Eastern belief systems have analogs, such as Tantric sex rites.

Holy Grail There are as many theories about how and where the Grail story originated as there are Grails: critics and writers have identified Celtic and western European pre-Christian myths, Byzantine mythologies and Eastern orthodox Christian traditions, a code for the secret bloodline of Christ, ancient Persian cult practices, nature worship ceremonies of the pre-Christian Middle East, alchemical symbology, and more, ad infinitum.

The modern version of the Holy Grail story was launched in the last quarter of the twelfth to the first quarter of the thirteenth century by a number of writers in an amazing variety of languages including French, English, German, Spanish, and Welsh. The earliest Grail romance still extant is the *Perceval* of Chrétien de Troyes.

The Grail as object is described differently by different authors. It has been depicted as a stone, an object made of gold with precious stones, a reliquary, and a cup. The quest for the Grail also has variations: one, where the guardian of the Grail is known as the Fisher King, finding it would mean a return to health and prosperity for the kingdom. The quest is also rendered more personally: it means for many a spiritual inner journey toward enlightenment and communion with God.

Whatever its history and meaning as relic or idea, every character in *The Da Vinci Code* is involved in its quest, and Brown's version of the legend goes where it has never gone before. "The greatest cover-up in human history," exclaims Teabing, "Not only was Jesus Christ married, but he was a father. My dear, **Mary Magdalene** was the Holy Vessel. She was the **chalice** that bore the royal bloodline of Jesus Christ."

Hugo, Victor Mentioned in *The Da Vinci Code* as one of many notable authors and artists whose key works secretly passed along the banished notion of the

Holy Grail, the **sacred feminine**, and Jesus and **Mary Magdalene** as husband and wife. Langdon cites Hugo's *Hunchback of Notre Dame* (along with Mozart's *Magic Flute*) as a work that was "filled with Masonic symbolism and Grail secrets." Hugo is often cited as having been a **Priory of Sion** member.

Hyssop "Purge me with hyssop and I shall be clean," Silas the **Albino** quotes from Psalms as he prays while dabbing blood from his back as the result of self-flagellation. John 19:29, describing Jesus' last moments on the cross, writes, "Now there was set a vessel full of vinegar; and they filled a sponge with vinegar, and put upon it hyssop, and put it to his mouth." Hyssop has culinary uses as well as medicinal ones: it is technically a vegetable and shows up in salads presented at restaurants. The biblical herb also is used in the making of the liqueur Chartreuse.

Iambic verse An iamb is a unit of alternating weak/STRONG emphasis in poetry, referred to as a foot. A line of iambic verse is built from such elements. If there are five in a line, the meter is referred to as iambic pentameter. While the pattern of accent on the second syllable is thought of as a particularly English-language feature, the iambic meter in poetry dates has Greek origins. Some feel the universality of this meter results from its similarity to the human heartbeat,

Icon From the Greek *eikon*, meaning "image," a picture that is a symbolic representation of something real. A religious icon is an artistic representation of anything holy or divine, and often employs extensive symbolism. Christians honor but do not worship icons; such worship was forbidden by the Second **Council of Nicea.**

Innocent II, Pope The pope who ruled from 1130 to 1143 and gave the **Knights Templar** carte blanche to be a law unto themselves, free of all interference from political or religious authorities, according to Dan Brown. Some theorize the Templars were bought off at the instigation the church so they would keep secret the documents supposedly found under the rubble of the **Temple of Solomon** that could embarrass the church. Others believe the Knights took the initiative and blackmailed Innocent II.

Irenaeus Leading theologian and polemicist whose arguments against **Gnostic** sects in the last half of the second century helped establish the doctrinal standards of Catholic Christianity: creed, canon of scripture, and apostolic succession of bishops. Irenaeus, along with other church historians such as Eusebius and **Tertullian**, are all charged in *The Da Vinci Code* as being coconspirators in rewriting Christian history and creating "the great cover-up."

Isis One of the oldest and most important female deities in the Egyptian pantheon, *The Da Vinci Code* emphasizes her status as the formative expression of the **sacred feminine**. Isis was considered the patroness of the family, of female fertility, medicine, and magic. Conceived by the God of Earth and the Goddess of Sky, Isis and her twin brother, Osiris, were married and ruled as king and queen over the Egyptian cosmos.

Langdon notes Saunière's extensive collection of Isis statuary in the Louvre (there are indeed many such statues there), implying that is so because of his connections to the belief in the sacred feminine. Isis also plays a role in Langdon's discussion of the *Mona Lisa*. The name is an anagram of Isis's ancient pictographic name—L'ISA combined with that of her male counterpart, the god Amon. L'ISA + AMON = MONA LISA. Some claim that Leonardo originally painted the *Mona Lisa* as wearing a lapis lazuli pendant depicting Isis, which he subsequently painted over. Whether or not this is true, there can be no doubt about the persistent echoes of Isis in many famous images of the sacred feminine.

The story of Isis and Osiris is first mentioned in the Pyramid Texts, religious hieroglyphics dating from 2600 B.C. Her cult lasted far into Roman times, and scholars speculate that the romantic, redemptive story at the heart of her myth provided a much-needed contrast with the severe and distant flavor of the empire's official religion. Worship of Isis was widespread geographically as well: the "Black Virgin" statues revered in some French cathedrals are likely to be figures of Isis. And ancient temples to Isis have been uncovered on the banks of the Danube and the Thames. There is said to have been a temple of Isis where the abbey of St. Germain-des-Prés in Paris now stands. This church was built by the **Merovingian** King Childebert to house holy relics.

Echoes of the Isis myth haunt the mythology and symbology of the Christian era. She is possibly the archetype for the high priestess of the **tarot**. The common representation of Madonna and Child is strikingly similar to countless images of Isis suckling Horus on her lap. Mary also assumed many of Isis's titles: Seat of Wisdom, Star of the Sea, and Queen of Heaven. Finally, the death and resurrection of Osiris is often credited as a precursor of Christ's resurrection, albeit with a feminine touch. Isis—the original sacred feminine—is the power that resurrects the god and continues his bloodline.

Isis is still worshipped by many New Age practitioners, giving her a lifespan of about five thousand years and counting.

Keystone Langdon describes the keystone as "the best-kept secret of the early Masonic brotherhood," which he means both literally and figuratively.

Literally, it is a wedge-shaped stone at the top of an archway that holds the other stones together and holds the weight (see **clef de voûte**). Symbolically, it is what opens the secrets of the **Priory of Sion**.

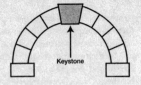

Keystone

"King of the Jews" Teabing, ever ready to impart reams of knowledge of early religious history from his point of view, recounts the history by which Jesus Christ is understood to be descended from King Solomon and King David and therefore to be the true, hereditary King of the Jews in addition to being the Messiah. When Jesus married Mary, according to *The Da Vinci Code* telling of history, he married into the **Tribe of Benjamin**, a line that carried on through Mary and their child to become the **Merovingian** dynasty. Part of the **Priory of Sion** legend is that whoever is the current heir to the bloodline of Jesus (pointed to as Sophie) is, in effect, the rightful King of Israel/Palestine (or France, depending on what point one is trying to make from these two thousand years of historical secrets).

Knights of Malta The only serious rivals to the **Knights Templar**, the Knights of Malta (also known as the Hospitallers of St. John of Jerusalem, and the Knights of Rhodes) were a monastic military order that originated in the Holy Land during the eleventh century. The order was dedicated to the relief of the sick and wounded, and established hospitals in the Holy Land to provide comfort and aid for pilgrims. The order considered itself the vassal of their patients; in some hospitals, the sick slept on linens and dined on silver services. Paradoxically, they also earned a reputation as fierce warriors, both on land and on sea. The Hospitallers wandered the Mediterranean, establishing bases in Cyprus, Rhodes, and finally Malta after the Holy Land fell to the Muslims. From these island fortresses they harried Muslim shipping and coastal towns.

Seizure of Hospitaller property during the Reformation and French Revolution deprived the Knights of their financial independence, and the weakened order surrendered Malta to Napoleon in 1798. The order was resurrected in various forms throughout the nineteenth century, returning to its Hospitaller roots as a refuge for the sick and wounded. Knights of Malta built operating theaters, organized nursing for various European wars, and ran field hospitals during the First World War. The order survives today as a sovereign state, much like the Vatican. Their headquarters in Rome is extraterritorial, meaning they can issue their own passports and exchange ambassadors with other countries (forty to date). It is the world's smallest independent state.

Knights Templar The Knights Templar are first mentioned in *The Da Vinci Code* as Sophie and Langdon drive through the **Bois de Boulogne**. Langdon gives a brief summary of their history, and how it relates to **the Priory of Sion**. The Knights play an overarching role in the book as one of the historical linchpins of the plot: the Priory, *The Da Vinci Code* maintains, created the Templars as a military arm charged with the recovery and protection of the documents and relics of the Holy Grail.

In 1119, nine knights, calling themselves the "Poor Fellow-Soldiers of Jesus Christ" took a vow to protect pilgrims journeying to and from the various holy sites in and around Jerusalem. This was a new kind of order: men of the church who were both warriors and monks and to whom shedding blood in the service of God was a joy.

King Baldwin II provided them with lodging in the al-Aqsa mosque, which was, according to the Crusaders, built on the location of the former **Temple of Solomon** (the debate continues about whether or not the mosque is actually above the original Temple of Solomon). From their lodgings above the temple, they derived their name: the Knights of the Temple of Solomon, or the Knights Templar.

As Langdon notes, the rise of the Templars after their inauspicious beginnings is indeed surprising. Conventional historians do not attribute this to secrets or treasures found beneath al-Aqsa; the general consensus is that genuine zeal for keeping the Holy Land in Christian hands led both secular and church authorities to make vast donations to the Templars. Additionally, Pope **Innocent II** issued a bull making the Templars accountable to the pontiff alone. This exemption from all secular and sacred governance—including taxation—increased not only the wealth of the Templars, but their power as well.

The destiny of the Templars was tied to the fate of the Holy Lands, which were constantly threatened by the armies of the Muslim kingdoms to the east. When the Holy Lands fell to the Muslims in 1291, the fortunes of the Templars waned. Sixteen years later members of the Templar order in France were arrested en masse, accused by King **Philip the Fair** of heresy, blasphemy, homosexuality, and other crimes against the church and God. Although the charges were probably false, the Knights confessed or were tortured into confessing; those that recanted their confessions were burned alive. The order came to an effective end in 1314 with the burning of the last grand master, Jacques de Molay, who recanted his initial confession and paid the price.

The *Last Supper* Along with the *Mona Lisa*, the *Last Supper* is Leonardo's most famous work. Leigh Teabing uses the *Last Supper* to illuminate his lecture on the **Holy Grail** and coded references to it in Western art, literature, and history. Teabing notes a variety of strange characteristics about the canvas—the feminine figure of **Mary Magdalene**, normally considered to be St. John, seated to Christ's right, the disembodied dagger pointing threateningly at Mary, the chalice and *M* symbols drawn by the bodies of Mary and Jesus. No major scholars would sustain Teabing's insights; Brown seems to have derived Teabing's unorthodox notions from Lynn Picknett's book *The Templar Revelation* and Margaret Starbird's *The Woman With the Alabaster Jar*.

Leonardo da Vinci Painter, sculptor, architect, engineer, writer, natural scientist, mathematician, geologist, anatomist—all words that describe the amazing variety of Leonardo da Vinci's interests and professions. Still, his fame rests most of all on his paintings, which were remarkably few in number. No more than thirteen existing paintings are generally attributed to Leonardo.

Biographical details of Leonardo's life are scarce, particularly of his youth. Born in 1452, he was the illegitimate son of a peasant girl and the son of a professional family in Florence. He apprenticed with the Florentine master Andrea Verrochio, and may have worked in his school with another apprentice who would become famous, Sandro **Botticelli**, painter of the *Birth of Venus* (like Leonardo, he has been connected to the **Priory of Sion** and his paintings are full of symbology).

Leonardo surpassed his contemporaries in almost everything to which he turned his hand. Over the next four decades he offered his services to the various lords of Milan, Florence, the king of France, and the church. He died, possibly of a stroke, in 1519 while living and working in France.

Some of Dan Brown's points about Leonardo come under strong scrutiny from Leonardo experts. Mainstream scholars have doubts about the use of coded messages, his association with secret societies, and even his homosexuality. No one, however, disputes the mastery of his paintings.

The Louvre The Louvre is the alpha and the omega of *The Da Vinci Code*. Saunière's murder takes place in the Louvre's Grand Gallery. Clues are hidden by the dying curator in some of the museum's most famous works. Finally, after a wild ride of deepening conspiracies, obscure clues, and narrow escapes, an exhausted Robert Langdon has an epiphany about the true nature of the Louvre's greatest treasure.

The history of the Louvre is enormously complex. Monarchs and governments have left their mark on the complex for almost eight hundred years, and it has suffered long periods of neglect as well as its accustomed glory. It was constructed in 1190 as a fortress for Phillip Augustus. Phillip ordered a rampart built around Paris to protect it from attack, and on the banks of the Seine, he built a castle, protected by a fortress overlooking the river—the Louvre. The tower of the Louvre became the royal treasury and held prisoners as well. Through its history the Louvre has served, as Catherine Chaine and Jean-Pierre Verdet describe in *Le Grande Louvre*, as

> a prison, an arsenal, a palace, a ministry ... [it] has contained a menagerie, a printing press, a postal service, the national lottery,

workshops and academies; it has been the home of kings, artists, provost officers, guards, courtesans, scientists and even horses … These rooms—surprise can no longer enliven them—witnessed life and its movement, festivities, trials, plots, crimes.

President **François Mitterrand**'s triumph was to consolidate the massive, run-down, labyrinthine building into the national treasure house it had often aspired to be. When he began considering changes to the complex, the Louvre was in poor condition for a preeminent cultural institution. Administration was lax and funding was scarce. Boasting over 250,000 works, the galleries were laid out in ways that baffled even the most familiar visitor. The works themselves were suffering. Dust accumulated on paintings without ever being cleaned off; some pieces languished in storage, never exhibited at all. The windows of the Louvre were so dirty that they were no longer filtering pure light—the cleaning schedules for the exterior of the windows were handled by a different ministry from the cleaning schedules for the interior of the windows!

Mitterrand changed all that, reorganizing the administration and providing funding for massive renovations—one of the "grand projects" of his administration that focused on rejuvenating many of France's cultural and civic monuments. The finance ministry was moved out of the north wing of the museum, opening that space for gallery use. I. M. Pei was hired, not only to construct a new and unified entryway for the museum (see **La Pyramide**), but to reinvigorate many of the existing galleries by rearranging their placement and expanding display surfaces. Works are laid out in an intelligible, ordered sequence, making the visitor's experience of the museum pleasurable instead of mystifying.

Madonna of the Rocks The name of one of two paintings, both technically called *Virgin of the Rocks*, both painted by **Leonardo da Vinci**. The *Madonna* has come to be shorthand for the one hanging in the Louvre, while the second, a "watered down" representation, hangs at the National Gallery in London.

Led by the solution to the anagram "so dark the con of man," Sophie searches the back of this painting for clues her grandfather might have left behind and finds the key with the **fleur-de-lis** on it as well as the initials *P.S.*—a fulfillment of his promise that one day she would get the "key" to many mysteries. As Sophie and Langdon escape the Louvre, chased by a security guard, they jump into her **Smart Car** and dash off to her grandfather's house. On the way there, Langdon muses to himself and out loud about this added "link in the evening's chain of interconnected symbolism."

What he in the novel, and scholars in the real world, have remarked upon, is the complex history of the painting and its windfall of possible hidden meanings, all them adding up to what Langdon calls "explosive and disturbing details," some of which he enumerates—the John-blessing-Jesus scenario and Mary making a seemingly threatening gesture over John's head.

Magdala The small town in the region of Galilee which scholars have identified as the place **Mary Magdalene** (also known as Mary of Magdala) most
likely would have come from. There is controversy over the location of the
town, but many scholars identify it with a village known to the Talmud as
Magdala Nunayya, or Magdala of the Fishes, likely named so because of its
proximity to the lake of Galilee. Magdala in Hebrew means "tower" or "fortress." Jesus may have retired to Magdala after the multiplication of the bread
and fishes.

Malleus Maleficarum Literally, the Witch's Hammer, recalled in a bit of interior dialogue by Langdon as he contemplates the anagram "so dark the con
of man" scrawled on the Plexiglas protecting *Mona Lisa*. The *Malleus Maleficarum* was published in 1486 and created untold misery by providing the
Inquisition's inquisitors with a guidebook on the identification of witches
(see Chapter 5). Such people were identified, prosecuted, and generally
turned over to civil authorities to be burned alive at the stake.

Marcion Marcion, a second-century heretic, was born the son of the bishop
of Sinope. He pronounced a heresy that proclaimed that the god of the Old
Testament was actually a demiurge who had created the material world and
invested it with his own inherent evil. Jesus, in Marcion's heresy, was the son
of another god, a greater god than the one who fashioned the world in seven
days. This greater god sent Jesus to mankind in order to free them from the
evil of the material world; therefore Jesus could not be a man at all, but was
wholly immaterial and not incarnated in flesh.

In order to resolve contradictions between his beliefs and those of the
standard Gospels, Marcion heavily edited the New Testament, creating a
shortened version of St. Luke that removed all references to Christ's birth.
He also included in his canonical works ten epistles of St. Paul, whom he
considered to be the only pure interpreter of the word of Christ. He advocated vegetarianism, and by some accounts, sexual abstinence. Marcionism
persisted into the fifth century, with significant modifications that brought it
closer to traditional Gnosticism than Marcion himself intended.

Tertullian, another church father who fought heresy, gives us an idea of
how much anger Marcion inspired in the early church, when he writes,
"fouler than any Scythian, more roving than the wagon-life of the Sarmatian,
more inhuman than the Massagete, more audacious than an Amazon, colder
than its winter, more brittle than its ice, more deceitful than the Ister, more
craggy than Caucasus. What Pontic mouse ever had such gnawing powers as
he who has gnawed the Gospels to pieces?"

Mary Magdalene Follower of Christ, understood by modern scholarship to have been his "companion." What the word is supposed to mean is a recurring theme at the heart of *The Da Vinci Code*. Orthodox tradition has portrayed Mary as a sinner, often as a prostitute; newer interpretations of the Magdalene, mainly derived from the **Gnostic Gospels** found at **Nag Hammadi**, position her as an influential and intimate companion of Jesus, perhaps even his wife (see Chapter 1).

Merovingians The Merovingians, according to Leigh Teabing in *The Da Vinci Code*, were the Frankish royal family that the descendents of Jesus and **Mary Magdalene** married into, thus perpetuating the holy bloodline. The bloodline supposedly reached down to **Godefroi de Bouillon**, the founder of the **Priory of Sion**.

The Merovingians traced their ancestry back to Merovée, a semimythical personage who was born of two fathers: a king named Clodio and a sea monster that seduced his mother when she was swimming in the sea. Because of their ancestry, Merovée and his descendents were reputed to have supernatural powers and unnaturally long lifetimes. Other legends connected their origins to Noah and other Jewish patriarchs as well as ancient Troy. Other claims—that the Merovingians were descended from aliens, that they were the progeny of "nephilim" or fallen angels, and that George Bush and Jeb Bush are both descendents of Merovée—have received less attention. One homage to the red-haired monarchs almost made Merovingian a household word: a character in the blockbuster *Matrix* series is named "the Merovingian."

Historically, King Clovis consolidated the Merovingian hold over the Franks in the last part of the fifth century. During a battle with another tribe, Clovis swore to convert to Catholicism if he was allowed victory. He did, and France was won for the Catholic Church. From this point on, the Merovingian line became more and more diffused, ruling over a group of tiny, warring countries. The conflict between these groups culminated in the murder of **Dagobert II**, the last effective Merovingian king. Within a few generations the kingship passed to the Carolingian line, most famously in the reign of Charlemagne. Leaving no connection unturned, the infamous *Dossiers Secrets* supposedly claim that Dagobert's child survived and carried the Merovingian bloodline into the present-day family of . . . **Pierre Plantard**.

Miriam Another name for **Mary Magdalene**.

Mithras Teabing mentions Mithras as a "pre-Christian god" whose attendant mythology closely resembles church legends about Christ. Mithras was a popular deity in ancient Rome, flourishing especially during the second through the fourth centuries A.D. Mithras was derived from an older, Middle Eastern god named Mitra or Mithra who was worshipped across Persia and India. Originally Mithra was a minor deity who served the Zoroastrian god Ahura-Mazda.

Mithras was identified with the light of the sun, and was often worshipped along with or as Sol Invictus, the conquering sun, another popular
Roman god. Devotion to Mithras was especially widespread among Roman
troops and garrisons, where their prolonged stays outside of their home territory exposed them to new ideas and new deities. Mithras was one of the
most successful "imported" gods.

The origins of many traditions about Christ and Christian worship practices may be related to the worship of Mithras. The celebration of the winter
solstice, the nativity of the sun, which occurred on December 25, was central
to Mithras's worship. In many societies Mithras was reported to be born
to a virgin, and was, in some traditions, a member of a holy trinity. Ritual
baptism and a last supper legend permeate Mithraic worship. Some scholars
believed that the burgeoning Christian faith appropriated the practices
and beliefs of Mithraism, allowing the new religion to subsume
the old.

Mitterrand, François Reluctantly riding to the **Louvre** with Lieutenant
Collet, Langdon reflects on François Mitterrand, former president of
France. He notes that Mitterrand's affinity for Egyptian culture earned him
the nickname "the Sphinx." Later, inside **La Pyramide**, he debates whether or
not to tell Captain Fache that Mitterrand commanded that 666 panes of
glass be used in the structure (a claim unsupported by the facts; see Chapter
11)—a claim that cannot be true, since the pyramid is constructed of 698
panes of glass.

Born in 1916, Mitterrand was a powerful figure in twentieth-century
French politics. An infantryman in World War II, he was wounded and captured by the Germans. After escaping, he returned to France and joined the
French Resistance. After the liberation, Mitterrand was appointed the youn-
gest minister in the new government of the French Republic. He gradually
relinquished his conservative leanings and became the first socialist president
of France on his third run in 1981.

One of Mitterrand's "Grand Projects"—a series of renovations focused
on restoring and rejuvenating France's cultural and civic monuments—was
the completion of the grand **Louvre**.

Mitterrand's nickname "the Sphinx" seems to have been derived from his
enigmatic and elusive character as a politician, not from his love of Egyptian
art. His main nickname was "the Fox," or "the Florentine," for his masterful—
some would say Machiavellian—manipulation of his opponents. The ubiquitous **Pierre Plantard** planted stories that he was also a member of the **Priory
of Sion**.

Mona Lisa The *Mona Lisa*, perhaps Leonardo's most beloved masterpiece (he
carried it with him for years) is considered by many to be the world's most
famous painting. In *The Da Vinci Code*, Jacques Saunière leaves an anagram

scrawled across the painting's Plexiglas cover. While Sophie and Langdon approach the painting to read the message, Langdon ruminates on a lecture he once gave to a group of convicts about the mystery and popularity of the painting.

Many prominent scholars agree that the painting is of a young Florentine woman, one Lisa Gherardini del Giocondo, a wife of a Florentine merchant. It is from the name Giocondo (which has the felicitous meaning of "happy") that the painting receives the name *La Joconde* or *La Gioconda*. Near the end of da Vinci's life the painting was sold or given to King Francis I of France, da Vinci's patron, and it remained in the possession of the French royal family, who placed it in the Louvre.

Langdon seems to diminish the artistic mastery of the painting, crediting its fame with the secret it supposedly carries behind its smile. Many scholars and art historians have speculated on the nature of this smile and the secret it hides. Some maintain that the secret is the sitter's identity: the painting is a well-disguised self-portrait in drag, a possibility that Langdon mentions in his lecture. Others suggest that Mona Lisa is a Medici princess, a Spanish duchess, and several other women of historical note. Scholars tend to dismiss Langdon's claim that *Mona Lisa* is an anagram of the names of the Egyptian fertility god **Amon** and the Egyptian goddess **Isis**. It may be that the secret of *Mona Lisa* is her secrecy. Perhaps she owes her enduring popularity to the fact that she does have a secret, and we will never know what it is; and not knowing is far more intriguing than knowing will ever be.

The *Mona Lisa* was stolen in 1911 as part of an art-reproduction plot by a remarkable Argentine con man named Eduardo de Valfierno. Once the painting went missing, a talented art restorer named Yves Chaudron would produce as many copies as possible; Valfierno would sell the copies to eager art collectors, and then return the original to the Louvre. Paris went into a frenzy on news of *La Joconde*'s disappearance; numerous suspects were rounded up, including most of the Louvre's staff and a confused Pablo Picasso, who came under suspicion because he had purchased two stolen sculptures from a friend who had stolen them from the Louvre.

The scheme worked for a while, and copies were sold; but one of the workmen that Valfierno enlisted to help steal the original tried to sell it to a Parisian art dealer. The dealer turned him in to the authorities. The *Mona Lisa* was discovered in the false bottom of a wooden trunk in the workman's apartment, not far from the Louvre. Valfierno, who had not revealed his identity to his henchmen, pocketed the money from his illicit sales, and lived out the rest of his life in satisfied opulence, giving the *Mona Lisa*, perhaps, a new reason to smile.

Montanus A second-century convert to Christianity who, around the year 156, told his followers he was a prophet and the sole bearer of divine revelations. Montanus prophesied the second coming of Christ, and imposed a very severe form of asceticism and penitential discipline. Montanus had many followers, and as his popularity spread, opposition grew ever more strident. Some people considered Montanism to be caused by a demon, and attempted to exorcise it. Eventually, Montanus and his followers split from the church.

Mozart, Wolfgang Amadeus A renowned late-eighteenth-century composer, Mozart (1756–91) was an avid Freemason, and Masonic elements appear in many of his works, one of which is forthrightly titled *Masonic Funeral Music*. Mozart is also reputed to have been associated with the **Priory of Sion**, in part for works such as *The Magic Flute*. While enjoying the music, many may not recognize that the words carry themes of Christian symbology reflecting the struggle between darkness and light, good and evil, and incorporating Egyptian and hermetic elements as well.

Nag Hammadi Library The name of the town where, in 1947, some of the most important texts relating to early Christianity were found (see **Gnostic Gospels**, as well as Chapters 1 through 5). The texts were bound as pages (as contrasted to early written works on scrolls; e.g. the **Dead Sea Scrolls**) and had covers of leather—the first known use of that material for books. While these **codices** do much to enrich understanding of that period, some scholars estimate that of all the texts from the early Christian tradition that are known to have existed, only 15 percent have been recovered. Many more interpretations of Mary's story may be awaiting discovery—and another potential bestseller.

Newton, Sir Isaac The sheer number of titles that Newton (1642–1727) can rightfully claim—mathematician, physicist, philosopher, natural scientist, theologian, political philosopher, to name a few—would make him a leading figure in the intellectual life of any era. But the revolution he staged in physics and mathematics establishes his preeminence among history's greatest thinkers.

Newton's achievement is often understood as the triumph of the Enlightenment values of reason and science over the still dominant, "superstitious" medieval conception of physical science. Despite this identification with the intelligible, scientific values of the Enlightenment, Newton was heavily steeped in esoteric learning and the occult. Before his breakthroughs in physics in the mid-1660s, Newton was a scientist of his time— an alchemist who spent years trying to unlock the divine secrets of the natural world through experimental chemistry, a discipline that at the time was not differentiated from magic. Not surprisingly, he conducted his studies in secret.

Newton has been identified as one of the grand masters of the **Priory of**

Sion in *The Da Vinci Code*, probably based on the controversial *Dossiers Secrets*. Although this assertion cannot be confirmed, Newton was known to associate with leading Masonic figures and his beliefs share many similarities with Masonic doctrine.

Although technically a heretic who denied the holy, he was granted a special exemption by King Charles II which allowed him to pursue his studies without having to have direct involvement in the Anglican Church. He did try to unlock what he saw as the hidden secrets of the Bible, and also attempted a reconstruction of the floor plan of the **Temple of Solomon**, which he regarded as a cryptogrammatic symbol for the universe itself. Intriguingly, one scholar has uncovered what he believes are various Christian and heretical symbols hidden in the diagrams of *The Principia*—Newton's crowning work in the physical sciences.

Nicene Creed The brief statement of faith, created during the **Council of Nicea**, that summarized the orthodox beliefs that made up the backbone of the church's teachings. The creed explicitly rejects Arianism (see **Arius**):

> And in one Lord Jesus Christ, the only begotten Son of God, and born of the Father before all ages. (God of God) light of light, true God of true God. Begotten not made, consubstantial to the Father, by whom all things were made.

The Nicene Creed is still spoken in Christian worship services.

Olympics The Olympics started out in 776 B.C. as a religious festival honoring the chief Greek deity Zeus. Originally staged in Olympia, near Zeus's sanctuary, the games had clearly **pagan** origins. The original Olympics were designed to be a unifying event among Greece's otherwise fractious city-states. Although the early Olympics had only one event, much time was taken up with a religious festival that included sacrifices to various and sundry deities major and minor. This pattern persisted for twelve centuries, until A.D. 393 when the Holy Roman emperor Theodosius declared "Games over." The modern Olympic games were revived in 1896 at the urging of Frenchman Baron Pierre de Coubertin. It was de Coubertin who, in 1913, designed the five interlocking rings that are the symbol of the modern Olympics. De Coubertin said the rings stood for the five participating continents, and the colors were those of the flags of every nation of the world. There are those who see in the Olympic symbolism a subtle homage to the polytheistic pre-Christian era.

O'Keefe, Georgia When Teabing explains to Sophie and Langdon that the **rose** has long been considered the "premier symbol of female sexuality," he suggests the best example for understanding how the "blossoming flower resembles the female genitalia" is to look at the work of Georgia O'Keefe, who has long been associated with this theme. O'Keefe herself, however, long denied there was symbolism in her work, and that the sexual and often erotic associations with her work were, in effect, in the eyes of the beholder.

Opus Dei To sharpen his plot, Dan Brown conveyed what are arguably the extremes of the differing paths of religious belief since the life of Jesus. On one side, represented by Sophie's grandfather and the mysteries the protagonists are trying to unlock, is the "radical" branch of the **Gnostic** tradition that believes in the marriage between Jesus and Mary and acknowledges humankind's long legacy of **paganism**. On the other is Catholic orthodoxy, represented by what many consider to be the most conservative voice, Opus Dei. Both sides seek the evidence of the **Grail**, albeit for opposite reasons.

The objective of Opus Dei, in its own words, is "to contribute to that evangelizing mission of the Church. Opus Dei encourages Christians of all social classes to live consistently with their faith, in the middle of the ordinary circumstances of their lives, especially through the sanctification of their work." Founded in 1928 by Josemaría Escrivá de Balaguer, Opus Dei was dedicated to the notion that holiness was achievable for lay Catholics. This holiness involved a sanctification and perfection of the "normal" life of the layperson where every action is sacrificed joyously to God. Opus Dei members are required to follow the strictures and teachings of Catholicism rigorously.

Opus Dei won a powerful ally in pope John Paul II, who made the organization a personal prelature: its members are under the authority of a prelate, who reports in turn to the Congregation of Bishops, entirely independent of geographical location or dioceses. Additionally, the pope canonized Father Escrivá in 2002. The attention paid to this organization was not merely related to the conservative roots that John Paul and St. Josemaría shared, but also to the growing popularity and power of the group. It is estimate that Opus Dei boasts has between 80,000 and 90,000 members worldwide, with estimates for the United States ranging from 3,000 to 50,000.

Controversy has dogged the group, mostly related to the practice of corporal mortification and what some critics consider the cultlike control the group is alleged to assert over its membership. There are two types of Opus Dei members: supernumerary and numerary. Supernumerary members make up about 70 percent of the membership; they concentrate on the sanctification of their work and family duties. Numeraries, on the other hand, often live within Opus Dei centers, isolated from members of the opposite sex. They pledge celibacy and hand over their income to the group. They also practice corporal mortification, ritualized self-punishment meant to purge one of sins and the urges that lead to them, using hairshirts (**cilices**), or disciplines.

Opus Dei has fought back against what it considers unfounded characterizations of its belief system and, in that connection, has provided Web links to articles critical of Dan Brown's interpretation of the Bible in general, and the organization in particular.

Opus Dei Awareness Network (ODAN) The anti-**Opus Dei** group which, as *The Da Vinci Code* mentions, attempts to warn the general public about the "frightening" activities of Opus Dei. It, too, has its own website.

Paganism In its most general application, paganism is a set of religious beliefs that recognize a polytheistic (multigod) ethos. Paganism predates Christianity, and is considered to be intertwined with it, at least in its early history. Indeed, much of the history of Christianity has been a struggle to establish itself against the forces of paganism. In *The Da Vinci Code*, Sophie's falling away from her grandfather began with her witnessing as a young woman his participation in a pagan ceremony. Not understanding what she was seeing—a replication of the pagan rite of *hieros gamos*—she was shocked at her grandfather's engaging in sex before a group. Langdon later explains to her that sexual intercourse was considered to be the act through which male and female experienced God. The physical union with the female remained the sole means through which man could become spiritually complete and ultimately achieve **gnosis**. Since the days of **Isis**, sex rites had been considered man's only bridge from earth to heaven.

Pentagram The pentagram first appears in *The Da Vinci Code* as a bloody symbol scrawled by Jacques Saunière on his stomach shortly before his demise. Langdon, brought to the scene of the crime, explains its significance as a symbol of Venus, the goddess of love and human sexuality, as well as its continuing association with nature worship.

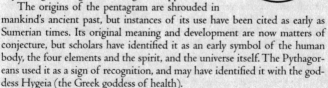

The pentagram is one of the oldest symbols known to man. Its most recognizable form is a five-pointed star, possessing equilateral arms and equal angles at all of its points. When inscribed within a circle it is referred to as a pentacle. The pentacle was commonly known as a Venus or Ishtar pentacle, depending on the goddess being worshipped.

The origins of the pentagram are shrouded in mankind's ancient past, but instances of its use have been cited as early as Sumerian times. Its original meaning and development are now matters of conjecture, but scholars have identified it as an early symbol of the human body, the four elements and the spirit, and the universe itself. The Pythagoreans used it as a sign of recognition, and may have identified it with the goddess Hygeia (the Greek goddess of health).

The pentagram as symbol is still in use today. Wiccans and other esoteric organizations employ it as a symbol in worship and ritual. It appears in the decorations and rankings of military organizations, as a symbol of the five pillars of Islam, and, most infamously, as a symbol for the worship of the devil and other demonic forces—a use, as Langdon notes, that is historically inaccurate.

Peter the Apostle (St. Peter) St. Peter's name was Simon when he initially met Jesus, who renamed him Cephas ("rock"); the Latinized version of this name is Peter. In the New Testament gospels Jesus seems to have had a special preference for Peter, who appears at certain key episodes in Jesus' story. Famously, the New Testament has Jesus turning to Peter saying, "Upon this rock I will build my Church."

Peter is mentioned in *The Da Vinci Code* during Teabing's long-ranging lecture on the nature of the **Holy Grail**. He quotes a passage from the *Gospel of Mary*, where Peter expresses disbelief that Jesus spoke to **Mary Magdalene** without the knowledge of the other **apostles**. "Did the savior really speak with a woman without our knowledge ... did he prefer her to us?" he asks. Teabing goes on to say that Peter was jealous of Mary because Christ actually entrusted the continuance of the church to her, and not to him. While, according to the *Gospel of Mary*, Peter may indeed be upset that Jesus spoke to Mary privately, there is no indication from this text that Jesus' message to Mary had anything to do with the founding of the church.

Phi Phi (pronounced "fye") is the never-ending, never-repeating number 1.6180339087. It is better known to nonmathematicians as the Golden Ratio, the Golden Section and, in Brown's terminology, the Divine Proportion. It appears in *The Da Vinci Code* as the centerpiece of a lecture that Robert Langdon recalls as he runs down a set of stairs to flee the **Louvre** with Sophie Neveu. (Not coincidentally, "phi" also forms the center of Sophie's name.)

Langdon explains to his students that it represents a "fundamental building block of nature," present in everything from honeybee populations to nautilus shell spirals, from sunflower seed heads to the human body (e.g., in the ratio of a body's total height to the height of the belly button from the floor). And, in an echo of this natural beauty and proportion, Phi has been used widely in art (Dali's *Last Supper*), architecture (the Parthenon), and music (Mozart, Bartok).

While this general description reflects reality, there are a few nits to pick. Dan Brown puts the term in all capitals in the book: PHI. In practice, mathematicians use "Phi" to mean the Divine Proportion and "phi" to mean its reciprocal. Symbologists—such as Langdon—would write the pairing as Ø and ø. Langdon also says that "the number PHI was derived from the **Fibonacci sequence**" but the historical record indicates the number was known long before Fibonacci derived it from his famous sequence.

The first clear definition of what was much later to be called the Golden Ratio was "given around 300 B.C. by the founder of geometry as a formalized deductive system, Euclid of Alexandria," according to the scientist Mario Livio. The Greeks labeled the ratio with the letter *tau*. The names

"Golden Section" or "Golden Mean" were likely not to have been used until the nineteenth century. The word *Phi* did not appear until it was quoted by the American mathematician Mark Barr at the beginning of the twentieth century as a tribute to the Greek sculptor Phidias, whose achievements included the Parthenon and the *Zeus* in the temple of Olympia.

The Golden Ratio is said to be a technique used by **Leonardo** in some of his most famous works. Not all experts are persuaded. The mathematical model for the Divine Section was not known in Italy until it was published by Pacioli in the last decade of the fifteenth century, after Leonardo painted or drew many of his most important works.

Philip the Fair, King (also known as Philipe IV) Philipe IV, King of France (nicknamed "the Fair" because of his striking good looks) is mentioned in Langdon's brief summary of the Templar persecution while he and Sophie drive through the **Bois de Boulogne**. Langdon claims that **Pope Clement V** devised a plan to bring down the **Templars** because they had amassed so much power and wealth. Philip the Fair (Langdon calls him King Philipe IV) acted in concert with the pope, and on the appointed day of Friday the thirteenth, October 1307 the Templars were arrested en masse and subjected to a trial infamous for its sensational charges of heresy and blasphemy, torture, and execution.

Langdon seems to have some of the details wrong. Philip the Fair, and not Clement V, is generally seen as the prime mover behind the arrest of the Templars. Philip initiated the persecution; in fact, many historians believe, his initial Friday the thirteenth arrest was executed without Clement's knowledge. Clement strongly rebuked Philip, but was politically weak and, some say, too beholden to Philip to have countered this move against the Templars.

Plantard, Pierre While Pierre Plantard is not mentioned in *The Da Vinci Code*, he is essential to the mythology that pervades it.

Pierre Plantard (1920–2000) was a real person, a citizen of France and the self-proclaimed grand master of the **Priory of Sion**, having been elected in 1981. He came to widespread public attention when he became one of the focal points of the investigations of Michael Baigent, Richard Leigh, and Henry Lincoln in their bestselling book, *Holy Blood, Holy Grail*. Their book inspired Dan Brown and Plantard's place in the *Holy Blood, Holy Grail* investigations would be analogous to Jacques Saunière—last grand master of the Priory of Sion and a descendent of Merovingian kings.

It is often hard in the case of Plantard to find the line between what is known and what is good story. The *Dossiers Secrets* supposedly deposited in the Bibliothèque Nationale in Paris purportedly claim that Pierre Plantard is a descendent of Jean de Plantard, who was himself a lineal descendent of **Merovingian** kings.

Baigent, Lincoln, and Leigh declared that in the course of their investigations into the legend of the **Holy Grail** that "all trails seemed to lead ultimately to [Plantard]." He appears to have been the chief source of information for many stories surrounding **Rennes-le-Château**, and provided investigators with many snippets of enigmatic information concerning the Priory of Sion—usually raising more questions than he answered. A representative example is that when interviewed about the Priory by the French magazine *Le Charivari*, Plantard said merely that "the society to which I am attached is extremely ancient. I merely succeed others, a point in a sequence. We are guardians of certain things. And without publicity." He is described in *Holy Blood, Holy Grail* as "a dignified, courteous man of discreetly aristocratic bearing, unostentatious in appearance, with a gracious, volatile but well spoken manner." He disassociated himself publicly from the conclusions drawn by Baigent, Lincoln, and Leigh, yet offered to correct the French edition of the book. He remained equivocal, however, on the descent of the Merovingians from Jesus' bloodline.

There also seems to be a dark side to the Plantard story. Plantard has been accused of being a Nazi sympathizer and an anti-Semite, associated with several right-wing publications and organizations before and during World War II. He may have been imprisoned for embezzlement and fraud in the 1950s; he may have fed the **Bérenger Saunière** story to the author who popularized the Rennes-le-Château mysteries as part of a financial arrangement. His claims of Merovingian descent have been discredited; many of the documents he used to prove the bloodline were created by him or his associates and deposited pseudonymously in the Bibliothèque Nationale.

It seems that for every assertion put forward by Plantard and the Priory, there are immediate counter assertions; and those, in turn, are undermined by further accusations. Codes within codes, stories within stories. The twists and turns of the myth of Pierre Plantard are an appropriate foundation for *The Da Vinci Code*.

Pope, Alexander Sophie and Langdon's trail of clues includes a poem, penned by Sophie's grandfather, one line of which says, "In London lies a knight a Pope interred".

At **King's College** they come to realize that "a Pope" was not a Catholic Pope, but rather famed eighteenth-century poet Alexander Pope (1688–1744), and that the knight was **Sir Isaac Newton,** whose funeral, Brown says "was presided over" by the poet, who "gave a stirring eulogy before sprinkling dirt on the tomb." It is true that Pope admired and knew Newton, but while he was undoubtedly at the funeral, there is no record that he presided—Newton was such a prominent figure that the pallbearers included a lord, two dukes, and three earls. The bishop of Rochester read the service.

There is no question whatever that Pope wrote Newton's epitaph about four years later when a monument was erected to the scientist. One of the most famous epitaphs in history, partly in Latin, partly in English, these lines read:

> Nature and nature's laws lay hid in night;
> God said Let Newton be! and all was light.

Poussin, Nicholas Considered by many to be the greatest French painter of the seventeenth century, Poussin achieved his notoriety in Rome, painting romantic and poetic works out of classical mythology. Poussin is remembered by Sophie as her grandfather's second favorite painter after Leonardo, and plays an interesting role in some of the source material Dan Brown uses for *The Da Vinci Code*. In the book, Poussin is the subject of several textbooks written by Jacques Saunière. These textbooks, it seems, are some of Langdon's favorites, dealing specifically with hidden codes in the works of both Poussin and Dutch painter **David Teniers**.

One of Poussin's paintings, *Les Bergers d'Arcadie (The Shepherds of Arcadia)*, executed in 1638, features a group of shepherds standing before a tomb. The Tomb has on it the Latin phrase *Et in Arcadia Ego*, or in English, "And in Arcadia I." The phrase has often been interpreted as a romantic allusion to the presence of death even in the idyllic realm of the shepherds; however, there is a connection between the painting and the **Rennes-le-Château** mystery. One of the parchments supposedly recovered by **Bérenger Saunière** from the parish church of Rennes-le-Château contained a coded message that read:

> SHEPHERDESS NO TEMPTATION THAT POUSSIN TENIERS
> HOLD THE KEY; PEACE 681 BY THE CROSS AND THIS HORSE
> OF GOD I COMPLETE [DESTROY] THIS DAEMON OF THE
> GUARDIAN AT NOON BLUE APPLES

There seems to be a reference to *Les Bergers d'Arcadie* in the message. Several authors on the Rennes-le-Château mystery have claimed that a tomb in the vicinity of the hamlet resembles the tomb in the painting. Was Poussin connected to a hidden secret in Rennes-le-Château? Baigent, Leigh, and Lincoln, in *Holy Blood, Holy Grail* mention a letter sent from Abbé Louis Fouquet to his brother, the superintendent of finances to Louis XIV. The letter describes a visit Fouquet had with Poussin in Rome:

> He and I discussed certain things, which I shall with ease be able to explain to you in detail—things which will give you, through Monsieur Poussin, advantages which even kings would have great pains to draw from him, and which, according to him, it is possible that nobody else will ever rediscover in the centuries to come

Shortly after receiving this otherwise unexplained letter, Nicolas Fouquet was arrested and imprisoned for the rest of his life.

Priory of Sion Dan Brown announces, on page 1 of *The Da Vinci Code*, that the Priory of Sion is a real organization, founded in 1099, and that parchments in the Bibliothèque Nationale reveal in their membership a list of the leading lights of literature, art, and science. The Priory is certainly a real organization, but what more can be said of it with certainty is open to question. The Priory can claim a documented existence in France beginning in 1956 (nothing existed before then), when the Priory registered and submitted statutes for the organization of the group with the government. Its spokesperson for most of its modern history was **Pierre Plantard**, a man whose claims about himself were as confusing as the claims the Priory made about itself. Indeed, it often seems unclear how much real difference there was between Plantard and the Priory of Sion.

The Priory, through what is said to be contained in the *Dossiers Secrets* and the public statements of Plantard and his associates provides a sketchy history at best. It is claimed the secret organization was founded in the last decade of the eleventh century by **Godefroi de Bouillon**. In seems generally accepted that the Priory ordered the formation of the **Knights Templar**, and then split with them almost a hundred years later, beginning their own line of autonomous grand masters. Around this time, the Priory began to also name itself "le Ordre de la Rose-Croix Veritas"–The Order of the True Rosy Cross, thereby connecting itself to the **Rosicrucians**. The group says that **Bérenger Saunière** discovered the parchments that sparked the **Rennes-le-Château** controversy on direct orders from Sion. And they list a series of grand masters from the 1188 split with the Templars to Thomas Plantard, Pierre's son.

Onto this bare sketch, presented in poetic, allusive language and quasi-historical formats, hundreds of authors have projected their speculations and theories regarding the Priory and its place in history. They are too numerous to list in their entirety, but *The Da Vinci Code* is based on one of the more famous and persistent notions, exhaustively described in *Holy Blood, Holy Grail*—that the Priory is the age-old guardian of the bloodline of Christ and **Mary Magdalene**. Other theories hold that the Priory is a front for several other esoteric organizations; others still claim that the group advocates a theocratic "United States of Europe."

Every accusation about the real origin or nature of the group, from the mundane to the vicious, has been defended by counter-assertions from the Priory and its defenders. It would seem that the Priory exists in what one commentator calls "a hermeneutical hell"—a nether land of conflicting interpretations, hypotheses, and evidence that seems, by its very scope and inclusiveness, to undermine the possibility of discovering any truth at all. Perhaps that is where the continuing appeal of the Priory lies; its very nature, as far as we know, is so indeterminate that it allows anyone to bring their hopes, fears, and fantasies to bear on its interpretation.

"Q" Document "The Q document," Teabing tells Sophie and Langdon in the instructional he gives them on the secret history of Christianity and its cover-up while they are all gathered in his library, is "a manuscript that even the Vatican admits they believe exists. Allegedly, it is a book of Jesus' teachings, possibly written in his own hand." Moving beyond his just-spoken caution, he puts a rhetorical question to Sophie, "Why wouldn't Jesus have kept a chronicle of his ministry?"

Whether he did so or not has preoccupied scholars since an Englishman, Herbert Marsh, first hypothesized a Q-like source in 1801, based upon the belief that someone wrote an Aramaic version of the sayings of Jesus. He labeled it *beth*, a Hebrew letter fashioned after the shape of a house. Several German scholars took up the cause later in the century, generating great controversy: since the Gospels of Matthew and Luke show some independence of each other, could there be a different source other than the synoptic Gospels for the sayings of Jesus? If so, which was the "right" one? As some doubt arose about the authenticity of the collection of sayings, the German scholar Johannes Weiss devised the more neutral *Q*, after the German word *quelle*, meaning "source." There things stood, with scholars adding layer after layer of reconstructions until the 1960s, when translations of the **Nag Hammadi** documents in 1947 revealed a *Gospel of Thomas*, which was translated by James Robinson and Thomas Lambdin.

Does the *Gospel of Thomas* really reveal itself as the direct source of Jesus' sayings? The answer lies in part on determining the dating of the documents, an unsettled issue. If it comes from the mid-first century, the link can seem persuasive. If, as the more conservative scholarship has it, the *Gospel of Thomas* was written after the first century, then there is a greater chance it was composed by accumulated memories (i.e., a less direct history).

Professor Robinson, the "godfather" of this debate answers the question this way: "The reference to Q, and as to whether Jesus himself wrote it? Of course Jesus didn't write it. That is another one of those places where Dan Brown sort of fudges the evidence to make it more sensational than it is." The debate will continue, with the hope that more texts from the early Christian era can be found to clarify this and many other controversies.

La Pyramide La Pyramide is the glass pyramid designed by I. M. Pei as the new entrance to the **Louvre**. It is one of the first things seen by Robert Langdon as he is summoned to the murder scene. La Pyramide also has an inverted counterpart, Pyramide Inverse, extending *into* the earth as the original stands above it; this is the pyramid which figures prominently at the end of Brown's book.

La Pyramide is the signature of the Louvre's makeover and emblematic of the wide-ranging architectural changes in the building instigated by Chinese-born architect I. M. Pei. La Pyramide centered all the entrances in one location, leading to a new underground concourse that provides access to the galleries as well as restaurants, shop spaces, and vital new storage and support areas for the museum itself. Pei's structure, while now generally accepted and even admired by Parisians, was met by uproarious public debate and outright attacks in the Parisian press when the plans were announced.

La Pyramide is constructed out of 698 panes of tempered, very light, transparent glass—not 666, the so-called "Satan's number" as claimed by Brown/Langdon and many conspiracy buffs. The lightweight panels, connected by equally lightweight steel supports, combine to create an extremely powerful form—a squat pyramid that only stands seventy-one feet high and is at once lofty yet powerful. The glass reflects the Parisian skies, a mood-stone for France's capital.

Rennes-le-Château Few places on earth, from Stonehenge to the Bermuda Triangle, have been the focus of as many conspiracy theories as Rennes-le-Château, a small French village situated on a mountaintop on the eastern edge of the Pyrenees. While it makes no appearance in *The Da Vinci Code*, it is at the center of the conspiracy that concerns the book.

Rennes-le-Château, like most of Europe's villages and cities, has a deeply layered and complex history, passing from prehistoric camp to Roman settlement to medieval stronghold. By the eve of the French revolution, the village had, through a complex series of intermarriages, fallen into the hands of the Blanchefort family. It is rumored that Marie, Marquise d'Hautpol de Blanchefort, a titular descendent, at least, of the **Templar** grand master of the same name, passed a secret to her parish priest upon her death. This priest, an Abbé Bigou, whom the revolution forced into exile in Spain shortly after her demise, was the clerical predecessor of the most intriguing resident of Rennes-le-Château: **Bérenger Saunière**.

Rose The rose is rich in symbolism and *The Da Vinci Code* explores quite a bit of it. The cryptex in the rosewood box Sophie holds as she and Langdon escape the Swiss bank in an armored truck has a rose on the lid, which she associates with great secrets, and which Langdon immediately links to the Latin phrase *sub rosa* (literally "under the rose"), meaning whatever is said has to be kept confidential. The rose has also been the symbol used by the **Priory of Sion** as a symbol for the **Grail**. One species has five petals, associating it with pentagonal symmetry, the movement of Venus in the sky, and the **sacred feminine**. Then there is its use as a compass rose, meant to point one to the "True Direction."

As he explains all this, Langdon has an epiphany, grasping that the Grail is likely to be hidden sub rosa, that is, underneath the sign of the rose in some church with its rose windows, rosette reliefs, and *cinquefoils*, the "five-petaled decorative flowers often found at the top of archways, directly over the keystone."

Later in the book, Teabing ties the rose closely to womanhood, the five petals representing "the five stages of female life—birth, menstruation, motherhood, menopause, and death." He also tells Langdon and Sophie that the word *rose* is identical in English, French, German, and other languages and that the anagram of the word is Eros, the Greek god of sexual love.

Many other meanings have been given to the rose—an emblem of Christ, a symbol of the nativity, and the messianic prophecy. In Greco-Roman culture, the rose represented beauty, spring, and love. The rose also referenced the speedy passage of time, and thus the approach of death and the next world. The Roman feast of Rosalia was a feast of the dead. Gothic cathedrals feature rose stained-glass windows, with Christ at the center of each, at the three entrances of these churches. The rose in this context is said to symbolize the salvation that lies within, and which has been revealed by God. Later Christian art, from the thirteenth century forward, often portrays Mary holding a rose, or in a rose garden, or in front of a tapestry of roses. The rose symbolically represents the union of Christ and his church and God and His people.

Finally, the rose is the same color as the **apple**, which ties it right back into the plot of *The Da Vinci Code*. In the last line of the poem penned by Sophie's grandfather that leads to Newton's tomb, we find the words

You seek that orb that ought to be on his tomb.
It speaks of Rosy flesh and seeded womb.

Langdon finds this last sentence a clear allusion to **Mary Magdalene**, "the Rose who bore the seed of Jesus."

Rosicrucians The Rosicrucian doctrine was first expounded in *The Universal and General Reformation of the Whole Wide World*, published in 1614. It claimed that Christian Rosenkreuz, a German noble, journeyed as a youth to the East, gathering knowledge and becoming an adept of secret wisdoms. These wisdoms amounted to an ecumenical approach that advocated simple, moral living and the common worship of a supreme being or god. Alchemical metaphors were deployed to symbolize the magical transformation of the human soul.

Some scholars believe that Rosenkreuz was merely an invention of the German theologian Johann Valentin Andreae, claimed by the **Priory of Sion** as grand master from 1637 to 1654. Many claim that Andreae wrote one of the Rosenkreuz books, *The Chemical Wedding of Christian Rosenkreuz*, as a satire of occult obsessions of the era. Fictional progenitor or not, the Rosicrucians still thrive today as an esoteric society based on the Rosenkreuz writings. Rosicrucianism became popular within Freemasonry in the eighteenth century, when it incorporated many Rosicrucian symbols, the foremost of which were the **rose** and the **cross**. (The most prominent use of the rose and cross symbol before that was probably as it appeared on Martin Luther's coat of arms.) The order continues to exist, albeit in a great variety of forms.

Rosslyn Chapel Heading toward the final scenes of *The Da Vinci Code*, Saunière's second cryptex leads Robert Langdon and Sophie Neveu to the Rosslyn Chapel outside Edinburgh, Scotland. Various occult and New Age commentators have, for years, believed that the **Holy Grail** resides at Rosslyn, having been taken there after the massacre of the **Templars** in France in the 1300s. Scottish Masonic groups have been seen as some of the heirs to the Templar tradition.

Work on the Rosslyn Chapel—also known as the Cathedral of Codes— began in 1446 at the behest of Sir William St. Clair, or Sinclair, a hereditary grand master of the Scottish Masons, and a reputed descendent of the **Merovingian** bloodline. Sir William exercised personal control of the chapel's construction, which halted shortly after his death in 1484. Only the choir—the part of the church occupied by the choir and the clergy, where services are performed—is completed. The chapel is filled with codes, symbols, alphabets, and imagery that suggest a sort of universal symbolic language. Christian and Jewish symbols coexist, as do Greek, Latin, Hebrew, and other languages, and references to Norse, Celtic, and Templar history. At the end of their visit to Rosslyn, Robert and Sophie seem to learn that the Holy Grail, if it ever was at Rosslyn, has been moved.

Sacred feminine The sacred feminine is an important thematic element of *The Da Vinci Code*, providing the linchpin for the various **Grail** seekers in the novel. Saunière's **Priory** worships it, Langdon studies it, and the fanatical followers of **Opus Dei** are trying to make sure that the sacred feminine tradition in Christianity stays suppressed, as it was by the early Roman church leaders, from Peter to Constantine. According to the novel, Jesus was a believer in the notion of the sacred feminine, as inherited from Egyptian, Greek, and other eastern Mediterranean traditions. The whole battle over **Mary Magdalene**'s role among the **apostles** and in church history afterward, is viewed in the novel as part of the "great cover-up" of Christianity's origins in the world of gods *and* goddesses.

The first mention of the sacred feminine in *The Da Vinci Code* is when Robert Langdon arrives at the scene of Jacques Saunière's murder. Interrogated by Captain Fache, Langdon tries to explain the iconography that Saunière used to "decorate" his death scene.

Sangreal/Sangraal Sangreal is the name identified by Langdon as the common historical name for the documents and relics that constitute what we today know as the **Holy Grail**. Teabing later explains that the word became split throughout its use in legend and theology, producing San Greal: Holy Grail. But if the division were made in a different place—sang real—then the words would read *royal blood* instead. *Holy Blood, Holy Grail* authors Baigent, Leigh, and Lincoln claim that the Grail is called the Sangreal or the Sangraal. The split in these words could also produce San Greal or San Graal (Holy

Grail) or sang real or sang raal (royal blood). However, Sir Thomas Malory, author of *Le Mort d'Arthur* and the first cited user of the word in English, deploys Sangreal and sang royal (which is derived from middle English real or rial) in two separate senses: Sangreal as the Holy Grail, and sang royal as holy blood, perhaps undermining Teabing and Langdon's etymology.

The *Oxford English Dictionary* claims that the etymology of dual meanings, first introduced in the seventeenth century, is spurious.

Saunière, Bérenger Parish priest of **Rennes-le-Château** installed there in 1885, and the historical touchstone for *The Da Vinci Code*'s Jacques Saunière. During a routine restoration of the village church, Saunière (1852–1917) supposedly discovered four parchments with coded messages stuffed into a column supporting the church altar. The messages, when deciphered, made oblique references to seemingly unconnected people and things: painters **Poussin** and **Teniers**, the **Merovingian** King **Dagobert**, **Sion**, "blue **apples**." Intrigued, he presented the documents to his superiors, who instructed him to travel to Paris to present the parchments to other church dignitaries, including the Abbé Bieil, director of the **Saint-Sulpice** seminary.

Little is known about what happened during Saunière's visit to Paris (many dispute he ever went at all), but upon his return to Rennes-le-Château, it is said he began spending exorbitant amounts of money on restoration projects and large new house for himself. His changes ranged from the mundane to the bizarre. He effaced the inscription on the tombstone of Marie, Marquise d'Hautpol de Blanchefort's (it had been designed by the Abbé Bigou for her grave, and the inscription was a perfect anagram of one of the coded messages that Saunière found in the altar). He constructed a tower, called the Tour Magdala, after **Mary Magdalene.** He built an opulent country house, the Villa Bethania, which he never occupied. He renovated and redecorated the church as well, but his new artistic touches were somewhat unorthodox: a statue of a demon upholds the holy water basin; "This place is terrible" is chiseled over the church door; and the Stations of the Cross painted on the walls of the church are filled with incongruous and disquieting details.

Rennes-le-Château was a provincial town, and Saunière's salary as parish priest was quite modest. Where did Saunière get the money for his renovations and construction? Why did he spend it in the way he did? He took the answers to these questions with him to the grave, and at that point, even wilder speculation begins.

Saunière's wealth, so the tale goes, could have been attributed to the discovery of ancient Visigothic treasure; to payoffs from a secret society with something to hide in the area; to the secret location of the **Holy Grail**; to the famed Money Pit of Oak Island, Nova Scotia. Links have been drawn among Saunière, the **Priory of Sion**, the Masons, and the **Knights Templar.** Astronomers and geometers have catalogued an incredible number of figures—triangles, **pentagrams**, pentagons—through and around Rennes-le-Château, all with some sort of esoteric significance. There are connections drawn between Rennes-le-Château, Stonehenge, and countless megalithic sites throughout Europe and Britain, and claims that the village hides some sort of mathematical doorway to another dimension.

The parchments that sparked this intrigue have never been recovered; although one person—**Pierre Plantard**, the late grand master of the Priory of Sion—claimed to have placed them in a safe deposit box in London for safekeeping. Saunière and his mysteries have been fodder for a great deal of historical speculation and spellbinding stories offered by authors such as Henry Baigent, Richard Leigh, and Henry Lincoln (individually as well as collectively in books such as *Holy Blood, Holy Grail*), Lynn Picknett and Clive Prince, and Tim Wallace-Murphy.

Clearly *something* strange is in the air of Rennes-le-Château, but is it an actual conspiracy or the conspiracy theories themselves? Does there come a point where conspiracy theories wind up burying whatever knowledge of actual events we could have achieved? Bérenger Saunière isn't telling.

Senechaux French plural of the (also English) word *seneschal*, meaning an official or administrator to whom important duties are entrusted, normally associated with ecclesiastical or feudal societies or groups. In *The Da Vinci Code*, the *senechaux* are three officials in the **Priory of Sion** who report to Jacques Saunière, the grand master of the Priory. They appear to be a trusted "inner circle." The senechaux are murdered, one by one, by Silas, the agent of **Opus Dei**. Each of the three senechaux, along with Saunière, are guardians of the secret location of the **Holy Grail**. They are also trained to deceive interrogators with a coordinated lie about the location of the Grail, ensuring that even if their identities are revealed and they are questioned, the Grail will remain safely hidden. Sister Sandrine calls them, one by one, when she realizes that Silas has arrived at **Saint Sulpice** to uncover the **keystone**, but is shocked when each of her calls indicates that the senechaux are dead. The concept of the senechaux in *The Da Vinci Code* are taken from the questionable list provided by **Plantard** and listed on websites.

Shekinah *Shekinah* is a Hebrew word meaning "God's presence," and many hold that it is the feminine aspect and attributes of that presence. The closest Christian concept would be that of the Holy Spirit. Shekinah was believed to be the physical manifestation of God's presence in the Tabernacle and later in **Solomon's Temple**. When the Lord led Israel out of Egypt, he went before them "in a pillar of a cloud"—shekinah.

Sheshach In *The Da Vinci Code*, Sophie uses her knowledge of the **Atbash cipher**, a substitution code in which the first letter of the alphabet is replaced with the last, second is replaced with next-to-last, etc. The Hebrew letters for what was transliterated as "Scheshach" yield a word that can be rendered as "Babel" when adding in the vowels that Hebrew lacks.

Smart Car Langdon and Sophie, following their escape from the **Louvre**, jump in Sophie's Smart Car and speed away. This is a micro, compact car originally developed in 1994 as a joint venture between the Swiss watch company Swatch and Mercedes-Benz. A Swatch watch was the design inspiration for the car, which in its basic configuration sells for around $20,000 and is available throughout Europe and many other parts of the world

Solomon's Temple David, the first king of Israel, wanted to build a temple for the King of kings, his God. In a dream, God told David that the temple could not be built by him because he was a man of war and had spilled too much blood. The temple would be built by his son, Solomon, who would enjoy peace during his reign so that the temple might be built.

Although he did not build the temple, King David planned it and gathered much of the materials. After David's death, Solomon issued orders for construction of the first temple. He called upon the Phoenicians, who were expert builders, to assist, and the temple was in fact modeled on Phoenician temples of the time. Construction of Solomon's Temple on Mount Moriah in what is now Jerusalem was an enormous task, involving tens of thousands of people and requiring seven years, being completed in 953 B.C.

The Solomonic temple differed from other temples in the ancient world by virtue of having no idol. This reflected the belief that idols were not needed for God to be present; the temple was built because of the people's needs, not God's.

Subsequent history of the temple involves a regular cycle of destruction. The original temple was destroyed by Nebuchadnezzar in 586 B.C. Seventy years later, the second temple was built on the same site, and expanded in 19 B.C. by King Herod, only to be destroyed by the Romans in A.D. 70.

Enter *The Da Vinci Code*. Langdon tells Sophie the **Knights Templar's** primary mission in the Holy Land was not to protect pilgrims, but to set up lodging in the Temple so they could "retrieve the [secret] documents from beneath the ruins." He goes on to say no one knows for sure what they found, but it was "something that made them wealthy and powerful beyond anyone's imagination."

Today the site is the location of al-Aqsa Mosque, the third holiest site in Islam.

Sophia From the Greek word for wisdom. Associated with the virgin goddesses such as Athena, and for the allegorization of wisdom in the Holy Spirit and **Mary Magdalene**.

Sub rosa Literally, "under the **rose**." The origin of this phrase is likely to have come from Roman times when, in formal dining, tables were set in a U configuration, with the guest of honor and his host at the side opposite the opening. Over the center of the U hung a rose. It was a reminder that a rose had been given by Eros to Harpocrates, the god of silence, to keep him from talking about the indiscretions of Eros's mother, Venus. Anything said sub rosa (under the rose) was to remain a secret.

Symbology Symbols were described by the late anthropologist Leslie White as "the arbitrary assignation of meaning to form," and one of the few things that truly distinguished humans from other creatures. Symbols are abstractions. The Bible and of course *The Da Vinci Code* are filled with symbology: from the **Vitruvian Man** whose pose Saunière adopts in death, to the **cross**, to the **apple**—tangible objects are made to stand in for intangible and sometimes complex concepts.

Symbols are a shorthand means of communicating. Just as the **rose** over the Roman table was a symbol of Eros's gift to Harpocrates and thus the need for secrets to be kept secret, symbols such as the cross provide a compact way of reminding people of a complex reality.

In *The Da Vinci Code*, Langdon was at work on a paper about the symbols of the **sacred feminine**. At the end of the book, while at **Rosslyn**, he stands with Saunière's widow, Marie, pondering the papyrus that bears the inscription:

The **Holy Grail** 'neath ancient Roslin waits.
The blade and chalice guarding o'er Her gates.

> Marie traces a triangle, point up, on his palm. An ancient symbol for the blade, and the masculine. Then she traces a triangle point down. An ancient symbol for the chalice and the feminine. She takes him to the church, where he finally sees in the Star of David the combination of blade and chalice—male and female, Solomon's Seal—marking the Holy of Holies, the place where both **Yahweh** and **Shekinah** were thought to dwell.

Tarot cards The origin of **tarot cards** is a subject of some debate. Some scholars trace their earliest appearance to a very specific time and place: northern Italy in the early fifteenth century. The first practical use of the deck seems to have been a game that was somewhat like our modern bridge. Since alchemical, astrological, and hermetic philosophies were part and parcel of medieval intellectual life, the illustrators of the first decks may have used them to code hidden meanings in the iconography of the cards. The many different interpretations and correspondences that tarot cards have inspired suggests that tarot is more than just bridge.

Occultists, fans of esoterica, and even modern bestseller writers believe instead that the cards have a much longer history (dating back to ancient

Israel or ancient Egypt) and a far deeper meaning. Kabbalah, the Jewish form of mysticism, is said to have a connection. Robert Langdon avers that originally the tarot "had been devised as a secret means to pass along ideologies banned by the Church" and that the pentacle suit of the tarot deck is the indicator "for feminine divinity." Critics debunk these types of theories, believing that the tarot was invented for "innocent gaming purposes." "The notion of diamonds representing the pentacles is a deliberate misrepresentation," contends Sandra Miesel, who wrote a long article harshly critical of the "so-called facts" in *The Da Vinci Code*.

There seems to be no hard evidence tying the origin of the decks to ancient traditions. History seems to tell us that the tarot cards do not appear as a *systematized* occult system until late-eighteenth-century France. Tradition can triumph over history, of course, and it is not hard to began speculating all over again about "coincidences" such as the arrangement of the major arcana: the High Priestess (**Female Pope**) card is normally given the number two and card number five, the Pope, is its logical opposite; just as the Empress and the Emperor (three and four respectively) counterbalance one another.

Teniers, David the Younger Dutch painter, son of David the Elder, also a painter. Born in 1610, he painted historical, mythological, and allegorical subjects, including a series of paintings depicting St. Anthony. Langdon mentions him early on in *The Da Vinci Code* as a subject, along with painter **Poussin**, of several textbooks written by Jacques Saunière.

These textbooks, it seems, are some of Langdon's favorites; they deal specifically with hidden codes in the works of both painters. This is a direct reference by Dan Brown to coded messages found by Saunière's historical namesake: **Bérenger Saunière**, parish priest of **Rennes-le-Château**. One of the coded messages that Bérenger Saunière found buried in the altar of the Rennes-le-Château parish church reads thus:

> SHEPHERDESS NO TEMPTATION THAT POUSSIN TENIERS
> HOLD THE KEY; PEACE 681 BY THE CROSS AND THIS HORSE
> OF GOD I COMPLETE [DESTROY] THIS DAEMON OF THE
> GUARDIAN AT NOON BLUE APPLES

Bérenger Saunière is said to have traveled to Paris after finding the coded documents, and during his trip supposedly purchased reproductions of a work by Teniers, a portrait of Pope Célestin V, and Poussin's *The Shepherds of Arcadia*.

Tertullian The first great writer of Latin Christianity whose extensive works covered the whole theological field of the time: paganism and Judaism, polemics, polity, disciple, morals, and the whole reorganization of human life under his interpretation of Christian doctrine. He was also a determined advocate of strict discipline and an austere lifestyle—believing that women should put away precious ornaments as they help lure men into sin, and that being unmarried and celibate were the highest state of being.

Todger "Teabing's eyes twinkled. 'Oxford Theatre Club. They still talk of my Julius Caesar. I'm certain nobody has ever performed the first scene of Act Three with more dedication . . . my toga tore open when I fell, and I had to lie on the stage for half an hour with my todger hanging out.'" Todger (aka tadger), is 1950s British slang for penis.

Tribe of Benjamin One of the twelve tribes of Israel, descended from Jacob's son Benjamin, part of whose inheritance, according to the Bible, is the city of Jerusalem. The tribe plays a part in Teabing's lecture to Sophie regarding the true nature of the **Holy Grail. Mary Magdalene,** he tells her, was of the tribe of Benjamin, and therefore her union with Jesus—a descendent of the royal house of David and the tribe of Judah—was of immense political importance. The Bible reports in the book of Judges that the tribe of Benjamin was attacked by the other tribes of Israel because of the protection they afforded certain criminals and "sons of Belial." The decimated tribe survived, but the *Dossiers Secrets* maintain that a portion of the tribe relocated to eastern Europe, first in the Greek province of Arcadia, and then up the Danube and the Rhine. *Holy Blood, Holy Grail* suggests that the tribe could be the forbears of the Franks, and, hence, the **Merovingians.**

Vatican Library Bishop Aringarosa visits **Castel Gandolfo,** and passes the Biblioteca Astronomica, the library of the Vatican Observatory. While hints of an organized library date back to the fourth century, the Vatican Library as it is known today dates from the reign of Pope Nicholas V, who ascended to the throne in 1447. Nicholas expanded the library from a few hundred works to over fifteen hundred, which made it the largest library in Europe at time. At present, it houses over a million books and 150,000 manuscripts which contain such works as the oldest known Greek texts of the Old and New Testaments, and early surviving examples of works by Dante, Virgil, and Homer, among others.

Venus Pentagram One of the most intriguing theories explaining the origin of the **pentagram** is astronomical: the planet Venus traces a pentagram in the night sky. How? When the movements of the planet are charted against the stars, it appears to move against them in a regular pattern. The ancients imagined that the stars that they saw wheeling through the sky were "fixed" on a sphere with Earth at its center. They used these fixed stars as a reference point to measure the movement of the planets, which moved independently of the fixed stars—appearing in different areas of the sphere at different times. If an observer records the position of Venus against the fixed stars on the same day for six years, and connects these positions in order across the sphere, a pentagram is produced (Venus returns to her original position on the sixth year, beginning the cycle again). This observation has not stood the test of later astronomical science: it is true that tracing the planet from the Near East would trace something of a pentagram, albeit a rather imaginative one. It would not look the same in other parts of the world and, as we now know, the laws of planetary motion have long dispelled the notion that the Earth is at the center of the universe.

Vitruvian Man A famed drawing by **Leonardo** of a man, front view and side, standing in a square within a circle. The first clue to the mysteries in *The Da Vinci Code* is Saunière having sprawled out his dying, naked body in emulation of this famous iconic Leonardo image. Vitruvian Man is named after Marcus Vitruvius Pollio, the Roman writer, architect, and engineer active in the first century B.C. He was in charge of the aqueducts of Rome and wrote *The Ten Books of Architecture*, perhaps the first work on architecture ever written. Vitruvius's study of human proportions was in his third book, and he left this guide for artists and architects to follow:

> The measurements of the human body are as follows that is that 4 fingers make 1 palm, and 4 palms make 1 foot, 6 palms make 1 cubit; 4 cubits make a man's height. And 4 cubits make one pace and 24 palms make a man. The length of a man's outspread arms is equal to his height. From the roots of his hair to the bottom of his chin is the tenth of a man's height; from the bottom of the chin to the top of the head is one eighth of his height; from the top of the breast to the roots of the hair will be the seventh part of the whole man. From the nipples to the top of the head will be the fourth part of man. The greatest width of the shoulders contains in itself the fourth part of man. From the elbow to the tip of the hand will be the fifth part of a man; and from the elbow to the angle of the armpit will be the eighth part of man. The whole hand will be the tenth part of the man. The distance from the bottom of the chin to the nose and from the roots of the hair to the eyebrows is, in each case the same, and like the ear, a third of the face.

Leonardo's contribution was to solve this ancient algorithm known as "squaring the circle," a geometric problem whereby a pair of compasses and a ruler are used in an attempt to construct a circle and square of equal area. Theoretically, a perfectly proportioned human would fit within the figure and while Vitruvius's efforts apparently remained crude, Leonardo's rendering is perfect and a work of mathematical as well as artistic genius.

Yahweh The personal name of God in the Old Testament. From the

Hebrew letters Yod, Heh, Vav, and Heh (the tetragrammaton—see **Adonai**). Speaking God's name in prayer is forbidden among Jews, who substitute Adonai. This restriction results from an interpretation of the Third Commandment that says it is forbidden to "take the name of God in vain." In writing, LORD or G-d replaces Yahweh.

The rendering of the ancient Hebrew as Yahweh reflects the difficulty of deciding how a language not spoken for more than two thousand years and lacking any vowels might have said the letters Yod, Heh, Vav, and Heh, and then transliterating that into modern English (or any other language). According to the argument in *The Da Vinci Code*, YHWH was actually a Hebrew acronym that combined archaic male and female names for God, and "Haveh," the Hebrew version of "Eve" is intermingled into the Yahweh.

Web Resources
Digging Deeper into The Da Vinci Code

By Betsy Eble

Copyright © 2004 by Betsy Eble.

Raise your hand if you looked up the *Last Supper* to see who was really sitting at the right hand of Jesus? Hands up if you'd never heard of Opus Dei? There's a royal bloodline? Priory of Sion? Am I the only person in the world who didn't know this stuff? Just your luck, answers to all those questions and many more have been search-engine-indexed, metadata-enhanced and rated by hundreds of prior users. If you're just dipping your toes in the water of a new concept, the Web is a perfect place to get started.

This morning there were 460,000 results on a Google query of "Da Vinci Code." With 460,000 results, you can find information to corroborate or invalidate just about any statement in the world.

I spent the summer of 2003 researching the literary, artistic, and historical references in *The Da Vinci Code*. I then assembled a collection of material found exclusively on the Web and published it as a compilation reader, *Depth & Details, A Reader's Guide to Dan Brown's* The Da Vinci Code. In *Depth and Details*, I highlight interesting sites relating to each chapter of the book so that the reader can cross-reference as they read. A summary of some of the more interesting sites are provided for you here.

Symbols

www.symbols.com is worthy of being deemed a site for sitting with a cup of coffee and just soaking in the significant research and beautiful presentation. Although I am not completely sure who goes there looking for symbols visually, describing the symbol by its symmetry, line softness, etc., it is fun to see what symbols.com comes up with when you give it a try. For their word index—a much better approach for the verbally inclined, all that's required to start hours of endless reading is to begin with one of the alphabetical tabs, pick a word and go! As it relates to *The Da Vinci Code*, you will find symbols of the chalice, Venus, the pentacle, pagan and Christian crosses, Masonic symbols, and more.

Olga's Gallery

Online Art Museum, www.abcgallery.com. If you are looking for high-quality images of famous artwork, this is a great site to browse. The only drawback is that you will get some pop-unders. They are a small price to pay to see such a vast collection of artwork. Most of the artwork is annotated and linked to other sources. You'll be able to view all of the referenced da Vinci art here, like *Virgin of the Rocks*, the *Last Supper* and the *Mona Lisa* as well as referenced Monet, Caravaggio, Picasso, and Bosch paintings.

Opus Dei

Opus Dei is a prelature of the Catholic Church, which plays a significant role in *The Da Vinci Code*. The first place to look for information on the controversial Opus Dei is the organization's own website, www.opusdei.org. The FAQ section will help you to quickly scan for areas of interest. For a more in-depth study of why Opus Dei was created, you can read works written by the founder of the prelature, Josemaría Escrivá, at www.escrivaworks.org.

To find a more independent view on the role of Opus Dei, visit www.rickross.com/groups/opus.html. The Ross Institute has gathered a collection of stories and articles that have been written about Opus Dei. Most come from generally reliable sources, such as *U.S. News*, the *New York Daily News*, the *Guardian*, and the Associated Press, and they provide a balanced discussion on Opus Dei's activities.

The biography of Opus Dei member and spy Robert Hanssen, referenced in *The Da Vinci Code*, is available on Court TV's website at www.crime-library.com/terrorists_spies/spies/hanssen/5.html?sect=23.

Louvre

If you vowed to polish up your French after reading *The Da Vinci Code*, you can give your newly polished skills a whirl at www.louvre.org. If you're like me, high school French was enough to get me through most of the French passages in the book, but navigating the Louvre website is quite out of my league. Use the following URL for the English version of the site: www.louvre.org/louvrea.htm and be sure to take a few virtual tours of their galleries. The Grand Gallery and the *Mona Lisa* are both viewable from their site. I can just imagine Robert Langdon and Sophie Neuveu sneaking through the Grand Gallery in the dark looking for clues left by Jacques Saunière.

After you've toured the Louvre, visit another virtual site with twenty-five webcams set up around Paris that provide real-time views of many of the locations referenced in *The Da Vinci Code*. www.parispourvous.net/index.php3?wpe=c3 is the English version of the parispourvous.com (Paris for You) site.

Mary Magdalene

Author of *The Woman With the Alabaster Jar*, Margaret Starbird, who is referred to in *The Da Vinci Code*, is a major article contributor to the popular website www.magdalene.org. This site hosts articles, devotionals, poetry, and all things Mary Magdalene. www.beliefnet.com also includes a section dedicated to Mary Magdalene, www.beliefnet.com/index/index_10126.html, with articles about the writings and biblical references to Mary Magdalene. Of particular note is the link to a gallery of artwork featuring Mary Magdalene. Also included are sections on Gnosticism and *The Da Vinci Code*. One of the enjoyable aspects of www.beliefnet's coverage of the topic is their presentation of opposing points of view on both Mary Magdalene's role in Christian history and the content of *The Da Vinci Code*.

Da Vinci

Whereas most of the topics in *The Da Vinci Code* are somewhat controversial in nature, content on Leonardo da Vinci has been widely researched and published for centuries. Bill Gates even purchased the Leicester Codex—a book of sketches by da Vinci—several years ago that has been bought and re-bought by the wealthy for centuries. Da Vinci's art, architecture, sculpture, and engineering are well documented on the Web, too. A very comprehensive site covering da Vinci's life and works are located at www.lairweb.org.nz/leonardo. It covers topics such as his apprenticeship to Verrocchio, questions of da Vinci's sexual orientation, his works and even his death on May 2, 1519, at sixty-seven years old. The site has many interesting factoids, such as claiming that da Vinci invented scissors and took ten years to paint Mona Lisa's lips.

Math, Art, and Architecture

The father of the Fibonacci sequence—the code at the murder scene in *The Da Vinci Code*—Fibonacci is detailed beautifully at www-groups.dcs.st-and.ac.uk/~history/Mathematicians/Fibonacci.html. Interestingly, most of the links on the Web regarding Fibonacci will reference this site. This is a pretty good indicator that the content is highly regarded as being accurate.

The divine proportion, also known as the Golden Mean (or PHI) is also documented very well on the Web. Any basic art history or architecture history class always includes a lecture on the Golden Mean in the design of the Parthenon and da Vinci and Durer's paintings. A good website with dozens of links on PHI, art and architecture can be found at www.mcs.surrey.ac.uk/Personal/R.Knott/Fibonacci/fibInArt.html. It's not a visually pleasing website which is somewhat ironic since it is about the beauty of the golden mean in works of art, but it is highly readable and the links are all very informative.

Cryptology

For those of you looking to learn more about cryptology and ciphers, a primer exists at www.murky.org/cryptography/index.shtml. You'll find information on classical and modern cryptology as well as puzzles. If you'd like to make your own anagram or cryptogram, try the following two sites: anagram builder www.wordsmith.org/anagram/advanced.html and cryptogram builder www.wordles.com/getmycrypto.asp.

Priory of Sion

The Priory of Sion is a quasi-secret society based in Europe which claims to have powerful secrets about the origins of Christianity. They founded the Knights Templar and possibly Freemasonry. Former grand masters are said to have included Isaac Newton and Leonardo da Vinci. You will find comprehensive information on the Knights Templar and the Priory of Sion at www.ordotempli.org/priory_of_sion.htm the official website of the International Knights Templar.

Royal Bloodline—Merovingians

Wikipedia.com's entry for the Merovingians states: "According to the esoteric version of history promulgated by Michael Baigent, Richard Leigh, and Henry Lincoln in their book *Holy Blood, Holy Grail*, the Merovingian kings were direct descendants of Mary Magdalene and Jesus Christ once they arrived in southern France following Christ's crucifixion and resurrection." The authors further claim that the Roman church killed off all remnants of this dynasty—the Cathar heresy of Languedoc and the Templars—during the Inquisition, in order to gain power through the "spiritual" dynasty of Peter instead of the "holy blood" (i.e., *sangreal*) of Mary Magdalene's descendants. Most historians do not accept these theories. The Merovingians were, in fact, a dynasty of Frankish kings ruling between the fifth and eighth centuries. The Knights Templar website contains a family tree of the Merovingian kings www.ordotempli.org/the_merovingians.htm.

Knights Templar

The authors of *Templar History* magazine have created a very readable website at www.templarhistory.com. It has in-depth articles on all aspects of the Knights Templar, ranging from fact-based historical discussion to an investigation of all the myths and tall tales that have cropped up around the monastic order. The site also provides reviews of books written about the Templars, if you want to delve even further into the topic.

Churches

Many of the scenes in *The Da Vinci Code* take place in churches such as Saint Sulpice, Rosslyn Chapel, Temple Church, and Westminster Abbey. Most of these churches have their own websites with floor plans and photographs. The Rosslyn Templars have built a site with images and comprehensive detailing of the architecture and symbolism in Rosslyn Chapel (www.rosslyntemplars.org.uk/rosslyn.htm). A fascinating and creative assertion that the Solomon's Temple is actually in the shape of a human body (with diagrams) can be found at home.earthlink.net/~tonybadillo/. Although the images are a little too small to see *The Da Vinci Code*–referenced "knights entombed," the Temple Church on Fleet Street in London www.templechurch.com/ does have a section dedicated to the church's history and origin that is worth perusing. Saint Sulpice is evidently a frequently photographed and published location. The photo sharing and posting website, pbase.com, has several high-resolution and compelling images of the church and Paris in general. Using their search tool with keywords such as *Paris*, *Louvre*, and *Sulpice* will yield dozens of beautifully photographed images. Picsearch (www.picsearch.com) is also a valuable resource for finding images.

Da Vinci Code *Websites*

Since first starting research on the *The Da Vinci Code* for my reader's guide, several *Da Vinci Code* websites have emerged. Of note, there is the www.danbrown.com website, established by the publishers (Doubleday) and dedicated to the book and its characters. The publisher is also running an "Uncover the Code" contest, which can be found at www.randomhouse/doubleday/davinci. Where the www.danbrown.com site contains links to images, historical research, etc., a slightly less polished website with many links can be found at www.darkprotocols.com/darkprotocols/id36.html. The presentation of the content is jumbled and disorganized; however, there are plenty of visual references and well as links to interesting *Da Vinci Code* supporting content.

Contributors

Dan Burstein (editor) is founder and managing member of Millennium Technology Ventures Advisors, a New York-based venture capital firm that invests in innovative new technology companies. He is also an award-winning journalist and author of six books on global economics and technology.

Burstein's 1988 book *Yen!*, about the rise of Japanese financial power, was an international bestseller in more than twenty countries. In 1995 his book *Road Warriors* was one of the first to analyze the impact of the Internet and digital technology on business and society. His 1998 book *Big Dragon* (written with Arne de Keijzer), outlined a long-term view of China's role in the twenty-first century. Burstein and de Keijzer recently launched their own publishing enterprise, Squibnocket Press, and are currently working on a series, *The Best Things Ever Said*, that will soon include new titles on the future of the Internet, blogs and blogging, and nanotechnology.

Working as a freelance journalist in the 1980s, Mr. Burstein published more than a thousand articles in over two hundred publications, including the *New York Times*, the *Wall Street Journal*, the *Los Angeles Times*, the *Boston Globe*, the *Chicago Tribune*, *New York Magazine*, *Rolling Stone*, and many others in the United States, Europe, and Asia. He also served as a consultant to ABC News, CBS News, *Time* magazine, and other leading media organizations.

For the last decade, Burstein has been an active investor in venture-backed startups, assembling a portfolio of more than twenty-five technology companies. From 1988 to 2000, he was senior advisor at The Blackstone Group, one of Wall Street's leading private merchant banks. He is also a prominent corporate strategy consultant and has served as an advisor to CEOs, senior management teams, and global corporations, including Sony, Toyota, Microsoft, Boardroom Inc., and Sun Microsystems.

Arne de Keijzer (managing editor) is a writer, former China business consultant, and Dan Burstein's partner in Squibnocket Press. He is author of five books, including a bestselling travel guide to China and two books with Dan Burstein, *The Rise, Fall, and Future of the Internet Economy* (one of the *Best Things Ever Said* titles from Squibnocket Press) and *Big Dragon: China's Future—What It Means for Business, the Economy, and the Global Order*. He has written for publications ranging from the *New York Times* to *Powerboat Reports*.

Diane Apostolos-Cappadona is an adjunct professor of religious art and cultural history in the Center for Muslim-Christian Understanding, and an adjunct professor and core faculty in art and culture in the Liberal Studies Program, both at Georgetown University. Dr. Apostolos-Cappadona was guest curator and author of the catalogue for *In Search of Mary Magdalene: Images and Traditions* (2002). She is preparing the introduction for the reprint edition of *Sacred and Profane Beauty: The Holy Art* by Gerardus van der Leeuw; two edited volumes, *Sources and Documents in the History of Christian Art* and *Sources and Documents in the History of Religious Art in 19th-century America*; and a textbook, *The Art of the World's Religions*. She teaches courses including Art, Creativity and the Sacred, Eastern Orthodox Christianity: History and Theology, and The Medieval Synthesis: Art and Religion in the Middle Ages. With Deirdre Good, she has presented a series of workshops and special lectures on the theme of the truth of *The Da Vinci Code*.

Michael Baigent, born in New Zealand in 1948, obtained a degree in psychology from Canterbury University, Christchurch. Since 1976, he has lived in England. He is the author of *Ancient Traces* and *From the Omens of Babylon*. He joined with authors Richard Leigh and Henry Lincoln on two international bestsellers, *Holy Blood, Holy Grail* and *The Messianic Legacy*. He has coauthored, with Richard Leigh, *The Dead Sea Scrolls Deception, Secret Germany,* and *The Elixir and The Stone*. His latest book, cowritten with Richard Leigh, is *The Inquisition.*

Amy D. Bernstein is a writer and academic who specializes in Renaissance literature. Her doctoral work comprised a new edition of the sonnets of Jacques de Billy de Prunay, a Benedictine monk and a bestselling author and translator of Gregory of Nazianzus and other Patristic writers.

Peter W. Bernstein, a partner with Annalyn Swan in A.S.A.P. Media, was a consulting editor for this book. Peter has served as an editor at *U.S. News and World Report* and *Fortune* magazines. He was also publisher of Times Books and Random House. In addition, he is a bestselling author. He is the creator and currently the editor and publisher of *The Ernst & Young Tax Guide*. He co-authored *The Practical Guide to Practically Everything* and coedited, with his wife Amy, *Quotations from Speaker Newt: The Red, White and Blue Book of the Republican Revolution.*

Esther de Boer studies theology at the Free University of Amsterdam and is currently a minister of the Dutch Reformed Churches in Ouderkerk aan de Amstel.

David Burstein is a high school Latin student and author of the forthcoming book *Harry Potter and the Prisoner of the* New York Times *Bestseller List*. He has written a book of poetry, seven feature-length plays, and has performed leading roles in high school productions of *Noises Off, The Wind in the Willows, Much Ado About Nothing, Cinderella,* and *Fiddler on the Roof.* Burstein also serves as fundraising chairman of the Westport Youth Film Festival.

Denise Budd is a graduate of Rutgers University in New Brunswick (B.A.) and Columbia University (Ph.D.). In 2002 she completed her doctoral dissertation on Leonardo da Vinci, a study that focuses on a reinterpretation of the documentary evidence from the first half of the artist's career. Dr. Budd has taught the core curriculum at Columbia University and is currently teaching at Rutgers University, while continuing her research.

John Castro is a New York City-based writer, editor, and researcher. He has worked on publications by civil rights leader Jesse Jackson, journalist Marshall Loeb, and Internet entrepreneur Charles Ferguson. John is also a theater director, actor, and playwright, with a particular love of Shakespeare. He is a graduate of St. John's College in Annapolis, Maryland.

Michelle Delio writes on a wide variety of technology subjects and is a regular contributor to *Wired* magazine. She has also contributed to Salon.com, on subjects from blocking spam to Harley-Davidson motorcycles.

Jennifer Doll served as research and editorial associate for this book, a role she has carried out for various other books and magazines. She is currently an editorial consultant for *Reader's Digest.* She's also contributed her talents to McKinsey & Company, *Continental* magazine, and The Teaching Commission. In her spare time, she's a fiction writer, at work on her first novel.

David Downie is a Paris-based freelance writer, editor, and translator. For the last twenty years, he has been writing about European culture, travel, and food for American and British magazines and newspapers and, occasionally, for French, Italian, and Dutch publications. His work has appeared worldwide. His latest, critically acclaimed book, *Cooking the Roman Way: Authentic Recipes from the Home Cooks and Trattorias of Rome,* is about the food and culinary culture of contemporary Rome. He is currently at work on a collection of travel essays titled *Paris, Paris.*

Betsy Eble has been creating things for as long as she can remember—at least as far back as making her own Cabbage Patch dolls. During the day, she builds information architectures and interfaces for online applications. At night and on weekends, she paints, writes articles for her blog, and collects research on historical fiction. Her *Depth & Details—A Reader's Guide to Dan Brown's* The Da Vinci Code was the first guidebook to provide research keys to the novel.

Bart D. Ehrman is the James A. Gray Distinguished Professor of Religious Studies at the University of North Carolina at Chapel Hill, where he has taught since 1988. An authority on the New Testament and the history of early Christianity, he has appeared on CNN, the History Channel, A&E, and other television and radio programs. He has taped several popular lecture series for The Teaching Company and is author or editor of thirteen books, including, most recently, *Lost Christianities: The Battles for Scripture and the Faiths We Never Knew* and *Lost Scriptures: Books that Did Not Make It into the New Testament*.

Riane Eisler is a social scientist, cultural historian, and evolutionary theorist. Her books include the bestseller *The Chalice and The Blade: Our History, Our Future*, a multidisciplinary study of human culture. Her other books include *Sacred Pleasure, Tomorrow's Children*, and *The Power of Partnership: Seven Relationships That Will Change Your Life*. Eisler is president of the Center for Partnership Studies, has taught at UCLA, and addressed keynote conferences worldwide.

Glenn W. Erickson has taught philosophy at Southern Illinois University, Texas A&M University, Western Carolina University, and the Rhode Island School of Design, as well as at five federal universities in Brazil and Nigeria, sometimes as a Fulbright Scholar. He is author of a dozen works about philosophy (*Negative Dialectics and the End of Philosophy*), logic (*Dictionary of Paradox*, with John Fossa), literary criticism (*A Tree of Stories*, with his wife, Sandra S. F. Erickson), poetry, short fiction, art history (*New Theory of the Tarot*), and the history of mathematics.

Timothy Freke has a degree in philosophy, is the author of more than twenty books and an authority on world spirituality. He has coauthored five books with Peter Gandy, including *The Jesus Mysteries* and *Jesus and the Lost Goddess*. He lectures and organizes seminars internationally, exploring *gnosis* or spiritual enlightenment. For more information on Mr. Freke and Mr. Gandy's books and seminars contact www.timfreke.demon.co.uk.

Peter Gandy has an M.A. in classical civilizations, specializing in the ancient pagan mystery religions. He is especially known for his works on Jesus, written with Timothy Freke, including *Jesus and the Lost Goddess* and *The Jesus Mysteries*.

Deirdre Good is Professor of New Testament at the General Theological Seminary of the Episcopal Church in New York City. She has published and lectured widely on Miriamic traditions and the female in Coptic and Gnostics texts. Her latest book is *Mariam, the Magdala, and the Mother*.

Collin Hansen is an editorial resident with *Christian History* magazine. With an academic background in journalism and church history, Hansen has covered topics including European secularism, the Iraq war, and Christian higher education.

Susan Haskins is an author, editor, researcher, and translator. She has given lectures around the world, appeared on various television programs to discuss Mary Magdalene, and is currently translating from Italian and editing *Three Marian Writings* (texts on the life of the Virgin by three sixteenth-century Italian female writers). She is the author of *Mary Magdalen: Myth & Metaphor* and editor-translator for *Three Sixteenth-Century Marian Writings*.

Stephan A. Hoeller, Ph.D., is a bishop of the Ecclesia Gnostica and the senior holder of the English Gnostic Transmissions in America. He is the author of several books, including *Gnosticism, Jung and the Lost Gospels* and *Freedom: Alchemy for a Voluntary Society*. Dr. Hoeller held the chair of Comparative Religions at the College of Oriental Studies in Los Angeles for sixteen years.

Katherine Ludwig Jansen is an associate professor of history at Catholic University. She is the author of *The Making of the Magdalen: Preaching and Popular Devotion in the Later Middle Ages*.

Karen L. King, Winn Professor of Ecclesiastical History at Harvard University Divinity School, is the author of *What is Gnosticism?* and *The Gospel of Mary of Magdala: Jesus and the First Woman Apostle*. Trained in comparative religions and historical studies, she pursues teaching and research specialties in the history of Christianity and women's studies. Her latest books, *The Gospel of Mary of Magdala* and *What Is Gnosticism?* have been widely acclaimed. Her particular theoretical interests are in religious identity formation, discourses of normativity (orthodoxy and heresy), and gender studies.

David Klinghoffer is the author of *The Lord Will Gather Me In* and *The Discovery of God: Abraham and the Birth of Monotheism*. He is also a regular contributor to *National Review*.

Richard Leigh is a novelist and writer of short stories. With Michael Baigent, he has coauthored a number of books, including *Holy Blood, Holy Grail* (with Henry Lincoln), *The Dead Sea Scrolls Deception*, *The Messianic Legacy*, *The Temple and the Lodge, Secret Germany: Claus von Stauffenberg and the Mystical Crusade against Hitler*, *The Elixir and The Stone*, and, most recently, *The Inquisition*.

Henry Lincoln began his career as an actor, but by the early 1960s he was writing for television, turning out more than two hundred dramatic scripts. His early fascination with Egyptology (he taught himself to read hieroglyphs) led to an exploration of historical mysteries, mythologies, and comparative religions. Since his imagination has been captured by the mystery of Rennes-le-Château, he has presented a number of documentaries for the BBC on other historic mysteries, including *The Man in the Iron Mask*, *Nostradamus*, and the *Curse of Tutenkhamun*. He is also a coauthor, with Michael Baigent and Richard Leigh, of *Holy Blood, Holy Grail*.

James Martin, S.J., is a Jesuit priest and associate editor of *America*, a national Catholic magazine. He is author of numerous books on religion and spirituality, including the memoir *In Good Company: The Fast Track from the Corporate World to Poverty, Chastity and Obedience*.

Richard P. McBrien is Crowley-O'Brien Professor of Theology and former chairman of the Department of Theology (1980–91) at the University of Notre Dame. He was also a past president of the Catholic Theological Society of America. McBrien's scholarly interests include ecclesiology, the relationship between religion and politics, and the theological, doctrinal, and spiritual dimensions of the Catholic tradition. Father McBrien's latest book is *Lives of the Saints: From Mary and St. Francis of Assisi to John XXIII and Mother Teresa*. He is a priest in the Archdiocese of Hartford, Connecticut.

Craig M. McDonald, an award-winning journalist and editor, has interviewed numerous authors, including James Ellroy, Anne Rice, Dennis Lehane, Walter Mosley, Alistair Macleod, and Dan Brown. His interviews are featured in *Writers on Writing*, accessible on the Web at www.modestyarbor.com.

Brendan McKay is a professor of computer science at the Australian National University. He achieved notoriety a few years ago by debunking *The Bible Code* theory.

Laura Miller writes about movies, books, theater, digital culture, and social issues for newspapers and national magazines. Her work has appeared in the *New York Times*, the *San Francisco Chronicle*, *Harper's Bazaar*, and *Wired*. She is also a regular contributor to Salon.com.

Sherwin B. Nuland is the author of *Leonardo da Vinci*, as well as the bestseller *How We Die*, which won the 1994 National Book Award for Nonfiction. His other books have included *The Mysteries Within: A Surgeon Reflects on Medical Myth*, *Doctors: The Biography of Medicine*, and *The Wisdom of the Body*, published in paperback under the title *How We Live*. He is Clinical Professor of Surgery at Yale University, where he also teaches medical history and bio-ethics.

Lance S. Owens, M.D. is both a physician in clinical practice and an ordained priest who serves a parish of the Ecclesia Gnostica. He completed his undergraduate degree in history at Georgetown University and Utah State University and received his doctorate from Columbia University. He also maintains the website, www.gnosis.org.

Elaine Pagels is the author of the bestselling *The Gnostic Gospels*, which won the National Book Critics Circle Award and the National Book Award, and is now available in a new edition. She earned a B.A. in history and an M.A. in classical studies at Stanford University and holds a Ph.D. from Harvard University. Professor Pagels is the author of *Beyond Belief*, another bestseller, as well as *Adam, Eve, and the Serpent* and *The Origin of Satan*. She is currently the Harrington Spear Paine Professor of Religion at Princeton University.

Lynn Picknett and Clive Prince are writers, researchers, and lecturers on the paranormal, the occult, and historical and religious mysteries. Their book *The Templar Revelation* is a bestseller and served as an important source for Dan Brown's book. With Prince, Pinknett also has cowritten *Turin Shroud: In Whose Image? The Truth Behind the Centuries-Long Conspiracy of Silence*, which propounded the thesis that it was Leonardo who staged the revered shroud as a hoax. Picknett wrote *Mary Magdalene*. She and Prince live in London, England.

James M. Robinson is Professor of Religion Emeritus, Claremont Graduate University, and general editor of the *Nag Hammadi Library*. As one of the world's leading authorities on early Christianity, he supervised the team of scholars and translators who brought the Nag Hammadi finds to life.

David A. Shugarts, a journalist with thirty years' experience, has served on newspapers and magazines as a reporter, photographer, desk editor, and editor-in-chief. His fields of expertise include aviation and marine writing. He has received five regional and national awards from the Aviation/Space Writers Association. He was the founding editor of *Aviation Safety* magazine in 1981 and of *Powerboat Reports* in 1988.

Margaret Starbird holds a master's degree from the University of Maryland and has studied at Christian Albrechts University in Kiel, Germany, and at Vanderbilt Divinity School. She has written extensively on the concept of the sacred feminine. Her books include *Magdalen's Lost Legacy: Symbolic Numbers and the Sacred Union in Christianity*, *The Goddess in the Gospels: Reclaiming the Sacred Feminine*, *The Feminine Face of Christianity*, and *The Woman With the Alabaster Jar: Mary Magdalen and the Holy Grail*.

Kate Stohr served as a research and editorial associate for this book. She is also a freelance journalist and documentary producer whose work has appeared in the *New York Times*, *U.S. News & World Report*, the *Christian Science Monitor*, *Time Digital*, *People*, *Rosie*, and *In Style*. Her recent reporting has covered such topics as urban farming, retirement migration, waste management, labor issues, and environmental justice.

Annalyn Swan, a partner with Peter Bernstein in A.S.A.P. Media, served as a consulting editor to this book. A professional writer and editor, she has been a staff writer at *Time,* music critic and arts editor of *Newsweek,* and editor-in-chief of *Savvy.* With the art critic Mark Stevens, she has also written a biography of the artist Willem de Kooning, to be published by Knopf in the fall of 2004.

David Van Biema is a senior writer for *Time* magazine, specializing in religion.

Brian Weiss has written books and articles for almost thirty years on a wide variety of topics, including technology, trade, aviation, and pharmacology. He has held senior editorial positions on several national publications, written a nationally syndicated newspaper column, and assisted in the writing of many books. His company, Word'sworth, is based in Pasadena, California, and provides marketing communications and consulting services to a wide array of businesses.

David Wilk was a consulting editor for this book. He has worked in the book business in many capacities, including writer, editor, publisher, and distributor. He was Literature Program Director for the National Endowment for the Arts and is currently a senior executive at CDS, in New York City.

Kenneth L. Woodward, a contributing editor at *Newsweek* and frequent writer on religion, is the author, most recently, of *The Book of Miracles: the Meaning of the Miracle Stories in Christianity, Judaism, Buddhism, Hinduism and Islam.*

Nicole Zaray was a researcher and editorial associate for this book. She is a New York-based writer and filmmaker who produced and directed the independent documentary *Work Life and The Unknowable,* cowrote the upcoming feature *Monopolis,* and the off-off Broadway show *Bread and Circus 3099.*

Acknowledgments

Special thanks and deep appreciation are due to a stunning array of people who became excited about the project of assembling this book and leaped with us over the chasm of all the obstacles to get it done in record time.

First and foremost, we must extend our thanks to Gilbert Perlman, Steve Black, and their colleagues at CDS, for their vision, support, and spirit of partnership. They moved mountains and made things happen on a schedule we have never seen before in two decades of doing books. David Wilk proved to be the best friend authors could have, coordinating the nearly infinite number of fibers involved with this project into a cohesive piece of papyrus. Thanks also to Kari Stuart, Hope Matthiessen, Kipton Davis, Lane Jantzen, Elizabeth Whiting, and Kerry Liebling.

We could not have produced this book without a terrific team of consulting and contributing editors, as well as research and editorial associates. John Castro, David Shugarts, and Brian Weiss performed yeoman's service on innumerable aspects of the book.

We were greatly aided by our editorial team at A.S.A.P. Media, which included Peter Bernstein, Annalyn Swan, Kate Stohr, Jennifer Doll, and Nicole Zaray.

The production team worked feverishly to give physical life to this book. Special thanks to George Davidson, Jaye Zimet, Leigh Taylor, Lee Quarfoot, Nan Jernigan, Gray Cutler, Suzanne Fass, David Kessler, Mike Kingcaid, Ray Ferguson, and Jane Elias.

Our families provided intellectual, artistic, and moral support throughout, helped us with key ideas, information, and design. Love and thanks to: Julie O'Connor, Helen de Keijzer, Hannah de Keijzer, David Burstein, and Joan O'Connor.

Numerous friends and professional colleagues championed the project, pitched in when the going got tough, helped us with key bits of information, gave us new ideas about how to tell the story, or generally helped us manage the rest of our lives while we were trying to put this book together: Ann Malin, David Kline, Sam Schwerin, Peter Kaufman, Marty Edelston, Susan Friedman, Carter Wiseman, Stuart Rekant, Ben Wolin, Bob Stein, Gregory Rutchick, Cynthia O'Conner, Petra Talvitie, Ilene Lefland, and Jen Prosek. Best wishes for a cancer-free life to Craig Buck and Phil Berman.

Elaine Pagels, one of the leading scholars in the field of Gnostic and alternative gospels, provided encouragement and support to us at the very beginning of this journey. She is a true Renaissance woman. We also want to thank all of our other authors and contributors. As a group, they are the backbone of this project: Diane Apostolos-Cappadona, Michael Baigent, Amy Bernstein, Esther de Boer, Denise Budd, Michelle Delio, David Downie, Betsy Eble, Bart D. Ehrman, Riane Eisler, Glenn W. Erickson, Timothy Freke, Peter Gandy, Deirdre Good, Susan Haskins, Collin Hansen, Stephan A. Hoeller, Katherine Ludwig Jansen, Karen L. King, David Klinghoffer, Richard Leigh, Matthew Landrus, Henry Lincoln, James Martin, Richard P. McBrien, Craig McDonald, Brendan McKay, Laura Miller, Anne Moore, Sherwin B. Nuland, the Opus Dei Awareness Network, Lance S. Owens, Elaine Pagels, Lynn Picknett, The Prelature of Opus Dei, Clive Prince, James Robinson, Margaret Starbird, David Van Biema, and Kenneth Woodward.

—DAN BURSTEIN AND ARNE DE KEIJZER